CUMBERLAND PRESBYTERIAN BIOGRAPHY

THE WRITINGS OF

RICHARD BEARD

HISTORICAL FOUNDATION CPC

MEMPHIS, TENNESSEE
2015

CUMBERLAND PRESBYTERIAN BIOGRAPHY: The Writings of Richard Beard. Edited by Matthew H. Gore. Cover design by Matthew H. Gore. Entire contents ©2015 by the Historical Foundation of the Cumberland Presbyterian Church and the Cumberland Presbyterian Church in America.

World rights reserved. This book may not be reproduced in whole or in part, or transmitted in any form, or by any means electronic, mechanical, photocopying, recording, or others, without written permission from the publisher, except by a reviewer who may quote brief passages in a review.

Second Printing, June 2015

ISBN-13: 978-0692464977
ISBN-10: 0692464972

Historical Foundation CPC, 8207 Traditional Place, Cordova, Tennessee, 38016

Contents

Introduction. vii

Preface (1867) by John C. Provine. ix

Preface (1874) M. B. DeWitt. ix

Alexander Anderson. 1

Sumner Bacon. 10
Robert Baker. 13
John Barnett. 20
William Barnett. 25
John Beard. 30
Richard Beard. 35
Robert Bell. 52
John McCutchen Berry. 66
Milton Bird. 75
Joseph Brown. 83
Alfred McGready Bryan. 94
Reuben Burrow. 101

Thomas Calhoon. 115
Alexander Chapman. 126
Ezekiel Cloyd. 139
Francway Ranna Cossitt. 142

Claiborne Albert Davis. 160
Silas Newton Davis. 175
George Donnell. 184
Robert Donnell. 192
Alexander Downey. 201

Finis Ewing. 203

David Foster. 210

James Smith Guthrie. 216

Robert Guthrie. 223

William M. Harris. 230
Hugh Bone Hill. 242

James Johnson. 253
Francis Johnston. 257
Laban Jones. 261

Samuel King. 270

Jacob Lindley. 277
William Calhoun Love. 290

Samuel McAdow. 299
Hiram McDaniel. 309
William McGee. 314
James McGready. 319
John Morgan. 324

Herschel S. Porter. 333
James Brown Porter. 339
John Provine. 352

INTRODUCTION

Richard Beard (1799-1880), the first professor in the Theological School at Cumberland University, received the A.B. degree from Cumberland College, Princeton, Kentucky, in 1832. On graduation he was named Professor of Greek and Latin at Cumberland College. He remained at Cumberland for six years before moving to Sharon College in Mississippi. Beard returned to Princeton as president of Cumberland College in September 1843, and held the position to February 1854. His inauguration as Professor of Systematic Theology in Cumberland University took place on March 13, 1854. He was still teaching for Cumberland University at the time of his death.

Beard wrote two volumes of Cumberland Presbyterian biography. The first, **Brief Biographical Sketches of Some of the Early Ministers of the Cumberland Presbyterian Church**, was self-published by the author in 1867, but the second, **Brief Biographical Sketches of Some of the Early Ministers of the Cumberland Presbyterian Church: Second Series**, was published by the Cumberland Presbyterian Board of Publication in 1874. Both volumes have now been out of print for over 130 years. Rare book dealers demand over a hundred dollars for either volume in sound readable condition.

Montana's Kessinger Publishing sells an unauthorized low-quality reproduction of the first volume for $30.95. According to the publisher, "In the interest of creating a more extensive selection of rare historical book reprints, we have chosen to reproduce this title even though it may possibly have occasional imperfections such as missing and blurred pages, missing text, poor pictures, markings, dark backgrounds and other reproduction issues beyond our control. Because this work is culturally important, we have made it available as a part of our commitment to protecting, preserving and promoting the world's literature."

The volume you are holding collects all of the biographies from both of Beard's volumes. They are free from missing text and the other problems that trouble the Kessinger edition. The 41 biographies are presented in alphabetical order along with Beard's autobiographical sketch, *Fifty Years a Teacher*, from **The Theological Medium, A Cumberland Presbyterian Quarterly** as it was originally presented in 1879.

    No attempt has been made to modernize the language Beard used and it may sound stilted to modern readers. Some of his terms, the use of "Scotch" to refer to a person from Scotland or "Scotch-Irish" for Ulster-Scots, for example, are now considered to be incorrect but they are retained as Beard originally penned them.

Matthew H. Gore
Memphis Tennessee, 2007

Preface to the First Series: 1867

The fruits of Christianity constitute its excellency. It is the developments and ameliorating influences of religion that give character and importance to its claims upon the confidence and consideration of man. The tree that produces no good fruit is hewn down and cast into the fire. That system of religion that does not improve the intellectual and moral condition of its subjects, is without intrinsic merit—it has no recommending qualities, and as a consequence, the intelligent mind, in its pursuit of happiness, turns from it to something that promises positive good in this life, and salvation in the life to come. That the Christian Religion is a positive benefit; that it does better the condition of man; that it does elevate him in the scale of moral and intellectual being, may be regarded as axiomatic truths. If, however, evidence be necessary to illustrate this, the lives of the good and the useful of every age may be presented; for their pious walk, holy conversation, "work and labor of love," is Christianity in its practical developments.

In the following "Biographical Sketches" we have our holy religion exemplified. The characters of twenty-one ministers of the gospel are introduced. They were in some respects peculiar men—raised up in the providence of God, it may be, for a special and an important purpose. Some of them were the instruments in the organization of the Cumberland Presbyterian Church. They lived to see the vine which, in the hands of God, they planted, spreading its branches "far and wide," and the precious seed of truth which they had sown yielding a most bountiful harvest. Having finished their work, they were gathered into their fathers, to be followed by others no less consecrated to the great work of saving souls. In the perusal of the following pages, the reader will discover interesting portraitures, drawn by a faithful hand—portraitures of the Fathers and their immediate successors in the ministry of our beloved Church. He will learn something of their early history, their incipient efforts in the ministry, their pious walk, their extensive labors, and their triumphant death. He will see what animated them in their progress through a world of suffering—how they endured hardness as good soldiers of Jesus Christ—what enabled them to resist temptation, to overcome difficulties, and to brave persecutions. He will see in the lives of these worthies the great truths of our holy religion elucidated, not merely in the morality of their actions, but in the purity of their principles. Finally, he will see them witnessing a good profession, and in the darkest hour of trial bearing their testimony to the truth of Christianity, living by faith upon the Son of God, and dying in the triumphant assurances of his salvation. These things being true, we trust that this volume may receive a hearty welcome into hundreds and thousands of Christian families, and that it may be read with profit by them all, and that it may prove a blessing to the Church and the world.

J. C. Provine (Nashville: April 1867)

PREFACE TO THE SECOND SERIES: 1874

On many accounts, the following Sketches are very interesting and valuable. The period of time which they cover was one of astonishing movements in social, political, and religious affairs. The opening of the nineteenth century was an important era among the nations, and especially was it important in the history of our own country.

In various departments of human interest, the period since then has been very full of both thought and action. The ecclesiastical world has been all astir with vital forces which have accomplished, already, wonderful things at home and abroad, and which promise to do even greater things in future times. The wide field of Christian missions, which previously to the year 1800 presented such a sad picture to the benevolent heart, has since then become the area of most cheering and happy influences and effects. A state of things existed in the Church of Christ such as to afford small comfort and hope to the lover of his race; but the Spirit of God was richly poured out upon the hearts of true men and women, and the result has been most glorious.

In every branch of the Church new life and power have been inspired and developed, and the cause of Christ marches forward, with rapid and steady strides, to ultimate victory. The Presbyterian household of faith has, since A.D. 1800, expanded without a parallel in its previous history. The Cumberland Presbyterian portion of that household was organized into a separate family since that date, and, by God's abundant blessing, has grown into quite a considerable body of believers. Rev. Samuel McAdow, the sketch of whose life is first in this volume, was one of the three ministers who constituted its first presbytery, on the fourth day of February, 1810, now near sixty-four years ago. The whole intervening space in our Church's history, from then until now, is here surveyed in the lives of some of its devoted men, including those of the man of wondrous pulpit power, C.A. Davis, D.D., and the man of broad and truly catholic views, Milton Bird, D.D.

Not the least interesting thought connected with these Sketches is that their venerable author, whose long life in his Church's service has been so fruitful of good works, whose eighth decade of years is beautifully iklustrating the Psalmist's words, "They shall still bring forth fruit in old age," was himself a participant in much of the experience of the times he records, and that he intimately knew many of the noble characters he presents to our view. This, his last book of Sketches, must some day be followed by one written by another hand, in which his own excellent career shall be prominently portrayed by a faithful and loving pen.

M. B. Dewitt, *Book Editor* (Nashville: January 1, 1874)

REV. ALEXANDER ANDERSON
(1764 - 1804)

Sources: Rev. T. C. Anderson, D.D.; Smith's **History of the Cumberland Presbyterians**; **Life and Times of Finis Ewing**.

Mr. Anderson did not live to witness the organization of the Cumberland Presbytery in 1810, and, properly speaking, therefore, was never a Cumberland Presbyterian. But for the reason that he was fully identified with the difficulties from which the Cumberland Presbyterian Church arose, and, had he lived, without doubt, would have been connected with it, and furthermore as he is considered to have been eminently worthy of such a memorial as these sketches are intended to preserve of their several subjects, he receives a place here.

Alexander Anderson was born in Orange County, North Carolina, October 28, 1764. His father, James Anderson, was a Scotch-Irish emigrant who settled in Orange about the middle of the eighteenth century. James Anderson subsequently married the sister of General James Mebane, of revolutionary memory. Alexander Anderson was the eldest son of this marriage. His mother was a member of the Presbyterian Church, and the son was brought up in the faith and according to the usages of that Church. The Sabbath was observed as a holy day. The Bible was read, and the Catechism was studied; these were the principal exercises of the Sabbath.

Having been thus religiously instructed, and raised by a pious mother, Alexander's mind in early youth was brought under religious impressions, but at what period, and under what circumstances, he became experimentally a subject of religion is not now known. It appears that he did not attach himself to the Church till after his marriage. His wife was a Miss Phebe Hall. She was also of Scotch-Irish descent, and a member of the Presbyterian Church.

Shortly after his marriage he became a member of the Presbyterian Church himself, and immediately established the Christian and Presbyterian usage of holding prayers in his family. From the beginning he was remarkable for his power in prayer. A Church was organized in his neighborhood, and he was chosen a ruling elder, and became one of the most active and influential men in the congregation. This was the Hawfield's congregation. It was one of the congregations of which Rev. William Hodge had charge previous to his removal to Tennessee.

In this congregation Mr. Anderson lived and labored until he became the father of six children. In the fall of 1797 he emigrated to Tennessee, and settled in Sumner County, three miles south of Gallatin.

Here in the midst of what might be called, almost without exaggeration, an interminable forest, with an immense undergrowth of cane, he literally "began in the woods." A house was to be built, a field to be cleared and fenced, and the cane to be cut and burned; and then the plowing of the new ground would have terrified a man of this generation. Still the crops produced compensated for the severe labor. Twelve or fifteen barrels of corn, and ten wagon loads of pumpkins, per acre, were common in the fall gatherings.

Mr. Anderson and his wife became members of Shiloh Congregation. The old meeting-house was situated about a mile from Gallatin. He was also elected a ruling elder in that congregation. The first pastor was Rev. William McGee. He was succeeded by Rev. William Hodge, who had left his old charge in North Carolina and settled in Tennessee. Mr. Hodge served the Shiloh congregation for many years after the disruption in 1810.

Mr. Anderson's piety was not of the fashionable type—a piety which can be kept out of sight during the business of the week and brought out on Sabbath for exhibition—but it was a living principle which reigned in the heart, subjugating the lower and baser passions, and developing itself in a godly life and Christian activity, and in sympathy with the souls of men. Consequently, when the great revival of 1800 began to develop itself in its wondrous-working power, he at once recognized the presence and power of God, and entered earnestly into the work of its promotion. By exhortation, singing, prayer, and conversation with serious persons, he made himself eminently useful. Says my informant:

> No secular engagements could keep him from his place in the prayer-meeting, the more public service of the sanctuary, or the camp-meeting. Wherever God's people were assembled for his service there was Mr. Anderson in the midst ready to do, or try to do, whatever duty seemed to demand. Blessed with a melodious voice, he could sing like a seraph; in prayer he talked with God, and pleaded with him in most melting strains for the salvation of sinners; in exhortation he drew the penitent to Christ, and subdued the stouthearted, and constrained him to humble himself before god. These labors were so effectual that the impression soon became general in the Church that he was destined for a higher work.

In the meantime the visit of Mr. Rice to the revival ministers in the Green River and Cumberland countries occurred. His counsels to these ministers and the congregations in their great exigency have often been referred to. They have become matters of history. One of the young men encouraged, in conformity with his counsel, to look forward to the ministry, and to try to prepare for it as well as his circumstances would permit, was Mr. Anderson. It would have been an appalling undertaking to any ordinary man. At home were a wife and a family of seven children. None of the children were able to do much in the cultivation of the farm. The country was new, and severe labor was necessary for the support of a large family. His education was limited. To come up to the requirements of the Presbyterian form of government in relation to probationers for the ministry was simply impossible. There were no schools; and had there been schools in abundance, he had no time to spare. Yet the Church was calling; and the providence and Spirit of God seemed to be calling in like manner. What was he to do? The congregations were suffering, and could not be supplied with the word and ordinances, unless extraordinary measures were adopted. The friends of the revival resolved to step over the chasm which seemed to be before them. They did so, and Mr. Anderson was one of the first that was called out. He and Finis Ewing and Samuel King were encouraged to make such preparation as they could with a view to the ministry. At the meeting of the Transylvania Presbytery, in October of 1801, the case of these men was brought before that body. They were not then received as candidates for the ministry, but were licensed to catechise and exhort in the vacant congregations, and directed to prepare discourses to be read at the next sessions of the Presbytery. At the next meeting, which is supposed to have been held in the spring of 1802, Mr. Anderson was received as a candidate by a bare majority, whilst the others were rejected by the same bare majority. In the fall of 1802, however, they were all licensed to preach as probationers.

In May of 1803 Mr. Anderson was ordained at Shiloh, Mr. McGready preaching the ordination sermon, and Mr. Hodge giving the charge. At his licensure he was appointed to a field of labor extending from Russellville, Kentucky, to Shelbyville, Tennessee, embracing the central district of Tennessee and the south-western portion of Kentucky. Of course his whole time and strength were called into requisition in supplying the wants of so extended a field.

It is difficult for us to appreciate the self-denial and moral heroism of a man placed in such a situation. His farm had been but newly opened; at home were a wife and seven or eight children. Human reason inquires, How could he leave his home, and thus commit himself to a work of such magnitude, and a work, too, which in a pecuniary point of view promised so little remuneration? Still he did confide his earthly all to God, and went into the work. His mission, however, was soon fulfilled: he died in 1804, a year and four months from his licensure, and nine months from his ordination. His death occurred in Kentucky, and his remains now lie about midway between Elkton and Russellville, in that State. The disease which carried him off overtook him while engaged in his appointed work. He was considered a great loss to the revival interest in the Church.

In relation to the acts of the Presbytery in his advancement to the ministry my informant says:

> They knew their man; they knew what he could do in exhortation, and prayer, and other religious exercises: nor were they disappointed. He drew crowds wherever he preached, and the writer has heard old veterans of the cross repeat large portions of his sermons after he had been in heaven half a century. There are yet a few old mothers in Israel lingering upon the shores of time who still weep at the mention of the name of Alexander Anderson. No man has ever made such a record in Tennessee in so short a time. That reputation still survives.
>
> The good providence of God has been around his family, too, till this day. His widow lingered with the children through fifty years, but she always had a comfortable home, and the kind regard of all who knew her. Two of his sons [Rev. T. C. Anderson, D.D., and Rev. John Anderson] have been active ministers of the Cumberland Presbyterian Church. One of his grandsons, [Rev. S. T. Anderson, D.D.] in the prime of life, is also a respectable minister of the same Church. All of his children have been members of the Church. Those who have gone died in hope. Two still linger awaiting the summons which shall call them home. All will doubtless meet in heaven. God will take care of the family of the faithful minister, whatever may be the term of his service.

The sketches given in these paragraphs of the promise and reputation of Mr. Anderson as a preacher, if tradition is reliable, are not overwrought. In the days of my boyhood his name was a household word within the circle of my own family connection. They were nearly all identified with the revival interest, and Mr. Anderson was always spoken of as an attractive and lovely preacher, and his early death was deplored as a great calamity, and a remarkably dark providence, all the circumstances being considered. In my early ministry I met the echo of these sentiments wherever I went within the bounds of his labors. I was trained up to respect his character and revere his memory. And whilst I write this imperfect tribute to his unusual worth, the impressions are still vivid in my mind which were deeply wrought there sixty years ago, in the days of my early boyhood.

I annex the following in relation to Mr. Anderson from the Appendix of Smith's **History of the Cumberland Presbyterians**;

This eminently pious and beloved minister of the gospel of Jesus Christ was born in Orange county, in North Carolina, A.D. 1764. His parents being pious, he enjoyed the high privilege of having been taught the Scriptures from his infancy, and at a very early period he became deeply impressed with a sense of his lost estate, and felt great anxiety for the salvation of his soul. After remaining in this condition for some time, he became the subject of the comforting influences of the Holy Spirit, and took great delight in reading the sacred Scriptures. But being very young, and none of his youthful companions having the same views and feelings with himself, and as he lived in a neighborhood where the life and power of religion were scarcely known, he relapsed into a state of coldness, and caught somewhat of the spirit of his associates. In this condition he remained until the period of his marriage, when he aroused himself from his lethargy, became a man of prayer, and spent his leisure hours in reading the Scriptures and other religious works. For some time he was the subject of much perplexity concerning the reality of his change of heart; but becoming satisfied on this important subject, he attached himself to the Presbyterian Church, and made such advances in piety and religious knowledge that in a short time his influence was felt by all with whom he associated. Such was his zeal for God that many of his friends were led by his example to forsake their sins, and to receive the Lord Jesus as their sovereign Lord, and a flourishing society was established in his neighborhood, and he was made a ruling elder.

Mr. Anderson removed to Tennessee A.D. 1798, and became a member of the Shiloh congregation. When he heard of the strange work in progress in Mr. McGready's congregations he determined to see it for himself, and was one of those who were present at the camp-meeting [The first camp-meeting ever held in Christendom.] at Gaspar River Church from Shiloh. He was convinced that the astonishing effects upon the people were produced by the mighty power of God. He returned home glorifying God for what his eyes had seen, and his heart had felt; and was zealously and actively engaged in the blessed revival that immediately after appeared in Shiloh and the neighboring congregations. Being often called upon to pray at the social prayer-meetings, and the Spirit within him constraining him to exhort the unconverted to flee the wrath to come, it was soon discovered that he possessed no ordinary gifts, in consequence of which, when the people in the neighboring settlements, who had no minister settled among them, became aroused to a sense of their exposure to misery, they would earnestly entreat Mr. Anderson to visit them, and hold prayer-meetings among them, at which he often exhorted with great power, and his humble efforts were owned of Heaven in the salvation of many precious souls. As the Presbyterian ministers in the country were very few, they encouraged Mr. Anderson and others to visit the distant congregations with license to catechise and exhort.

Before his removal from North Carolina, Mr. Anderson labored under serious impressions that he ought to preach Christ, but he shrank from the thought, owing to his want of literary attainments and the impossibility of procuring them, circumstanced, as he was, with a helpless family looking to him for support. The exercise of his gifts at the commencement of the revival in the Cumberland country renewed his impressions. Still, however, he could not bear the thought of devoting himself to the ministry; and to quiet his conscience he continued to exhort. This, however, only tended to deepen his impressions. He was in this embarrassed state of mind when he was informed that, owing to the destitute state of the country, the Presbytery were willing to license those who appeared to possess an aptness to teach, although they had not acquired the literary attainments required by the book of discipline; and that if he would present himself as a candidate for the ministry, his want of classical learning would constitute no serious objection. This information deprived him of his chief apology. And although he had a numerous and helpless family depending for support upon his exertions, God having opened such a door before him that he could no longer keep peace with his conscience, he committed his family to the protection of Him who feedeth the young ravens, and clothes the lilies of the field; and he devoted himself to the great work to which he believed the Head of the Church was calling him. Immediately upon being licensed he hired a person to superintend his farm, and he acted as an itinerant preacher, traveling over a large extent of country, exposed to many trials and privations. In this new sphere Mr. Anderson manifested great zeal for the cause of his Divine Master. Nor did he labor in vain, and spend his strength for naught, for such a holy unction attended his ministrations that many, very many, precious souls, through his instrumentality, were savingly converted to God. He continued to labor with great success, and without receiving any, or very little, pecuniary remuneration until the time of his death, which was in February, 1804, and while traveling in Kentucky, proclaiming salvation through Christ to perishing sinners.

Mr. Anderson was a man of no ordinary mind. He possessed very clear views of divine truth, and a happy facility of communicating his ideas in an interesting manner to his hearers. He had a commanding voice and a tender accent. While he could thunder the curses of the law like the voice of God upon Mount Sinai, he could moisten his words with tears. Whilst he was a bold man, and could put scoffers to shame, he could also clothe his ideas in the most familiar language, and was an instructor of babes in Christ. He, on no occasion, indulged in controversial theology, but uniformly preached Christ, and him crucified. He carefully cultivated a spirit of love and friendship with all denominations. By all parties he was beloved. By the churches under the care of the revival members of Cumberland Presbytery he was idolized. Therefore, for good and wise reasons, no doubt, he was removed from the walls of Zion, and that, too, immediately before that fearful storm burst upon the Church for whose benefit he labored, and nearly crushed and annihilated all its prospects. The approach of that storm Mr. Anderson saw, and, being a man of a meek and quiet spirit, he frequently expressed his desire that, if consistent with the will of Heaven, he might not witness it. God heard and answered his prayer by removing him from the evil to come. His career was short, but bright; and at the resurrection of the great day many, who will be his crown of rejoicing, will arise and call him blessed."

Such is the testimony borne to the great worth of this good man near forty years ago. A bustling and noisy generation has passed away since that time, but the testimony still stands. "The memory of the just is blessed." This is as true now as it was a thousand years before the commencement of our era. It will be true forever. The examples of her great and good men and women will be the best earthly legacy of the Church in all ages. Mr. Anderson was no doubt taken from the evil to come, but the good name of all such men is better than precious ointment.

I embody here also a paragraph from Dr. Cossitt's **Life and Times of Finis Ewing**.

About this time the revival party were called to mourn the death of Rev. Alexander Anderson. It seemed an inscrutable providence. He was one of the first of the young men licensed by the Transylvania Presbytery, and the first ordained by the Cumberland Presbytery. His great zeal and eminent usefulness had been witnessed. Of his services to the Church high hopes had been entertained. On his being licensed he had employed a person to superintend his farm, and, from that time to his death, had devoted himself to the work of the ministry. Nor were his sacrifices and labors in vain. A holy unction attended his ministrations; and, during the few years of his ministerial life, he was the acknowledged instrument of saving many, very many, precious souls. He had been much respected and beloved by all who knew him. It is even said that he was almost idolized by those who knew him best; and some have supposed that it was for this reason that the Lord saw proper to remove him to his inheritance on high. He had seen the cloud of opposition rising, which portended the approaching storm, and was heard to express a wish that, if consistent with the divine will, he might not live to witness it. His prayer was answered, and the Church was doomed to mourn. His uprightness and amiability of character had won the confidence and love of all parties. He died at his post while itinerating as a preacher in Kentucky, February, 1804.

We have a single printed sermon of Mr. Anderson. It was published in the **Cumberland Presbyterian Pulpit** of 1834. I add to the preceding sketch some extracts from this sermon as a specimen of the sermonizing of the young men whose licensure and ordination created such a storm in the Presbyterian Church in the early years of the century. At what time, or under what circumstances, the sermon was delivered is not know. The manuscript was found among his papers after his death. The text is Rom. v. 21: "That as sin hath reigned unto death, even so might grace reign through righteousness unto eternal life by Jesus Christ our Lord."

The preacher introduces his subject by a single remark: "The ruin of mankind by the fall of Adam and redemption by Jesus Christ are subjects of the utmost importance in the Christian religion."

The follows the division. "In discoursing upon the text I will speak," says he:

    I. Of the primitive state of man.
    II. Of his present degraded state.
    III. Of salvation through Jesus Christ.

'Of the primitive state of man,' it is said, 'he was made in the image of God.' In what, however, did that image consist? This is an old inquiry. The preacher considers it in several particulars:

1. The dignified form of man bespeaks him a noble creature. Not that his body is in the image of God, for God is a spirit, and consequently without bodily form. But man's erect position indicates his high origin, and the dignity of his nature. This thought is expanded: man looks up; other creatures look down.

2. Man is the most wonderful part of all creation. In this respect he is like God, who is the wonder and admiration of all

intelligent beings. Man is, as it were, the universe in miniature, a compound of heaven and earth—an abridgment of the works of Jehovah—material and immaterial, corporeal and spiritual, visible and invisible.

3. Man is the miniature likeness of Jehovah in regard to the dignified authority conferred upon him. God governs all worlds with unlimited dominion. Man was made subordinate ruler of this world. God rules all; man rules in his own sphere.

4. Man was made in the likeness of God as it respects the nature of his soul. The soul is a substance that can exist without communion with, or dependence upon, matter. It can and will exist without the body. This subject is extensively discussed. God exists an eternal spirit without body or bodily parts. Angels exist without bodies.

5. The soul is invisible. This follows necessarily from its immateriality. Was there ever a man so stupid as to doubt the existence of the soul because he cannot see it? But God is invisible, and man is like God, in one of his aspects, invisible.

6. It is also immortal. Nothing can extinguish its existence, but God himself, and he is pledged to perpetuate it in his promise of eternal life to the believer, and in the award of everlasting death to the unbeliever. The immortality of the soul is another feature in which it bears the image of God.

7. Thus far we have considered the natural or physical image of God in which man was created, and man in his fallen state still retains all this similitude of his Creator, though considerably marred. But the most distinguishing feature of the divine image remains yet to be considered. Man was made in the moral image or holy likeness of God. This point is contested, and our preacher enters into an extended discussion. Reason and Scripture are brought into requisition, and the argument is well sustained.

8. Man was not only a holy and happy being, but he was exceedingly glorious. How bright, how majestic his appearance! Did the face of Moses shine with dazzling splendor after he had been with God in the mountain? What must have been the appearance of Adam when he came from the forming hand of his Creator, dwelt in his immediate presence, and enjoyed the most intimate communion with him? He was the image of the divine glory.

9. Man was not only glorious, but the peculiar favorite of Heaven. God dwelt with him in very deed; a free intercourse existed between heaven and earth; there was no need of Jacob's ladder, or Elijah's fiery chariot.

10. To complete the dignity and happiness of man he was created a free moral agent." Here again the preacher was upon contested ground. I mean it was contested at the time. It is hardly contested now by any of the schools of philosophical theology.

However the subject may be explained, very few modern theologians deny, in distinct terms, the freedom of man. The old men did not understand the question—they hardly understood themselves.

Our examination has extended through the first division of the sermon. This will serve as a specimen. It will be readily perceived that the discussion of the various topics was intended to be exhaustive. This was the character of the preaching of those days. The sermons were long. Repeated now, they would weary out the patience of hearers of this restive generation. But the specimen of sermonizing here presented is a sufficient illustration of the ability and great promise of the man. The introduction of such men as Mr. Anderson into the ministry was one of the best results of the old revival of 1800. The Church was practically taught that God was wiser than man in the selection of agencies for the accomplishment of a great work. We educate men now for the service of the Church. We should do it. They ought to be more thoroughly educated than they are. Our education ought to be profound, thorough. It ought to train mind, heart, and body. The Church can impart such an education as this. But after all, if "the root of the matter" is not in the man we will have poor preaching. It is God who makes the good and the great preachers, even among our scholars. The anointing must come from him. "The Spirit of the Lord God is upon me," said the prophet, "because the Lord hath anointed me to preach good tidings unto the meek; he hath sent me to bind up the broken-hearted, to proclaim liberty to the captives, and the opening of the prison to them that are bound; to proclaim the acceptable year of the Lord, and the day of vengeance of our God; to comfort all that mourn." This is a great mission. The prophet personated the Saviour, and the Saviour is the model of all preachers. Whilst we are struggling for the cultivation of mind, and heart, and manner, when we enter fully upon our work, we must, in like manner, seek not less earnestly—yea, far more earnestly—for the anointing of the Spirit of the Lord God.

REV. SUMNER BACON
(1790 - 1844)

Sources: Revs. J. B. Renfro, John Buchanan, and W.G.L. Quaite

Sumner Bacon is supposed to have been a native of Massachusetts. The first account we have of him is as a regular soldier in the army of the United States. The regiment with which he was connected was stationed at Fort Smith, Arkansas, about the years 1823 and 1824. In 1824 his term of service expired, and he was discharged. Says my informant: "He spent two years as a hired hand in a family in Arkansas, dressed in buckskin—pants and hunting-shirt—as were myself and most of the day-laborers at that time in Arkansas." He seems to have been very profane. It could hardly have been otherwise, after an experience of some time in the army; but in 1826 he professed religion, and in a short time was received by the Arkansas Presbytery as a candidate for the ministry. In a year or two he was licensed by that Presbytery. The date, however, of his licensure is not known. The records are lost.

His early efforts in the ministry were not very satisfactory. The Arkansas ministers at that time were John Carnahan, Josephus A. Cornwall, James H. Black, Andrew Buchanan, and Jesse M. Blair—all solid, serious, and thoughtful men. Bacon was considered to be rather erratic.

In 1828, he went to Texas, and penetrated into the country as far as San Felipe. This was the field for him, so true it is that when God calls out a workman he always finds a work suited to the character of him who is thus called. In traversing the wilds of Texas he preached whenever and wherever an opportunity was offered. He bore a high character of scrupulous honesty, great energy, and punctuality in fulfilling his engagements. Though of a rough exterior, and unpolished manners, he had a soul which gleamed with the noblest affections, while he was a stranger to fear. It required a heroic spirit to bear what Protestantism was compelled to bear at that time in Texas. That spirit he possessed in large measure.

In 1832, he was appointed an agent for the distribution of the Scriptures in Texas. "He scattered," says my informant, "the Word of Life from San Antonio to the Sabine with an industrious hand." Of course this brought him into collision with the Roman Catholic prejudices of the country. On one occasion he was taken by a band of desperadoes, and threatened with death. He asked permission to pray. Permission being granted, he threw himself upon his knees and poured forth an earnest prayer for the men who were threatening to take his life. Concluding his prayer, he opened his eyes, and his persecutors were gone. The appeal was too strong to be resisted. The tradition is, that when the ringleader of the band returned to his home, his savage mother asked him if he had succeeded in killing the preacher. He replied, with earnestness: "I would not hurt a hair of that man's head for this cabin filled with gold."

On another occasion, while he was distributing the Bible, Colonel James Gains reported him to Colonel Bean. The latter told him to go on and distribute as many Bibles as he pleased, with the injunction that he should not disturb the peace.

On still another occasion, Mr. Bacon and others were preparing to hold a camp-meeting near San Augustine, and a number of wicked men conspired to break it up. Colonel Bowie, one of Texas's noblest men, providentially was present at the meeting, and being so deeply impressed with the simplicity and solemn earnestness of Bacon, that he said to the ruffians in his expressive manner, "Captain Bowie is in command to-day," and, making the sign of the cross upon the ground, he told the preachers that they could proceed with the meeting. This, of course, settled the matter.

About the year 1835, Mr. Bacon was ordained by one of the South-western Presbyteries, perhaps the Presbytery of Mississippi. I make this statement on my own authority, still not being certain that I am correct. I have a distinct recollection of having heard of the occurrence about the time, and that Thomas B. Reynolds and William A. Scott were present and promoted and participated in the ordination. These were then recent graduates from Cumberland College, but earnestly favored the measure from the consideration of Mr. Bacon's great usefulness in his field of labor, although in literary attainments he was known to fall below the requirements of the Form of Government. It was certainly an indulgence to be granted.

In 1836, Mr. Bacon organized the second Cumberland Presbyterian Church which was organized in Texas. In the fall of that year he attended the meeting of the Mississippi Synod, and succeeded in procuring an order of the Synod for the organization of a Presbytery as soon as three ministers of the country could be collected together in that capacity. In the winter of 1837, a Presbytery was organized, holding its first meeting five miles east of San Augustine. In 1841, three Presbyteries were formed out of this one, the Texas Presbytery. The names were Texas, Red River, and Colorado Presbyteries. In 1842, these Presbyteries were organized into a Synod, which held its first meeting near Nacogdoches. Rev. Samuel Bacon was Moderator. In a short time after the meeting this pioneer of Cumberland Presbyterianism, and of Protestantism in Texas, died at his home in San Augustine county.

I close this brief and imperfect sketch of the life and labors of one of our good men with a letter From Rev. W. G. L. Quaite, one of the successors of Mr. Bacon in Texas. It will be seen that a little fire has kindled a great matter in that country. God works wonders, and sometimes, too, by agencies which men would not have selected. The following is the letter:

WAXAHATCHIE, TEXAS.

BROTHER BEARD:—I inclose you a sketch of the life and labors of Rev. Sumner Bacon, by Rev. J. B. Renfro, with additional statements by Rev. R. O. Watkins, who was the co-laborer of Mr. Bacon for several years in Texas.

For several years before his death his great anxiety and prayer was that God would spare his life to see a Synod organized in Texas. This God permitted him to see, and preside over, in the fall of 1842, in Nacogdoches county, Texas.

This was the last time he and Watkins ever met. Bacon told Watkins that his work was done. He said he had a presentiment that he should die soon. He called Brother Watkins his Texas boy;

committed to Watkins his mantle; told him he was going home to die.

Bacon returned to his home in San Augustine county, and in December, 1842, closed a long, and laborious, and eventful life.

In the latter part of the year 1836, he married Miss Elizabeth McCrosky, of Middle Tennessee.

Rev. Sumner Bacon left a wife, one son, and two daughters, who all became worthy members of the Church he labored so faithfully to plant in Texas.

The Cumberland Presbyterian Church numbers three Synods in Texas, fourteen Presbyteries, and one Presbytery in the Indian country, one hundred and eighty ministers, and more than twenty thousand communicants, with an institution of learning second to none of its age, and a large number of young men of fine promise preparing for the ministry.

The labors of this faithful man of God, with those of the sainted A. J. McGown, and others, will tell for the Cumberland Presbyterian Church in the great day of God Almighty.

REV. ROBERT BAKER
(1795 - 1845)

Sources: **Watchman and Evangelist**; Minutes of Nashville and Lebanon Presbyteries; Manuscript Letters of Rev. J. C. Provine and Thomas Hamilton, Esq.

Robert Baker was born in Orange county, North Carolina, on the 28th of December, 1795. His parents were James and Sarah Baker. In 1799 they moved from North Carolina to Tennessee, and settled first in Sumner county. After remaining in Sumner a year, they moved again, and settled permanently in Wilson county, in the neighborhood of the Big Spring.

Mr. and Mrs. Baker, the father and mother, were members of the Presbyterian Church in North Carolina. In the revival of 1800, however, they became unsettled in their religious hopes. After a long and careful course of self-examination and prayer, "the Lord was pleased," says my authority, "to open their eyes to a brighter and better light." They became the steadfast friends of the revival, and entered fully into its spirit. The father was an elder in the Presbyterian Church whilst the Old Cumberland Presbytery was in existence. After the organization of the Independent Cumberland Presbytery in 1810, he and his family became Cumberland Presbyterians. The Big Spring congregation was for many years one of the leading congregations of the Cumberland Presbyterian Church, and James Baker continued a ruling elder in it till his removal, in his old age, to Western Tennessee.

The parents of Mr. Baker were unusually pious persons. They raised their children with great care. They dedicated them to God in baptism, and believed in the promise which was made to them and to their children. We have a striking illustration of their faith in an incident which occurred in the early life of the son. When he was six or seven years old, he had the misfortune to get a substance of some kind lodged in his windpipe. His friends at the house were alarmed, of course, and thought his life to be in danger. The boy was himself alarmed. In this state of mind he went to his father, who was at work in the field, told him what had happened, and that he feared he would die, and that he did not feel prepared for death. He asked his father to pray for him. They kneeled down together in the field, and the father committed the son to God. At the same time the mother at the house was engaged in a similar manner. The parents retired to bed that night with full confidence that all would be well with their son. When the awoke in the morning they found him entirely relieved. They regarded the whole matter as a very special providence, and from that time seemed to feel that their son belonged to God. This anecdote is worth something, inasmuch as it illustrates the views of our fathers on the subject of prayer. They believed in the efficacy of prayer. A volume might be filled with illustrations of this truth.

At a very early age Robert Baker became seriously concerned on the subject of religion. He was a regular attendant upon the means of grace, and was for years an earnest inquirer. When about eighteen years of age he volunteered for a campaign against the Creek Indians. Of this portion of his life all that is known is, that he was faithful in the discharge of his duties, and secured the confidence and esteem of both the officers and private soldiers with whom he was connected. Amidst all the temptations of a soldier's life his religious impressions remained.

Soon after his return home, these impressions were rendered deeper by the exhortations of a sister, who urged him in her dying moments to prepare to meet her in heaven. At a camp-meeting at the Big Spring he was in deep distress. His distress continued through the meeting, and at its close he went home with a heavy heart. He spent the day of his return from the meeting in earnest prayer for the salvation of his soul. About dark his parents, who had become uneasy about him, started to the grove where he had passed the time to look after him. In the meantime his mind had become relieved, and he met them in their search with the glad intelligence. I suppose his profession of religion to have been made in 1817, or in 1818, when he was of course in his twenty-second or twenty-third year.

Mr. Baker's mind was turned toward the work of the ministry soon after he professed religion. He endeavored, however, to suppress the thought. His health was frail, and the work seemed above his strength. A minister's life at that time, too, was considered a hard life. It involved much labor and self-denial, and presented no prospect of earthly compensation. He shrunk from its trials and its responsibilities. At the meeting of the Nashville Presbytery in the spring of 1819, the great destitution of ministerial laborers in the bounds of the Presbytery was seriously considered, and a day of fasting and prayer was appointed in view of that destitution. The congregations were recommended to pray for an increase of ministers, and the preachers were to preach upon a call to the ministry. On the fast-day, Thomas Calhoon preached at Fall Creek, upon a call to the work. The sermon was delivered on Monday of a camp-meeting. It was a powerful effort, and made a deep impression. Robert Baker and another young man acknowledged their spiritual struggles on the subject, and, it was understood, gave themselves up to God that day for the work of the ministry.

At the fall meeting of the Presbytery of that year, on the 14th day of October, at the Big Spring Meeting-house, he was received as a candidate for the ministry. The text for his first trial sermon was Heb. ii. 3. The text assigned at the next Presbytery was Rom. vi. 23. At the following meeting of the Presbytery Mr. Baker, in conjunction with the writer, was licensed. This occurred at the Beech Meeting-house, in Sumner county, in October, 1822. Rev. Thomas Calhoon officiated. At this meeting of the Presbytery he was assigned for the whole of his time to the Nashville Circuit. This circuit extended through the most cultivated portion of Middle Tennessee. At the next meeting of the Presbytery he was assigned to the same work. At the fall meeting of the Presbytery in 1821 he was still continued, in conjunction with William Etherly, upon the Nashville Circuit. In the course of his first year's labor, he received what was considered a striking testimonial of his popularity as a preacher. Some of the ladies of the circuit combined, and presented him with a cloth suit. Other circuit-riders considered themselves high favored to be supplied with socks, and very common clothes—such as the ladies made themselves. A present of a cloth suit was a new thing under the sun. It was, however, well deserved on this occasion. His labors had been very useful, and he was greatly beloved.

In the fall of 1822 the Lebanon Presbytery was organized. It had been stricken off from the Nashville Presbytery by the preceding Synod. Mr. Baker lived within the bounds of the new Presbytery, and of course was transferred to its care.

At the meeting of the Lebanon Presbytery in 1823, he was set apart to the whole work of the ministry.

In the spring of 1823, in company with Abner W. Lansden, a licentiate of the Lebanon Presbytery, he was sent to East Tennessee. "Amiable, conciliatory, easy, and agreeable in his manners, sedate, deeply pious, affectionate, and sympathetic, he was a model missionary. Possessing respectable talents, a voice combining with the volume of the trumpet the soft melody of the lute, and a sympathy of soul that wooed his audience in the tenderest strains of the gospel, he was such a preacher as we are apt to imagine the beloved disciple was, who reclined upon his Master's bosom."[1] He labored in East Tennessee for twelve months, in conjunction with Mr. Lansden and others. In the winter months, however, his health suffered, and at the spring session of the Presbytery in 1824, he was assigned to the Lebanon Circuit, that he might be in the vicinity of his home in the event of his being unable to prosecute his labors from a farther failure of health.

In the fall or winter of 1825 Mr. Baker's father moved to Western Tennessee, and settled in Carroll county, first on Clear Creek, and afterward in the neighborhood of what is now McLemoresville. Robert Baker moved with him, and became a member of Hopewell Presbytery. From that time his labors were confined chiefly to Western Tennessee. He attended the last meeting of the Cumberland Synod. Its sessions were held at Franklin, Tennessee, in the fall of 1828. The following spring he was a member of the first General Assembly. Its sessions were held at Princeton, Kentucky, in May, 1829. He was also a member of the General Assembly of 1838, which met at Lebanon, Tennessee. It must not be inferred from the mention of these particulars that he was ever remiss in his attendance upon the judicatures of the Church. He was punctual in the discharge of these as well as other duties. He was trained in a school in which punctuality was required.

In the early part of the summer of 1829, Mr. Baker was married to a young lady, a member of the Church, and of very respectable family. In a few months, however, it was developed that he had bestowed his affections upon a very unworthy object. A separation was the result. His feelings and his happiness had been cruelly trifled with. It was a dark cloud over the path of a good man. He felt it to be a terrible blow. I performed the marriage service myself, and became fully acquainted with the feelings of the sufferer. Let the curtain of oblivion, however, drop upon a scene which was at the time so full of sadness and disappointment. In process of time, I believe in the winter of 1829 and 1830, he was divorced from his wife by the action of the Legislature of Tennessee.

On the 27th of December, 1831, he was married a second time, to Miss Sarah C. Hamilton, of Carroll county. He settled immediately in the neighborhood of his father-in-law, and remained there until his death. In the meantime he became the pastor of the Shiloh congregation, in the bounds of which his father-in-law's family had lived from the time of its organization. Here he labored as long as he had strength for any public service. I suppose the pastoral connection was dissolved by his death.

From the time Mr. Baker entered the ministry his health was feeble. His friends thought that he could not bear the labors and hardships of the service many

---

[1]**Life of George Donnell**.

years. He was himself under the impression that his race would be short. Still, he held up against encroaching infirmities until 1845. I spent two days at his camp-meeting in the fall of 1844. I had not seen him for years. His health and strength seemed at least equal to what I would have expected. Still he was very feeble. In the course of that winter he failed rapidly. Some time before his death his brother-in-law, who lived some miles distant, removed him to his own house, hoping that the change would afford some recreation and relief. The invalid soon, however, became worse, his family were sent for; he declined rapidly, and on the sixth day of March, 1845, he breathed his last. My informant says that "while he retained the proper exercise of his mind, all was peace and comfort." His remains were borne to what had been his home, on the day following his death, and on the next day were buried in the burying-ground at Shiloh. On the day of the burial, whilst the religious service connected with the occasion was conducted in the church by Rev. A. E. Cooper, his wife fainted. With considerable difficulty she was relieved of the affection, and revived. She witnessed the burial, and was taken to her home in a carriage by some friends. When she reached the house, seeming to be overpowered by a sense of her desolation, she fainted again, and never revived. She had appeared previously to be in perfect health, and to bear her bereavement with unusual presence of mind. Thus died a good man, and certainly a most devoted wife. Six fatherless and motherless children were left behind. Two of them have since died. The others, with one exception, are members of the Church. It was said at the time that Mr. Baker's friends, and the members of his congregation, were unusually kind and liberal in making provision for his children.

I append the following account from a respected minister, an eye-witness of the last hours of Mr. Baker, and of the melancholy circumstances which followed. The circumstances were so remarkable and afflicting, that a more detailed statement of them will be interesting:

> It was my privilege to meet with Rev. Robert Baker frequently during his last illness. I had just entered the ministry. Being inexperienced, and subject to many discouragements, I esteemed it indeed a great privilege to be welcomed to his hospitable home, and there to have the benefit of his counsel and instruction. I found his home a resting-place and a quiet retreat for the young preacher, and that there was no one to whom he could go with more reliable assurances of sympathy and kindness. He talked to me frequently of the trials of his early ministry. Often have I listened for hours at the recital of his sufferings, both physical and mental. He was indeed a man of many sorrows. A few of his intimate friends knew something of these; but the world will never know what he suffered, for the reason that the history of his sufferings never will, never can be written. Yet in the midst of all, be it said, that he was the same patient, self-poised Christian philosopher, never murmuring, or repining, or at any time evincing a spirit of insubordination to the Divine will. His lamp was at all times trimmed and burning, and doubtless at any hour during the last few years of his life he could, in its full spirit, have adopted the language of the great apostle of the Gentiles, 'I am

now ready to be offered.'

I was present and witnessed the closing scene of his earthly pilgrimage. He was at the house of his brother-in-law, near McLemoresville, in Western Tennessee. he had been declining for some time previous to his removal there. His death, which soon occurred, was therefore no matter of surprise, either to his relatives around him, or to his friends more remote. In his last hours he was calm and self-possessed. His arrangements had all been made, and he only awaited the call of his Master. His wife and children had been previously committed to that God who has promised to be a friend to the fatherless and the widow. With an unshaken confidence in the faithfulness of Him who thus promises, he closed his eyes in death. The scene was indeed impressive, especially to the writer, who had never witnessed such an occurrence before.

There was a circumstance connected with the death of this great and good man of a very remarkable character. While he was breathing his last in the presence of a concourse of weeping friends and relatives, the writer, with others present, observed that his wife, an excellent Christian lady, sat by the bedside apparently unmoved. She looked steadfastly into the face of her dying husband without shedding a tear or heaving a sigh. No satisfactory explanation could be given at the time of what seemed so strange, and, we may say, so unnatural. In the course of the proceedings, however, of the funeral solemnities, the mystery was explained. While listening to the funeral-sermon of her deceased husband in the Shiloh church, where he had so often ministered himself, she fainted and fell on the floor. She seemed to be lifeless for a time. But the attention of friends and attending physicians restored her to consciousness, and when the burial was over, she was able to ride in a carriage to her lonely and desolate home, which was but a few hundred yards distant from the church. Having walked into the house, at the suggestion of her friends she lay down on a convenient bed to rest. She asked her sister for some water. In less time than would be requisite for writing this sentence, the water was brought to her couch, but, lo! she was not there. The spirit had departed: Mrs. Baker had joined her sainted husband in a better world. Several physicians were called in with the utmost dispatch. They labored to a late hour in the evening to restore animation and consciousness, but their labors were unavailing. Death had done its work. She had gone to heaven, and would not return.

The physicians present decided that her death was the result of excessive grief, which could not find expression—that if she could have given vent to her feelings by shedding tears, and other customary means, she might have lived.

Robert Baker belonged to what might be termed the third generation of

Cumberland Presbyterian preachers. He was brought into the ministry by the fathers of the Church, and trained in their school. He had imbibed much of their spirit: from the time he entered the ministry he felt himself to be a consecrated man. He never, during his subsequent life, lost a sense of the holy obligations which the vows of his early manhood had imposed upon him. If a man could inherit religion, he would certainly have been one of the heirs. His father and mother were Christians of the old school, which flourished fifty years ago. Religion with them was an earnest matter—it was a business of life. He was brought up under the ministrations of Thomas Calhoon. The impressions made by Mr. Calhoon were deep and abiding. Mr. Baker was always a favorite with Mr. Calhoon, and if the sentiment had been reciprocated, it would not have been a matter of surprise, nor would the character of the teacher have been likely to impair that of the disciple.

Mr. Baker had many natural endowments which were favorable to the ministerial work. His mind, though not cultivated in the schools, was active and vigorous. What he read he understood, and retained in memory. He could use his acquisitions, too, with great readiness and freedom. He had an excellent spirit—he was kind, conciliating, unselfish—everybody loved him. His manner in the pulpit was natural and agreeable; it was more than agreeable—it was pleasing. His voice was unusually good. He delivered his sermons with an earnestness and a holy unction which seldom failed to make an impression.

I recollect the time of his first visit to Shiloh, where he ultimately settled, and was buried. It was upon the occasion of a camp-meeting. He had been unwell, but reached there on Saturday evening. He preached on Sabbath from the apostolic injunction, "Examine yourselves whether ye be in the faith; prove your ownselves; know ye not your own selves how that Jesus Christ is in you, except ye be reprobates." It was a sacramental-sermon. It became a favorite sermon with him afterward. On that occasion it made a fine impression. He preached again on Monday, from the first Psalm. There were two good old men present, who had recently settled in the neighborhood with their families. They had been members of another Church, in Kentucky, and had been in the habit of hearing good preachers from their youth. They were captivated, however, with the preaching which they heard in the wilderness. They expressed earnest wishes that their old friends in Kentucky could be there, to hear what they were hearing. I need hardly add that these two old men with their families became members of Shiloh congregation. The old men have passed away, but their descendants are still there, earnest and laborious members of the Church.

At a certain time, whilst Mr. Baker and myself were cooperating in Western Tennessee, we were directed to hold a two-days' meeting in Huntingdon. No congregation had been organized in the place. There was no house of worship, and the community were thought to be rather impracticable on the subject of religion. The meeting was appointed, and the time came. We preached in the courthouse. The attendance was fair. The next day we preached in the court-house in like manner. The congregation was large. We felt serious in prospect of the responsibility. I recollect on our way to the meeting on Sabbath morning, I repeated to him the words of Abishai to Joab, when they were about entering into battle with the enemies of Israel: "Be of good courage, and let us behave ourselves valiantly for our people, and for the cities of our God; and let the Lord do that which is good in his sight." I preached that morning as well as I could. Mr. Baker followed. He preached from a passage in the Lord's Prayer: "But deliver us from evil." He denounced what were said to be the evils and vices of the place, and especially of the young men, with great boldness and severity. It was an earnest and terrible philippic. The people listened with respectful and profound attention. Of course some curiosity was excited to know how the last sermon would be received. In a few days the question was settled. The young men, instead of becoming offended, were so much pleased with the boldness and fidelity of the preacher, that they made him a present of a suit of fine clothes. Public attention was turned to the subject of religion to an extent to which it had never been turned before. Beyond that immediate result, we cannot tell what the more remote results may have been. One of those young men is now my neighbor, and a respected member of the Church.

Mr. Baker and myself were intimately connected a number of years in Western Tennessee in the work of the ministry. I knew him well. A small volume might be filled with incidents. The country was new. We were young men. The members of the Presbytery were nearly all young. The work imposed a heavy responsibility. Still, from the harvest which has been reaped, we may diffidently infer that some good seed was sown.

In the winter of 1829 and 1830 John C. Smith and James McKee died. They were both members of the Presbytery—men of promise, and greatly beloved. We were desired by their friends to deliver sermons as memorials of the deceased. The sermons were to be delivered together. We preached at Huntingdon, Trenton, Sandy Meeting-house, and Shiloh. It was a melancholy series of services. They related to the dead. With them, too, our cooperative labors came practically to a close. In a few days after the meeting at Shiloh we separated. He remained in Tennessee, and continued a faithful, laborious, and honored preacher and pastor. I went to Kentucky, and entered upon a course which, in the providence of God, has led to what was certainly not of my own devising. God rules as he will.

REV. JOHN BARNETT
(c. 1784-1853)

Of the early life of John Barnett, as in the case of his brother, nothing is known to the writer. Even the time and place of his birth are unknown. It was always understood the John Barnett was the older of the two brothers, whilst William was first in the ministry, and, of course, the older preacher. I have therefore placed him first in the order of my arrangement. It has always been understood, too, that John, as well as William, entered the ministry some time after he became the head of a family. His wife's name was Polly McAdow. She was at least a remote relation of Rev. Samuel McAdow. The McAdows were of North Carolina origin, but lived chiefly in Tennessee.

John Barnett was received as a candidate for the ministry by the Cumberland Presbytery at the Beech Meeting-house, in Sumner county, Tennessee, April 9, 1813. At this meeting the Presbytery was divided, and he was placed under the care of the Logan Presbytery. By that Presbytery he was licensed August 31, 1813, and ordained August 11, 1815. He is first mentioned as a member of the Cumberland Synod in the records of its sessions in October, 1816.

At some time in the early part of his ministry he settled in lower Kentucky, which was considered at that time a frontier of the Church in that direction. His settlement was made in the neighborhood of what is now the Bethlehem Congregation. He originated that congregation, and in early time they built a log meeting-house of very moderate dimensions, in which, as pastor of the congregation, he ministered for near thirty years. Camp-meetings were introduced very early, and kept up forty years. Great numbers have been converted at these meetings. Bethlehem in now a flourishing congregation. They have been worshiping for twenty years in a capacious brick church. A neat brick academy stands hard by the church—a realization of the proper theory of Presbyterianism, the theory of a church and school combined.

During all the years of his connection with Bethlehem Mr. Barnett was also the pastor of Piney Fork Congregation. A modest house of worship was built at Piney, and camp-meetings were held annually, and mostly with great success. At Piney these meetings are still continued.

Whilst Mr. Barnett was pastor of these congregations, he was at the same time one of the best farmers in his neighborhood. He was a strong man, had fine health, and labored daily with his own hands. He also kept every one around him busy. It is a matter of tradition that he frequently labored on his farm all day, and in the evening rode four or five miles, and preached in some private house in his congregation, continued his meetings till eleven or twelve o'clock at night, returned home, and was ready for another day's work in the morning. By labors of this kind Bethlehem and Piney Fork Congregations were gathered and strengthened from year to year.

In 1826 Cumberland College commenced its operations. Mr. Barnett had an active agency in its location, and in the organization and direction of its exterior system. I allude to the management of the farm and boarding-house. He moved tot he College, and for some two or three years had charge of these. After his connection with them ceased, he moved to Christian county, and lived a few years, near Salubria Spring, in the neighborhood in which his brother William had once lived, and perhaps upon the same farm. After a few years he returned to the neighborhood of his former home near Bethlehem. In 1831 the Trustees of Cumberland College, by the advice of the General Assembly, leased the institution to him and Rev. Aaron Shelby for a term of years. This was an extraordinary measure, but the exigences of the College were considered to require something extraordinary. It was deeply involved in debt, and still was not self-sustaining irrespective of its debts. Of course it was becoming more deeply involved every year. The lessees of the institution were to keep up the farm and boarding-house, manage its general finances, keep up its Faculty, and pay its debts. To enable them to do all these things, they were to have the proceeds of the farm and boarding-house, and the customary labor of each student two hours per day. The proceeds of the tuition department were to be set apart of the payment of the instructors. Mr. Shelby continued his connection with the institution two or three years, and sold his interest to Mr. Harvey Young. A new brick building had been put up, a very coarse and inferior one, it is true, but still an improvement upon the previous condition of things. Every thing seemed to go forward rather prosperously till the summer of 1834, when the cholera visited the town. It did not reach the College, but it was followed by a most malignant fever, which spread all over the country, including the College community. Mr. Young died; three-fourths of the students were sick. Recitations were discontinued for some time. Myself and wife were both prostated for several weeks. I was myself evidently near the door of death. It was a terrible infliction upon the College. Mr. Barnett considered it the turning-point in his administration of the financial affairs of the institution. It was a prostration from which he never recovered.

After the death of Mr. Young, his interest reverted, of course, to the Trustees, and the partnership henceforward was a partnership of the Trustees and Mr. Barnett. He, however, became practically the administrator of the business. Things worked badly; a great deal of dissatisfaction grew up all over the Church; he was sometimes unhappy in the temper in which he conducted his business; the wisdom of his measures was thought in some cases to be very defective, and a few began to call in question his personal integrity. He and Dr. Cossitt, the President of the College, differed in their views of measures, and, unfortunately, became estranged from each other. I have told this unhappy story elsewhere. They were both good men, earnest in their opinions, and unwavering in their fidelity to the Church; but they did not harmonize; it was a misfortune. With regard to Dr. Cossitt, my esteemed instructor and friend, my testimony is before the world. With regard to Mr. Barnett, and his connection with the College, I have a few things to say, but for the present hold them in reserve.

It will be readily perceived that these difficulties must have had a disastrous influence upon the College.

At the General Assembly of 1837, a new plan was adopted, with a view to the relief of the institution from its difficulties, which were rather increasing than diminishing. An association was formed under the style and title of The Cumberland College Association, after the manner of a joint-stock company. Mr. Barnett and the Trustees surrendered their interest in the College to the Association. It was to do the same things which Barnett and Shelby were to have done, and after accomplishing them, to have pro rata dividends of the proceeds, should it ever turn out that there were such proceeds to divide. This plan was expected to be a success, whilst the preceding one had proved a disastrous failure. The history is known, and needs not be repeated here. To say every thing in the fewest possible words, an experiment of three years proved its utter insufficiency. It, too, was a failure. In 1834, in the midst of the prevailing sickness, Mr. Barnett lost his eldest son, a young man of rather unusual promise. He was one of the early graduates of Cumberland College. Some time between 1838 and 1843, he lost his wife, and third and fourth sons. From this time he became unsettled for several years. After the lapse of a few years, however, he was married a second time, to an estimable widow lady, of Henderson county, Kentucky. His constitution was very much shattered, and his health soon failed, and in a few years his life of unusual trial came to an end. Of the circumstances of death nothing is known to the writer. The most of his latter years had been passed under a cloud. A great many of his expectations had been thwarted. His providential discipline had been severe. When death came, it was doubtless a release. A life very much made up of clouds and storms was, we must confidently believe, exchanged for a companionship of the four and twenty elders, the hundred and forty and four thousand, and the great multitude that no man can number.

    My first recollection of Mr. Barnett goes back to the fall of 1819. He was attending a camp-meeting at the Big Spring, in Wilson county, Tennessee. His first sermon there was delivered on Saturday evening. It had rained in the forenoon, and meeting was held in the house, and William Bumpass preached. The rain had ceased, however, and we removed to the stand, as it was called; there was no shelter. Mr. Barnett was the preacher. I had never heard or seen him before. His text was the prophet's personation of the Saviour as a preacher: "The Spirit of the Lord God is upon me; because the Lord hath anointed me to preach good tidings unto the meek; he hath sent me to bind up the brokenhearted, to proclaim liberty to the captives, and the opening of the prison to them that are bound; to proclaim the acceptable year of the Lord, and the day of vengeance of our God." The preacher and the text were both new to me. The preacher was certainly in a good spirit. It seemed to me that the fitness between him and the text was perfect. The solemnity, and tenderness, and earnestness of his manner, and the unction which seemed to rest upon him, were altogether unusual. I have seldom, in a long life, been more deeply interested, or more favorably impressed; and I have often called to mind the apparent tenderness and gentleness of that occasion when, in subsequent years, I have witnessed his struggles with the difficulties of the College, and his excusable impatience with the impertinence and impracticability of men with whom he was thrown into contact in his business transactions. The descent appeared to be very great. He felt it to be so himself; yet Providence seemed to him to lead him into that line of duty. On Monday of the same camp-meeting he preached again, from the text in First Corinthians: "And ye are not your own, for ye are bought with a price; therefore glorify God in your body, and in your spirit, which are God's." The text was familiar, and the sermon was good, but not equal to that of Saturday.

    In 1824, or 1825, Mr. Barnett and Rev. David Lowry made a visit to Western Tennessee, to assist William Barnett in two or three camp-meetings. They preached with great interest and power, and left a deep impression behind them. In that visit Mr. Barnett was condescending enough to make me a sort of companion in one or two of his excursions outside of his regular movements, in visiting some of his old acquaintances and friends. I say, "condescending enough;" I really thought it a privilege and an honor to be permitted to attend him. He seemed to me tender, and kind, and even paternal in his manners.

I had but little connection with him after these occurrences, until I went to Cumberland College, in 1830. At that time he was living in Christian county. In the spring of the following year, as it has been said, he became connected with the College as one of the lessees. My own connection with the College continued to 1838. From 1831 to 1837, his connection, as general administrator of its business affairs, continued. We were frequently thrown together under circumstances of great trial. A large part of the period was passed under discouragement, darkness, and distress. In these he, of course, shared very largely. He had embarked every thing in the experiment of trying to improve the financial condition of the College. If he failed, poverty was staring him in the face, whilst yet he had a heavy family on his hands. As it has been mentioned, he lost his eldest and most promising son in the midst of those years. He had fondly expected help from that son, and the loss on that account seemed the more severe. The Church complained of his general administration; the students complained of his stringency in providing for the boarding-house; the teachers complained that they did not receive much more than half pay. He was made answerable for a great many evils. The year 1837 came around, and public sentiment seemed to require a change of the outward administration of the affairs of the College.

It is fitting that I should say here, in my place, that no man could have labored more earnestly for the accomplishment of the great objects of a mission than Mr. Barnett did, in those years, for the fulfillment of his engagements with the General Assembly. He did not succeed. No man could have succeeded in his circumstances. He had entered upon a Herculean task; he was a strong man, but still only a man. He was no Hercules. He committed errors, without doubt; but they were the errors of a man governed, upon the whole, by good intentions. He meant well. Of this I have no doubt. His personal integrity was sometimes impeached; but the best possible vindication that could have been offered was the fact at last disclosed, that whilst he entered into his connection with the College a prosperous man, and bringing into it a respectable property, he left it with his temporalities in ruins, and from these ruins he never recovered. After the lapse of thirty-six years, I have no patience with charges which affect his personal integrity. I am ashamed of him who reiterates them.

He though the Church owed him something in consideration of his losses. He pursued that thought for years, but without success. I do not pretend to decide upon the justice of his claims from this source, but there are a few living who can recollect the persistence of his efforts in prosecuting those claims, which we all thought, whether just or unjust, to be hopeless.

No man in the Cumberland Presbyterian Church was ever so generally misunderstood. It rarely happens to a man, in any of the relations of life, to be so generally misunderstood by those who ought to understand him. Public sentiment took a wrong direction. There were, of course, reasons for it, but still the direction was wrong. The Church, instead of quarreling with a man who had taken one of its heaviest burdens upon his shoulders, should have reached out a helping hand, and, if possible, lightened that burden. Such a course, however, was not pursued. He was in the ditch, and was left very much to take care of himself.

I make one farther remark in this connection. Other men have quarreled with the Church, and have left it. In one or two cases the quarrel has been very bitter. Mr. Barnett, however, in the midst of all the vituperation and reproach, and, as he thought, ingratitude and unkindness which he endured, never faltered in his fidelity and devotion to the Church of his early choice to his dying day. In illustration of this a fact may be stated, which, of course, is not known generally, but which, for the sake of his memory, should be known. In making a final settlement of his shattered affairs, he set apart a thousand dollars for the use and benefit of Cumberland College, in the service of which he had suffered so much, and of which he had at that time high hopes. This is an argument which any man can appreciate.

After Mr. Barnett's second marriage I seldom saw him. His home was remote from mine, and he did not travel much. The infirmities of age were closing in upon him. In a few years he ended his stirring and stormy life. He had left home with the view of traveling some time, in hope of an improvement of his health. In a few days he reached the residence of his son-in-law in Western Tennessee, and stopped to rest. It proved to be his last resting-place. He died there.

The case of Mr. Barnett brings up to our minds the darkest chapter in our history as a Church. The history of Cumberland College has never been written. Most likely it will never be written. In twenty years from this time it cannot be truthfully done. The actors in the transactions will all have passed away, and no man can write it who has not, to some extent, been one of those actors. Dr. Cossitt, Mr. Barnett, Judge Morrison, Aaron Shelby, and Harvey Young, have all been removed from among us. A few still remain, but will not remain long. The College has ceased to exist. Many will say that a great deal of labor has been lost, and a great deal of money has been expended in vain. So thought Judas and the other disciples which the anointing oil was poured upon the Master's feet. He gave them to understand, however, that they were mistaken. It was not a waste. Nor has the labor and money expended upon Cumberland College been a waste. It has fulfilled its mission. In many respects it was a noble mission. Some of those connected with it were never appreciated. Even time itself may not fully vindicate them; still, their works follow them. The seed sown there is producing a harvest all over the West. Our pioneers in the work of education have been amongst our benefactors. Their work has been silent, but it has been none the less effective and vital in its influence on that account. It will live forever in its results.

William and John Barnett had a younger brother, or, rather, half-brother, Rev. James Young Barnett, who entered the ministry in early life. He was a man of fine ability, and was thought in his early life to be the equal of his older brothers. He never filled so wide a space, however, in public estimation. He married the daughter of Mr. David Usher, of Christian county, Kentucky, and settled in the neighborhood of his father-in-law, where he lived till his death, which occurred some years ago. he was an estimable and useful man. His widow still lives.

There was a fourth brother, Robert Barnett, who also entered the ministry, in Western Tennessee, in his early life. He married the daughter of Hon. Adam R. Alexander, but of his subsequent history I have no knowledge.

REV. WILLIAM BARNETT
(1785-1827)

William Barnett was born April 24, 1785. Of his early history nothing is known to the writer. It is supposed that he grew up, as ordinary boys in his time did, with limited means of education. He married early; according to the family record, November 17, 1801, when he was in his seventeenth year. His first wife was Jane Owen. The following memorandum, said to have been written with his own hand, has been kindly furnished to me:

> William Barnett professed to be regenerated, or born again, August 2, 1803; was licensed to preach the gospel October 10, 1810; was ordained, or set apart to the whole work of the ministry, in February, 1813.

According to the records of Cumberland Presbytery, which vary from his own account, he was received as a candidate for the ministry March 20, 1810, at the Ridge Meeting-house, in Sumner county, Tennessee. The meeting of the Presbytery at which this occurred was the first after its constitution in the previous month. The text assigned him for trial was John x. 9. The sermon was read at the meeting of the Presbytery at the Big Spring, March 22, 1811. A second text was assigned him—Rom. v. 9. From this he read a discourse at the sessions of the Presbytery held at the Ridge, October 11, 1811. On this occasion he was licensed as a probationer for the holy ministry. At a meeting of the Presbytery held at Mount Moriah Meeting-house, in Logan county, Kentucky, February 13, 1813, he was ordained. His trial-sermon was from John iii. 16. Rev. Thomas Calhoon preached the ordination-sermon—Rev. Finis Ewing presided and delivered the charge.

It will be observed from these data that Mr. Barnett's Christian and ministerial life was one of the fruits of the old revival of 1800. Mr. Smith, in his **History of the Cumberland Presbyterians**, mentions him as one of the candidates for the ministry that met the Cumberland Presbytery at the Ridge Meeting-house in March, 1810. It appears, however, from the records of the Presbytery, that he was received as a candidate at that meeting. His own memorandum confirms the truth of the record. He had no doubt been exercising his gifts as an exhorter, under the direction of the Council, previous to that time. He was ordained, as it appears from the records, and from his own memorandum, in February of 1813. His name appears on the minutes of the Cumberland Synod of that year. The meeting was held in October, at the Beech Meeting-house, in Sumner county, Tennessee. The next meeting of the Synod occurred in April, 1814. The sessions were held at Suggs's Creek Meeting-house, in Wilson county, Tennessee. Mr. Barnett is recorded in the minutes as having been present. This meeting of the Synod is memorable from its having been the occasion upon which the present Confession of Faith and Form of Government were reported by the committee appointed at a previous meeting to prepare them. They were examined and adopted in conformity with the report. At the next meeting of the Synod, in October, 1815, at the Beech Meeting-house, Mr. Barnett was appointed Moderator. In October of 1816 he delivered the customary opening-sermon of the Synod from Jer. xxiii. 22. In 1825 he was again the Moderator of the Synod. Its sessions were held that year in October, at Princeton, Kentucky. This meeting is memorable from its having originated our first literary institution. Resolutions were passed, and arrangements were made, which led to the organization of Cumberland College. The organization took place in March following. He delivered the opening-sermon at the following Synod in 1826, from Col. iv. 17.

In the division of the Cumberland Presbytery into the three Presbyteries, with a view to the formation of a Synod, he became a member of the Logan Presbytery. He remained in Kentucky, and a member of that Presbytery, until 1823. Whilst in Kentucky, he lived first in Christian county, near Salubria Spring. After some years, perhaps about 1821, he moved to the town, or county, of Henderson, and remained there about two years. In Kentucky he lost his wife and the mother of his children. He afterward, August 17, 1820, married the widow of Colonel Shelby, of Montgomery county, Tennessee, a lady of some property and of great personal worth. His last wife survived him a number of years. In the fall of 1823 he moved to Western Tennessee, and settled about twelve or fifteen miles above Jackson, where he remained to the close of 1825. In January, 1826, he moved again, and settled in Hardeman county, twelve miles west of Bolivar. He there collected a congregation around him at Mount Comfort. In August of 1827 his annual camp-meeting occurred at Mount Comfort. He was taken from his home to the camp-ground sick. At the close of the meeting he was removed home with increasingly unfavorable symptoms, and in a few days died of the common fever of the country. This occurred on the 29th of August, 1827. His death was felt to be a heavy blow on the infant Church in that country, as the ministry who were left were all young men. Still it was found that seed had been sown which produced a rich harvest. The Cumberland Presbyterian Church has up to this time held a strong position in Western Tennessee. How much of this is due to the influence of Mr. Barnett, and to his few years of labor in that country, none of us can tell. Certainly he labored with great earnestness, power, and apparent success.

My personal recollections of Mr. Barnett go back to 1812. He attended the camp-meeting at the Ridge Meeting-house in August of that year. I received my first distinct impressions of the Church at that meeting. Several ministers, of whom sketches are presented in this and the preceding series, were present on that occasion. As I have said, the meeting was held in August. In the fall of that year he had an appointment for preaching at a private house in the neighborhood one evening. The reader will recollect that our second war with Great Britain commenced in 1812. My father and myself attended the appointment for preaching. After reaching the place of preaching we heard for the first time of the first great reverse of the American arms in that war. I allude to the surrender of General Hull. The event had just occurred, and the intelligence spread with great rapidity over the country. I was but a boy, but was very much of a patriot, as boys usually are. The intelligence of the surrender distressed me very greatly. It made me sad. The hour for preaching came on, and the preacher was sick, and could not preach. The meeting was converted into a prayer-meeting. Several of the old brethren prayed. Mr. Barnett came out of his room to close the meeting. A song was sung, and he prayed. I had never heard any thing like it, and I have certainly heard very few such prayers since. Perhaps I was in a favorable state of mind just then to hear a prayer. It seemed to me that the very heavens and the earth would come together. He was at that time a young preacher, and full of spirituality.

In 1817 Mr. Hodge, pastor of Shiloh Congregation, which had been greatly blessed in the early part of the revival, projected a union meeting at Shiloh. Mr. Hodge, and the men who constituted the Cumberland Presbytery, and originated the Church, had separated in 1809, and he had given in his adhesion to the Synod of Kentucky. Still he was a good man, and his heart remained warm with the old fire of 1800. The Cumberland Synod was in session somewhere in Kentucky within convenient distance from Shiloh. Mr. Hodge sent to the Synod for help. He called in a prominent Methodist minister, Rev. James Gwynn, of the neighborhood, and Rev. Dr. Blackburn, and one or two other Presbyterian ministers, and so we had the first union meeting that I ever attended or heard of. William Barnett and David McLin were sent by the Synod to cooperate with Mr. Hodge and others at the union meeting. Mr. Gwynn and a young Presbyterian minister preached on Saturday. Mr. Gwynn preached a fitting sermon from the prophet's prayer, "O Lord, revive thy work." On Sabbath Mr. McLin and Dr. Blackburn preached, and on Sabbath-night William Barnett filled the pulpit. He preached on the shortness of time, from a familiar text. He did not succeed so well. His friends said that his manner and spirit seemed to be cramped. Indeed, it was thought that all the preachers of the occasion suffered in that way, except Mr. Gwynn and Dr. Blackburn. They were old heroes in the war. Mr. Barnett, however, had some mourners and a considerable movement at the close of his sermon. But the good old pastor did not realize his hopes from the meeting. It was well intended, but was considered a failure.

In the winter of 1819 and 1820 I was attending a school at Suggs's Creek, in the course of my preparation for the ministry. On a certain Saturday evening Mr. Barnett came into the neighborhood. He expected to spent the Sabbath with the Suggs's Creek Congregation, of which Rev. David Foster was pastor. It turned out that a Baptist minister had an appointment for preaching at the house of one of his brethren in the neighborhood that day, and Mr. Foster and his people had thought proper not to interfere, but to worship with the Baptist brethren. Mr. Barnett came to the meeting, and worshiped with the brethren in like manner. He was not known to the officiating minister, and of course was not invited to preach. But an appointment was made for him for Sabbath-night at old James Law's. It was one of the most convenient and roomy houses in the neighborhood. Expectation was excited, and a large crowd attended. The house was filled to its utmost capacity. Among the rest was a young man who had recently come into the neighborhood, very wicked and thoughtless. He anticipated a crowd, and something of a stir, and came to meeting with his coat turned wrong side out to attract attention, and to have some fun. Mr. Barnett preached also on that occasion on the shortness of time: "But I say, brethren, the time is short." It was a terrific sermon. The young man's fun was all spoiled. Mourners were invited forward for prayer, and he was among the first. He fell upon the floor with bitter cries for mercy. A great many others followed the example. I have never witnessed a more solemn night. These things occurred fifty-three and a half years ago, but the recollections have all the vividness of recent events. Our young friend professed religion in a short time. He thought himself called to preach, but he was very illiterate, and could not endure what we thought the necessary discipline connected with a preparation for the work, and transferred his relations to another Church. It is probable, however, that the sermon of that night was the means of saving his soul.

In October of 1822, the Cumberland Synod held its sessions at the Beech Meeting-house. I was ordained in the July preceding. It was, of course, the first Synod that I attended. There was an unusual number of young men in attendance on that occasion. They were some of the earliest of the third generation of Cumberland Presbyterian ministers. Mr. Barnett was appointed by the Synod to preach a sermon especially to the young men. I have no particular recollection of the sermon, except that it made a good impression. James B. Porter followed with an exhortation, and John Barnett with a general shaking of hands, according to the custom of those days.

It has been mentioned that in the fall of 1823 he settled in Western Tennessee. In the providence of God, I was at that time on a circuit which passed through the neighborhood of his settlement, and had a two-days' meeting at Adley Alexander's, in the neighborhood, including the first Sabbath after his arrival. He attended, and, of course, preached. The sermon was based upon the inquiries which the servant of Elisha was instructed to address to the Shunamite woman: "Is it well with thee" Is it well with thy husband? Is it well with the child?" It may be supposed that it was a good introduction into a new field of labor. It was indeed so.

Mr. Barnett was exceedingly popular in Western Tennessee. He was an extraordinary preacher, and had lost none of his pulpit power when he settled in that country. If any man in the Cumberland Presbyterian Church was entitled to the distinction of a Boanerges, I suppose William Barnett, in his time, by common consent would have been considered as holding the highest claim. When in the spirit, as it was customarily said in former times, and ought always to be said, he was very powerful. He had a celebrated sermon on the value of the soul and the danger of its loss, which in those times he preached a great deal, and which always attracted attention. On the subjects of conversion and a call to the ministry he was very searching, sometimes possibly cutting down those that he ought to have built up. If he erred, however, on such occasions, the error was on the safe side. There is more danger of healing a spiritual hurt slightly, than of not healing it at all. He had some of the highest characteristics of the fathers of this Church developed in unusual fullness. He had an iron-like bodily frame, a voice like a trumpet, and the courage of a lion. He was sometimes rough with the "boys," as they were usually called, but the pupils, many of them, were rough as well as the teachers. The writer knows all about the severity of that school; he sometimes smarted under it, but it was the school for the times.

Nearly four years transpired between Mr. Barnett's removal to West Tennessee and his death. These were years of labor. I recollect some of the circumstances of the last camp-meeting at which he performed any labor, with great distinctness. The meeting was held at McLemoresville. He preached on Sabbath upon the choice of Moses, "To suffer affliction with the people of God rather than to enjoy the pleasures of sin for a season." It was a pleasant sermon; of course a testimonial in favor of an experimental and practical Christianity. It made a fine impression. It was, however, as I have intimated, a pleasant, rather than a terrible, impression. On Monday he preached on the subject of the Judgment. It was a sermon of great power, very much of the character of the sermon described which he preached at old Mr. Law's. It was terrific. The crowd trembled under the influence of his awful and overwhelming appeals. Such appeals are seldom heard, and such impressions are seldom made now. He closed with a great movement in the congregation. Many were convicted, and hopefully converted that evening. It was the last sermon that he ever preached. His own camp-meeting commenced the following Friday. He rode home on horseback from McLemoresville, in the heat of August, a distance of seventy-five miles. When his own meeting commenced he was complaining. He went, however, with his family, to the ground, and remained till the close. He had to be taken home in a carriage; he went to bed, and never rose again. The strong man and the iron will yielded to the inevitable call. He fell with his armor on.

Mr. Barnett's last wife survived him a number of years. He left three sons and two or three daughters. His eldest son entered the ministry, and acquired, I suppose, some respectability. He was a member of the General Assembly from some one of the Texas Presbyteries in 1853. He has been dead some years. His second son, who was named for himself, was educated at Cumberland College, and graduated in 1832. He afterward studied medicine, and after a practice of a number of years, first in Missouri, and then in Kentucky, died in Caldwell county, Kentucky. The youngest son, I suppose, still lives. After spending some time at Cumberland College, he went to Missouri. One of the daughters is the wife of Rev. Samuel Lambert, of Mississippi.

Mr. Barnett was an extraordinary man. He had imperfections, and some of them were striking. Every thing about him was striking. His greatness was natural. His education was very limited. He seemed to live at the proper time, and the theater in which he acted was certainly providential. In all such cases we are deeply impressed with the thought that God, in his providence, selects his own agencies for his own work. If the history of the Cumberland Presbyterian Church teaches any thing, it teaches this lesson. We receive it and record it with profound gratitude and humility, that he has condescended to use agencies so unworthy, in the accomplishment of what we cannot call otherwise than a great work. Some mighty men, too, have been engaged in that work.

REV. JOHN BEARD
(1800-1866)

John Beard was born December 25, 1800, in Sumner county, Tennessee. His parents were David and Jane Wallis Beard. His grandfather, Captain David Beard, emigrated from Bedford county, Virginia, two or three years after the close of the Revolutionary War, and settled first in Kentucky, where he spent one year; he then moved to Tennessee, and, after being unsettled a few years, located in Sumner county, about seven miles from where Gallatin now stands. Captain Beard was a Revolutionary officer, and commanded a company of volunteers in the regiment of the famous Colonel Lynch, from whom Lynchburg received its name, and who is said also to have given name to what we popularly term Lynch-law. This company shared with their regiment in the battle of Guilford Courthouse, and likewise in the siege of Yorktown. At the close of the battle at Guilford Court-house, in the retreat of the Americans, a fellow-officer of Captain Beard was shot down at his elbow, and he very narrowly escaped being taken prisoner. In his old age he frequently referred to the adventure with thrilling interest. In Tennessee his eldest son was killed by the Indians; his other sons he succeeded in settling around him. John Beard was the eldest child of his parents. His boyhood was spent with the younger brothers, on his father's farm. His early educational advantages were limited. Reading, writing, and arithmetic constituted the educational course in the neighborhood, and in the country generally; and the time spent in these was what could be spared from the farm. The girls could go to school in the summer, but the boys were confined to farm-work until after the crops were laid by, and then again there was another season of labor in gathering the crops, and after that, their schooldays extended through the winter. Those were good days for promoting industry, economy, rural simplicity of living; but not favorable to advanced education. Good spelling was a distinguished attainment; the committing of the catechism to memory was a daily, or rather a nightly, exercise; English Grammar was hardly thought of, and the Rule of Three, as it was then called, was the general limit in the study of arithmetic. The people labored all week, and as many of each family as could be provided with conveyances attended church on Sabbath. If a casual sermon was to be heard in the immediate neighborhood, all, except the aged and infirm, generally went on foot—the boys and girls, in the summer, barefooted, or carrying their shoes and stockings in their hands, in order to save them, until they came to some suitable point near the congregation, where they were accustomed to stop and complete their equipage. In a state of society of this kind, as near as a hasty description can reach, John Beard spent his boyhood. His parents were members of the Presbyterian Church, and raised their family with great care. Rev. William Hodge, pastor of Shiloh Congregation, to which the family belonged, customarily preached in the neighborhood once or twice a year, and catechised the children of members of the congregation. On these occasions infant baptism was administered to children that could not be conventiently taken to the church, which was several miles distant. David Beard's house as frequently used for these religious assemblages. Scarcely any thing was wanting to the promotion of morality and good order. John Beard could hardly have grown up otherwise than a well-behaved and good boy. He was such in a very high degree—a model of morality, filial obedience, and industry.

In the meantime, the Cumberland Presbyterians were making progress in the country, and on the 20th of August, 1820, he professed religion at one of their camp-meetings at Stoner's Creek, in Wilson county. He had been serious, and deeply engaged on the subject of religion, for two or three months. A characteristic anecdote is told of him, which grew out of this part of his history. Some years after these occurrences, some ministers were holding a meeting at a church near the neighborhood in which he was raised, and some young men of rather unpromising character were professing religion in what seemed to the old-fashioned observers to be too short a time. A gentleman of the neighborhood, who was not himself a professor religion, and, moreover, not very well versed in those matters, observed the new order of proceeding, and decided earnestly that those young men were not converted at all—that the thing was out of the question. His argument was, that it took little John Beard[2] three months to get religion, and that he never did any thing wrong. The conclusion was, that these bad boys, who had so many misdeeds to account for, must be deceived when they thought of settling up the question in two or three hours.

Of course, the reasoner knew very little about the day of Pentecost, or the case of the jailer. It indicates, however, the estimate in which the subject of this sketch was held in the community in which he was brought up.

After his profession of religion, the question of a choice between Churches, of course, came up. He very properly sought the counsel of his parents, and they as properly submitted the matter to himself, advising him to unite himself with the Church in which he thought he would be most happy and most useful. The result was, he selected the Cumberland Presbyterian Church, and connected himself with the Dry Fork Congregation in February, 1821.

On the first day of April in the same year, he was received as a candidate for the ministry by the Nashville Presbytery. The Presbytery held its sessions at that time at Moriah Meeting-house, in Rutherford county. After being received as a candidate, he spent some months at school in Gallatin, under the instruction of the Rev. Mr. Bayne, a pious and well-qualified teacher of the Presbyterian Church. At this school he made his principal preparation for his work, in addition to his early education, which has been described.

He was licensed a a probationer for the ministry by the Nashville Presbytery, on the third day of April, 1823, and ordained on the sixth of April, 1826.

While a candidate for the ministry, he spent one winter with the writer on a circuit in what was then called the Western District of Tennessee. It is now Western Tennessee. The country was new; we were compelled often to make long rides, the houses were sometimes open; and occasionally the fare was hard. Still, I suppose we both felt that we were laboring under a providential and spiritual appointment, as well as the appointment of the Church, and the order of things in those days, on the part of the young men, was to obey; and we did try to obey,

---

[2]The good old people sometimes called our subject Little John Beard, rather than otherwise as a sort of affectionate and parental interest in him. The epithet, too, was descriptive enough of his exterior. In this respect he was a small man.

although compelled to confront showers of rain, heavy snows, and deep, and often overflowing streams.

After his licensure, he traveled as a circuit-rider, with very slight intermissions, four years and a half. His labors were greatly blessed during that time. Few men were more useful in that department of service, and certainly few were more beloved, in those years, than he.

In the spring, or early summer, of 1827, the last year of his service as an itinerant preacher, he visited, with some one else, the Charity Hall institution, in the Chickasaw Nation of Indians. These visits were made by appointment of the Cumberland Synod. On his return homeward, he called at McLemoresville, in Western Tennessee. I was making my home at McLemoresville at the time, and the chief object of his call was a visit to myself. He reached there sick, and immediately went to bed. It proved to be a protracted and dangerous illness. It was thought for several days that he would die. He rallied, however, and after a few weeks was able to prosecute his journey homeward. The trial from his sickness was greater from the fact that before he left home he had made an engagement to be married, and the day was fixed upon, time being allowed for his return. It turned out that when the appointed day arrived, he was in his sick-bed at McLemoresville. Of course, he seemed to himself to recover very slowly. Through several long and weary weeks I waited at his bedside myself, watching the lazy symptoms of his recovery. He did recover, however, and reached home, and the marriage, although having been delayed, was consummated. He married Miss Margaret S. Cloyd, daughter of the Rev. Ezekiel Cloyd, of Wilson county, Tennessee. The Rev. David Foster performed the marriage-service.

Soon after his marriage, he settled at Suggs's Creek, and took charge of that and Stoner's Creek Congregations. Mr. Foster had been his predecessor in these congregations for twenty years. He was now, however, preparing for a removal to Illinois. The successor labored in Sugg's Creek Congregation nineteen years. My informant says, "During this time many precious camp-meetings were held; a number of revivals occurred; hundreds of souls were converted, a goodly number of whom afterwards became able and useful ministers of the gospel."

In the fall of 1832, he settled in the Stoner's Creek neighborhood, still ministering to the same two congregations, until the spring of 1848, when he moved to Illinois. The want of adequate support, and tahe demands of a growing family, sent him westward.

After one or two unimportant removals in Illinois, he settled at Cherry Grove, where he became a member of the Rushville Presbytery. Here he labored with his accustomed activity and zeal, until the spring of 1859, when he moved to Missouri, where he found a field of usefulness in the bounds of the Lexington Presbytery. Here he remained a year and a half, and in the fall of 1860, when listening to the calls for help from the opening settlements in Kansas, he removed thither, and became a member of Kansas Presbytery. Here he labored, extending the usefulness of himself and family among the enterprising population of this new and opening country as far as he was able. In process of time the Kansas Presbytery was divided, and the Leavenworth Presbytery was constituted. He became a member of the new Presbytery. It held its first meeting according to appointment; but previous to the second appointed meeting, he, with another member, was called to his rest. As a matter of history, it may be mentioned that the death of these two members left the Presbytery without a quorum. Other ministers, however, have come in, and the Presbytery has been reinstated, and is doing a good and vigorous work.

A short time before his death, he had been preaching regularly to four congregations—Round Prairie, in the bounds of which he lived; Wolf River, forty miles distant; Pleasant Grove, eight miles distant; and High Prairie, twelve miles distant—besides doing much outside work at other points. The field was so large, the harvest so white, and the laborers so few, that he felt himself urged to more ministerial labor than one of his age could long endure.

On Saturday, July 28, 1866, in holding a sacramental-meeting, assisted by another minister, he preached his last sermon. The meeting was held at Pleasant Grove, near Atchison City, and the sermon is said to have been one of more interest and power than usual. He went home on Monday, and immediately to his bed, from which he never arose a well man. He became very sick. A physician was called in; then another; and still a third. No permanent relief, however, was afforded. From affliction of the throat he spoke but little, and with difficulty. A few hours before his death he had some select Psalms read, and songs sung, which seemed to give him great spiritual comfort. He then had his family and friends present gathered around him, and gave each one a parting word, asking all to meet him in heaven. In a few hours more he breathed his last, on the 15th of August, 1866, universally lamented by his friends and acquaintances. I would suppose he had no enemies.

My personal knowledge of John Beard was, of course, very intimate. We were near the same age, he being but about a year the younger. Our early boyhood was spent almost together. In those years I lived with my grandfather, and his father's home was but a few hundred yards distant. We went to school together to my father's unpretending school, when we could be spared from the labor of the farm. We went to mill together, and on the Sabbath, when both families were gone to the customary meetings, we sometimes met and talked over our reading. He was always fond of reading hymns, and read the hymn-book a great deal on the Sabbath, whilst I read the "Pilgrim's Progress," and the "Travels of True Godliness." He was three years behind me in his profession of religion, and the same length of time in his entrance upon the ministry. In our ministerial work, with the exception of the six months with me on the circuit which I have mentioned, we were far separated, but I still knew him well, and kept up with the history of his work. With his local ministrations, labor on a farm for the support of his family, I believe, was always connected. It was so, at least, while he lived in Tennessee. He thus labored through the week, and preahced on Sabbath. He was always beloved, and notwithstanding the difficulties he must have encountered in preparing his sermons, he was always heard with interest and pleasure. In fact, as far as his pretensions went, when in the prime of life, he was one of the best preachers of his day. He never aspired to greatness or leadership, yet, whilst most men fall below their pretensions, he was generally above the line which he had fixed for his measure. The wonder always was, that he could preach so well. In all the relations of life he was a model. He respected his parents, and as a brother, husband, and father, he filled up his obligations with a kindness and fidelity which are unusual.

His widow and five of his children still live. A son and daughter preceded him to the grave. Both of these promised usefulness, but were cut down in early life. One of his sons graduated at Cumberland University several years ago, and another is, and has been for several years, the endowing agent of Lincoln University, in Illinois. They are worthy representative of one of the best of fathers.

With interest I add the following to what I have written of this good man. He kept a record of his work. According to this record, he administered two hundred and ninety-four infant baptisms; two hundred and eight adult baptisms; married one hundred and twenty couples; and preached three thousand seven hundred and ninety-two sermons.

John Beard had a younger brother, Adam Meek Beard, who entered the ministry, and promised usefulness, but died in early life. His remains lie in the old family burying-ground in Sumner county. A modest head-stone tells of his birth, something of his life, and of what seemed his premature death. "Blessed are the dead which die in the Lord from henceforth. Yea, saith the Spirit, that they may rest from their labors, and their works do follow them."

REV. RICHARD BEARD
(1799-1880)

Fifty Years a Teacher[3]

Should the writer live to complete the present collegiate year in June next, he will have terminated his fiftieth year in the work of instruction. It would perhaps be remarkable if he did not contemplate such an event with some degree of interest. There have been two or three years of interruptions in the series of the years which has been mentioned, but I speak of the years which have been devoted to the actual work. My work in this respect has corresponded very closely, and has to a considerable extent been identified, with the work of the Cumberland Presbyterian Church in this line of labor. When I thus speak I certainly do not intend to claim the "quorum magna pars fui" of the classic hero, but that I have been a sharer, however humble, in a department of service which has very properly occupied much of the time and attention of this Church for more than half a century. A consideration which has some influence upon me in the preparation and publication of this sketch is, that it may be of some service to the Church in the way of suggestions derived from an experience of unusual length in a particular departm4ent of enterprise; and, furthermore, that it may encourage other young men in what may seem discouraging labors in promoting the great interests of truth and righteousness among men. When I commenced the work of life I was young, and thought myself called to the ministry of reconciliation. I hope still that I was not mistaken on this subject. I desired no other work, nor did I crave any other honors or emoluments that what such a work would bring. Before, however, I reached the prime of life, what seemed to be an irretrievable failure of health compelled me to a partial change in the work of my remaining years. That guidance which I regarded as Providential I have followed with a few, but very few, interruptions to the present time. I have always, however, regarded my first work as having paramount claims upon my time and strength, as far as my time and strength were able to respond to those claims. I have always felt that the highest honor that could be conferred upon man would be to preach the gospel of salvation to a dying world, and that the highest rewards that man could desire would be the rewards of such a work. I have thought it proper that I should here, and thus, give a distinct expression of my views of the work of the ministry. I regard it as the greatest of works. I place the business of instruction next in the order of importance in the line of a minister's life. Under this impression, when compelled partially to turn aside from the one, I, to the same extent, have given myself up to the other.

Perhaps before I enter upon my sketch proper, I should explain that while I am fully aware of the delicacy of the position of a writer or speaker before the public, who expresses himself very freely in the first person, thus laying himself liable to the charge of egotism, I shall be compelled from the nature of my subject

---

[3]Beard, R. *Fifty Years a Teacher*, **The Theological Medium, A Cumberland Presbyterian Quarterly** (January 1879), pages 1-27.

to forego the beautiful privilege of using the style of Moses and Xenophon and Caesar, and ask the indulgence, without being misunderstood, of expressing myself in the first person. I hope by this explanation to disarm, in the outset, fastidious criticism, should I have the honor of attracting the attention of critics. I now proceed to the brief sketch of my fifty years' work.

    My first school was commenced in the summer of 1818, and extended into the following winter. This was a mere experiment with a special object. We occupied a house which was connected with the old Ridge camp-ground, in the western end of Sumner county, Tenn. The Ridge meeting-house, or camp-ground, had acquired an extended notoriety in the revival of 1800, and in the early days of the Cumberland Presbyterian Church. The second meeting of the Cumberland Presbytery was held there about a month after its organization in Dickson county. My father had taught in the same house six years before, and in that school I had finished my early education. Of course it was limited, to have been completed in my thirteenth year. In the spring of 1818, I had attended the meeting of the Nashville Presbytery, with a view of offering myself to the consideration of the Presbytery as a candidate for the ministry. I was not received as a candidate, and did not expect to be, at that meeting, but was particularly advised to go to school and wait to a subsequent meeting. I had no means of supporting myself at school, and, furthermore, was needed at home on my father's farm. In the summer, however, after the crop was "layed by," as we used to express ourselves in those days, I undertook the school at "The Ridge." It was a very common school, of course, but was well attended. There were but three features connected with it of any interest. Whilst attending to my duties as teacher, all my spare time was employed in studying the elements of English grammar in connection with James S. Guthrie. Neither of us was teacher; we were both learners helping one another, and acquired in that way our knowledge of the principles of the language in which we expected to preach. I boarded at his father's, and of course we could be together every day. The next noticeable feature of the little school was that there were three boys in it who afterwards became useful and highly respected ministers of the Cumberland Presbyterian Church. I speak of them as boys; one was, however, about my own age. They were Eli Guthrie, William H. Guthrie, and Allen W. Guthrie. Eli, as I have said, was near my own age; William H. was younger, and Allen W., although now a man venerable in age, was then a very little fellow in his primer. The sad circumstances of the death of Eli Guthrie are known. William H. Guthrie is also dead. Allen W. Guthrie still lives, the only representative of an extraordinary family of young men. I have described them more fully elsewhere. The third fact connected with this school, perhaps worthy of being mentioned, is that from its proceeds I procured a horse with a very moderate outfit, which enabled me two years afterwards to start on the circuit a licensed preacher. The school, however, contributed nothing towards my own education, except what little I learned of English grammar by my own efforts, together with my friend and brother, James S. Guthrie, who was working on the same line with myself, being a year, however, further advanced in his preparations for the ministry. James S. Guthrie, Eli, and William have all been dead several years, whilst I, the frailest of the four, still live. I ask myself involuntarily, Why is it so? Still I know that it is not for the thing formed to say to him that formed it, Why hast thou made me thus? God rules.

In 1822 my health began to fail under the severe labor of successive camp-meetings. I was ordained in July of that year, in connection with my friend James S. Guthrie, and we were immediately directed to camp-meeting work. By the last of October I was very much broken down. We were expected to preach long and loud, and we did so, up to our full measure. We had but little help, and the strain upon us was very great.

I continued my work, however, upon the circuit to the summer of 1824, when I was partially laid aside with chills and fevers, which, after a short respite, terminated in the bilious fever. The fever came upon me at a camp-meeting in Stewart county. I was hauled from the meeting in a wagon, and confined to the neighborhood about two months. There was a partial recovery, but I was threatened, or seemed to be threatened, with a pulmonary disease. I preached no more till the following spring. I struggled through the spring and summer of 1825, preaching a little and making two or three excursions over the ground which I had been occupying, but the understanding was with both myself and my friends, that my work was substantially done. The school-room was, by common consent, my only resort. I had improved my education through the liberality of friends while a candidate for the ministry, and considered myself capable of teaching a decent school. My father died in the summer of 1825, leaving a family of small children who needed a teacher, and that circumstance seemed to make it necessary that the school should be near my step-mother's home. Everything considered, there appeared to be but one course for me.

Accordingly I went around among the neighbors and solicited their patronage. I received but little encouragement, but it seemed to be a point that was not to be yielded, and in November of that year, in a house almost as inadequate as it could be, in one of the darkest corners of Henry county, in Western Tennessee, I opened my school. I mean to say that it was a dark corner then; no doubt it is greatly improved now. It had, indeed, greatly improved when I ceased to be acquainted with it. But certainly no man ever commenced an enterprise under more gloomy prospects. The literal truth could hardly be believed, if it were made known, and I take no pleasure in dwelling upon it now, at the expiration of fifty-three years. Still the hesitation of the people is not a matter of so much surprise when it is considered that they knew very little of men, except that I was a young circuit rider and a partial invalid. Furthermore, I had not denominational influence to support me. In that respect everything was positively against me. But I have forgiven the good people long since for their hesitation in acknowledging my claims. I knew they were very excusable.

It turned out, however, that the school was one of the most agreeable that I ever taught. Soon after it was commenced, the neighborhood seemed satisfied to co-operate in the experiment. They sent their children. The little schoolhouse was crowded. Several boarders came in; four or five young ladies of excellent character and habits, and from good families, became pupils, and one of the best young men that I ever knew turned in with us. Besides, there were two young men preparing for the ministry—John McKee, who died some years since, and Thomas P. Stone, who still lives in an honored old age. It was a signal but noiseless triumph, and to this day I reflect upon that year's work with an interest altogether unusual. I remember, too, with gratitude the spirit of kindness and personal respect towards myself which seemed to grow up among the people, and which appeared unabated as long as I continued to visit them. I receive some tokens of these even now.

In the fall of 1826 I went to what afterwards became McLemoresville, in Carroll county. I was earnestly solicited to do so; it was a Cumberland Presbyterian community, and I thought the prospect for establishing a permanent school there better than in Henry county. The personal influence, too, of R. E. C. Doherty, a prominent man in society, and also a prominent member of the Church, contributed largely to my removal. He was a generous man, and I do not think that I ever had a more sincere friend. His kindness and even liberality continued as long as I knew him, and although I have understood that his latter days were passed under a cloud, I take this opportunity of bearing my public testimony to his unfaltering fidelity in all his relations to myself during our enter acquaintanceship, which continued through several years. During all these years I am certain he never faltered in his feelings; at least, he never faltered in his expressions of kindness. If he committed errors, I mourn over it, but I should be ashamed of myself if I did not spread the mantle of charity over them.

In November of 1826 I commenced my school at what was then called Doherty's Office. Everything worked well enough through the first year, but at the commencement of the second year an opposition school was originated under sectarian influence. The community, of course, became divided. I did not feel happy in such a condition of things; I did not think a victory in the case worth the time and annoyance of a conflict, and at the close of the second year I closed my labors there. In the course of the two years at Doherty's Office, which in the meantime became McLemoresville, Silas N. Davis, John McKee, a young brother Ward, James McKee, and William A. Bryan were members of the school, the two latter preparing for ordination. The others were not so far advanced in their preparation for the ministry. They all became good and useful preachers. James McKee died early, after a brief but brilliant promise. The others all reached maturity and usefulness, and left honored names behind.

On leaving McLemoresville I returned to the home of my step-mother, and fitted up a little room for the purpose, and spent the winter in teaching her children and young brother Ward, who spent the winter with us. In the meantime I engaged to commence a school at Huntingdon, the county-seat of Carroll county, in the spring. Accordingly, about the first of March, I entered upon my engagement at Huntingdon. I was to teach a year, allowing a short vacation in the fall. Early in that year, through the agency of a friend and merchant with whom I boarded, I secured Horne's "Introduction to a Critical Study and Knowledge of the Holy Scriptures." In reading this work I became so deeply impressed with a sense of the insufficiency of my own knowledge of what it seemed to me every minister ought to know, that I began seriously to consider the subject of taking some decided measures towards supplying what I felt to be my deficiencies. About the same time Mr. Campbell's version of the New Testament fell into my hands, and the reading of that work deepened the impression which had already been made upon my mind. Another consideration came in also for its share in my thoughts, not quite so spiritual, it is true, as those already mentioned, but still not without its influence. I seemed to be doomed to the school-room for life, as a means of keeping myself from want. If it were to be so, I reasoned that it would be worth while to spend some time in improving my stock of knowledge, in order that, if I must teach, I might be able to do so on a larger and more liberal scale, and make the work, I will frankly acknowledge, more respectable and more lucrative. As I have said, this last argument did not base itself so fully upon considerations of duty, but rather looked to interest, and perhaps appealed to a chastened ambition, but I have never seen anything wrong in it. Whatever considerations, however, might have been mixed up in my mind, my great object was to be able to read the New Testament in the original language. This consideration, I know, was controlling, and, at the time, was the utmost limit of my aspirations.

The work of my school at Huntingdon went on very well. I had some good boys and girls under my care. I recollect several of them with great pleasure, and have the satisfaction of knowing that many of them have done well for this life, and still more for the life to come. My friend and fellow-laborer, Robert Baker, was in the school awhile preparing himself for teaching, at least temporarily, in order to supplement his other resources.

The result of all my reasonings with regard to the future, which I have mentioned, was that I borrowed the only Latin grammar and lexicon which I suppose were in the town, if not in the county, and in the course of my summer session commenced the study of Latin. This was the starting point in my new departure. I made no explanations to any one. It was my own counsel. In my short vacation I attended the customary camp-meetings, generally carrying my borrowed Latin grammar with me, and improving my spare time upon it. A young lawyer of the town, a well educated man, learned by some means that I had taken up the study of Latin, and encouraged me, and, furthermore, offered me any assistance that he could render in my new pursuit. I went to his room occasionally at night and recited a lesson. In this way I passed through the second session of my school, teaching all day and reading Latin as well as I could at night. When the school closed in the spring of 1830, I had made up my mind to spend some time at Cumberland College, and had made my arrangements to go to Kentucky in a few weeks. I was now in the thirty-first year of my age and in the tenth of my ministry. It is at present a common thing for young men of such an age to attend our institutions of learning, but then I suppose it was nearly, if not wholly, unprecedented. There were difficulties in my way, however, more serious than my age. My step-mother had been in the habit of looking to me for yearly assistance from the time of my father's death; but I had counted the cost and the purpose was fixed. In May of 1830 I entered Cumberland College. How I met my obligations to my step-mother's family I need not explain, but I met them.

As I have intimated already, I did not think at first of a full course of college studies, but only of so much Latin as would serve as a stepping-stone to Greek, and so much Greek as would enable me to read the Greek Testament with some degree of confidence and satisfaction. As I have written elsewhere, however, the way was providentially opened before me and my interest in the course of studies increased, and in two years and a half I had finished the college course, with the exception of a single branch of study, and by way of compensation I made that the subject of my graduating address. So I went over the whole ground acceptably, at least to the College authorities. The day after graduation in September of 1832, I was appointed Professor of Languages in the College. It was the first regular Professorship of Languages that was officially recognized in the institution. It was a position which I had too much self-respect ever to have asked, but which I would have desired above all others. I thus stood upon a new plane, and looked out upon life with a new interest.

I remained at Cumberland College, happily enough associated with Dr. Cossitt and Prof. Lindsay, from 1832 to the fall of 1838. We had but little trouble, except what arose out of the operations of the farm and the boarding-house. But the students were constantly coming into collision, especially with the manager of the farm, and sometimes with the superintendent of the boarding-house. The troubles became so serious and frequent that I learned to have a dread of the approaching footsteps of the manager of the farm. My recitation room was in the second story of the building, and I could hear his footfalls as he approached, and I became accustomed to regard them as presages of trouble. I was, too, more annoyed, as for the most of the time I was the only member of the faculty who lived on the premises, and of course was more accessible.

My work in the department of instruction was agreeable. I have a particular recollection of the highest class I had in Latin when I commenced my course of instruction in the College. They were reading in Cicero's Orations. They were all young men, well matured, and very much interested in their work. They roomed in the Brick Row. A few of my readers will know what I mean by the Brick Row. Some of the classes were slow in moving when the bell rang, but this class were generally out of their rooms and on their way to the recitation by the time the sound of the bell had died away. It was a pleasure to hear their recitations. Noble young men they were. Some of them died early, and of the others I have lost sight. A great many interesting incidents occurred there in the course of my first years of service in the College. I labored very hard to raise the standard of scholarship, and hope that I contributed something to that end. On two occasions in the course of my six years I was brought very near to the border of the grave from sickness.

In the summer of 1838, very unexpectedly, I received a call to the Professorship of Languages in Sharon College in Mississippi. This was projected as a Union College, in which Presbyterians, Cumberland Presbyterians, Methodists, and Baptists were represented in the Board of Trustees, and to be represented in the faculty. The President of the College came all the way from Mississippi to Kentucky with a certified copy of my election by the Trustees of Sharon College, and with authority to stipulate with me for an annual salary of fifteen hundred dollars. My salary at Princeton was six hundred dollars, and I was not receiving really more than five hundred. I was discouraged and thought I foresaw what occurred to Cumberland College in the course of two or three years. There were other reasons of a personal character that operated on my mind; and notwithstanding I had not much confidence in the success of enterprises based upon the assumption that sectaries were too public spirited, and had too much of the spirit of Christ, to be sectarian, I accepted the call to Mississippi and determined to change my field of labor. The trustees and students were both kind enough to give me written testimonials of respect and confidence, and some of the business men of the community, I have no doubt, regretted the step I was taking. I hope I may be allowed to mention one case without seeming to be desirous of attaching importance to myself. A leading merchant of the place took me quietly into his room one day, after the business had made some progress, and told me that if money was the consideration which was influencing me, he was authorized to say to me that the difficulty could and would be removed-that what might be necessary would be forthcoming. I replied to him that money was not the whole consideration, and that my mind was made up.

On the 19th day of October, 1838, I started with my little family through the country to Mississippi, a distance of about four hundred miles. A common barouche and two very common horses carried us all. When I reached Sharon the prospect seemed rather unpromising. The President, Rev. Alexander Campbell, a Presbyterian clergyman from Delaware, was on the ground, together with the preparatory teacher. The school was in operation and they were giving instruction in the male department. The College included two departments, male and female, under the control of one Board of Trustees and one President, but otherwise entirely distinct and occupying separate buildings at some distance apart. Of course I took my place in the male department, as the young ladies were not ready for Latin and Greek. Several efforts were made to secure Professors from the other Churches but without success. A disposition, which I might have expected, and which I really did apprehend from the beginning, soon began to develop itself. It seemed to the other Churches that whilst the institution was to be organized and carried on upon union principles, it was likely to be wholly Presbyterian. Jealousy arose. Twenty-five thousand or thirty thousand dollars which had been subscribed in the county, as an endowment of the school, was nearly all withheld. At the expiration of the first year we received our stipulated salaries, but from that time we were thrown upon the resources from the uncertain patronage of the school for our support.

As I am writing history, however, I take occasion to say that I believe the trustees acted in good faith in making their appointments and stipulating to pay the salaries which they promised. They relied upon the subscriptions to the endowment to enable them to make payment. They elected two distinguished Methodist ministers in succession and a distinguished layman of the Baptist Church to Professorships in the institution, but none of them accepted. As I have mentioned before, it seemed likely to become a Presbyterian school, and this was very conveniently used by the subscribers to the endowment as a pretext for not paying their subscriptions, and consequently they had not means of paying the teachers beyond the patronage of the school. We carried forward the operations of the institution under the forms of a college two or three years, but of course it soon ran down to nothing.

Rev. Alexander Campbell was of course of Scotch descent, as the name imports; was a fine scholar and a most estimable gentleman, but not very popular in his address. He was, however, an excellent and successful teacher. He was, moreover, one of the most unselfish fellow-laborers with whom I was ever associated. He had great physical endurance, compared with myself, and was always willing to take the heaviest share of the burden that was upon us. He became discouraged, however, at length, and resigned, and, together with the Presbytery with which he was associated, endeavored to revive the old Mississippi College, which had been neglected for some years, and had ceased to be regarded as an institution of learning. It had very good buildings and some property in addition. The Presbytery was strong and there was some hope of infusing life into an institution which seemed to be dead, whilst one that had been thought to promise life was evidently about to die. The Presbytery contemplated a theological department in connection with the Mississippi College, and my good friend, Mr.

Campbell, was kind enough to offer me the Professorship of Theology in their institution. This is a small item in my own history which I suppose has never been known to half a dozen Cumberland Presbyterians. The offer was not made in a selfish, proselyting spirit. It originated, I am sure, in personal kindness and the partiality, perhaps undue and undeserved, of a friend. I have mentioned this, as I have intimated, to a very few persons, but have always regarded it as one of the most agreeable and flattering incidents of my life. I did not accept the offer, of course, and my attention was soon turned to my old field of labor.

I have always reflected with satisfaction upon my experience, as a whole, in Mississippi. Sharon College failed, but I had become acquainted with new men, and with a new phase of society, which, however it may have been misunderstood at a distance, and sometimes maligned, too, developed a great many interesting features. I do not speak here of slavery. I had spent my entire previous life in slave-holding States. But I allude rather to features of society which perhaps grew our of slavery, more fully developed than it ever was in Kentucky or Tennessee. The people were generous, liberal, hospitable, and rather a high order of intelligence was common. My new literary associations were also profitable. I met with men who were outside of the literary range to which I had been accustomed. Besides, I had two of the most loveable little congregations to which any ordinary minister ever ministered. One of these I organized myself. My heart was united to them, and I had some reason to believe that my feelings were reciprocated. I have said elsewhere that the darkest day of my previous life was the day in which I determined to turn my back upon Mississippi. I found my reasons in what I thought considerations of duty, but these need not be detailed here.

I took one step forward in my literary life while connected with Sharon College, upon which I have ever since congratulated myself. I might have taken this step elsewhere, but, however this may have been, the measure turned out to be a Mississippi development. Upon the close of my first collegiate year in the College, which occurred the first week in August, 1839, we had a vacation of three months. I was afraid to travel much, from apprehension of the heat of a Mississippi sun. It was considered perilous to persons not acclimated. Furthermore, there was not inducement to go abroad. My family and myself were boarding. I was consequently not burdened with domestic cares. The vacation was at my own disposal, and the question was as to the manner of spending it. It occurred to me that in the three months I could acquire a sufficient knowledge of Hebrew to enable me to read the first chapter of Genesis. I had a deep anxiety to be able to read that chapter for myself, from the recent attack which had been made upon it in the interest of geology. There was a young minister connected with the female department of the College, a graduate of a New England university, who had pretended to study Hebrew; but finding that the young ladies had no need of instruction in that language; and not being much addicted to the work of the ministry, he was willing to dispose of his Hebrew outfit. I bought, I suppose, his entire stock of Hebrew books-Bush's Hebrew Grammar, Gibbs' Hebrew Lexicon, and a good, sound Hebrew Bible. The grammar was a good deal dilapidated, but I have it yet, together with both the others. I thereupon set in, without the aid of an instructor, with the view of the mastery, if possible, of the first chapter of Genesis. I need not pursue the subject further. I did, however, accomplish my task, and read the first chapter of Genesis. I did not find, nevertheless, much more satisfaction in the original than I had found in our own version upon the question of its geology. Still I had made a start, and found that the Hebrew Scriptures were not a sealed book. I have always considered it a vacation most fortunately spent. I did not stop with the first chapter of Genesis, but more than this I consider that delicacy forbids me to say, except that if the outgrowth of that vacation's work were a merchantable article, no man could buy it from me. I am thankful to God that he turned my mind, when I had leisure, although I was carrying years upon my shoulders, to the study of the grandest and most sacred of the languages of antiquity. Some of my good friends were surprised that I was not contented with what I had acquired, and wondered if I thought my Hebrew would be of any service to me in heaven. Still I held on to my Hebrew and to some extent, at least, hold on to it yet. My last vacation at Princeton had been improved in a similar way, and the improvement has been a matter of interest to myself and others, but I do not wish to say more than to allude to the fact, and now return to the thread of my narrative.

In 1842 the revulsion occurred at Princeton. Early in 1843 my attention was called, as I have said, to the old College as the forlorn hope of its friends and a small part of the Church. The authorities there urgently invited me to their assistance. I was fully aware of the responsibility of accepting the call, and of the labors and trials which it would bring upon myself. Considerations, however, were connected with the call which I did not feel myself at liberty to overlook, and I accepted. These considerations were chiefly known to myself. Had the full weight of them been known, I cannot tell how I might have acted. They proved, however, to be of little weight. But I had accepted and acted before the proof was made. In September of 1843 I started from Sharon for Kentucky, and on the first day of October I reached Cumberland College. Rev. F. C. Usher, who had been appointed Professor of Languages, was on the ground, and seventeen students. Six or eight students came with me from Mississippi, and so we had something of a beginning for a school. But the buildings were dilapidated; the Brick Row, which I have mentioned, was a mass of ruins; and the college bell was broken, and everything had the appearance of a chaos on a small scale. It was, upon the whole, a dark prospect, but I was there and committed, and well knew that if light came, it would have to come from the future, and that nothing but hard work would bring it. But I was in the prime of life, and had some strength of body, and, I think, more heart. I never had so much energy before nor since. Nine years I labored there. They were the best years of my life. It was quiet labor, but if the Church knew it, the labor was not in vain. Some of its fruits are in their turn bearing fruits to-day, and certainly in no small measure. We added to the buildings a value of five thousand or six thousand dollars, more than had ever been expended there in that way before, and collected and invested in bank stock about seven thousand dollars. We educated some men whose worth is not to be estimated in dollars and cents. But I have gone over this chapter before and need not enlarge.

I should do great injustice to my own feelings were I to neglect to call to mind the estimable men who co-operated with me at Cumberland College. Professors Usher, Riley, and Biddle have passed away. Their memories deserve to be honored. Rev. F. C. Usher was a good and worthy man, well educated by the liberality of his parents, who were old and honored members of the Church. Mr. Usher was not appreciated and encouraged as he should have been. Rev. J. G. Biddle was, as well as Mr. Usher, a graduate of the College under its first administration. He was a Pennsylvanian and an estimable gentleman. He became prominent as a teacher, and was an excellent preacher. William S. Delany was a son of one of the oldest preachers, an excellent scholar, and is now a prominent lawyer and civilian in Texas. Rev. Dr. Azel Freeman was with us several years-a scholar, a superior teacher, and a Christian gentleman. In more important positions, his works have commended him. Philip Riley entered Sharon College soon after I reached it. I started him in the Latin grammar. He came with me to Kentucky. I was personally almost his sole teacher through his whole college course. He was a natural gentleman, and one of the purest men that I ever knew. He died two or three years ago in Texas. These were my fellow-laborers. In all our intercourse a sharp word never passed between any of us, nor was there ever an unkind thought of one towards another, as far as I knew. I honor the memory of the dead, and hear with deep interest of the successful struggles of the living in the great battle of life.

I should add also that our esteemed friend, Rev. W. G. L. Quaite, afforded us efficient aid in procuring notes for the endowment of the institution and for improving the buildings, and Mr. Charles T. Caskey in making collections. And it affords me great pleasure to say, after all has passed off, that I have no recollection of a single note or subscription, large or small, made for either of these purposes, which was not paid sooner or later, and generally with promptitude. This is a testimony which I could not in justice to my own feelings withhold. Every one that acted seemed to be in earnest. It was a noiseless work, but we worked.

In 1852 the General Assembly determined, after several years of deliberation, to establish a Theological School. A plan was matured by a committee previously appointed, and being submitted was adopted, and it was determined to locate the school at Lebanon, Tenn., as a department of Cumberland University. In the spring of 1853 the writer was nominated to the General Assembly by the Board of Trustees of the University as Professor of Systematic Theology. The General Assembly, which met two or three weeks after the action of the Board, confirmed the nomination.

The following is a copy of my letter of conditional acceptance, written as a reply to the Secretary of the Board on the occasion of my being informed of my nomination. It will be perceived that Dr. Cossitt was first nominated by the Board to the General Assembly, but he having declined in consideration of his age and increasing infirmities, the appointment was tendered to myself:

CUMBERLAND COLLEGE, May 4, 1853.

BROTHER McCLAIN-Dear Sir: Yours of the 22d ult. came to hand a week ago. I have not replied before for the reason that I wished a meeting of our Board of Directory previous to my doing so, and have not been able to secure a meeting until last evening. I regret very much that Dr. Cossitt did not accept the nomination. But as the matter is now before me, I hasten to make the following response:

First. I have never desired the nomination, and do not now desire the appointment.

I involuntarily shrink from it. I am certainly somewhat aware of the responsibility which he incurs who takes the position. I would have preferred its being assumed by another.

Secondly. I will find it difficult to disengage myself here. The subject was distinctly presented to the Board last evening. To the rest of the community nothing is known of it. The Board seem very unwilling to give me up. I hope further reflection will lead them to juster views of the question than they seem at present to entertain. But it would be a great trail to me to leave here under circumstances which would be likely to endanger the vital interests of this institution; and certainly I might be expected to consider such a question presented in such aspects as a question of duty.

Thirdly. I do not feel at liberty, however, yet to decline the nomination. The way before me is dark. I am willing to let the nomination come before the Assembly. Of course, the spirit manifested by that body would contribute very much towards inclining or disinclining me to a final acceptance of the situation. I make this statement in view of the probability of the Assembly's confirming the nomination. They might, however, reject it altogether. They might also confirm under such circumstances as would make me consider it unsuitable to accept. I will try to obey the call of duty in whatever direction it may lead me. Duty combines, however, many things. My first duties I owe to the Church; but there are duties more grave and imperative which I owe to myself and family, and I will certainly be allowed to feel myself under some obligations to this institution and this community. Could all questions be settled, however, in any considerable degree to my satisfaction, notwithstanding I would assume its responsibilities with unfeigned hesitation and self-distrust, still I would consider it my duty to make trial of the situation which you propose, in the event of the nomination being confirmed.

Respectfully yours, RICHARD BEARD.

I have introduced this letter that the Church and other readers may know, as far as it may be read, something of the spirit and temper with which I undertook my present work, which I regard as the most important of my life. I have often doubted whether I should have undertaken it, but I did so under the circumstances and with at least something of the spirit indicated in this letter, and the steps are not to be retraced now. What has been done, has been done.

I did not leave Princeton until the following February, allowing the Board of Directory there time to supply my place in the College. On the 12th day of March, however, in 1854, I was regularly introduced into my new field of labor in Cumberland University. I readopted the Confession of Faith and Form of Church

Government ex animo, and pledged myself to teach in conformity with the principles of both. The questions were propounded and a very impressive charge was delivered by my old friend and instructor Dr. Cossitt. I prepared a schedule of studies for three years; but objection was made to the length of time, and the course was reduced to two years, and it was finally reduced to one year. It is now, however, brought back to two years of forty weeks each. Two years of forty weeks each are nearly equal to three years of the ordinary theological schools of the country.

The prospects of the school were very unpromising from the beginning. For two or three years there was hardly what could be called a patronage. There were thirty candidates for the ministry in the College; but it seemed to me that some of them regarded me with distrust, as though I had come in with a scheme formed mainly to extend the time of their education—additional time, too, which was not likely to be of much service. They generally, however, attended my lectures very respectfully, and by degrees some of them entered the department for the study of theology. The prospect began to be encouraging, when the war came on, and that threw everything into confusion.

As I stated in my letter of conditional acceptance, I undertook the work with hesitation. In my expression on that subject I was sincere, but if I had been able to foresee all the future, my hesitation would have been still greater. I was told by a distinguished layman of the Church that he considered the prospect of success in establishing and enlarging the school almost hopeless. He thought the Church was not ready for it. In the course of the first session a good minister who knew something of the difficulties of the work, gave me to understand that the general impression of those favorable to the enterprise was, that it would wear out at least one man before it could be made a success. He meant that the time, and labor, and the sickness of hope deferred would be more than one man could bear. Of course I knew that the one man was to be myself. In a very few cases personal discouragements came from sources from which, least of all, I wold have expected them. Still, no one has been quite worn out, and the Church, as a whole, has responded to the efforts of the instructor with as much generosity and Christian sympathy and liberality as could have been expected. It wold be a gratification to myself to mention a few names in this connection, but delicacy forbids and I forbear. I have lived to see the Theological School occupy a status of respectability before the Church and before the country. I thank God and take courage.

I beg leave to add a few paragraphs to this brief sketch, which reflections upon my quiet experience have suggested. And,

First. In the providence of God it has been my experience since I turned my attention to a higher order of educational attainments and labor, to be connected with struggling enterprises. I have sometimes said that I have been under sheriff's hammer ever since 1832. This is not literally true, but it is a very near approach to a general truth. In the first summer of my connection with Cumberland College as a student-the summer of 1830-there were great discouragements in regard to the condition and prospects of the College. It was, too, only in the early part of the fifth year of its existence. It was known to be in debt. It owed a debt even then, the result of which was feared, and which only twelve years afterwards temporarily crushed out its life. In the course of that summer a few good young men were in the habit of meeting together and talking over the affairs of the College, and making conjectures as to what its future would be. That was a sort of informal club. Many a half hour did Cyrus Haynes and Elim McCord and John D. Perryman and John Napier, and others, spend in that way. I was admitted, of course, to their councils and to a share in their sympathies. We were deeply concerned for the destiny of our Alma Mater, and for the honor and prosperity of the Church whose fortunes seemed to be closely connected with the fortunes of the College.

Dr. Cossitt, too, was greatly discouraged. From my age and previous experience, he was kind enough to admit me, although a student, to his friendship and, in some degree, to his counsels. He never tired of speaking of his discouragements. His labors and responsibilities were great and his compensation was small. He thought, too, that his labors were not appreciated by the Church. It took nearly all the money accruing from tuition to meet other demands against the College. Of all the debts contracts, those to the teachers were the last paid. At least this was his construction of the prevailing economy. He had a large family of children growing up around him, and a frail wife who was soon to leave them motherless, and he hardly knew what the end was to be.

In 1832, with my eyes open, I stepped in under the College burden myself, as a sharer with others. My object was not money, or I would have sought other locations or other pursuits. My nominal salary was small, but my real salary was smaller, as I have related. It worked well enough while I had no family, or a very small one. When it became larger the condition of things was changed. I went to Mississippi with the prospect of a liberal remuneration. It was realized the first year, but after that I received what I could get, and our bubble of a College, as any of us might have expected, came to nothing.

The second experience at Princeton was a struggle for life. We taught, not two or three, but six or seven hours a day, and gained something, but all was lost at last.

Of the trials of Cumberland University I need not speak. They are familiar to most of those who will read this article. Of those which have been experienced, the Theological Department has certainly had its full share. Still, it has not been sold out, nor has it begged its way, and its prospects, as it has been already stated, are more promising than they have ever been before. It is due to truth, however, to say that we have reached this condition of things under a strain. One of the instructors performs his work as a labor of love; another is supported by private subscription; of the third I have not been in the habit of saying much, and I shall say nothing here. Of the Theological School I hope it will not be considered impertinent or indelicate in me to say that it ought to be one of the most interesting and cherished agencies connected with the Church, and that I do most sincerely believe that the neglect of it, should it be neglected, on the part of the Church and our young men preparing for the ministry, will prove to be suicidal. This is my last word on this subject to my older and to my younger brethren alike. The Church to-day needs men more than she needs anything else.

Secondly. Our age which is just closing, has been an age of transition from an imperfect itinerancy to the permanent pastoral system of supplying the congregations with the word and the ordinances of the gospel. It is true, many of the old preachers were pastors, yet they divided their time often, and the young men generally received a training on the circuit. The pastoral system is, however, the natural system of Presbyterianism, and is the system upon which it must mainly rely for its growth and strength. This does not include the labors of evangelists or home missionaries, of whom every Presbytery ought to have one, if possible, and every Synod one or two. But the pastoral system is the system natural to Presbyterianism, and, as I have said, must be its main reliance for the fulfillment of its mission. This implies a reasonable support of the pastor on the part of the people. "Even so hath God ordained that they that preach the gospel should live of the gospel." Now, when I went to the school-house we had no rule on that subject. The rule was in the New Testament, but we had not reduced it to practice. While I was on the circuit I received forty or fifty dollars a year, and socks enough perhaps to fill my saddle-bags. But when I engaged in teaching these resources were dried up. But I loved to preach-thought my mission in that line was not yet fulfilled. I took more delight in seeing the Sabbath dawn than any other day of the week, and I preached, although I neither received nor expected to receive money nor anything else. I suppose I preached as regularly on the Sabbath, sometimes connecting Saturday with it, as any pastor in the country or anywhere else. I kept up the habit while a student at college. Hardly a Sabbath passed in which I did not go out and preach to some country congregation. I had the advantage, it is true, of ordinary students-I had preached ten years before I went to college, and had a good deal of old material on hand which I used very freely. It is becoming the common theory now that if a man is not wholly devoted to the work of the ministry, he has, therefore, no business in the pulpit. What I wish to urge is that if a man is called to preach, he has business in the pulpit, and he ought to be there, as a general rule, on all suitable occasions. And then if the school-house or the corn-field is between him and starvation, he is an honest man if he goes into the school-house or corn-field, and he is not to be scouted and despised because he does so; but he ought to preach, preach, preach, as well as he can. I once heard a prominent elder in the Cumberland Presbyterian Church jestingly allude to a preacher who was a farmer on a small scale, and express a wonder where he found material for his sermons and how he prepared them; yet that was a faithful preacher, and preached with almost constant regularity. I knew him well from his boyhood to his grave. He unfortunately entered upon his work before he was well prepared, and married early, but the people who heard him preach forty-five years ago, remember him and speak of him with interest yet. He was, however, one of the most earnestly spiritual preachers that I ever knew. He was attacked with the disease which carried him off at a sacramental meeting, and died at his post in the far West. His call to the ministry never exhausted itself. The memory of such men is to be honored. If he had had the advantages which our schools and colleges are now offering in vain to three hundred and fifty young men,[4] he would never have been under the necessity of resorting to a farm for the purpose of supplementing a meager salary. There were congregations even tehn that would have kept him in the pulpit. We have enough such now.

    Thirdly. I hope I may be allowed to say that a controlling thought with me,

---

[4]The Stated Clerk of the General Assembly reports four hundred and forty candidates and licentiates belonging to the Presbyteries. Perhaps ninety of these are at school.

at least for thirty-five years, has been the education of the ministry of the Church to which I became providentially united at first, and with whose doctrines and order I have been in hearty and earnest sympathy since I became capable of understanding and appreciating them. I have always regarded this Church, in its origin, as a providential necessity. It became an agency for reaching and bringing under religious influence, thousands of the best people of the West and Southwest who could hardly have been brought under such an influence by any other agency. I told Dr. Archibald Alexander in his room in the Seminary at Princeton a few weeks before his death, that I regarded the Cumberland Presbyterian Church in such a light, and in illustration of it, that from my own surroundings in early life, and from early influence exerted upon me, I did not know how I could ever have been brought into the fold of Christ by any other agency, and that there were multitudes of men and women in this country in the same condition. It was, therefore, a very natural conclusion with me that the existence of the Church was providential. I thought the good man believed me. He was a little more susceptible than some of his brethren have been. But let me not wander. I have been burdened with the impression that such an organization, if really of providential origin, and bearing such truths as it does bear, and offer to a dying world, ought to be furnished with religious teachers who would be able to represent it in the most effective manner before the world. I have believed, and still believe, that with such a ministry this Church could collect congregations anywhere, not by making inroads upon other denominations, but upon the great empire of Satan. I make no apology for expressing myself thus. We have many preachers, and I will add, many good ones, but it is plain that we have not enough of such as I have described. If we had, why have we not congregations in Philadelphia, in Louisville, in Cincinnati, where we have made failures? Why have we not three or four in Nashville, in Memphis? Why is there such a struggle at St. Louis? Why have we not resident pastors and flourishing congregations in Fayetteville, and Shelbyville, and Clarksville? All these latter points belong to our own Middle Tennessee, in which our Church was organized. And outside of Tennessee, besides those I have mentioned, there are fields innumerable, both towns, cities, and country places, where our ministry would be made welcome and useful. Why are they not in all these places and at work? Those of us who understand the condition of things a hundred miles from home, know the reason well enough. Pardon me while I say it: I sincerely believe, and have believed for forty years, that we need to some extent, and I will say to a very considerable extent, a more highly cultivated ministry in our Church. They are an absolute necessity. My reader will mark my words; I say, to some extent at least. I respect the feelings of good men, and unless I lose my senses or forget myself, I shall never treat them rudely. It is not intended that this high culture should be universal on the part of the ministry, but that it should be largely increased among us. This is the necessity which I call absolute. A man of high culture can preach anywhere, as well among the low as the high; a man of indifferent culture cannot preach everywhere. He is restricted, of necessity. I mean he is socially restricted. But we need a larger proportion of men who can preach anywhere and everywhere. Furthermore, we owe to the world and to ourselves, great and learned expounders of the truth-men who can stand shoulder to shoulder with the highest and the best. My reader must pardon me; I never exhaust myself when I enter upon this subject. Let me add, however, that we need men for the foreign missionary work, and we cannot escape the call of Providence.

I beg leave to introduce here an extract from an article written by myself and published in the Banner of Peace thirty-seven years ago. It expresses what were my views and feelings on this subject then. The experience and observation of the thirty-seven years since have produced no change, except in strengthening the convictions expressed then. The article was the close of a series written and published in 1842:

AN EDUCATED MINISTRY-THE CONCLUSION.-NO. XIII.

With this paper I shall be compelled to conclude this discussion, at least for the present. It is the first subject that I ever brought before the Church, and it will perhaps be the last. I am not seeking notoriety. I am an obscure member of the body, and hope that I will be contented with my obscurity. I can certainly say as Paul said, "I seek not yours, but you." I have been cradled in the Cumberland Presbyterian Church. I was taught from my infancy to revere its ministry. I considered them the greatest and best men in the world. I embraced religion and entered the ministry in early life. I took my first lessons and received my first training on the circuit. I have climbed mountains, swum creeks and rivers; have been drenched with the showers of heaven; have shivered through the drifting snow; have eaten coarse food and lain upon hard beds in open houses, and still preached day and night, I am a Cumberland Presbyterian of the old school. These statements are made that my readers may know that I am no ecclesiastical exotic, bringing into the Church sentiments and sympathies acquired elsewhere; or inexperienced student, fresh from college, or laureated tyro, still under the impression that his college is half the world, and his degree the chief end of man.

The views and feelings expressed in these papers are, as far as I am able to determine, the result of experience and observation. My conviction is deeply settled that our ministry ought to be more thoroughly furnished; that unless they are, they cannot be what the ministry were designed to be, "the salt of the earth" and "the light of the world." My conviction is as thorough that they ought to be furnished from original sources. Biblical literature ought to be made a primary matter. I look prospectively. The young men are mainly interested in this subject. One word must be said, however, in relation to the past. I love the fathers. I honor them. They were raised up for a crisis, and well and nobly did they meet it. They were formed by their circumstances. There is a Providence in all these events. They were men of power and spirituality, and Heaven blessed them. But the crisis is past-the circumstances have changed. We must rely mainly upon a settled ministry. I speak of the body of the Church. Let the frontier Presbyteries manage their own matters. A settled ministry cannot be useful without a more thorough preparation than has been common with us. Twenty years will decide whether I am right or wrong on this subject.

As I have said, this is an extract from the last of a series of articles for the Banner of Peace of 1842, in which I entered very fully and earnestly into an argument for an educated ministry upon the basis of our Confession of Faith. In order to understand the extract fully, the reader must be informed that I did not write under my own but under an assumed name. Whether twenty or thirty-seven years have confirmed my argument or not, I leave to the decision of others.

Fourthly. I could hardly have been expected to go over the ground which I have thus briefly sketched, without at least a mixture of sadness and melancholy in my feelings. A public life of near sixty years, fifty of which have been devoted to a laborious and responsible profession, and partially to another, equally laborious and more responsible, would bring a mixture of events and experiences. It has, of course, been so with myself. Entering the ministry young, with some prospects of success and usefulness, before I had been able to make full proof of myself, I was laid aside, as it seemed for a time, hopelessly by a failure of health. Taking up another profession under the pressure of necessity, I had to undergo a new discipline in order to be prepared for it. As a result, I suppose, of this change, at least in part, the eight or ten years which succeeded 1825, in which I commenced my work as a permanent teacher, were the most gloomy and despairing years of my life. I look back upon them as the valley of the shadow of death. It was not known to the people or my friends that my experience was so bitter. I look back upon those years, as I have said, to-day with a sort of irrepressible sinking of heart. God was good and had, I suppose, something better in store for me, or I should have sunk under my burden. I take no pleasure in details, and doubtless my readers would take less, and I forbear. In 1829 my mind, from some cause, turned itself to new thoughts, and in 1830, as I have related, I entered Cumberland College. I found new friends there and new sympathies. A new class of pursuits opened out before me. At length employment came congenial with my taste and suited to my health. It has always seemed to me providential, and I am thankful to-day that my steps were thus directed, as I think they were, from under the gloomy cloud which had covered them during the few preceding years. Through the remaining years up to the present, I have labored hard, but with as much cheerfulness and satisfaction as most men experience in fulfilling the tasks assigned them in this world of service. The shadows of the evening are growing long with me, but I bear my armor still. I hope to bear it quietly and cheerfully, standing in my lot while God requires, and awaiting the end of the days. **Laus Deo.**

REV. ROBERT BELL
(1810-1853)

Sources: Rev. C.H. Bell, D.D.; Smith's **History of the Cumberland Presbyterians, Banner of Peace**.

Robert Bell was born in Guilford county, North Carolina, December 16, 1770. His father's name was Robert; his mother's family-name was Walker. He had but one full brother. This brother was the father of the Hon. John Bell, of Tennessee. There were several full sisters, besides a number of half brothers and sisters.

When he was twelve years old his father moved to the Cumberland country. The first settlement of the family was north of Cumberland River, in what is now Sumner county. In a year or two they moved to the neighborhood of what is now Nashville, and settled there.

At some time early in the revival of 1800 he made profession of religion. The exact time, however, is not known. At the sessions of the Transylvania Presbytery, in October of 1802, Mr. Bell was licensed as an exhorter and catechist. At the same Presbytery Hugh Kirkpatrick and Ephraim McLean were received as candidates for the ministry. At some time between the fall of 1802 and December of 1805 he was received as a candidate for the ministry, and licensed as a probationer. This is inferred from the fact that, in the proceedings of the Commission of the Synod of Kentucky, which met early in December, 1805, he is recognized as a licensed probationer, and was one of those who were forbidden to exercise any ministerial functions derived from the authority of the Cumberland Presbytery. The licentiates and exhorters were included in the prohibition.

It is supposed that his education was perhaps better than that of most of the young men of his time who came into the ministry, but its extent cannot be distinctly stated. The probability is, that it was irregularly acquired, as the circumstances of the country would allow, and as his own disposition would prompt. A man of his habits of mind would be apt to make the most of his circumstances in the way of improving himself. It is certain that, by his own application, after he entered the ministry he became a good English and Latin scholar.

It is said, upon his own authority, that when the Commission of Synod was in session, considering the cases of the young men, he was privately approached, and assured that if he would adopt the Confession of Faith without reservation, his license as a probationer for the ministry would be continued. He, however, declined the proposition.

It appears from the history of the proceedings of the Commission that when the question of submission to a reexamination was put to the young men individually, he and Samuel K. Blythe, a candidate for the ministry, "requested a short time to consider the subject." No one who knew the character of Mr. Bell would be surprised at the request on his part. He was an unusually thoughtful and conscientious man. The result of the consideration was that both the men refused to submit, as did all the others. The ground of the refusal was a constitutional one. It was, "That they believed the Cumberland Presbytery was a regular judicature of the Church, and competent to judge of the faith and ability of its candidates; that they themselves had not been charged with heresy or immorality—and if they had been, the Presbytery would have been the proper judicature to call them to account." The question was, as I have said, a constitutional one, and the young men were clearly justifiable in their refusal. The proceedings of the Commission were obviously unconstitutional and anti-Presbyterian. The New Brunswick Presbytery had taken the same view of the subject more then half a century before.

The same difficulties were in the way of Mr. Bell's advancement in the ministry, which were in the way of others. The action of the Commission left the Presbytery in a state of confusion. Nothing was done presbyterially until after the organization in 1810. We have nothing official on the subject, but Mr. Donnell says that he was licensed in 1804, and ordained in 1810. His ordination appears, therefore, to have been one among the first Presbyterial acts of the new Presbytery.

From his licensure in 1804 to 1807 he lived in Logan county, Kentucky, and his labors were partially, at least, confined to that section of country. In 1807 he moved to Bean's Creek, near Salem, Tennessee, and settled there.

In the Minutes of the old Cumberland Synod, which met on the 19th of October, 1819, at Suggs's Creek Meeting-house, in Wilson county, Tennessee, we have the following record:

> Whereas several letters have been directed to the Moderator informing the Synod that a number of societies have been formed, the object of which is to raise funds for the purpose of establishing schools for the literary and religious instruction of the Chickasaw and Choctaw Tribes of Indians, and appointing the ordained ministers of this Synod their Board of Trustees; therefore,
>
> Resolved, That this appointment be accepted.

This preamble and resolution is the first public indication of a measure which, in its time, attracted a great deal of attention in the Church. Mr. Bell, too, spent some of the best years of his life in efforts for its promotion. A sort of spontaneous feeling began to develop itself in different parts of the Church in favor of endeavoring to civilize and Christianize the Southern Indians. The Creek war had passed over, and the Chickasaws and Choctaws had maintained such relations to the whites during that struggle that a favorable public attention was naturally directed to them.

From the report on the state of religion to the Synod at its sessions in the same year I make the following extract relating to this subject:

> By the heaven-born charity and zeal of some female members of the Church, funds have been raised, which have enabled the Missionary Board to employ several missionaries a considerable part of their time, by which your bounds have been much enlarged in the South and West. This has multiplied the calls and cries to our Presbyteries and Missionary Boards for help. The people desire the word and ordinances. Among the most

impressive calls we hear is one from the tawny sons of the woods in the South. One of them has recently given satisfactory evidence that he has obtained the 'one thing needful,' and he has been admitted to the sealing ordinances of the Church.

This Indian man was brought from the Chickasaw Nation of Indians last winter by Revs. Samuel King and William Moore, two of our missionaries. He has been boarding with Brother King, and going to school from his house, and has made almost unparalleled progress in his education. Your committee anticipate great good to his nation from his education and conversion, especially if it should please the great Head of the Church to call him to the work of the ministry.

It seems that, in consequence of the opening condition of things, and the state of feeling developed in the Church, the plan was conceived of a school in the Chickasaw Nation which should combine at once instruction in letters and religion, together with domestic, agricultural, and mechanical pursuits.

Accordingly, on the 11th of September, 1820, the following articles of an agreement were entered into by Revs. Samuel King, Robert Bell, and James Stewart, as the representatives of the Cumberland Presbyterian Board of Missions, which consisted of the ordained ministers of the Cumberland Presbyterian Church on the one part, and the chiefs of the Chickasaw Nation on the other part:

Articles of Agreement between Samuel King, James Stewart, and Robert Bell, missionaries, and the chiefs of the Chickasaw Nation, viz.:

Article 1. We, the said Samuel King, James Stewart, and Robert Bell, on the part of the Board of the Cumberland Presbyterian Missionary Society, do promise to teach the people of the said nation reading, writing, and arithmetic, and a knowledge of agriculture and the mechanical arts. Also those who resort to them for instruction shall be boarded and clothed gratuitously, provided they are not able to clothe themselves.

Article 2. We promise that we will not take more land than will be necessary for the support of the institution. And should we leave the institution, the houses and land which we have occupied shall revert to the Indians.

Article 3. We, the chiefs of the Chickasaw Nation, on the part of said nation, do permit said society and missionaries to come into our nation to teach our young people.

Article 4. We do hereby bind ourselves to allow said society as much land as may be necessary for the support of their missionaries, which land they shall hold as long as they continue to teach our children.

Sept. 11, 1820.

These articles were signed by Messrs. King, Stewart, and Bell, on the part of the Missionary Board; and on the part of the Chickasaws, by Stako Tookey, King of the Nation; and Tisho Mingo, Appa Suntubba, Samuel Sealy, William McGelbra, James Colbert, and Levi Colbert, chiefs.

In the month of November a school was opened, under the name of Charity Hall, within the limits of what is now the State of Mississippi, about seven miles from the present city of Aberdeen, and three miles from Cotton Gin Port. Mr. Bell was appointed superintendent. He taught a few weeks in a private room furnished by one of the chiefs until suitable buildings were prepared for the use of the school. The buildings erected were plain and cheap, costing in all about $1,500. Thirty acres of land were cleared, and put under cultivation. The Indians learned with some facility, and labored with as much readiness as would have been expected. The Government of the United States contributed liberally toward paying for the buildings, and also made an annual contribution of $300 or $400 toward keeping up the school. But great difficulties were experienced in carrying forward the work. Mr. Bell, in his communications, complains especially of the depreciation of the currency in those parts of the Church from which he received his principal supplies. Of course a great many members of the Church were indifferent toward the enterprise. Some were even opposed to it. There were lingering prejudices against the Indians. Still great efforts were made. Many of the preachers and people cooperated earnestly with the good man in the work upon which his heart was deeply set. I have before me files of subscriptions of money from men and women scattered all over the Church—subscriptions ranging from ten dollars to twenty-five cents—also of clothing, from a jeans coat to a pair of socks.

I transcribe a copy of one of the appeals to the Church. It is from William Harris, who never spoke otherwise than earnestly on such a subject:

> Friends, who have felt the sweets of learning and religion, suffer a call to be made on the benevolence of your hearts in behalf of the poor heathen children of the Chickasaw Nation now under the care of the Cumberland Presbyterian Missionary Board at Charity Hall School. Will you aid in bringing them from under the gloom of heathen darkness by giving some of the abundance with which you have been blessed, in money, school-books, or country-cloth suitable to clothe the naked children of the woods? Any thing of the kind will be thankfully received by
>
> WILLIAM HARRIS,
> Agent for Logan Presbytery.
> May 17, 1825.

Notwithstanding these efforts the enterprise dragged heavily. Some of my first recollections of the old Cumberland Synod, which commenced in 1822, are recollections of troubles and discouragements connected with Charity Hall. My feelings at those times were, and they still are, that Mr. Bell's patience, and perseverance, and Christian forbearance, under all the trials arising out of his situation, were almost superhuman. The trials were very great. One thing has affected me much in examining the old papers relating to Charity Hall. I allude to the respectful consideration in all transactions with the Federal Government with which he was treated by its officers. There are repeated communications from Hon. John C. Calhoun, a portion of the time Secretary of War; from Hon. John B. McKinney; and again from Hon. William B. Lewis, as well as others. Every intimation in every communication indicates that they consider themselves communicating with a high-minded, honorable, Christian man. Whilst his brethren were sometimes impatient and fretful, not always fully respectful, and sometimes fault-finding, there is no intimation of the kind from these high government officials. Mr. Bell's descendants and the Church which he so nobly represented through all these years of trial ought to regard such testimony from such a quarter, although indirect, as an imperishable treasure.

The Synod were in the habit, from year to year, of appointing a commission of their own body to visit Charity Hall, and make report of its condition, system of operations, and general prospects. I transcribe here one of those reports as an illustration of the general operations and prospects of the school. The Commission on this occasion consisted of Revs. James S. Guthrie, David Foster, and James Stewart. Mr. Stewart did not attend. Messrs. Foster and Guthrie report the following:

> According to the appointment of the Cumberland Presbyterian Missionary Board, David Foster and James S. Guthrie met at Charity Hall Missionary Establishment, Chickasaw Nation, on Friday, the 20th of May, 1825. James Stewart was absent.
>
> **THE STATE OF RELIGION AT THE ESTABLISHMENT**
>
> On Friday evening after the arrival of your committee we had preaching. On Saturday two discourses were delivered, and, toward the close, the little congregation manifested great solemnity and deep concern—tears were flowing, and six or eight came forward for prayer, one or two being Indians. About as many were whites, and the remainder were blacks.
>
> On Sabbath, after preaching, the ordinance of the Lord's Supper was administered, at which your committee were rejoiced to see some of the first-fruits of missionary labor in the Chickasaw Nation seated at the Lord's table. At the evening preaching a considerable company collected. They received the word of life with more than ordinary interest; many wept; some came to join in public prayer, and it is hoped that one black woman raised in the nation found peace with God. About four connected themselves with the Mission Church as seekers of religion. Your committee are sorry to say that some of the Chickasaws, both male and female, who, as they are informed, had appeared to be deeply concerned, were during the occasion but little affected, though others appeared anxious to know and understand what was done on the occasion. Upon the whole, your committee think the prospect of religion to be flattering about the establishment, and particularly so among the black people, who are much

concerned about the state of their souls, through the nation, as far as they had information. The black people generally can speak and understand English, and this your committee think to be the reason why they feel more interest about religion than the Indians. It is but just to observe that the black people in this nation have less extravagance connected with their religious feelings than the committee have witnessed in other places. During preaching, many of the Indians seemed inattentive and restless, though not as much so as we frequently find among the white people. The Indians view the white people as their superiors, and it is probable that their example has its influence with the Indians.

After describing the locality and appurtenances of the farm, the report proceeds to the

STATE OF THE SCHOOL.

The school consists of thirty scholars, who attend, in general, regularly. A few, however, are not perfectly regular in their attendance. We heard a small class of beginners spell in two syllables, and a larger class spell in different places in the book. when the words were given out, the little fellows seemed ready to catch the sound, and apply suitable letters, though they sometimes missed the spelling of the word. Others, however, who were farther advanced, never missed the spelling of a single word, though the words were selected from different tables in the book. The small class in the New Testament read imperfectly, though we think, for the time they have spent, they are in a good way of improvement. The next Testament class read well, yet all read too low.

The class in the English Reader read very correctly. They all appeared to understand the Key to Webster's Spelling-book.

Two are studying English Grammar who have begun to parse. It does not appear that they will improve in grammar as rapidly as in spelling, reading, and writing. We observed no symptoms of quarreling among the scholars, nor of doing mischief to one another, as we frequently find in schools among the whites. They appeared, however, full of mirth and play, and this we were informed was generally the case.

GENERAL RULES

About day-light the trumpet is blown—the signal for all to rise. In half an hour it is blown again, that all may attend family-worship in the dining-room. Within five minutes from the close of the worship, Mr. Bell, with the boys, repairs to the field until eight or nine o'clock, and Mrs. Bell, with the girls, to sewing or other employments. They are then called to breakfast, where

Mr. Bell is seated at the head of the table, with the boys on one side and the girls on the other. When breakfast is over, they repair to school until twelve o'clock. After an interval of an hour, they are called by the trumpet to dinner. After dinner, until four o'clock, they are at school. They then go to the field until night, when all are called to supper and family-worship. Throughout the whole, the scholars appear to be under strict discipline, which they observe with promptness and cheerfulness, except that they seem a little slow to start to work in the morning, but when at work they seem brisk and cheerful.

REMARKS

Mr. and Mrs. Bell have more labor to perform, and more business of different kinds upon their hands by far than they should have. They have more to do than they can do in justice either to themselves or to the interest of the establishment, and unless they have some assistance in future, their days must certainly be shortened. We hope and believe, however, from various indications, that the needed assistance will be supplied, and that measure will be vigorously prosecuted to make the school a blessing to the nation, and a means of salvation to hundreds of poor Indians.

I omit a part of this report because of its length, but have embodied what I present here for three reasons.

First. The source from which it comes makes it reliable. I knew the men most intimately, and have no doubt that in every statement they were faithful. There is no varnishing in the document.

Secondly. It sets forth something of the labors and self-denial of Mr. Bell. In 1825 he was fifty-five years old, and yet we find him in the field at work with the Indian boys, and in the school-room teaching dull children the spelling-book and the English Reader, whilst his wife, of corresponding age, is endeavoring to indoctrinate the Indian girls into the mysteries of spinning, and sewing, and weaving, and cooking. And the committee say, they are wearing themselves out at this work.

Thirdly. It will be useful to the present and succeeding generations of members of this Church to know something of what their fathers and mothers have done and suffered. Fifty years ago the Cumberland Presbyterian Church had a Foreign Mission, and although they perhaps did not discharge their whole duty toward it, still they were sustaining it. How far have we advanced in that direction in these fifty years? The committee mention in this report a fact which I have omitted—the loss of a beloved son on the part of these old people at the Mission. This son most likely fell a victim to a sickly climate and locality. Yet the parents labored on. There are a few men in the Church, and but a few, who, with myself, will recollect the intense and undying interest which Mr. Bell manifested on all suitable occasions in the prosperity of the Mission. He evidently felt his work there to be the great work of his life. Nor was all this labor lost. Without doubt there was seed sown at Charity Hall which will bring forth fruit forever.

The last report on file from Mr. Bell, as superintendent of the Mission, was made in 1830. This report was made to the Cumberland Board of Missions, or rather at that time to the General Assembly. There is a copy of a document transmitted to the General Government in 1832. This is the latest document which I find on file. About this time the removal of the Indians to their present locality became a subject of agitation. This, of course, would unsettle every thing connected with the Mission. The actual removal of the Indians at last is a subject for the national historian. In some of its aspects it will be a dark chapter in our record.

After the close of the Mission-school, Mr. Bell settled in the interior of Mississippi, in what is now Pontotoc county. The last twenty years of his life were devoted earnestly and laboriously to preaching the gospel. His labors ended only with his life. On the 9th of November, 1853, this life came to an end. He died in his eighty-third year. He had an appointment for preaching the Sabbath previous to his death. Being upon his death-bed, he was, of course, unable to fill it, and it was filled by his grandson, Rev. C. H. Bell, now of Oxford, Mississippi. After the return of young Mr. Bell, the old man inquired particularly about the meeting, indicating still an unflagging interest in the welfare of the Church and the salvation of his fellow-men.

Mr. Bell married, some time in the earlier part of his life, a Miss Grizzell McCutcheon, of Logan county, Kentucky. They had four children—two sons and two daughters. The younger son died at Charity Hall, or while his parents were connected with the Mission-school. The event has been already mentioned. The other son was the late General John Bell, of Mississippi. The daughters still live—one in Mississippi, the other in Texas. The latter is the wife of Rev. John Haynes, of Pilot Point, Texas.

Says a correspondent:

> Mr. Bell was a great man; great because he was faithful and good—good so far as it may be said that a mere man is good. He loved the gospel, loved the Church, loved the souls of men, and was himself universally beloved. 'An excellent spirit was in him.' He was characteristically modest and retiring in his habits. It is perhaps not proper to say that a man can be too modest, otherwise I should say he was too much so. He was remarkably conscientious, even scrupulous, in the observance of the Sabbath. He prepared for the day of rest, and required others of his household to do the same. He was not rich, but God in his providence had favored him, and he was in what would be called independent circumstances.
>
> At a meeting of the Presbytery to which he belonged, two or three weeks before his death, he seemed to be under the impression that it would be his last Presbyterial meeting on earth. An order was passed for the ordination of his grandson. The young man hesitated, but his reluctance was overcome by the obvious anxiety of the grandfather that the ordination should be consummated, and his own apprehension that it would be the old

man's last meeting with the Presbytery. The ordination proceeded, and the aged patriarch participated. Never shall I forget his noble, venerable, and benevolent countenance: how it beamed with joy while he participated in the solemnities of the occasion. It seemed as though one of the fathers of apostolic times had come down among us. O that the grandson may be as good, as holy, and as devoted as his predecessor?

His domestic relations were of the happiest kind. Not long before his death he remarked to a circle of friends, in the presence of his wife, that "they had lived together fifty-four years, and no unkind word had ever passed between them." She was a few years his junior, and survived him about six months.

Mention has been made of the extent of Mr. Bell's early education. Of course, but little is known on this subject. But Rev. Dr. C. H. Bell, of Mississippi, says: "He was a close student through life, and a careful reader even in his old age. On his death-bed he gave me his copy of Scott's Commentary, in five volumes, with Cruden's Concordance, to correspond with it. The Commentary is marked throughout with his pencil." The pencil marks are the indications of close reading.

I copy the following letter from the Banner of Peace, of December 15, 1853. It is from Rev. Robert Donnell:

ANOTHER OF THE FATHERS OF THE CUMBERLAND PRESBYTERIAN CHURCH GONE TO HIS REWARD.

ATHENS, ALA., November 23, 1853.

MESSRS. EDITORS:—The Rev. Robert Bell, near Pontotoc, Mississippi, departed this life on the 9th of October, in the eighty-third year of his age. He was a subject of the revival of 1800. He was received as a candidate for the ministry soon after Anderson, Ewing, and King. He was licensed about 1804, and ordained in 1810. The delay of his ordination was produced by the protracted difficulties with the Mother Church. Through that whole struggle he was firm and prayerful. No one labored harder to promote religion, and no one was more rejoiced to hear of the organization of the Cumberland Presbytery by McAdow, Ewing, and King, than Brother Bell.

He was a man of retiring modesty, sound sense, and humble deportment, and was untiring in his efforts to do good. His fidelity would not suffer him to impose on others, and his prudence prevented others from imposing on him. He was firm, but not obstinate; he was humble, but not mean; he thought for himself, but was cheerful in allowing others to think for themselves. He was contemporary with the great and good men, McGready, Hodge, McGee, McAdow, Ewing, and King, as well as younger brethren in the ministry. He planted many churches, and fed the flock over which the Holy Ghost had made him overseer. He was an indulgent master, a kind father, an affectionate husband, a consistent Christian, and a devoted minister of Jesus Christ. He lived long; he labored hard to the last, a when on his bed of death, had an appointment out which a grandson, at his request, filled. May the mantle of the grandfather remain on that son, who, by the trembling hand of a grandfather, with others, had just been set apart to the whole work of the ministry of the gospel! Were I able to write, I would move, if I could, the whole Cumberland Presbyterian Church, especially its ministry, by his example, to redoubled diligence in the cause of God. The Church, of which he was a member, was raised up to aid other Christian Churches in hastening on the latter-day glory. We have no time to idle away, no Sabbaths to spend without preaching. A minister's call is for life. Old ministers, like old David, want to show to the present generation, and to every one that is to come, the power and glory of God.

I would say to his congregations, He has left you a minister of his own family. To his family I would say, Trust in the lord, and he will be to you a father that will never die. To his aged and Christian companion, I would say, Your husband, in all your removals, has been the pioneer, and he has gone before you now, to prepare, or see first, the place prepared for you, and until you are called home—to your happy home—your strength shall be equal to your day. With your departed husband, you have borne the burden and heat of the day. Your reward shall be as his; he had gone first, but you will not be long behind him. It must have been consoling to him, and to you both, to see the Church, for which you have labored so long, in a prosperous state.

Brother Bell was emphatically one of the fathers of the Cumberland Presbyterian Church. I have been indisposed for some time, and am not now able to write. Those capable, and who have promised a history of the fathers of the Church, will give a full history.

Brothers Kirkpatrick,[5] Porter, Calhoon, and McSpadden

---

[5]Rev. Hugh Kirkpatrick was born in Orleans county, North Carolina, May 8, 1774, and was brought up in the Presbyterian Church. He married Isabella Stewart, of the same county and State, July 2, 1795. Both professed religion in 1797, and soon emigrated to the South-west, spent one year in Kentucky, but finally settled in Sumner county, Tennessee. They were two of the first four that joined the Beech Congregation. He was licensed to preach by the Transylvania Presbytery at its sessions in October, 1803. His education was better than that of the ordinary young men, as they were called. After 1805, he followed the fortunes of the Council, and was one of the first who was ordained after the organization of Cumberland Presbytery in 1810. He was a good man, and spent the most of his life and ministry in Sumner county. His wife died in 1859, and in his old age he married Nancy Grizzard. He died in 1863, leaving an only son, who still survives him.

are on the list before me—on the list of the ministry-but I may be first on the list of mortality. May we all depart out of this world as tranquilly as Brother Bell, and all the fathers of the Church who have gone! R. DONNELL.

The following is a copy of a letter addressed to Rev. Robert Donnell, by the surviving son of Mr. Bell, in relation to his father's death. It was published in the Banner of Peace, of January 12, 1854. Every thing on the subject is interesting:

REV. AND DEAR FRIEND:—In father's death, all his children, and relations, and friends that were around him feel a great bereavement. They are consoled alone from the fact of his great resignation, his patient endurance of his affliction and suffering, and the undisturbed sereneness of his mind in his dying hour; and from the reflection that he has made, we doubt not, a happy exchange of bodily suffering for that unalloyed happiness which we most confidently believe is to be the reward of a long life devoted diligently, faithfully, and continually, down to his last moments, to the service of Him who promises to reward the good and faithful servant. Few die as he did. He had prayed for dying grace, and it was given him. He breathed out his life without a struggle, or a groan, or the distortion of a muscle of his face, perfectly in his senses, closing his own eyes and his own mouth, leaving a serene and smiling expression upon his face which he took with him to the grave. Better evidence of a full preparation for death could not have been afforded, and it is sinful in us, perhaps, to lament our bereavement.

Father, for a good many years, was afflicted with rheumatic pains in both his hip-joints, also with asthma, and considerable nervousness, especially in his right arm and hand. Of this you are, perhaps, aware; otherwise his health was generally good. For a long time he was unable to ride on horseback, but with the aid of a staff he could walk about. In riding he used his buggy; and, for several months before his death, to enable himself to walk, he had frequently to use two staves.

Although his voice had become very weak, he continued to preach nearly every Sabbath up to the time he was taken down; but, standing in the pulpit, to preach even a short sermon, fatigued him very much, and often after preaching, on account of his asthmatic affection, he would have great difficulty in breathing. For many years, on account of the nervousness in his right arm and hand, he was compelled to write with his left hand.

The attack of sickness of which he died arose evidently from exposure and cold, which brought on what is called here typhoid pneumonia. The Presbytery to which he belonged sat at the church, where he preached to the congregation under his care, near his home. The Presbytery met on the third Friday in September, and, contrary to advice, he would attend the meetings day and night until it closed. In the meantime a change of weather took place, and the nights became cool. He was up several nights until after midnight. The cold he contracted at this meeting was no doubt the occasion of his death. He was taken sick on Friday, after the adjournment of the Presbytery, and lived seventeen days after he was taken down. Having had frequent attacks of a similar kind, and from the same cause, and attended with more pain—for he did not complain of much suffering, his cough being the worst—he indulged the belief that he would recover until the evening before his death. For more than a week, however, he was well aware that his case was a critical one, and always expressed himself with perfect resignation to the will of Providence in regard to him. He died on Sunday, and on that day he was to have preached the funeral-sermon of an old revolutionary soldier, who had died a few weeks previously, and who had requested that father should perform that service. Although unable to fulfill the engagement, he kept it in mind to the last. Also the morning before he died he urged my son, who did not wish to leave him, to fill his place at one of his stated appointments for preaching about three miles off, and when my son returned and reported to him that he had done so, it seemed to relieve and satisfy him. His whole mind appeared to be absorbed in the interests of religion, giving himself little concern about the things of this world.

  Before leaving this branch of the subject I cannot refrain from relating an incident or two which took place during the sessions of the Presbytery. On account of his infirmity, father petitioned the Presbytery to release him from the pastoral charge of the Church which had been under his care ever since he had been living here, which, I believe, was not granted. At the same Presbytery the ordination of my son, Claibourne, took place. I was not present, but it was said that the scene was an unusually interesting one, and that the whole congregation was bathed in tears. When it came to the laying on of hands, and when my old father came tottering forward, supported by his staff, to lay his weak and trembling hand upon the head of his grandson, a deep and solemn sensation was produced. All felt that his work was about done, and that this would be perhaps the last ministerial act of his life. It seemed a transfer of his mantle to a younger branch of the family for continuing and carrying on the good work in which he had been so long engaged.

  Of father's early history, and particularly from the time he engaged in the ministry, I suppose you are rather well acquainted. He was born, I think, in North Carolina, and I have often heard him say that he was nine years old when the battle of Guilford was fought in that State, and that his father lived nine miles from that place at the time. About the year 1784 or 1785, when he was fourteen or fifteen years old, his father moved to the Cumberland country, and settled near Nashville. This was in the midst of the troublesome times with the Indians, against whom my father, with others, made several excursions. In 1795 he married, and moved to the State of Kentucky, and settled in Logan county. About the year 1804 or 1805 he commenced the ministry as a circuit-rider. In the fall of 1806 he moved back to Tennessee and settled in Franklin county; and in 1820 he moved to the Chickasaw Nation, and engaged in the missionary work among the Chickasaw Indians under the patronage of the Cumberland Presbyterian Church. He continued in that business until about the year 1830 or 1831. In 1836 he settled a few miles from Pontotoc, Mississippi, where he spent the remainder of his days. It appears from the record of his age that he was born on the 16th of December, 1770. Consequently, had he lived to the 16th of December next, he would have completed eighty-three years. Your sincere friend and relative,

JOHN BELL

My personal knowledge of Mr. Bell was very limited. I never heard him preach but once. In 1817, in the month of October, I attended a camp-meeting at the Beech Meeting-house, a place frequently mentioned in these "Brief Sketches." I had professed religion but a few weeks before. Mr. Bell was at that meeting, and preached on Sabbath. He was then, of course, in the prime of life. I recollect his appearance very distinctly. He was well dressed, and had altogether a gentlemanly aspect. His text was: "Fear not, little flock, for it is your Father's good pleasure to give you the kingdom." It may seem strange, but I have recollected ever since, and still recollect the train of thought presented. He first made a statement of the estimated population of the earth. He then took out the pagans, and then the Mohammedans, and then the Jews. This left him Christendom. Christendom was small in comparison with the whole. He then cut off a great many from Christendom, and came down to the visible Church. Of course a great many members of the Church were unsound, whilst the sound membership was small. The flock was a little flock. I suppose my mind was in a situation to receive vivid impressions then. I thought of nothing but preaching, and preachers, and connected subjects. Robert Donnell followed Mr. Bell with a sermon, having reference to the death of Rev. William McGee, one of the fathers who had recently been called away. It was a very solemn and interesting day.

I have no recollection of seeing Mr. Bell after that meeting, until the fall of 1822, at the first meeting of the Cumberland Synod which I ever attended. This meeting was also held at the Beech. Mr. Bell was there as the Superintendent of Charity Hall. On that occasion, I began to see a little of what I have seen my full share since. Charity Hall was an institution of the Church, and it was already in need of money. This was its condition during the eight or ten years of its existence which followed. The labors, and discouragements, and varied toils of the superintendent and missionary were very great. Yet he bore all heroically. He left a record behind which the Church ought to read. Year after year he urged the claims of Charity Hall and the benighted condition of the Indians before the Synod and the Church. A few of the old ministers and of the old men and women stood by him to the last. No man could have commanded more of their confidence, and the record shows that their confidence was never betrayed. It was a good work, and, as far as the limited means would allow, it was well done; and when history does full justice to the characters and labors of those who have devoted themselves to the elevation and evangelization of the savage tribes of this country, the name of Robert Bell will be found worthy of a place with those of John Eliot, and David Brainerd, and others who have made themselves benefactors of their race.

REV. JOHN MCCUTCHEN BERRY
(1788 - 1857)

Sources: Sketches by Rev. A. Johnson, published in the **Western Cumberland Presbyterian**, of 1864.

John Mccutchen Berry was born in the State of Virginia, on the 22d of March, 1788. Of his parentage and early education nothing in known. It is inferred, from some facts connected with his history, that his parents were religious persons, and perhaps stringent in some of their doctrinal views. His education, from the circumstances of his early life, must have been very limited. In his fourteenth year he came to Tennessee, and in his twentieth year professed religion, under the ministry of the fathers of the Cumberland Presbyterian Church. His age at the time of his profession would bring that event within the days of the Council. They were days of trial.

He had a hard struggle, while under conviction, with difficulties arising from early doctrinal impressions. The doctrine of Election and Reprobation had been taught him in his youth. This is generally a trying puzzle in the early experience of persons who are seriously inquiring for the way of salvation. If tendencies have been originated in such minds towards the conclusions of the theology which has been mentioned, the difficulties become greater. This seems to have been the condition of young Berry. The guilt of sin pressed so severely upon him that he could not believe himself to be one of the elect; of course, his reasoning was, that he was proscribed by an unchangeable destiny; that no blood had been shed on Calvary for him; that his case was hopeless. A conflict of this kind is terrible.

"Such thoughts," says my authority, "drove him almost into despair. Of his deliverance he was accustomed to say, that on a certain day, giving the day itself, which we have forgotten, the sun arose at midnight."

The reader, of course, knows what he meant. His spiritual midnight had been changed to the light and beauty of the morning. It would be difficult to forget such an experience as this. I suppose he never forgot it. He retained, in all his subsequent life, a great aversion to the doctrine of a limited gospel provision. He thought that it had nearly ruined his soul. He did not preach often in direct opposition to the system, but salvation, full and free to all, was a favorite theme with him. It was a sort of a spiritual indoctrination.

Shortly after his conversion his mind began to be agitated on the subject of preaching the gospel. He, however, very naturally drew back from the undertaking. He was utterly unwilling to enter upon the work. His inward conflict was so great that he sometimes thought of resorting to suicide in order to quiet it. It is said that he actually went out one night with the intention of laying hands upon himself, but was mercifully restrained. In order to hedge up his own way he married early, and, as it turned out, either intentionally on his own part, or providentially on the part of God, who intended to scourge him with the greater severity into his duty, he had selected a wife who was as much opposed to his becoming a preacher as he was himself to preaching, Of course he had thrown very strong fetters around his feet. This hasty act gave him trouble, as we would have supposed. For many years after he entered the ministry his wife was impatient under the hardships the family had to suffer, and although he was a pure and faithful husband, yet, under a sense of duty, he often left his home, to be gone for weeks, with no prospect of earthly reward, bidding adieu for the time to his wife struggling against discontent with the lot which Providence had assigned her. Great must be the trial of a good man under such circumstances.

In 1812 he joined the army, in connection with a regiment commanded by Colonel Young Ewing, of Christian county, Kentucky. He seems to have moved to Kentucky. Says my authority:

"He has told me that during the campaign he was in a cold and backslidden state, living in the neglect of prayer, and indulging in much vain and idle conversation, but was unable to efface the impression against which he was striving."

The expedition in which the regiment was engaged in a great measure miscarried. It was sent against Indians around Fort Clark, in what is now the State of Illinois. They found no Indians, and, after a very near approach to starvation, returned. Rev. Finis Ewing was with the regiment of his brother, in the twofold capacity of a soldier and a chaplain.

In 1814, Mr. Berry entered the public service again, under the command of General Jackson, and was in the celebrated battle of the 8th of January, 1815, below New Orleans. Whilst the battle was raging, and the missiles of death were flying around him, perceiving himself to be in a very exposed situation, and that he might in a few moments be hurried into the presence of God, he threw his mind back upon his past life. His former rebellion and obstinacy came up in full view before him. He wept, prayed, and confessed his sins before God. He then and there promised that, if the Lord would spare his life, and restore to him the joys of salvation, and bring him again to his home, he would consent to preach, or to do, or to suffer whatever God, in his providence, might see fit to require at his hands. His prayer was answered. For the time, he was filled with unutterable joy. Says my informant:

> Often in his preaching have I heard him tell that he had enjoyed the love of God in his soul, at home and abroad, around the fireside, in the closet and in the grove, in the corn-field and amidst the storm of battle. I never dared, however, to ask him whether he continued to carry on the work of death with his fellow-soldiers after his renewed reconciliation with God. Still, no one who knew him will believe for a moment that a mean cowardice had anything to do with his surrender of himself to God that day.

In the fall of 1817, Mr. Berry was received under the care of the Logan Presbytery as a candidate for the ministry. Two years afterward, or in the fall of 1819, he was licensed to preach as a probationer. The sermons which he wrote in the course of his trials of two years' continuance, are said to have been unusually interesting and impressive. Sometimes the Presbytery and the congregations were moved to tears in hearing them read. Sometimes, whilst he was exercising his gifts publicly, he made it a matter of special prayer to God that, if he was really called to preach, as an evidence of it, a soul might be converted at his next appointment. We can easily see how an earnest and sincere man, without experience, might be led to desire such proofs of the genuineness of his calling, and how desirable they might be to all Christian ministers; still, they are not the proofs which God always gives, nor are they such as we have always a right to expect.

In 1820, Mr. Berry moved to Indiana, from Christian county, Kentucky, where he had been living for several years. The country in which he settled was new, the people were poor, farms had to be opened, and, as a matter of course, even where congregations were organized, they were not able to do much toward the support of a minister and his family. Some were, no doubt, unwilling to do what they were able. He tells, himself, of some members of the Church who refused to let him have what he needed for his family, for the evident reason that they were ashamed to sell, and too stingy to give, him what he needed. Others, less sensitive, sold to him, and charged him for what they sold more than they could get from common buyers. He was a preacher and needy, and they made his necessities their rule in selling. This was cruel treatment, but good men have received such treatment, both before and since. Some men of the world, however, took an interest in the welfare of our young preacher in the midst of his troubles, and rendered him timely assistance.

He was ordained in 1822, and shortly after his ordination moved to Illinois, and became one of the original members of the Illinois Presbytery, which was constituted in the fall of that year by the Cumberland Synod. From that time to 1829 there was but one Presbytery in the State of Illinois. In April of 1829, the Sangamon Presbytery held its first meeting. There were five ministers in this Presbytery in its organization, of whom Mr. Berry was one. He was, therefore, closely identified with the origin and early operations of the Cumberland Presbyterian Church in that State. During the seven years in which there was but one Presbytery in the State, every one of its session, with a single exception, was held at a distance of from two to four days' travel on horseback from where he lived, and the sessions of the Synod were uniformly from three hundred to five hundred miles distant. Yet it was a matter of conscience with him to attend all the judicatures of the Church with which he was connected. Those old men have left us examples which ought to be a standing reproach to many of us. Think of a man's riding on horseback five hundred miles once every year to a meeting of Synod. Still, these long journeys were performed for conscience' sake. The first time the writer ever saw Mr. Berry was at a meeting of the Cumberland Synod in 1825, at a point which must have been three hundred miles from his home. It had never been, and was never afterward, held at a point nearer. It was generally one hundred or two hundred miles more remote. The rule was, and it was stringently urged in those days, that a plain providential hindrance, and nothing short of this, furnished a sufficient excuse for neglecting the judicatures of the Church.

After the settlement of Mr. Berry in Illinois, his life was spent very much as other ministers of his time and section of the Church spent their lives. Their labors were great, while their earthly remuneration was small. Whilst they dispensed the gospel to their fellow-men with great fidelity, they labored, like Paul and his fellow-laborers, with their own hands, and thus made themselves chargeable to no man. However we may reproach a congregation, or congregations, which permit such a condition of things, we admire the zeal and earnestness of the men who thus unselfishly devote themselves to the great work of saving souls. Men of such a spirit are those who have always kept, and will always keep, the Church alive.

In the winter of 1856 and 1857, Mr. Berry died, at his residence in Clinton, DeWitt county, Illinois. His last sermon was delivered at Sugar Creek, in Logan county, from the precious words of the Apostle: "And we know that all things work together for good to them that love God, to them who are the called according to his purpose." He had been assisting at a meeting at that place for several days, and was taken sick at the meeting, or shortly afterward, and died in a few days. He fell with his armor on. "Blessed are the dead which die in the Lord, from henceforth. Yea, saith the Spirit, that they may rest from their labors, and their works do follow them."

The subject of this sketch seems to have been what the world calls an original man, and all such men have distinctly marked traits of character Mr. Berry had his proportion of these. Some of them are brought out in the following letter from an intimate friend and fellow-laborer, written a few months after his death:

OREGON, July 1, 1857.

DEAR BROTHER:-I was in California, several hundred miles from home, when I first saw the account of Brother Berry's death. I could not restrain my tears, though I was in the house of a stranger. I directly sought the silent grove, where old associations rushed upon my mind, with many past scenes which can never return any more. I wept freely. But I asked myself, why should I weep? Could I have been so cruel and selfish as to retain him here any longer, had it been in my power, after he had labored so long and so faithfully, and done so much for his Master's cause? That he had his faults and frailties none will deny. But it is clear as noonday to my mind, that he had his sterling virtues, such as very few possess in the same degree. Among the natural gifts with which he was endowed, was a faculty of discerning or reading a man's character at first sight. We used to call this the gift of discerning spirits. You are aware that he and I were for many years confidential friends. And he never feared or hesitated to give me his opinion of any one. Sometimes I thought him mistaken; but, in every case, as far as I can now recollect, his judgment proved to be correct. He once pronounced a certain individual a snake in the grass. I thought him mistaken, but twenty years afterward, I found he was right, and I was wrong.

There was a nobleness of soul after him that never would stoop to any thing mean or low, even if it might not be considered sinful. I always considered him one of the fairest Presbyters that I ever knew, or with whom I ever was associated. If I ever knew a man entirely clear of jealousy or envy, it was John M. Berry. You inquire about, and request me to send you, all his short, pithy sayings which I can remember. As to these, they were always so original, and seemed to be suggested so naturally in illustration of his subject, that it is not easy for me to call them up, only as I can call up the subjects that suggested them. They were very natural to him, and so abundant that, unlike any other person, he never used any one of them more than once. You probably recollect his rejoinder to the man who took him to task for his manner of expounding the Scriptures, because Brother Berry did not take every passage just as it was written, saying what it means, and meaning what it said. 'You take it that way, do you?' said Brother Berry. 'Yes,' said the man. 'Well, which, then, was Herod-a man or a fox?' referring him to the passage in Luke in which our Savior calls Herod 'that fox.' I was not sure, at first, that this was original, but I have never found it anywhere else.

    I will now relate an incident that took place at the first Presbytery I ever attended, which has had a great influence in shaping my course from that to the present time. The Illinois Presbytery then embraced the State. Brother Berry and Brother Joel Knight were the only ministers north of White county. A special session of Presbytery had been appointed in Sangamon county, for the purpose of ordaining Brother Thomas Campbell. Brother Berry was the only ordained minister who attended. At the regular session of Presbytery the inquiry came up, Was the special session of Presbytery held? It was answered in the negative. The members were individually called upon, and reasons for non-attendance were demanded of all the delinquents. Some pleaded want of a suitable horse to ride, others lack of money to bear their expenses, and others had feared that it might rain and raise the streams, and make muddy roads. The youngest member of Presbytery made light of the whole matter; stated that he had been South, married a wife, and therefore could not attend-in short, he made a joke of the whole affair. Brother Berry insisted, against all of them, that none had offered a providential reason. He urged, with all the ardor for which he was famous, the great importance of sustaining government, and the strong obligation that a minister of Jesus Christ should feel himself under to let nothing hinder him from attending the judicatures of the Church, which was not strictly providential. Several of the members were considered more talented than Brother Berry, and at first they were all against him. Presbytery finally pronounced the young brother who had married the wife guilty of unjustifiable delinquency, whilst the others barely escaped censure.

    In his remarks he said that no excuse should be offered to, or sustained by, Presbytery that we would not offer at the bar of God with a reasonable expectation that he would sustain it. I have tried to live up to the above rule ever since, and in every case it has governed my vote upon reasons offered by others for delinquency. Brother Berry remarked, in the debate, that he never knew a minister that was not regular in his attendance upon the judicatures of the Church who was useful to any great extent, and that such often hindered more than they helped. My observation proves the same to be true.

Yours, as ever, NEILL JOHNSON

We have additional characteristics and anecdotes of Mr. Berry.

He was accustomed to use great plainness of speech with candidates for the ministry. In some cases he drew upon himself lasting opposition. A particular class of young men could not bear his plainness with patience. By the same candor and frankness he made others his friends. He was always ready to help the humble and studious; he was ever ready to uphold the modest and unassuming. He could not tolerate lifeless preaching. On a certain occasion a young man, recently from a distant theological school, came to one of his meetings. He was, of course, invited to preach. He did so, but the sermon was dull. There were some withered flowers of rhetoric-some well-rounded periods, but they were too well-rounded; they had no point. When the sermon was closed, Mr. Berry whispered into the ear of him from whom I have an account of the occurrence, 'That was a pretty corpse." Still, he thought it was but a corpse, a body without a soul. He was accustomed to say, that every sermon ought to have so much of Christ in it, that any sinner in the congregation, if, in the providence of God, he should never hear another, might still know how to be saved.

He was punctual in the fulfillment of his appointments for preaching. In his early days Illinois was a rough country. The winters were terribly cold. One worthy preacher of another denomination was actually frozen to death. "In the spring," says my informant, "there were oceans of mud; the streams were poorly bridged, and many not bridged at all. In the summer, the horse-flies were so numerous and blood-thirsty that to travel even a few hours in the day was to risk the life of a horse. Preachers and other travelers were compelled to travel in the night, at the risk of their own lives and health; yet he attended his appointments, and preached Christ through all these difficulties." Half of the time of the ministers of those days, from June to November of each year, was spent in attending camp-meetings. Some inadequate idea can be formed of the labors, and hardships, and self-denial of these men; yet they were the men who laid, broad and deep, the foundations of the Cumberland Presbyterian Church in Illinois. They labored, and other men are entering into their labors.

Mr. Berry was earnestly devoted to the temperance reformation. It seems that he found a powerful argument at home, in the aberrations of a wayward and perverse son. The evil course of the son was attributed by the father to the influence of a certain Church in the neighborhood, which opposed and ridiculed all the efforts of those who were trying to promote the cause of temperance. He had some success, however, in his work, as we shall see. Abraham Lincoln and Mr. Berry's prodigal son were at one time partners in a little store. It is not so said, but we should infer from the narrative that they probably sold whisky. Although Mr. Berry could not overcome the obstinacy of his son, he seems to have succeeded with the partner. On an occasion afterward, when Mr. Lincoln had risen to some eminence as a lawyer, a grog-shop in a particular neighborhood was exerting a bad influence upon some husbands. The wives of these men united their forces, assailed the establishment, knocked the heads out of the barrels, broke the bottles, and smashed up things generally. The women were prosecuted, and Mr. Lincoln volunteered his services in their defense. In the course of a powerful argument upon the evils of the use of, and of the traffic in, ardent spirits, whilst many in the crowded court-room were bathed in tears, the speaker turned, and pointing his bony finger toward Mr. Berry, who was standing near him, said, "There is the man who, years ago, was instrumental in convincing me of the evils of trafficking in, and using, ardent spirits; I am glad that I ever saw him; I am glad that I ever heard his testimony on this terrible subject." Tears ran down the venerable man's cheeks whilst he was thus brought so distinctly to the notice of the assembly. He was more honored that day than he would have been afterward had he been made Mr. Lincoln's Secretary of State.

Mr. Berry seems to have been deeply versed in a knowledge of human nature. We have a reference to this characteristic by our Oregon correspondent. It is said that he scarcely ever made a mistake in his estimate of the character of a man. An incident of this kind occurred at a certain time in the Presbytery to which he belonged. A young man came to one of their camp-meetings in a hunter's garb, and with a hunter's accouterments. He made a profession of religion before the meeting closed. This was all well enough. Hunters have, no doubt, often been converted. They are not worse than other men. After awhile he was an applicant to the Presbytery to be received as a candidate. Some of the good old people thought that his conversion was a sort of miracle-a partial parallel to the case of Saul of Tarsus. He was received, advanced, flattered. Mr. Berry, however, did not believe in him. He warned the Presbytery that if they advanced the young man they would regret it. Still, they persevered. The result was, he committed a flagrant wrong, and was deposed, and that was the end of his Cumberland Presbyterian history. We have had a number of such histories. The writer retraces more than one of them with sadness. We have sometimes succeeded, in our way, in making as far as men could make, very good preachers from very unpromising materials. Still, we have occasionally, in our attempts at miracles in this line, made miserable failures. We will learn, at last, that the general laws of Providence will not be contravened in our favor.

Every man who is a preacher, indeed, has something in his style and manner of preaching peculiar to himself. I present the following account of these, in the case of Mr. Berry, from the source from which I have chiefly derived my material for this sketch:

"Brother Berry," says my informant, "preached in a manner and style peculiar to himself. His discourses were made up of short, pithy sayings, which some of his friends called proverbs. Sometimes these would grow naturally out of his subject; at other times their connection with his subject was not so obvious. Sometimes he seemed to present a golden chain; at other times, a collection of golden links. He never said any thing which had no meaning; he was always easily understood, and when he became fully interested in a subject, critics who had a soul in them were obliged to forget their logic and their rhetoric. A whole congregation, at such times-the learned and unlearned, the old and young, all classes-would be borne away with a force nearly irresistible, whithersoever his powerful will chose to carry them. In the application of his sermons, he could contrast one thing with another with fewer words, and greater variety of them, than any man I ever knew. Heaven and its joys, contrasted with hell and its miseries; the death of a saint with the death of a sinner; life on earth with life in heaven, and life on earth with life in hell, were some of his terrible antitheses. On each successive occasion, too, on which he would use such a mode of presenting truth, he would use words and forms of expression which were wholly new, and still as forcible as others which were new when previously used. This characteristic of his sermons, whilst it rendered them exceedingly to the hearer at the time of delivery, was unfavorable to their recollection after the charm of the delivery had passed away."

Perhaps some allowance is to be made in reading this account, on the score of personal partiality; still, such preaching, if the reality approached what may seem to have had something of the ideal in it, must have been finely adapted to the earnest, practical sense of the hardy pioneers to whom it was addressed. And if such preaching is to be considered a specimen, it needs not surprise us to find new Synods and Presbyteries, and numerous congregations of earnest and devoted Cumberland Presbyterians in Illinois. Good seed was early sown.

An incident is mentioned, of a kind certainly to be deprecated, connected with an Illinois camp-meeting. It was characteristic of the times. I give it in the words of the narrator:

"The Eastern theological schools, in quite an early day, sent forth many of their students into Illinois, ordained as preachers; many of them filled with high notions of their own importance, and very contemptible notions of others. Some of these attended a Cumberland Presbyterian camp-meeting, and one of them, being invited to preach, undertook very unceremoniously to animadvert upon the doctrines which had been preached at the meeting, and the exercises and proceedings generally. It had been arranged that a young brother should follow with a sermon, but the programme was changed, and after a short intermission Brother Berry followed, and dealt as plainly with the stranger as he had dealt with the managers of the meeting. His objections were all met with a force and power which made him tremble like Felix or Belshazzar of old. Mr. Berry would up by referring to the spirit manifested by Christ whilst here on earth. 'I admit,' said he, 'that Christ was bold, but he was not impudent; he was humble, but not mean.' Then, pointing his finger toward the preacher, he said, 'Sir, you are both impudent and mean.'"

I have said that such incidents are to be deprecated. Sometimes, however, impertinent inexperience must receive instruction in a manner which is by no means agreeable to the instructor himself. Theological students, if they are taught nothing else, ought to be taught "how to behave themselves in the house of God."

I have a few personal recollections of Mr. Berry. I first met with him at the meeting of the Cumberland Synod in 1825; or, rather, I met with him on the way to the Synod. Some of his inquiries and conversations are not yet effaced from my mind. They were, however, not of a character to interest any one now. My next recollection of hi is connected with the General Assembly of 1845. Twenty years had elapsed. At the latter Assembly he was kind enough, as I thought, to manifest an interest in me which I had not expected. I was then connected with Cumberland College. He spoke of sending his son to the institution, expressing a hope that I might exert some good influence upon him. The young man, however, never came to the College.

In 1846, the Assembly met at Owensboro, in Kentucky. On his way thither he called at my house, and we went together to the meeting. On our way from Princeton, we spent a Sabbath in Madisonville, and he preached. It was a strong and well-expressed sermon. He was very companionable, and we had, of course, a great deal of conversation about men and things. He developed some of his idiosyncrasies. His judgments of some of our men were rather severe. It is certain that the men were not all perfect, and with regard to some of them he had made up his mind very distinctly. The parties have now, however, nearly all passed away. They understand each other, no doubt, better. They were all imperfect while here. We may allow, however, that they were equally honest; all meant well. He preached again at the Assembly, but I preached myself, at another house, at the same hour, and did not hear him. With that Assembly, and our return together to my house, our intercourse closed. His ability was very respectable, and his honesty in his opinions was, I suppose, unquestioned.

Mr. Berry published a sermon in the Theological Medium, of 1847, on the law and the gospel, or, man's fall and remedy; and another in the Medium of 1850, on the punishment of sin, and how to escape it. He also published, "Lectures on the Covenant and the Right to Church Membership," a volume of three hundred pages, which attracted some attention in their time. He was a good man, and Illinois, especially, ought to cherish his memory.

REV. MILTON BIRD
(1807-1871)

Milton Bird was born October 23, 1807, in Barren county, Kentucky. His parents were Robert and Rachel Bird. Of his parentage and early life little is known except the name of his parents. It is supposed that the worldly circumstances of his father's family were ordinary, and that his education was such as was common to boys in Kentucky in the early part of the century. It is certain that his early advantages were so restricted as to have made it necessary for him to become what he did become by his own personal efforts. He was, in the most practical sense of the expression, a self-made man. His principal literary attainments were made, too, after he entered the ministry.

On the 20th of February, 1824, he made a profession of religion. He was then in his seventeenth year. On the 13th of August of the same year he connected himself with the Cumberland Presbyterian Church.

On the 14th of October of the following year, 1825, he was received as a candidate for the ministry by the Logan Presbytery. Alexander Chapman and William Harris were the controlling spirits of the Presbytery at that time. It would be judged, from his subsequent life, and from the high estimate which he is known to have placed upon these men, that they succeeded in infusing a large measure of their own spirit him.

October 12, 1826, he was licensed as a probationer, and in April, 1830, he was set apart by ordination to the whole work of the ministry. Mr. Bird retained as long as he lived, and carried to his grave, a deep impression of the solemnity of this transaction, and of the obligations which it imposed. He sometimes referred to it in his sermons, and never without obvious interest and tenderness of feeling, often bringing tears to the eyes of his hearers. He was ordained as an evangelist.

In the early summer of 1831, a number of ministers, under an appointment of the General Assembly as missionaries, visited Western Pennsylvania. In the fall of that year they were joined by Mr. Bird, who, it will be perceived, was still a young man, and quite a young preacher. Cumberland Presbyterianism in Pennsylvania was a new thing, and it excited, of course, some awakening, and some opposition. The religious crust was broken which had hardened upon the surface of society, and some agitation followed. It was inevitable that the labors of the missionaries should receive something of a polemic cast. Mr. Bird was one of those who remained in the country. There were, consequently, frequent calls upon him, as well as upon the others, for their theological status, as well as the theological status of the Church. Explanations of subjects growing out of such inquiries could not be made without bringing them into collision with what was considered something like the established order of things. These circumstances threw Mr. Bird almost of necessity into the attitude of a controversialist. He retained something of this cast of character through life, always modified, however, by an excellent Christian spirit. When assailed, his replies, although not bitter and acrimonious, were always bold and fearless. His hearers knew where he stood.

He served for some time as pastor of the Waynesburg Congregation. After that he was for a number of years pastor of Pleasant Hill Congregation, in Washington county.

In 1840, he moved to Uniontown, and became connected with Madison

College, as Professor of Moral and Intellectual Philosophy and Natural Theology. He was appointed to this position as the successor of Rev. John Morgan. He gave instruction in that institution during the collegiate year of 1841-1842, and in the spring of 1842 resigned, in consequence of some difficulty between the President and some of the Trustees. This difficulty resulted in severing the connection between the Cumberland Presbyterian Church in Pennsylvania and Madison College—a connection which at one time promised to be a matter of some interest to the Church.

In 1841, Mr. Bird assumed control of the **Union Evangelist**, the publication of which had been commenced the previous year by Mr. Morgan. In connection with his other work, after the death of Mr. Morgan, he served the congregation in Uniontown for some time, as pastor or supply.

At this place he commenced, in 1845, the publication of the Theological Medium. This was published for several years monthly, in pamphlet form. It afterward became the Medium and Quarterly. This publication was continued, with one or two short intervals, to the commencement of the late war. It is said that for seven or eight of his latter years in Pennsylvania, Mr. Bird preached very extensively, and that his influence in all the congregations and judicatures of the Church was very great—almost supreme.

In 1847, Mr. Bird left Pennsylvania and moved to Louisville, or rather to Jeffersonville, Indiana, and took charge of the "Book Concern" in Louisville. The General Assembly of 1845 had taken the initiatory steps toward the entrance of the Church upon the work of publication. At Louisville, in July, 1850, he commenced the publication of the Watchman and Evangelist. This paper had a respectable circulation, and acquired altogether a respectable reputation.

In 1855, he removed to Princeton, Kentucky, and took charge of Princeton and Bethlehem Congregations. For some time, also, he held a nominal connection with Old Cumberland College, as its President. The connection, however, was nominal only, with the exception of his holding the customary religious services.

In 1858, he went to St. Louis, and for a year edited the St. Louis Observer, in connection with his Medium and Quarterly. When the war commenced he removed to Jeffersonville, Indiana. It was intended to be a retirement from the storm.

After the meeting of the General Assembly in Owensboro, in 1862, at the earnest request, it was understood, of some conservative leading members of the Church in Kentucky, he undertook a journey southward, with a view to conciliating and quieting the minds of Southern congregations and ministers, as far as he could reach them, and preventing a division of the Church. He visited Nashville and Lebanon, but, it is believed, went no farther. The passions of the people were very much inflamed, and he could have done but little. God in his providence, however, kept the Church together.

At the Assembly at Alton, in 1863, Dr. Bird was Moderator, and, of course, opened the next Assembly, which met at Lebanon, Ohio, with the customary sermon. The sermon produced some dissatisfaction, and was afterward published by Dr. Bird himself as a matter of self-vindication. This is mentioned as a prominent fact connected with the life of the author. It is not the place, however, to consider the merits of the sermon, or the circumstances out of which the publication arose.

In 1864, he returned to Caldwell county, Kentucky, and took charge of

Bethlehem Congregation, in connection with the congregation at Fredonia. The labor of his two last years was confined to Bethlehem.

Dr. Bird was a member of the General Assembly at Nashville, in 1871, and seemed to be in ordinary health and spirits. In the course of the preceding year he had been conducting a correspondence with prominent men of the Evangelical Union Church of Scotland. Both himself and the Assembly were deeply interested in the correspondence. It had been managed on his part to the satisfaction of the Assembly, and he was requested to continue it. No one could have anticipated what was so soon to follow. On the 18th of July, however, two months only after the Assembly, he was attacked with a violent form of congestion, affecting chiefly the stomach and bowels. From the first there was hardly a hope of his recovery. His vital powers seemed completely prostrated. He conversed but little. Says my informant, however: "In addition to the accumulated evidence of a long life, he left sufficient and satisfactory assurance of his readiness to depart." He died on the 26th of July, about 5 o'clock P.M. The funeral-services were performed by Rev. Wm. C. Love, the oldest minister of the Presbytery, and a former pastor of the congregation, at 3 o'clock the following day. Dr. Bird was a Mason, and his remains were buried with Masonic honors as well as sincere Christian respect. The spot selected for the burial was near where the old camp-meeting shed stood in former days. Where the shed had stood, camp-meetings had been held annually, until within a few years past, for the space of fifty years. Scores, scores of sinners had been converted on that ground. It is worthy of remark that Mr. Love, the officiating minister upon the occasion of the funeral, followed his friend to the grave in the course of a few months.

Dr. Bird was married on the 4th of November, 1834, to Miss Elizabeth A. Dunham, of Uniontown, Pennsylvania. He left her a widow with seven children. Five of their children had preceded him to the grave.

In 1857, in connection with Rev. A. M. Bryan, of Pittsburgh, he received the degree of Doctor of Divinity from the Trustees and Faculty of Cumberland University. This was the second occasion on which such a degree had been conferred by the authorities of the University, the first being the occasion on which Rev. Herschel S. Porter received the degree, in 1851.

Dr. Bird was remarkable for his punctuality in attending the judicatures of the Church. It is said that from his marriage to his death he was uniform in his attendance at the General Assembly with one exception, and at that time he was prevented by sickness. Thirty-seven Assemblies had intervened, and at thirty-six he was present. He was Moderator of the General Assembly at Owensboro, in 1842; at Memphis, in 1848; at Pittsburgh, in 1851; at Louisville, in 1856; and at Alton, in 1863. At Clarksville, in 1850, he was appointed Stated Clerk of the General Assembly, as successor of Rev. Cornelius G. McPherson. On eight occasions he preached the introductory-sermons to the General Assembly. The last occasion upon which he officiated thus was at the opening of the Assembly at Owensboro, in 1866. The Moderator of the former Assembly had died in the interim, Rev. Hiram Douglas, and Dr. Bird preached by request.

It will be observed from these statements that he acted a very prominent part in the operations of this Church during thirty-five or forty years. Dr. Bird is a conspicuous example of what industry, perseverance, and unfaltering fidelity to the great principles of truth and duty will do for a man under very great disadvantages.

His early education was defective; his habits of communication were embarrassed; he was always poor, and for years had the care of a large family; yet he early became one of our first men, and maintained that position by an unquestioned right for a greater number of years than most men are permitted to labor in the ministry. Nor were labor and earnest application wearing him out. As it has been intimated, in his place at the last Assembly which he attended he presented the prospect of years of labor still. When overtaken by the disease which carried him off, he had his armor on. His annual protracted-meeting had been appointed; the young man who had been called from a distance to assist him knew nothing of his affliction until he reached the neighborhood. It turned out that the young man came to see his father in the ministry die. During his sickness, although terribly prostrated in body and mind, the thoughts of the good man still turned occasionally to the appointed meeting. Says my informant, from whom I have received many of these particulars:

> I never witnessed a more distressing scene than that which followed his death. His family were much devoted to him, as was also the entire community where he has labored for the last seven years. No one could have been more universally respected and beloved. This was especially so with the young, to whom he had devoted a large share of his attention for the last two years. The funeral-service was attended by a very large audience—the largest that has assembled there since the days of camp-meetings.

Dr. Bird did something in the way of authorship. The most of the sermons delivered at the openings of the several Assemblies in which it has been mentioned that he thus officiated were published in the Theological Medium and in the Medium and Quarterly. The sermon delivered at Lebanon, Ohio, was published in pamphlet form.

In 1856, he published a work on the "Doctrines of Grace." This work is understood to have originally grown out of a controversy which commenced in Pennsylvania. A minister of another denomination, in a published sermon, endeavored indirectly to show that Cumberland Presbyterianism, theoretically at least, excluded the gracious features of the gospel, and when understood was nothing better than a legal theology. It was the old polemic resort—an attempt to make it appear that a people must believe what they never thought of believing, or that they stultified themselves. It was a pressing into service of the *odium theologicum* in an argument. Such is always a poor, and sometimes a mean, resort. The object of Dr. Bird's work is to show what a gracious system of theology is, and that Cumberland Presbyterians embrace such a system in its fullest and most scriptural sense. At his death he left in manuscript an extended biographical sketch of Rev. Alexander Chapman, which has since been published by our Board of Publication. It is a very respectable sketch of the life and labors of a good man.

My personal recollections of Dr. Bird are rather extended, and are certainly very agreeable. Our relations, however, were not very intimate—such only as men form at meetings of the judicatures of the Church; but I think I knew him well. I first saw him at the General Assembly at Princeton, Kentucky, in 1835. Our acquaintance there was merely a passing one. I heard him preach once on that occasion. I have a distinct recollection of the sermon and the text: "Pure religion and undefiled before God and the Father is this," etc. I had not been in the habit of hearing such sermons, and it appeared to me to be the work of a man of promise. He and John Morgan and Alfred M. Bryan were all young men from Pennsylvania.

My real acquaintance with him, however, commenced at the Assembly of 1843, at Owensboro, Kentucky. He delivered the opening-sermon on that occasion. It was rather a stormy Assembly. Old and difficult questions came before the meeting, arising out of the Assembly's former connection with Cumberland College. Mr. Bird and myself were on the same side of the Church politics, and our sympathies, of course, brought us into closer relations. We combined with others, and together we succeeded in an effort to keep off the meeting of the next Assembly two years, to give time for the passions of men to become cool.

Near the end of 1843, a few of us were called together at Russellville, Kentucky. In the call made upon us, it was expressed as the consideration that Judge Broadnax, an aged member of the Church, who had acquired considerable wealth, but had no family, desired some counsel on the subject of disposing of his property at his death. The understanding was that he desired to give it to the Church upon certain conditions, or under certain restrictions. Mr. Bird was called from Pennsylvania. I had the honor of being called into the conference myself, with Rev. F. C. Usher, at that time my colleague in Cumberland College. The other members were Rev. Thomas Calhoon and Rev. John L. Dillard. The meeting proved to be a great farce. We could not accept the conditions submitted by our friend. They seemed to us, whether designed or undesigned on the part of the Judge, to affect the integrity of the Church, and self-respect, as well as fidelity to our ordination-vows, required but one course on our part. The result was that Judge Broadnax soon left the Church, and took his money with him. He found new friends who very readily received his benefactions. Mr. Bird returned to his work in Pennsylvania, and the rest of us in like manner to our charges. The Church was no richer from the conference.

Mr. Bird was a prominent member of the Assembly in 1845. A memorial came before the Assembly praying an exposition of the tenth chapter of the Form of Government. This chapter was framed with a view to the Synod's continuing the highest judicature of the Church. When the General Assembly took the place of the Synod, the committee appointed to frame a chapter for the organization and government of the Assembly neglected to change the chapter relating to the Synod, and adapt it to the new order of things. It became a source of constant trouble. The memorial was referred to a committee, of which Mr. Bird was chairman. His report was an intelligent exposition of the whole subject conformed to the spirit of the Form of Government rather than to the letter. The report was adopted, and became at once practically the law of the Church. I speak of this occurrence here for the reason that I was myself the Moderator, and selected the committee with a particular view to the chairman.

I extract the following from the Minutes of the General Assembly of 1850:

Brother T. C. Anderson offered the following preamble and resolution, which were unanimously adopted:

WHEREAS, The Assembly of 1849 authorized and requested the Trustees of Cumberland College and Cumberland University to take measures for the establishment of Theological Departments in these institutions; and,

WHEREAS, The Trustees of Cumberland University have reported to this Assembly their acceptance of the overture of the last Assembly, and their readiness to cooperate with the Assembly in this enterprise, and it is understood that the Trustees of Cumberland College are also ready to cooperate with the Assembly; therefore,

Resolved, That a committee of seven, a majority of whom shall be competent to act, be appointed by this body to mature a plan for the establishment of Theological Departments in said institutions, and report the result of their deliberations to a subsequent Assembly.

On motion, Brothers Roach, Anderson, and _____ were appointed a committee to report suitable nominations to constitute said committee, who reported R. Beard, D.D., T. C. Anderson, Milton Bird, Hon. N. Green, Prof. A. Freeman, David Lowry, and R. R. Landsden, which report was unanimously adopted.

The day before the meeting of the General Assembly in 1852, a majority of this committee, consisting of the chairman and Messrs. Anderson, Bird, and Lowry, met at Nashville and framed the plan of the present Theological Department in Cumberland University.

It will thus be seen that Dr. Bird and the writer were connected in some of the most important transactions of the Church. I ought to have known him; and, as I have said, I think I did know him.

These recollections might be continued, but I forbear. A full sketch of the life and labors of Dr. Bird would enter largely into a history of the Cumberland Presbyterian Church for a quarter of a century, from his connection with it as Stated Clerk of the General Assembly, and from his attendance at its meetings, and his extensive influence upon its measures. Mention may be made before I close of his last introductory-sermon to an Assembly. It was delivered at Owensboro, in 1866. The occasion was a delicate one. It was the first Assembly of the whole Church after the war. It was largely attended. There was a great deal of inflammable material. In a very short time after we met he was kind enough to urge upon me that I should allow my name to used in connection with a measure in the organization of the Assembly, with a view to the promotion of peace. I yielded to what seemed to be an earnest desire, provided that he and other wise and good men thought that the measure would be promotive of peace. He preached the sermon by request. It was an effort to promote peace. There may have been extremists who were not satisfied, but the sermon was intended to be oil upon the troubled waters. By the mass of the assembled delegates it was certainly appreciated. The Assembly was organized in conformity with the plan for peace. We have had peace. How far these measures, which were at least well meant, may have contributed to this end, He alone knows who has overruled and directed all. We had to some extent a stormy Assembly, but still God gave us wisdom and grace, and we did not divide the Church. There was a triumph of principle over passion. Long may it be remembered as a matter of gratitude and thanksgiving!

I have great regard for Dr. Bird's memory. I loved him; I honored him. This Church has produced as good and as great men, but it has never produced one more unselfishly devoted to its great interests, or one less disposed to compromise the great principles of what he regarded as truth and duty, than Dr. Bird.

I add a paragraph from the Banner of Peace of August 19, 1871. It is a Masonic testimony. Dr. Bird was a Mason, but never substituted Masonry for Christianity:

> Brother Bird was an active, zealous, and faithful minister of the Cumberland Presbyterian Church. In the stormy period from 1861 to 1866, when other Churches were rent asunder, he, in the true spirit of a devoted Christian and Mason, 'spread the cement of brotherly love and affection over the surface of society—that cement which unites us in one sacred band'—and he died leaving his Church a unit, 'keeping the unity of the spirit and in the bonds of peace.' In view of this sad dispensation of Providence we recommend the adoption of the following resolutions.

Six resolutions follow, of which I extract the third and fourth:

> 3. Resolved, That we deeply sympathize with his bereaved widow and sorrowing children, and tender them a wide space in our feelings and affections.
>
> 4. Resolved, That we offer our condolence to his shepherdless flock, and join with a smitten community in mourning the death of one beloved, trusted, and revered by us all.

I add, also, from a leader in the **Banner** of August 5, 1871, in relation to the death of Dr. Bird:

> Truly a pillar of the Church has fallen, but, thank God, the superstructure remains in its majesty and strength. It defies the power of time, and the devices of man. Well said the prophet, 'I have set watchmen upon they walls, O Jerusalem, which shall never hold their peace day nor night.' In the heat of action a leader falls; instantly another, from the staff or ranks, assumes command. The battle goes on. So in the Christian warfare; a strong man may be stricken down, and the people, in grief and sorrow, may be ready to despond; but they may rest assured that the Lord will provide, that his standard will be borne full high and onward by other hands, and that final victory is sure. The fall of a captain of the host may call for greater devotion, for greater sacrifices on the part of the survivors, yet, as of old, champions will be raised up in God's own time, and the army of the Lord will continue to march steadily on from conquest to conquest.
>
> Dr. Bird was no ordinary man, as the many and various

positions of prominence he occupied in the Church in the course of his ministry fully testify. As a writer of note, and of marked ability, he is known to the whole Church. The amount of work which he performed in his career was immense. His industry was indefatigable. His wisdom, his correct judgment, his well-tempered views on all subjects pertaining to the welfare and progress of the Church, made him a trusted leader and a safe counselor. In our judicatories the vacancy caused by his death will be deeply felt. May his mantle fall on one worthy to fill his place!

The following is from the Cumberland Presbyterian of August 4, 1871:

Two notes this morning are at hand bringing us the sad intelligence of the death of the venerable father, Dr. Bird. This will send a thrill of sadness through the whole Church. Dr. Bird had served faithfully his allotted time, and we should not arraign the Providence that admits him to his crown, which is studded with many stars.

REV. JOSEPH BROWN
Otherwise, Colonel Joseph Brown
(1772-1868)

Joseph Brown was born in Surrey county, North Carolina, on the 2nd day of August, 1772. His father, James Brown, was brought from Ireland to Virginia when seven years old. He shared in the war of the Revolution as a soldier, and was at the same time a pious member and an Elder in a Presbyterian congregation in Guilford county, where he settled when Joseph was an infant. Joseph when very young learned to read, and, according to the custom of the times, committed to memory the Shorter Catechism and the Lord's Prayer. The family lived several miles from the place of worship at which they customarily attended, and Joseph, being the seventh child, did not attend preaching until he was about seven years old. He says of himself; "I asked my father to let me go to church. He consented to take me if I would ride behind him, which I was proud to do. The sermon was preached by Rev. David Caldwell, pastor of the congregation. The subject was, the parable of the rich man and Lazarus. Mr. Caldwell dwelt at considerable length upon the time which had intervened between the delivery of the parable and the occasion of the sermon, something more than seventeen hundred years, and upon the fearful truth that the rich man was still in that place of torment, and yet that seventeen hundred years was comparatively nothing to eternity. This, though the first sermon that I ever heard, made such an impression upon my mind that I then and there resolved to serve God whilst I lived. From that time I began to pray in secret, and have kept up the practice through life. I have abundant reason to thank God that I formed such a resolution, and established the habit of secret prayer so early."

In 1788, Colonel James Brown, the father of our subject, attempted to move his family from North Carolina to the Cumberland country. Lands had been allotted to him in Cumberland for military services. An account of this enterprise constitutes one of the bloody chapters of which the history of the settlement of the South-west is largely made up. I quote from Ramsay's "Annals of Tennessee." It seems that the emigrants had penetrated to East Tennessee, and at this point the narrative commences:

> Taking with him to the distant wilderness his family, consisting of his wife, five sons, two of whom were grown, and three younger; four small daughters, together with several negroes, he was unwilling to expose them to the dangers of the route through Cumberland Gap, or the more direct but no less unsafe passage over the mountain; and therefore determined to descend the Tennessee River, and reach Nashville by ascending the Ohio and Cumberland to that place. The boat was built on Holston, a short distance below Long Island. He took the precaution to fortify it by placing oak planks, two inches thick, all around above its gunwales. These were perforated with port-holes at suitable distances. To these measures of defense was added a swivel placed in the stern. Besides his two grown sons, James and John, Colonel Brown had with hi five other young men—J.

Bays, John Flood, John Gentry, William Gentry, and John Griffin. These were all good marksmen. The emigrants, or, rather, the adventurers, embarked on the fourth of May. On the ninth, the boat passed the Chickamauga towns about day-break, and the Tuskigagee Island town a little after sunrise. The head-man, Cuttey Otoy, and three other warriors, came on board there, and were kindly treated. They then returned to their town, from which they immediately sent runners across the mountain to Running Water Town and Nickajack, to raise all the warriors they could get, to ascend the river and meet the boat. The narrative of the capture of the boat, the massacre of most of the passengers, and the captivity of such as survived, will be given in the words of the narrator, the youngest son, the late Colonel Joseph Brown, of Murray county, Tennessee. It contains such a horrid recital of Indian cruelty and barbarism by the savage banditti that so long lay concealed in the fastnesses of Nickajack and Running Water towns—is withal so truthful and minute in its details of the captivity and sufferings of one of the prisoners, who himself, in the end, piloted the expedition in 1794, which penetrated these mountain recesses, and extirpated the miscreant land-pirates and murderers that infested them—and is, besides, now for the first time given to the public, that no apology is needed for giving it entire without condensation or abridgment.

I hardly need explain, that Colonel Joseph Brown is the subject of our present sketch. The narrative is a part of the history of the country, and of the terrible experience of one of our good and honored men, and it shall be given in his own words as they are recorded in the Annals, and in the manuscript autobiography which I have in my possession. They substantially agree.

Only four canoes came meeting us in the current of the river, which at the time was very high. Seven or eight came up through the bottoms, in some ponds, and after the Indians in the four first got on board, the other canoes came out through the cane, and the Indians in them also came on board. The first four came two and two, side by side, holding up white flags, but had their guns and tomahawks covered in the bottoms of their canoes. But as there were forty men in the four canoes, my father ordered them not to come nigh, as there were too many of them. We then wheeled our boat, leveled our swivel, and had our match ready to sink their canoes, when they claimed protection under the treaty, and said, through a man named John Vann, whom they got to come and talk for them, that it was a peaceable time, and that they only wished to see where we were going to, and to trade with us, if we had any thing to trade on. My father ordered the young men not to fire, as he was coming to an Indian country, and did not wish to break any treaty.

After they came to us, they appeared friendly until the

other canoes came around; and they then began to gather our property and put it into their canoes. My father begged Vann not to let them behave so, and he replied, that the head-man of the town was gone from home, but that he would be at home that night, and would make them give up every thing. He also promised that one of them should go with us, and pilot us over the Muscle Shoals, as the passage was dangerous for boats.

Before they had finished robbing the boats, however, a dirty, black-looking Indian, with a sword in his hand, caught me by the arm and was about to kill me, when my father, seeing what he was attempting, took hold of him and said, that was one of his little boys, and that he must not interrupt me. The Indian then let me go, but as soon as my father's back was turned, he struck him with the sword, and cut his head nearly half off. Another Indian then caught my father, and threw him overboard. I saw him go overboard, but did not know that he was struck with the sword; it astonished me, therefore, to see him sink down, as I knew him to be a good swimmer. As this took place in the stern, and my brothers and the other young men were with Vann in the bow, I went to them, and told them that an Indian had thrown our father overboard, and he was drowned.

Our boat was landed at the upper end of Nickajack, but before it reached the shore, an Indian wanted me to go out of the boat into a canoe, which I refused, not dreaming that I was a prisoner. As soon as we landed, the same Indian brought an old white man and his wife to me, who said, 'My boy, I want you to go home with me.' I inquired where he lived, and he said his house was about a mile out of town. I told him that I supposed I could go home with him that night, but that we would continue our journey in the morning. On his saying that he was ready to start, and wished me to go with him, I mentioned to one of my brothers the old man's wish that I should go with him, and told him that I would return early in the morning, to which he replied, 'Very well.'

I had not got half-way to the old man's house before I heard the report of the guns which were killing my brothers and the other young men, but I thought it was the noise of our guns, probably taken out of the boat to see how they would shoot. I had been at the old man's house but fifteen or twenty minutes, when a very large, corpulent old woman came in, the sweat falling in big drops from her face, who appeared very angry, and told the white people that they had done very wrong in taking me away, that I ought to be killed, that I would see every thing, and that I would soon be grown, and would guide an army there, and have them all cut off; in short, that I must be killed. This was said in Indian, so that I did not understand it, nor what she went on to say, that is, that all the rest were killed, and that her son would be there directly, and would kill me, she knew.

The old Irishman, however, told me that my people were

all killed, but added that I should not be hurt, although he squaw had just told him that her son would kill me immediately. He then directed me to sit on the side of the bed, and getting up, stood in the door, with his face outward, talking all the time to his wife and the old squaw in Indian, which, of course, I did not understand. In about ten or fifteen minutes, the old squaw's son arrived sure enough, but had not come up the road, so that the old man did not see him till he reached the corner of the house. He asked at once if there was a white man within. The old man answered, 'No; that there was a bit of a white boy in there.' To which the Indian replied that, 'he knew how big I was, and that I must be killed.' The old white man pleaded for my life, saying it was a pity to kill women and children; but the Indian used the same arguments that his mother had employed—that I would get away when I grew up, and pilot an army there and have them all killed, and that as a matter of self-defense I must be killed at once. This old fellow was a British deserter, who had come to America before the Revolutionary War, and had deserted several times, and had at length got into the Cherokee Nation, having been there about eighteen years. His name was Thomas Tunbridge; he had lived with his wife about sixteen years. She was a French woman, who had been taken by the Indians when a small girl, and had grown up, and had had children among them before she had an opportunity of returning to her people. Her name, she said, was Polly Mallet. She had had no children from her connection with Tunbridge, but it was an Indian son of hers who took me prisoner. He gave me to his mother, telling her that I was large enough to help her hoe corn. When, therefore, Cuttey Otoy insisted on killing me, old Tunbridge told him that I was his son's prisoner, and he was still in town, and that I must not be killed. No greater insult could have been offered to Cuttey Otoy, for he was a great man, and usually did as he pleased, while Tunbridge's son was only twenty-two years old—a mere boy, in Cuttey Otoy's estimation. Incensed at this insult, he came to Tunbridge with his knife drawn, and tomahawk raised, and asked him if he was going to be the Virginian's friend. In fact, he would have killed him immediately if he had admitted it, but Tunbridge said, 'No,' and stepping back from the door-sill into the house, spoke in English, 'Take him along.' Cuttey Otoy, who was a very large, strong Indian, followed in a rage, and came to me with his knife and tomahawk both drawn; but the old woman begged him not to kill me in the house, to which he agreed, and catching me by the hand, jerked me up and out of the house. Outside of the house were ten of his men surrounding the house and door, and one had in his hand the scalp of one of my brothers, and another those of the other men on a stick. Some had their guns cocked, and others their knives and tomahawks drawn, ready to put me to death. I requested Tunbridge to beg them to let me have one half-hour to pray, to which he replied that it was not worth while. But they concluded to strip my clothes off, so as not to bloody them, and while they were doing so, the old French woman begged them not to kill me there, nor in the road which she carried water along, for the road passed by her spring. They answered that they would take me to Running Water Town, as there were no white people there, and would have a frolic knocking me over. All this was said, however, in Indian, and I knew nothing of what they were discussing, and as soon as my clothes were off I fell upon my knees, and cried, like dying Stephen, 'Lord Jesus, into thy hands I commit my spirit,' expecting every moment to be my last. But I had not been on my knees more than a minute, when Tunbridge said, 'My boy, you must get up, and go with them; they will not kill you here.' He told me, however, nothing of what they said of having a frolic at Running Water Town.

We had not gone more than seventy or eighty yards, when Cuttey Otoy stopped his men, and said to them that he could not, and they must not, kill me, as they were his men, and it would be as bad for him, as if he himself had done it; for that I was a prisoner of Poor Job—the French woman's son—who was a man of war. 'Now,' said he, 'I have taken a negro woman out of the boat, and sent her by water to where I live, and if we kill this fellow, Poor Job will go and kill my negro, and I do not want to lose her; nor could all the Indians in the nation keep him from putting her to death.'

Now, when Cuttey Otoy spoke thus, the thought of my being one day a man, and leading an army there, and having them killed, and evidently given way to avarice, for the old woman as well as her son wanted the service of the negro. As I knew nothing of what they were saying, I was on my knees trying to give my soul to God, through the merits of the Saviour, and expecting every moment the tomahawk to sink into my skull. At length, the favor shown to Stephen in his dying struggle came to my mind, how he saw the heavens opened, and the blessed Saviour sitting at the right hand of God. I opened my eyes, and looking up, saw one of the Indians, as they stood all around me, smile. Then, glancing my eyes around, I saw that all their countenances were changed from vengeance and anger to mildness.

This gave me the first gleam of hope. Cuttey Otoy then called to old Tunbridge to come after me, saying that he loved me, and would not kill me then, but that he would not yet make peace with me, but if I lived three weeks, he would be back again, and then make peace with me.

Young Brown had thus passed the crisis. It was a terrible ordeal. He still experienced dangers from the jealousy and suspicions of the Indians. He was taken under the care of one of the head men of the town, named The Breath, whom he was directed to call uncle. Poor Job, who had captured him, he was to call brother. Under the shadow of these nominal relationships it was thought his life would be in less danger. In April of the next year, after being a captive eleven months, an exchange of some prisoners was made, and he was restored to freedom.

At the time of the disaster upon the river, Mr. Brown, two sons, and two sons-in-law, were killed. Joseph, the subject of this sketch, and a younger brother, three sisters, and their mother, were taken prisoners, The mother and one of the sisters were in captivity about seventeen months; the others were released at the expiration of eleven or twelve months. It seems a merciful and almost a miraculous providence that they all survived the dangers and horrors of their fearful experience among their savage captors.

Several incidents grew out of the connection of facts which has here been presented, in which the reader will feel some interest. The captivity of Joseph Brown extended from the spring of 1788 to the spring of the following year, 1789. On the night of the 30th of September, 1792, an attack was made by about seven hundred Indian braves, as they were boastfully called, upon Buchanan's Station, five miles from where Nashville now stands. The fort contained only fifteen defenders. Still the assailants were repulsed with heavy loss. Among their killed was the step-son of Tom Tunbridge. This was Poor Job, who had captured young Brown on the boat. He had become one of the Indian braves.

In 1794, the celebrated expedition against Nickajack and the neighboring towns took place. It turned out that what the furious old squaw, the mother of Cuttey Otoy, anticipated and predicted, and what Cuttey Otoy himself seems to have dreaded, was realized. In September of that year, a considerable body of men set out with the view of trying to break up the towns which have been mentioned. They reached the northern bank of Tennessee River after dark on the 12th day of September. The only method of approach to the Indian towns was by swimming the river. A part of the troops remained on the north bank to protect the horses and provisions; a part, who were the better swimmers, made light rafts, upon which they placed their guns, ammunition, and clothes. Colonel Brown says that about two hundred and thirty of the men swam the river in safety, pushing their light rafts before them. He himself, now a grown man, was their guide, fulfilling the prediction of his boyhood, that, "If he were not killed then, he would soon be grown, and would get away, and pilot an army there, and have them all cut off." They penetrated into the heart of Nickajack before they were discovered. The poor Indians thought that the white men must have come down from the clouds, the attack was so sudden, and their fright was so great. Some of those who were captured recognized young Brown, and seemed to be horror-stricken. "At length one woman ventured to speak to him, reminding him that his life had been spared by them, and importuning him to plead now in their behalf. He quieted her apprehensions by remarking to her that they were white people, and did not kill women and children." The destruction of the Indian towns was complete, and the war soon came to an end, which had been carried on for several years against the frontier settlements with all the atrocities which have commonly attended Indian warfare in this country.

Another incident deserves to be mentioned. I derive it from an Indian tale published by the Southern Methodist Publishing House in 1860. It is intended to illustrate the efficacy of prayer, and is considered reliable authority. Mr. Mitchell also confirms it in his sketch. During the Creek war of 1812, Colonel Brown, now about forty years of age, was with General Jackson in the character of aidde-camp and interpreter. He was experienced in Indian warfare, and understood the language of the Creeks. Learning that the old warrior, Cuttey Otoy, who was so anxious to kill him once, when Tunbridge befriended him, and old Breath adopted him, twenty-five years before, was now living on an island in the Tennessee River, he sought an interview with him, when he thus addressed him:

> Cuttey Otoy, you murdered my father and my two brothers when I was a boy. You robbed my poor mother not only of her husband and children, but of all the property she had, and left us orphans, and reduced almost to beggary, cast upon the world without a dollar to keep us from starving, causing us to suffer many hardships and cruelties. For all this you deserve to die, and some of my men would kill you this very moment if they had the opportunity.

Cuttey Otoy hung his head with shame and remorse, and replied, "It is true; I do deserve to be put to death. Do as you please with me." The soldiers around cried out, "Kill him! kill him!" But Colonel Brown was a Christian then, as well as a magnanimous soldier. He replied to the old, cruel warrior, "No, no; although you richly deserve death at my hands, I will not kill you. If I did not, however, worship and serve the Great Spirit who made the sun, the moon, and the stars, and who made us both, I would kill you this moment. But vengeance is His; I will leave you to answer to Him for you crimes; I will not stain my hands with your blood. You are old now, and will soon go down to the grave, and will have to give an account of the life you have led to that Great Spirit."

I bring this eventful episode of twenty-five years' duration in the life of our subject to a close here. In 1796, after the close of the Indian war in which he suffered his captivity, he was married to Miss Sally Thomas, and settled about three miles from Nashville, on White's Creek. Soon after this he united himself with a Presbyterian congregation under the care of Rev. Thomas Craighead, and in a short time was set apart as a ruling elder. His autobiography would leave the impression upon the reader's mind that he considered himself to have been converted in very early life, before he fell into the hands of the Indians, and perhaps from about the time of his hearing the first sermon from Dr. Caldwell. He seems, at least, from about that time to have borne with him always the Christian spirit.

He gives us an account of his first experience with the jerks. Bodily jerking was one the remarkable phenomena of the old revival of 1800. Mr. Brown was traveling through the wilderness across Cumberland mountain on some public business. He was in the habit of fasting in those days a considerable portion of each day. One day, on his journey, he turned aside a short distance from the road to give his horse some corn, which he was carrying in a sack for that purpose. While the horse was eating, he kneeled down and engaged in prayer, and while thus engaged, he was seized with a paroxysm of jerking. He regarded it as a visitation from God, and intended to convince gainsayers that the religious movement which was then just commencing in the country was from God. Under that impression he submitted to it, and his remark is, that in the very act of his submission, under the impression mentioned, he began to enjoy more of the light and comfort of religion than he had ever enjoyed before. He occasionally had paroxysms of jerking—not, however, of the most violent kind—through life, and always rejoiced in it as a lesson calculated to keep before the mind an illustration of man's utter helplessness, and, as he expressively says, his "nothingness" in the hands of God.

About this time the great South-western Revival began to develop itself. Mr. Craighead seemed to be in sympathy with the work at first, but soon became an opposer. His congregation was divided. A large party went with the revival ministers, and amongst them was, of course, Mr. Brown. He became an active supporter of the work, and labored in prayer-meetings and in exhortation, with great efficiency and success..

In 1806, he settled on Lytle's Creek, in Maury county, while the country was yet a wilderness, covered with an undergrowth of cane. It is said that he held the first prayer-meeting that ever was held in the county, and that he called in the whole population of the county, consisting of four men and three women in all. This was a small beginning.

When Rev. Dr. Gideon Blackburn organized the Presbyterian Church in Columbia, in 1810, Colonel Brown was elected one of his elders.

Some time in the year 1812, he joined the Cumberland Presbyterian Church, in which he also served as a ruling elder until he entered the ministry. During all that time he was an earnest and zealous promoter of the great religious interests of his fellow-men. He was in those days what we call a man of business, and, in that respect, a man of the world, but business and worldly interests were kept in subordination to higher considerations. It was understood that his life was in the highest sense a religious life.

About the year 1823, he was set apart to the whole work of the ministry by the Elk Presbytery. He continued a member of that Presbytery until the spring of 1835, when, by appointment, he became a member of the Richland Presbytery, and assisted in its organization. He continued a member of that Presbytery until his death.

Owing to the circumstances of his early life, his education was of necessity limited; still, he was a good English scholar. His practical education was better than his theoretical. This is the case with a great many of our most successful business men—they are men of the world, but still they are Christians, and can do great good.

In the providence of God, he was blessed with success in the administration of his temporal affairs. He was thus enabled to live comfortably and plentifully at home, and to assist the Church in its necessities. In this latter respect he was zealous and liberal. He had leisure, too, to preach much, and his ministerial labors were remarkably spiritual and useful.

He traveled a great deal, and his custom was to have prayers with families wherever he stopped, if permitted. He adhered to this rule whether amongst acquaintances or strangers. It was generally the case, too, that if there was any thing like a warm religious atmosphere about the houses where he held these services, they terminated with a shout, and a time of rejoicing. In one of his manuscripts he says, "I am now ninety-two years old, and still I try to pray, and ever have tried to pray wherever I have been. Since 1805, only two families have denied me the privilege of praying with them in all my travels in Georgia, both Carolinas, Virginia, Alabama, Louisiana, Mississippi, Florida, Arkansas, Texas, Kentucky, and Tennessee." It will be thus seen that he carried his testimony through a wide range as well as a long life. Few men in our country have filled up so large a strictly religious measure. Other men have preached more, and have produced better sermons, but there has never been a man in the Cumberland Presbyterian Church whose personal religious influence has been so extensively felt. In how many thousand families has his voice been heard in fervent prayer! "In this respect," says my authority, with undoubted truthfulness, "he has left a record, we suppose, without a parallel."

For more than five years previous to his death, it was his custom to read the New Testament through every week, and in all that time he said that he had failed in but two readings. A short time before his death he remarked, "Every time I read it, I find new beauties in it. Now, when my hearing is so dull that I cannot enjoy society, it is such a comfort to me to be permitted to read the dear, blessed word of God! Glory!" This latter ejaculation he used, I expect, more frequently than any man of his day. It was his continued note of thanksgiving. Every expression which contained any thing of spirituality ended with his customary "Glory!"

"He lived," says my authority, his honored pastor at the time of his death, "an unblemished life, fulfilling the responsibilities of the various relations of life as but few have ever done. As son, brother, husband, father, master, neighbor, citizen, soldier, Christian, ruling elder, gospel minister, he was above reproach. His piety was uniform, in private, in public, at home, and abroad." What a legacy to a surviving family, and to the Church!

When in his ninety-sixth year, he attended a protracted meeting of about three weeks' continuance, at Mount Moriah Meeting-house, two a a half miles from his home. He was present at every service except one. Near the close of the meeting he rose in the pulpit, in the course of the exercises with the mourners in the altar at an afternoon service, and delivered the last public exhortation which he ever gave in the house of God. And while he was talking, and urging the trembling mourner to open the door, and let the dear Saviour come in, an old, gray-headed man, following the counsel, was joyfully converted, and rose from his knees praising God for his great deliverance. "Was not this," inquires the narrator, "truly still bringing forth fruit in old age?"

In giving an account of his sickness and death, I quote from Rev. G. W. Mitchell, pastor of the congregation with which he was connected:

"On Saturday before the last Sabbath in January, 1868," says Mr. Mitchell, "I visited him, and spent most of the afternoon in his room. His mind was unusually lucid. He told me he was glad I had come to see him, for he thought that, at the rate at which he had declined for the last few days, he could last but two or three days longer. He told me his wishes with regard to his funeral, left some messages for some of his family and neighbors; said he had made all his arrangements, and was ready and waiting for the Lord to take him to his home and reward. He spoke of his past life, of his labors for Christ, of God's amazing goodness and faithfulness to him; of the preciousness of his word; of what a privilege it had been to him to be a servant of the Lord, and thanked God that he, unworthy as he was, had been permitted to lift up his voice as a witness for Jesus wherever he had gone, mentioning the cities of Richmond, Washington, New Orleans, and others;

mentioning, also, all the States through which he had traveled. He repeated many passages of Scripture appropriate tot he circumstances attending; quoted the familiar hymn, 'Hark, my soul, it is the Lord;' then remarked upon Toplady's prayer, expressed in the sweet hymn,

> 'Rock of Ages, cleft for me,
> Let me hide myself in thee,' etc.,

repeating the hymn.

I then read the first chapter of 2 Timothy, whilst he responded, according to the sentiment, 'Thank God!' 'Glory to God!' 'Bless the Lord!' 'Amen!' We then sung her favorite hymn, 'Rock of Ages,' etc., he joining with us in the singing through the hymn. During prayer his soul was on the mount. He seemed to stand in the very gate of heaven. After singing a few more hymns, I left him, This was the last conversation which he had with friends on earth. From this evening he sunk rapidly, and from the next morning ceased to be able to talk. On Tuesday morning, as it turned out, in the providence of God, the 4th day of February, 1868, the anniversary of the organization of the Church of his choice, he died, in his ninety-sixth year. His last articulate expression was his favorite ejaculation, 'Glory!'

Thus lived and died Joseph Brown, one of nature's noblemen, a singular subject of the providence and grace of God; a pioneer and leading spirit of the great South-west.

The funeral took place on the following day. The text for the occasion was the triumphant profession of the apostle: "For I am now ready to be offered, and the time of my departure is at and. I have fought a good fight; I have finished my course; I have kept the faith. Henceforth there is laid up for me a crown of righteousness, which the Lord, the righteous judge, shall give me at that day; and not to me only, but to all them also that love his appearing."

I have some personal memoranda of Colonel Brown, which I add to the preceding sketch. I first saw him in 1812. My father lived near the old Ridge Meeting-house, in Sumner county, Tennessee. I was a little fellow. It happened on a particular Sabbath that some one preached at the meeting-house. My recollection is that the preacher was William McGee. The family went to meeting, but I was left at home to take care of the house. The meeting was closing with a good deal of interest, and some noise. It was but a short way from the house, and my curiosity prompted me to go over and look through the cracks to see what was going on. A man as passing around among the people near the pulpit, rejoicing, and shaking them by the hand. I learned after the meeting closed that the happy man was Colonel Brown. He was a stranger there, I suppose, to all except my father and the preacher. He came to our house for dinner. He and my father had been fellow-soldiers in the Nickajack expedition. Their meeting that Sabbath was altogether unexpected, and, it may be supposed, created some mutual interest. This will account, in some degree, for my recollection so distinct of an occurrence far back. It will be observed, perhaps, by those who read these sketches, that I frequently refer to the year 1812, and to the Ridge Meeting-house and its surroundings. My recollections of these are very numerous and very sacred. This year was one of the years of my life.

I perhaps saw Colonel Brown occasionally in subsequent years, but have no distinct recollection of a meeting until 1837. That year he attended the meeting of the General Assembly at Princeton. It was in the days of old Cumberland College. From some cause he reached Princeton a few days before the meeting of the Assembly. One of those days was the Sabbath. We customarily had preaching on Sabbath-afternoon in the College chapel, and on that occasion Colonel Brown preached for us. Boys are sometimes hypercritical, but they heard the worthy old man with fine attention, and an obvious feeling of deep respect. He became a member of Cumberland College Association at that meeting of the Assembly, and, I suppose, gave some of his money before he left the place.

Some time previous to 1862, he had executed a note for five hundred dollars to what was then our Board of Education. A stipulation was, that it should be paid in Confederate money. In the spring, or early summer, of that year, he traveled in his buggy all the way from his home, in Giles county, to Lebanon, to pay off that note. No one in Lebanon had the note in possession, and, of course, no one felt authorized to receive the money. I seemed to me cruel that he should have taken such a journey, at his age, and still be disappointed. I took the money, or what we thought was the money, and gave him a receipt against the note. It all turned out unfortunately; the money became valueless, but the transaction illustrated the character of the man. A journey of near a hundred miles was made at the age of ninety years, to pay a debt which he considered himself in good faith to owe to the Church. His meeting with me on that occasion was very tender and interesting. The interest, on his part, did not seem to arise so much from his relations to myself as from his recollections of his former relations to my father, his old friend and fellow-soldier.

Colonel Brown raised a large and respectable family. Some of them have been pillars in the Church. The majority of them, however, says my authority, together with his aged companion, had gone before, and were awaiting his arrival in heaven. No doubt his long pilgrimage of more than eight-seven years as an earnest follower of Christ brought him at last to the desired home.

I write this sketch with unusual interest, but still it must have a close. I acknowledge my almost unbounded admiration of such a life and such a character as I have endeavored truthfully to describe here. No human mind can estimate the debt of gratitude which the world owes to such men. They are redeeming spirits of a race mainly given up to selfishness, sottishness, and sin.

Rev. Alfred McGready Bryan
(1805 - 1861)

Alfred Mcgready Bryan was born in Logan county, Kentucky, on the 19th of August, 1805. His parents were James and Anne Bryan. His father was an elder in the Presbyterian Church. His parents were both devotedly pious. In his later life he spoke more frequently of the piety of his mother; but this may have arisen from his unusually sensitive disposition, which would lead him to cling more tenderly to the recollections of his mother. The writer has heard him state that his parents were of those who signed Mr. McGready's celebrated Preamble and Covenant in 1796. The history of this transaction is familiar. It was one of the precursors of the great revival of 1800.

Of Mr. Bryan's early boyhood little is known, except his religious training. This would be inferred from the character of his parents. He also made frequent allusions to it himself, always with apparent earnest thankfulness to God for such a blessing. When about seventeen years old he professed religion. He had been attending a camp-meeting at Red River Meeting-house, not far from his home. On his return home one evening of the meeting, he was telling his mother, with some interest, of those who had professed religion, and of others who were mourners. She turned to him, and with great tenderness inquired, "And what of you, my boy?" The inquiry went like an arrow to his heart. He retired to a secret place, and sought and found peace. He returned to the meeting, which was still in progress, and was encouraged by the ministers to stand up and tell what God had done for his soul. He immediately developed unusual gifts, and his attention was directed to the work of the ministry. On application, he was accordingly received as a candidate for the ministry, by the Logan Presbytery, at Pilot Knob Meeting-house, on the 2d day of April, 1823. He was licensed at the Union Church, in Russellville, April 7, 1825. On the 8th of October, 1829, he was ordained, at Glasgow. His trial-sermon was from St. John i. 29. Rev. Alexander Chapman preached the ordination-sermon, and Rev. William Harris presided and gave the charge.

From the time of his licensure to the spring session of the Presbytery in 1829, Mr. Bryan labored in different parts of Kentucky—all the upper part of which was at that time included within the bounds of the Logan Presbytery. At the spring session of 1829 he was appointed to supply Russellville, Mount Moriah, Red River, and Liberty congregations, until the fall meeting. At this meeting, as it has been stated, he was ordained. By the Presbytery, in the fall of 1829, he was appointed to what was called the Mercer District, in the upper part of Kentucky. In April, 1830, he is noticed as an advisory member of the Logan Presbytery. It is supposed he had been attached to the Kentucky Presbytery, which was stricken off from the Logan Presbytery about the time of his ordination.

About this time also he took charge of a congregation in Nashville, Tennessee. Here he continued eighteen months or two years. I believe this was the first permanent effort made to establish a Cumberland Presbyterian Church in Nashville. Rev. Robert Donnell had held several meetings there, but his visits were occasional only.

In 1831 Mr. Bryan was appointed, in connection with four others, by the General Assembly, on a mission to Western Pennsylvania. His first sermon in Pennsylvania was delivered in Washington county, it is believed, in the same house in which the stroke of death fell upon him. After laboring as a missionary in Pennsylvania eighteen months, he determined to remain in that State, and took charge of a congregation, the nucleus of which had in the meantime been collected in Pittsburg. His labors in Pittsburg commenced about the close of the year 1832. From that time to his death his history is in a great measure identified with the history of the Pittsburg congregation.

Previous to the time of Mr. Bryan's settlement in Pittsburg, the few Cumberland Presbyterians who had been collected together occupied a building as a house of worship on First Street, and secured such ministrations as they could. A portion of the year 1832 they had been served by Rev. Samuel S. Sparks, who preached at this point in connection with his charge in Monongahela City. On the arrival of Mr. Bryan, a regular organization was effected. This occurred on the first day of January, 1833. The following is an extract from the records of the session:

> Whereas, the great Head of the Church, who works when, and where, and by whom he pleases, has condescended to bless the labors of the Cumberland Presbyterian missionaries in the city of Pittsburg, it has been thought expedient by the missionaries to constitute a society, especially as a number of respectable citizens have solicited them to do so;
>
> Therefore, on the first day of January, 1833, Rev. John Morgan and Rev. A. M. Bryan constituted a society, which was on the first day of April following organized by Rev. John Morgan, according to the discipline of the Church, and called the First Cumberland Presbyterian Church of Pittsburg. Simeon Bulford and James Watt were unanimously chosen and ordained ruling elders.

The church thus organized was composed of fifteen members. In December, 1833, the first year of their organization, the congregation had completed, and began to occupy, a commodious house of worship, located on the corner of Smithfield Street and Diamond Alley. Their house soon began to fill with hearers. Early in January, 1834, a series of meetings was commenced which resulted in the addition of more than one hundred persons to the Church. Similar meetings were held in several successive years, and were more or less blessed. These accessions of strength enabled the congregation to pay the debt incurred in building their house. This was finally effected on the fifteenth of February, 1838. The following is the grateful acknowledgment of the trustees, found upon their records:

> The Cumberland Presbyterian Church is now out of debt. May it ever continue to be a fold for Christ's flock; and may He, the Shepherd, watch over it, and make the members of the flock strong in the faith and in every good and perfect work; and may there be daily added to it of such as shall be saved; and to God we will give all the praise! February 15, 1838.

This building soon proved too small, and early in 1838 (about the time, it would seem, it which they had completed their payment for it) the trustees appointed a committee to look out a lot for a new building. They selected the lot on which their present house of worship stands.

Another revival occurred in the early part of the winter of 1839 and 1840, and continued through the most of the winter. The congregation were then engaged in building their new house. At the spring communion eighty-four persons were received into the communion of the Church. On the 26th of June, 1842, the new church was dedicated. The cost was about $15,000.

In 1845 another revival occurred. The Lutheran congregation united with Mr. Bryan in holding a union or joint meeting, which resulted in a number of accessions to each congregation.

In the spring of 1845 the great fire visited Pittsburg. Mr. Bryan lost his family residence; his church, however, escaped, but the debt contracted in its erection had not been all paid. His congregation had suffered from the fire, and of course were partially disabled. In May of that year he was a delegate to the General Assembly, which met at Lebanon, Tennessee. Many will recollect one of his short speeches on the floor of the Assembly, in which he alluded to the late fire in the city of his adoption, and to the terrible perils of his family while it was raging, and expressed his gratitude to God, with tears in his eyes, that although he had lost nearly every thing else, his wife and children had been spared to him. The losses of his congregation from the fire made it necessary for him to apply to his brethren in the South for assistance in paying their debt. Accordingly, on leaving the General Assembly, he spent some time in Middle Tennessee and Kentucky, in endeavoring to raise money for that purpose. It needs hardly be said, that he was met wherever he went with a generous liberality.

In 1848 his congregation was visited with another revival, which resulted in the addition of more than one hundred to their communion. His pastorate continued happily and usefully to the spring of 1856. In the course of that spring he received a call to the pastorate of the congregation in Memphis, as the successor of the lamented Porter, who had died there the fall before. He accepted the call, but the decision cost him a struggle. The tenderness of his attachment to his people of Pittsburg can readily be appreciated by those who were acquainted with the tenderness of all his sympathies, and the strength of his attachments. On the first of April he was dismissed from his charge. As an illustration of the feelings of his friends whom he left behind, I quote from his funeral-sermon, by Rev. Dr. Paxton. Says the preacher:

> He went regretted by all who knew him. His brethren in the ministry, of all evangelical denominations, were sad to bid him farewell. His uniform courtesy, kindness, and warm, brotherly sympathy, had endeared him to all hearts; and had it not been that he felt the call of duty, they would all have thrown around him the arms of affection, and said, 'Stay, brother—stay.'

On his way to Memphis an explosion occurred on board of the steamer. His eldest son, a lovely boy, was scalded to death, and himself and the rest of the family narrowly escaped. This fearful Providence is said to have made a deep impression upon the mind of Mr. Bryan. It was a terrible affliction to his sensitive soul. It staggered him in relation to the propriety of his removal.

He was cordially received at Memphis. His house of worship soon became crowded to excess—so much so, that the necessity of a new building began to be felt.

In the summer of this year, 1856, he was honored with the degree of Doctor of Divinity by the Trustees and Faculty of Cumberland University.

It has been said that Dr. Bryan was well received and popular at Memphis, but it now seems probable that his heart was never there. In February of 1858 he was called to the management of a protracted meeting at Lebanon, which had been commenced with very favorable promise by others. He continued the meeting about three weeks, preaching every night, and delivering a practical lecture every morning. It was a meeting of great interest. Many will recollect it in heaven. He had been often in Lebanon, and had many friends there, but the labors of that meeting greatly increased the interest of the community in himself and in his preaching. The congregation were then without a pastor, and he was twice called, with unusual unanimity, in the course of a few months, to the pastorate. It seemed afterward, however, that his heart was with his former charge of Pittsburg. In the spring of 1859 he was recalled to Pittsburg, and commenced his second series of labors there on the first of April. In his absence the congregation had undergone sore trials, and the wonder is, that it was not broken up. The nature of these trials needs not be mentioned. Even the recollection of them is afflicting. The people rallied, however, around their old pastor, and there was a prospect of extended usefulness; but in the providence of God it appeared that he came back rather to die.

On the third week in January, 1861, he attended the convention for prayer for the outpouring of the Spirit of God in the land. The convention was held in Pittsburg. He took a deep interest in the meeting. At the close of the last session of the convention, which was held in the First Presbyterian Church, he is said to have offered a prayer of unusual earnestness and fervor—so much so, that the remark became general with those who were present, "What a remarkable prayer Brother Bryan offered!" This was his last public service in Pittsburg. The following day, Friday, he started to Van Buren, in Washington county, to administer the Lord's Supper, by appointment of the Presbytery. A minister who was present at the meeting writes that "it was evident in all his preaching and private conversation, that he felt an unusual anxiety for the salvation of sinners. His labors were evidently blessed, and the prospect for doing good was well marked."

On Saturday he preached from Gen. xxxv. 1-3; on Sabbath morning, from 1 Cor. v. 7-8; on Sabbath night, from Luke xiii. 23-24; on Monday, from John iv. 29. Having closed his sermon on Monday, he invited the anxious to the seat prepared for them in order to prayer. To give them time to assembly, he commenced singing the hymn, "I'm not ashamed to own my Lord."

While singing his voice faltered, and he immediately fell back unconscious in his seat. In a few minutes he rallied for a moment, opened his eyes, and said to a lady who stood near, "O sister, I was almost in Paradise!" In another instant all appearance of consciousness departed, and he never spoke again. Having been removed to the house of a friend, he received every attention which Christian kindness and medical skill could bestow, but in vain. The spirit lingered through the night and to the following midday, when it took its departure, and a good man rested from his labors. He died January 22, 1861.

On the 8th of April, 1835, Mr. Bryan was married to Miss Ann Eliza Rahm, of Pittsburg. He left behind him six children, four of whom are members of the Church. His widow still lives respected, with the younger members of the family, in Alleghany City.

The records of the session show that in the course of his pastorate in Pittsburg, about eleven hundred persons were received into the communion of his congregation; and of these, eight or nine hundred were received upon examination. What a testimonial went before him to Heaven!

In relation to the character of Dr. Bryan, I quote from Dr. Paxton's funeral-sermon:

> He combined all the elements of a useful and effective minister of the New Testament. With a strong practical cast of mind, which made him wise in counsel; an energetic executive capacity, which gave him promptness and efficiency in his plans and purposes; a king, conciliatory address, which won friends, and seldom gave offense; a large heart, which drew out the sympathies of others—he combined all those peculiar gifts which gave force and impressiveness to his pulpit ministrations.
>
> As a preacher, he had unusual power in addressing unconverted men upon the value of the soul, the danger of their impenitent condition, and the preciousness and freeness of the salvation offered to them in the gospel. A number of things combined to fit him for such moving appeals. He had an awful conviction of the dreadful state of an impenitent sinner. He had a realizing apprehension of the perdition of the ungodly. To this he added a clear view and a precious experience of the Saviour's atoning work, and of the office of a simple faith in effecting the salvation of a soul. All this gave such deep feeling, and such an unmistakable earnestness to his entreaties, that few sinners could listen to his moving persuasions and go away unconcerned.
>
> As a preacher, he possessed another quality in an unusual degree—the faculty of bringing out and applying the consolations of the gospel to the distressed and afflicted. In all the sermons which it was my privilege to hear from his lips, this was the distinguishing characteristic. He had searched the Scriptures, and felt the consolations of God in his own soul, and therefore knew how to apply them with great tenderness and descrimination to the souls of others.
>
> As a pastor, he had all the qualities of heart and the graces of the Spirit to make him eminently effective. His sympathies were so ready and susceptible, that he was ever prepared to weep with them that wept, and to rejoice with them that rejoiced. In the families of his people his large heart would enter into all their trials, and feel them as if they were his own. At the sick-bed he had the gentleness that soothed the sufferer, and

a sweet voice that could speak comfort and inspire hope in the darkest hour. To all this he added those personal qualifications which underlie the outward functions of the ministerial life. He was a godly man, living before his Master's omniscient eye in all honesty and godly sincerity. He was a man of faith-living, working, walking, and preaching by faith; a man of prayer, feeling it his privilege to live in fellowship with God, and in every thing by prayer and supplication, with thanksgiving, to make his requests known to God.

For some years previous to Dr. Bryan's death, he was considered one of the most popular and useful preachers in the Cumberland Presbyterian Church. Without doubt he was justly so considered. He possessed many advantages. Although his education was limited, nature had done much for him. His person was fine. His voice was clear, strong, and musical. He had a ready command of language, and a tender heart, which expressed itself in his words. He rarely failed of keeping his audience in sympathy with himself. His hearers felt that his gifts were sanctified by grace. He could not have been otherwise than an effective preacher. The great ingatherings which attended his ministrations in Pittsburg are an illustration.

In 1843 he was Moderator of the General Assembly. The meeting was held that year at Owensboro. It was rather a stormy Assembly; but the dignity and energy with which he controlled its proceedings, were matter of remark by spectators.

But in the midst of his own family, I suppose, Dr. Bryan appeared to greater advantage than even elsewhere. No man was a gentler husband or a kinder father. A friend, too, found a pleasant shelter under his hospitable roof. The writer spent a few days with him in Pittsburg in the summer of 1851. Soon after I called, as an inducement that I should stay with him, and not at the hotel, he remarked pleasantly that they had "a little chamber on the wall, which was furnished with a bed, and a table, and a chair, and a candlestick, for the use of sojourning prophets." The religious services of the family interested me very much. They were so tender and impressive! Of course I occupied his pulpit on Sabbath. His closing prayer in the morning was a model of its kind. It may seem strange, but a portion of that prayer I still recollect. I could hardly forget a petition so earnestly offered up for "the beloved brother" who had ministered to them that day.

I have many pleasant personal recollections of Dr. Bryan, but I need to record them here. A concluding remark may, however, be made. His example is worth a great deal to the Church. A stranger, a young man partially without experience, he established himself in a great city, and by his own energy and influence brought hundreds into the fold of Christ, collected around him a large congregation, and made himself respected and beloved by all classes of persons, and especially by those who would have been considered his rivals in his work. I say, the example of such a man is a treasure to the Church. It shows us what can be effected by consecrated time and talents. Dr. Bryan labored for no selfish interest. He loved the Church, and labored for its interest. He selected his field, guided o doubt by the providence of God, and devoted himself to it. We have seen the result. Why should not scores of others imitate his example?

I must be indulged in a still farther remark. I have said that Dr. Bryan "loved the Church." He loved its primitive theology, primitive usages, and its old men. Every one acquainted with him knew how sensitive he was in regard to every thing affecting the character of any of these. I once saw him weep like a child, when he felt that the theological reputation of some of the fathers had been assailed. He felt that the character of the fathers, in all its aspects, together with the doctrines and usuages formed into a system by them, had been left to us as a sacred legacy.

Dr. Bryan died just at the commencement of our late national troubles. Before I had seen the announcement in the papers, a friend met me on the street and communicated the afflicting intelligence. In the course of our conversation, he remarked, in view of what seemed probably before us, that "it was a good time to die." Dr. Bryan's sympathies were largely extended over both sections of the country. To have witnessed the terrible struggle and sufferings which followed his death, would have been an inexpressible affliction, especially to him. His attachments were strong. Nothing but death could have broken them. A good and wise Providence, in regard perhaps to a tender spirit, removed him before these difficulties were fully developed. He was not allowed to see what he could not prevent, and what he could hardly have borne.

REV. REUBEN BURROW
(1798-1868)

Sources: Manuscript Autobiography; Rev. A. E. Cooper; Records of the Elk Presbytery.

All the facts in the following sketch up to 1852 are derived from a manuscript autobiography, prepared at the request of the Heurethelian Society of Cumberland University, and preserved by them to the present time. The sources of the remaining material are indicated in the customary manner. The autobiographical sketch is preceded by the following letter, which explains itself:

APRIL 12, 1852.

To the Heurethelian Society:

DEAR BRETHREN:—I have penned this sketch rather in compliance with your request than with a view of furnishing any means of perpetuating my name to posterity. Although I have labored hard to do good, regardless of ease and worldly comfort, and always with cheerful resignation, I could now wish my name, and any record of my life, which I feel to have been too unprofitable, might be dropped out of view, and given to oblivion, as soon as I shall have passed from the stage of action. If, however, any thing likely to be profitable in the future can be gleaned from my checkered life, the following sketch is hereby cheerfully submitted. In relation to my opportunities in early life I have said but little, yet as much as I have intended to say. Touching the means of my support, I have drawn a veil over the subject. I do not wish to leave the impression behind that I place a high estimate upon unrequited labors. Certainly I will not waste my time and strength in complaints. I am very sure the Church ought to do her duty; yet I am by no means certain that those for whom she does most are the men who do most for her prosperity, and for the honor of God. In a word, we ought to do our duty at all hazards, and at whatever sacrifice, committing results into the hands of God. Pursuing this course, we may be certain that he cares for us, in whatever manner that care may develop itself

Yours, most fraternally,

REUBEN BURROW.

I was born A.D. 1798, in the State of North Carolina, Guilford county. My parents, Ishmael and Catharine Burrow, were industrious persons, and moved in the humble walks of life. My father, by religious training, was a Methodist, but did not profess to be an experimental Christian until about the age of forty-five, at which time he connected himself with that Church. My mother was a Lutheran, and had been in connection with that Church from her infancy, and lived in its communion until our removal to Tennessee, but never claimed to know any thing of experimental religion until many years after my father became a member of the Methodist Church. When she became satisfied on that subject, she joined that Church with her husband, and they both continued in its fellowship until their death.

In 1806, my father, with his family, moved to Tennessee, and spent one year in Smith county. He then moved to Bedford county, and settled near the Three Forks of Duck River. This occurred in 1807. The country was new, and covered with a thick and heavy forest. I was trained to industry, but was surrounded on all sides by dissipation, irreligion, and the desecration of the Sabbath, and for several years the state of society seemed, instead of growing better, to grow worse. There were schools of the common kind, conducted by incompetent teachers, but very little, if any, improvement was made for some time. Consequently, the opportunities afforded for an education were very indifferent.

We had preaching at an early day by the Methodists and Baptists, but none by either of the Presbyterian Churches until the settlement of Revs. William McGee and Samuel King, near the Three Forks of Duck River, between the years 1810 and 1812. Not long after they settled there, the state of society began to improve. The Lord revived his work through their instrumentality, and a large Church was organized at that place, and others in different parts of the adjoining country. I frequently heard these men preach when a careless and wicked boy, but was never moved by the preaching of any one until after I professed religion. In a tender age I was frequently visited by remorse of conscience, but the first powerful alarm which I ever experienced I experienced at home, when, in the darkness of night, God shook terribly the earth, in 1812. I then prayed and vowed to the mighty God of Jacob, and continued to be thoughtful for a time, but finally my serious feelings subsided, and I became harder and worse than before. I continued in this condition about eight years, when I was nearly grown. About that time a revival of religion occurred in the neighborhood in my absence, and a number of my acquaintances shared in its blessings. On my return home I witnessed the change. I saw some, who had been my associates in sin but a short time before, actively engaged in the service of the Lord. This caused me to think of changing my course. One evening I visited a pious little family. The man and his wife were my relations, and had been subjects of the late revival. The woman, in passing to and fro, attending to the affairs of her household, inquired after the welfare of my soul. Her words were few, but God directed them to my heart. They were like arrows there, and remained until he who inflicted the wound employed his healing power. That dear woman died soon after this occurrence, went to her reward, and never knew what God had done through her instrumentality that evening at her own quiet fireside. From that moment I vowed to God to seek his grace. In a few days I left that country, and went to what was then called the Western District of Tennessee, with the intention of settling there, but prayed as I went, and after my arrival at my destination, until I found peace with God in the dreary forest of what is now Carroll county, about twelve miles from what is at present McLemoresville. This occurred in the spring of 1821. That summer I returned to Middle Tennessee, and joined the Cumberland Presbyterian Church. The congregation to which I attached myself was under the care of Rev. Samuel King.

In the fall of the same year I was received as a candidate for the ministry by the Elk Presbytery, at Mars' Hill, in Giles county. The next spring I was sent, with R. D. King,[6] to the State of Missouri, to travel there while Mr. Ewing was writing his lectures. I was not yet licensed in form, nor was I licensed until twelve months afterward, when I received license in the spring of 1823, in Missouri. The circumstances were the following: It was thought expedient that an intermediate Presbyterial meeting should be held in Arkansas, for the purpose of receiving some young men under the care of the Presbytery. With a view to that end, it was decided to ordain King, and license myself. Consequently, I went with Carnahan,[7] Long, and King, to White River, where they met, and held their Presbyterial sessions. Several young men were received as candidates for the ministry, some of whom have been long in the field, and have been greatly blessed of God.

After the close of the sessions of the Presbytery, and the camp-meeting which was in progress at the same time, Long returned to his field of labor in Missouri; Carnahan and King went to the settlements on Arkansas River, and left me on White River, where I formed a circuit, and preached until some time in July, when I joined them near Fort Smith, in the upper settlements of Arkansas. We were to hold a series of camp-meetings and sacramental-meetings, extending from that point back to White River. Shortly after I joined them, our first camp-meeting came on. Our pulpit was supported by logs on one side, and Judge Billingsly's fence on the other. Some bushes were spread over our heads to protect us from the heart of the sun. The other accommodations corresponded. There were but three camps, and these were made of rails and covered with bushes. God, however, came down into his broad temple, and lighted it up with

---

[6]Rev. R. D. King, now of Texas.

[7]Rev. John T. Carnahan, a pioneer Cumberland Presbyterian minister of Arkansas. He laid the foundation of the Church in that State.

his presence; and the little meeting closed with thirty-five rejoicing converts.

At the close of the meeting I was attacked with chills and fevers, but went with the brethren to the next appointment. The meeting was held on the bank of Arkansas River. There was great excitement, but being sick during the meeting, I cannot remember much of the result, except that it was good.

The next appointment was in the neighborhood of Crystal Hill, a distance of near a hundred miles from the point where we then were. I was unable to travel on horseback, and Brothers Carnahan and King bought a tan-trough, took the leather out of it, and converted it into a sort of canoe. They put me into it, in charge of two of the young men who were going to the next meeting, and in that way I was borne upon the surface of the stream, in the heat of summer, under a burning sun, unprotected from its rays, and suffering from a scorching fever, to the next appointment, a distance of one hundred and fifty miles by water. This meeting was owned of the Lord as one of his own; there were many converts.

I soon recovered from my illness, but Brother King was taken sick, and I waited on him as well as I could, until it was necessary for us to set out for the camp-meeting on White River. Brother Carnahan and I left King sick on the bank of Arkansas River, and went to the meeting, a distance of a hundred miles, accompanied by eighteen young persons, some of whom were professors of religion, and the most of those who were not, obtained a hope at the meeting. At the close of this meeting I set out alone, on Tuesday morning, for St. Michael, in the State of Missouri, through a dreary country, a distance of one hundred and fifty miles. The most of this journey I traveled on foot, as the day I left White River my horse was taken sick, and after my leading him and driving him alternately for some time, he died. By perseverance, however, I reached my destination the day on which our meeting was to commence. Here I met with, and embraced, Brother Long, with tears of joy. Here, also, we realized a refreshing from the presence of the Lord.

From this place Brother Long and I packed our baggage on his horse, girded on our sandals, and set out on foot for the next appointment; but from weakness and great fatigue I became unable to travel after the first day, and the next morning Brother Long left me sick, as he thought, unto death. The impression was that we should meet no more on this side of the resting-place of the pilgrims. But in the course of two weeks I had so far recovered as to be able to walk about. A dear friend loaned me a horse, and I set out for Presbytery, which was to meet near Father Ewing's, south of Boonville. On the first day I relapsed, but persevered at the rate of thirty or forty miles a day, with a burning fever on me all the way, except a few hours just before and after daylight.

When I reached Presbytery, I made a brief report, and went to bed in the house a Father Ewing, a very sick mortal. I remained there some two or three weeks, in the course of which time Brother King, whom I left sick on the bank of Arkansas River, came up with me. After my recovery, we set out for home, after an absence of eighteen months.

The reader will observe that at this point the progress of the narrative is arrested, and the autobiography goes back to the point of time at which the writer reached Missouri, in the spring of 1822. In this intermediate chapter we have the narrative from the spring of 1822 to the spring of 1823, when he was licensed, and set off with others for Arkansas, where he spent six months, of which we have just had the particulars. The writer says:

At this point I shall take up this unfinished narrative, and continue it, after narrating what occurred of moment in the State of Missouri from the time of my arrival to that of my licensure and departure for Arkansas.

The first place at which we[8] called to rest for more than a Sabbath, after we left Tennessee, was at the house of Father Ewing, who directed us to make our way to a camp-meeting which was to be held, in the course of a week, on Chariton River. He proposed to meet with us at this meeting. The meeting came on, and I thought it one of the most divinely sweet seasons in which I had ever participated; and a great many who came to the place in their sins were delivered from the power of sin, and returned to their homes full of hope. From some cause, however, my mind became enveloped in a cloud which covered me with darkness, and filled me with an unusual kind of feeling which I have no words to express. I was aware of the probable cause, but forbear to mention it, thinking such a course to be best. I will satisfy the curious, however, so far as to say that my state of mind did not arise from any feeling of rebellion in my heart against God, nor from any known sin which I had committed; but beyond this I say nothing. My darkness and distress continued several days and nights without any abatement. Indeed, they only grew worse, until the heavens seemed to be brass, and I feared that God had forgotten to be gracious.

In the mean time, I was directed to the western part of the State, to ride and preach on the same circuit with Brother John Morrow. King and myself left the camp-ground together. We had to cross the Missouri River, and while crossing, I became so overwhelmed by my feelings, that I should have fallen in the boat, had I not been supported by a circumstance not necessary to be mentioned here. Finally, we fell in with Morrow, at an appointment

---

[8]Himself and Rev. R. D. King.

at which King preached, and the next morning left us and went on to his destination. Morrow and myself went in company to the next appointment, which was in a settlement on the Missouri River. The service was held in the house of Captain William Jack, who was at that time a captain in the army of Satan. The congregation was composed of sinners, with the exception of two formal professors of religion, Jack's wife and a colored man. Brother Morrow preached, and called on me to conclude. I was still in darkness, and do not know that I had thought once of attempting to preach, but when Morrow sat down, I rose up, took a text, and commenced talking, and very soon, in my manner, reached the top of my voice. Morrow became alarmed, and trembled for the ark. I had forgotten all but Christ, and the salvation of souls. My darkness was gone, and the place was as awful and sweet to me as the gate of heaven. All in the house were in a state of high excitement, and entered into a solemn covenant to pray in secret night and morning, and seek the Lord, until the camp-meeting at Tabbo, about two weeks from that time. The most of them professed religion before the time, and came to the meeting happy in the love of God, but Captain Jack was yet groaning under an intolerable burden; but he continued to agonize, as he had done before, until Monday morning, when, as the day dawned, and while he was in his camp lifting up his soul to God in prayer, peace was spoken to his heart, and he came out of his camp praising God, while a heavenly light seemed to be beaming from his countenance. The people collected, and the work of the Lord went on so triumphantly that the people could not be collected that day for preaching at the stand, but fell in all directions, and cried to God for mercy; and many experienced his saving power that day. From the time of my deliverance from my darkness and trouble in the house of Captain Jack, I was happy in the love of God night and day, with scarcely any intermission, for twelve months. The number of converts reported from that circuit at the close of the year was over three hundred.

There is one more incident which I will mention in this connection. I went some eighty miles down the river, and that distance from my circuit, to attend a camp-meeting. It proved to be one of the Lord's own meetings, as nearly all camp-meetings were in that day, and many were born of the Spirit on the occasion. At the close of the meeting on Tuesday morning, some brethren, in getting their horses, let mine out, and he ran off. I hunted him for several days, but failed to find him. I then set out in the heart of summer, with my saddle-bags upon my back, for my circuit. The country through which I had to travel was mostly an open prairie, with only two or three houses on the way. The first day, hungry and thirsty, I traveled on till night, when I came to a small cabin where I was permitted to spend the night; but I was in so much pain, from weary limbs and blistered feet, that I could neither eat nor sleep. The next morning I started again, and traveled until late breakfast-time, when I came to another shanty, where I got some refreshment. There were then thirty-five miles before me to the next house, which was on the border of my circuit. About the middle of the afternoon I reached the edge of a prairie said to be twenty-two miles wide. Forward I went. Night came on; my feet were skinned; but about midnight, I reached the house of a friend. Next morning the good sister applied some soothing plasters to my feet; a message in relation to my distress was sent to Brother Jack, who came with a horse for me, and one for himself. He said to me, 'Take this horse and go on your circuit, and give yourself no uneasiness; I will find yours, if I have to follow him to Tennessee.' So we parted—I to my circuit, and he in pursuit of my horse. In eight or ten days he returned with him.

I have mentioned this incident as a memorial of Brother Jack, hoping that others, when they see a poor preacher bending under his burden, will extend a hand of relief; and, also that young men called of God may be stimulated not to flinch from their work, though it should give them pain in the flesh, and sometimes cost them the skin of their feet, but to go, and preach Christ.

The reader will observe that the intermediate chapter here closes. The writer takes up his narrative at the point which he had reached previous to its introduction. That point was the termination of his work in Missouri and Arkansas. He had been in the country eighteen months, having spent a year in Missouri, and six months in Arkansas. He proceeds with his narrative, and says:

The aid which I received in eighteen months amounted to about fifty dollars in cash, and some articles of clothing.

Let the money-lovers of the present time observe this; fifty dollars for eighteen months of hard service, and a horse, also, had died. Yet the young preacher held on.

"I shall now return," says the autobiographer, "and continue my narrative from the time when King and I set out from the house of Father Ewing for Tennessee. My horse having died on my way from Arkansas to Missouri, I bought another with what means I had, without any farther aid from brethren, and borrowed money from King to enable me to pay my way home.

After my return to Tennessee, I was directed to a circuit which extended through Giles, Maury, Bedford, and Lincoln counties. There I labored for twelve months, though my health was very feeble. Camp-meetings were common in those days, and signally owned by the great Head of the Church. The number of conversions varied from twenty to one hundred, and it was the custom to close on Tuesday morning, whatever the prospects might be. The circuits were all supplied with preachers, and young brethren were willing to labor as poor circuit-riders. There was no difficulty in finding laborers. While this was the state of things we had gracious outpourings of the Spirit, revivals were common, and the cause of Christ was triumphant. But when the circuits began to be neglected, and the young preachers too refined, and think themselves too talented to travel as circuit-preachers, camp-meetings began to decrease in numbers and usefulness, and worldly-mindedness and pride to seize upon both ministers and people. Camp-meetings are almost numbered with things of the past, and circuits have been given up to be trodden down of the Gentiles. There can be no sound objection to an increase of riches and knowledge in the Church of Jesus Christ; but worldly-mindedness and pride are to be watched as the mantle in which Satan will clothe himself when he approaches the temple of God. I am inclined, however, to wander from my narrative, and will return.

In the fall of 1824[9], as well as I recollect, I was ordained by the Elk Presbytery, where I continued to labor until directed by the old Synod[10] to another field. In the fall of 1825, the Synod resolved upon the establishment of the first College of the Church. The College was organized in the spring of 1826, and in the fall of that year it was decided by the Synod to send out agents for the purpose of collecting funds for its benefit. Brother Albert G. Gibson[11] and myself were directed to the Carolinas. We started the same year of 1826, and traveled through East Tennessee, preaching as we went. The ministers traveling in East Tennessee

---

[9] I derive the following from the records of the Elk Presbytery: "Reuben Burrow was received as a candidate for the ministry at Mars' Hill, Giles county, Tennessee, October 3, 1821. The first text assigned him was John viii. 36. At the same presbytery, an order was passed, directing him to travel with Rev. Robert D. King, on a Missionary tour in Missouri. He was ordained at Shiloh, Bedford county, Tennessee, April 24, 1824. The text of his trial-sermon, from 2 Tim. iv. 2; Rev. Samuel King presided and gave the 'charge.'" The reader will remember that he was licensed in Missouri.

[10] Cumberland Synod, before the organization of a General Assembly.

[11] *Rev. Albert G. Gibson commenced the ministry some time about the year 1820, or 1821. He attended the meeting of Cumberland Synod for the first time in 1822. He was raised, and spent his life chiefly, in Tennessee. His labors were chiefly confined to Lincoln county, in which he lived.

at that time were, George Donnell, Abner W. Landsden, William Smith, Samuel Aston, and the two Tates. They met with much opposition, but were much aided by the Lord. On our way we made an appointment for a camp-meeting east of Greeneville, to be held ten months from that time, on our return to the West, and also an appointment for a two-days' meeting in Abingdon, Virginia, to be held the week before the camp-meeting. We then proceeded on our way over the mountains to North Carolina. This was a new field for Cumberland Presbyterians, and they were a new people without congregations, or houses of worship. Of course we found in impossible to collect much for the College, and we concluded to give ourselves to the ministry of the word. We sent forward appointments, as well as we could, through the State, and went on until we reached the Atlantic. In the city of Raleigh, while we preached, the Lord came down in great power, and the large assembly appeared to be excited throughout. A gracious revival was the result, as we heard after our departure for Newbern and Wilmington. In Wilmington nothing special appeared, but in Newbern and in Fayetteville the Lord was present in a remarkable manner; but being in the midst of strangers, and occupying houses of worship belonging to others, we did not call the awakened to the anxious seat. From Fayetteville we went into South Carolina, and spent several weeks, chiefly in York District. Passing from thence, we spent our time, to the latter part of the summer, in North Carolina and Virginia, confining our labors mostly to Guilford, Orange, Caswell, and Rockingham counties in North Carolina, and to Patrick and Henry counties in Virginia. Here the field appeared white unto harvest, and many found peace in the Son of God. We were often and warmly urged to organize congregations, but declined doing so.

On our way to the West we attended the appointment at Abingdon, where we met with Brother Aston. The bell was ringing for worship when we arrived. The first day's service closed with a good degree of interest. On Sabbath there were clear and manifest displays of the Divine presence and power, which continued to increase until many hearts found peace. Brother Sparks[12], who left our Church, and connected himself with the

---

[12]Rev. Samuel Sparks, after his ordination, went to Pennsylvania, and labored there for some years, but becoming dissatisfied with his Church relations from some cause, he determined to change them; and the disruption in the Presbyterian Church taking place about that time, he united himself with the New School division of that Church. The understanding is, that the change was perhaps unfortunate for his happiness as well as for his usefulness.

New School Presbyterians in Pennsylvania, was awakened at this meeting, and professed religion at the camp-meeting near Greeneville, the week following. On Sabbath-evening of the meeting at Abingdon, when we went into the pulpit to commence the service, we found a letter in the Bible, directed to C.P., with a request, 'Read it before you preach.' The writer stated that he was a great sinner, and that he had been awakened in the course of the service that day. He requested us to pray for him, adding that at a suitable time he would make himself known. At the close of the service many of the people remained in the house, as if unwilling to leave. This young man, Sparks, approached us, and said that he was the man who wrote the letter. We gave him some counsel, and parted with him. Shortly after, being seated at the house of the friend with whom we lodged, a messenger came for us to go into town. When we reached the place to which we were called we found a house filled with people crying to God for mercy. We remained with them until a late hour of the night, when we left, promising to meet them at the same house early next morning. We met them in the morning, and after much exhortation and prayer, we left them for the camp-meeting near Greeneville, seventy-five miles distant. On Friday, at the first public service, Sparks, from Abingdon, and another young man who came with him, were present. They had walked all the way. They both found peace at the camp-meeting, and returned to Abingdon, and went to work for the promotion of the good work at home.

    The meeting in Greene county was very interesting. Forty or forty-five persons professed religion up to Tuesday morning, and a great many afterward. From this place we traveled westward, and attended several sacramental and camp-meetings on our way, which were mostly precious seasons. The funds collected for College were paid over. The sum was small, and we were released from that agency with a reprimand, and without any compensation for services, although we had each expended in the trip about seventy-five dollars.

    In the spring of 1827, I returned alone, and labored in East Tennessee, North Carolina, and Virginia until fall. On my return through Abingdon I had Brother Sparks for a traveling companion to the West.

    On the 5th day of February, 1828, I was married to Elizabeth Bell, of Franklin county, Tennessee, and lived in Giles county near Pulaski, until the fall of the same year, when I moved, and settled in Madison county, where I now live.

    After the old Cumberland Synod was superseded by the General Assembly, and Cumberland College had been in operation some years, a correspondence was opened between Rev. F. R. Cossitt, President of the College, and some persons in Western Pennsylvania, on the subject of the Assembly's sending some missionaries to that country. The correspondence was commenced by an application on the part of those persons for a visit of some Cumberland Presbyterian preachers. These communications were brought before the General Assembly of 1831, and urged upon its consideration. The result was, that five ministers were directed to go to that country as soon an practicable. The five selected were, Robert Donnell, Alexander Chapman, A. M. Bryan, John Morgan, and Reuben Burrow. Chapman, Bryan, and Morgan went through Ohio; Brother Donnell and myself went through East Tennessee and North Carolina, and thence to Pennsylvania. The first point at which we halted to preach was Greensboro, the county-seat of Guilford county. Here we held a meeting in the old Academy and surrounding yard. The congregation was large, attentive, and serious. We closed on Sabbath-evening with twelve converts, leaving between eighty and ninety penitent mourners. The interest was followed up, however, by the Methodists and Presbyterians, and resulted, as we were afterward informed, in four hundred or five hundred converts. At some other places our meetings were of nearly equal interest, and such was the urgency of the people in many places that we should organize congregations and remain with them, that we at one time concluded to separate, one remaining, and the other going on to Pennsylvania. But when the time for separation came we changed our minds, determining to remain another week, and then to go, both of us, to the North. From that point to Washington, Pennsylvania, near which we held our first camp-meeting, the distance was between four hundred and five hundred miles. The brethren who went through Ohio had been laboring for some time in the field to which we were all directed, and the camp-meeting at which we had agreed to meet was in progress when we arrived. The congregations were very large and attentive, and hundreds came forward at each call for mourners. The meeting closed on Tuesday morning, giving two hundred and fifty as the number of conversions, as well as now recollected. We held another camp-meeting, which closed with one hundred conversions. The other meetings were of two and three days' continuance, and mostly very interesting. Congregations were organized, and Brothers Morgan and Bryan remained, and Brothers Donnell, Chapman, and myself returned to the West. This was the introduction of our branch of the Church into Pennsylvania and Ohio. Two[13] of these dear brethren, Chapman and Morgan, have long since gone to their rest and reward.

---

[13]The others are now also gone. Dr. Burrow himself was the last. Donnell, Morgan, and Bryan are noticed in the preceding series of Sketches; the others, Chapman and Burrow, in this.

Brother Donnell and I attended the meeting of the Franklin Synod at Lebanon on our way homeward. A gracious revival followed the meeting of the Synod, and some of those who are now the old members of the congregation professed religion on that occasion.

At the time Father King visited the Churches in the South, in the years 1834 and 1835, Brother William H. Bigham and myself made an excursion to the State of Missouri, and spent four or five months in preaching there. This was about twelve years after my first visit to that country. We spent most of the time in the congregations where I had devoted the morning of my life. Nothing of special interest occurred in this tour, except that some of the camp-meetings and sacramental-meetings were favored with the Divine blessing.

In the spring of 1847, I went again to the State of North Carolina, visiting some portions of that country where I had labored before. This tour was undertaken at the solicitation of some of the old ministers of the Church, and in compliance with a pressing call from brethren in that country who had united with our Church, through the agency of some young men who had left them in a state of destitution after organizing them into congregations. I found the state of things greatly changed. The converts of 1831, and of former days, having despaired of any permanent organization and supply from our branch of the Church, had united with others, whose leaders had not failed to instill prejudice into their minds against those whom God had honored as the instruments of their conversion. I became fully satisfied, however, that all this might have been easily overcome, if we could have had faithful men permanently in that field. But men who had been raised in the West cannot be easily induced to locate in a country so old, while the field is both large and white unto harvest in the West, North-west, and South-west.

Brothers Carson P. Reed[14] and J. Kirkland came on when I had been in North Carolina four or five weeks, and we were all urged to remain there. We all left, however, for the West about the same time. Brother Kirkland and I spent some time in East Tennessee, where we found many flourishing congregations and faithful ministers of our denomination, who were doing well.

In the course of my labors in North Carolina, I found, from first to last, that our doctrines were more popular with the

---

[14] Rev. Carson P. Reed entered the ministry more than fifty years ago. He attended the Cumberland Synod for the first time in 1822. He lived a long and useful life, greatly beloved and honored, and died but a few months ago. He was born October 28, 1798, and died December 2, 1872. He was one of the representative men of the denomination which he served so long and so faithfully.

members of the Presbyterian Church than their own, and in many instances they so expressed themselves freely. On one occasion a Church-session urged us to organize, and proposed that they and the congregation would unite with use in a body. We, however, declined taking such a step.

Since my return home, in 1847, my labors have been mostly confined to Tennessee and Mississippi, in visiting and preaching to the more destitute, and in some cases visiting remote destitutions. During the course of my ministry my labors have been chiefly itinerant, and in no one place have I been stationary long; and now, while I am penning these lines, and thinking upon the past, I feel no disposition to wish that the circumstances which have surrounded me had been materially different from what they have been. Though I have done but little, I have done what I could.

I offer no apology for introducing this sketch substantially in the words of the subject himself. Dr. Burrow described his own life and labors better than they could have been described by another. Many of his friends, too, who will read this work, will prefer that he should have spoken for himself.

It will be observed that the sketch comes up to 1852. In February of this year a Theological Department was established in connection with Bethel College, at McLemoresville, Tennessee, and Mr. Burrow was appointed Professor of Systematic Theology. He commenced his labors in that department immediately after his appointment. In the fall of 1852, having moved to McLemoresville, he took charge of the congregation there as its pastor, and continued his labors in that capacity until 1864.

Some time in 1853, or 1854, he received the Degree of Doctor of Divinity from Bethel College.

From 1853 to 1864, by a special arrangement, he preached one Sabbath in each month to Shiloh Congregation, which was in the meantime under the pastoral care of Rev. A. E. Cooper. I have said that this was a "special arrangement." It was also mutual.

In 1863, he lost his wife, after a union of more than thirty-five years. Some time in 1867 he began to be afflicted with inflammatory rheumatism. The immediate cause of the disease was, most probably, his severe ministerial labors in the latter years of his life. During a few of those years, it was said by his friends that he preached with more spirituality and power than had been usual with him for years before. He was always spiritual and powerful, but he seemed to have received a new baptism of the Spirit for the closing out of his work. His disease ultimately assumed a dropsical form, and after great suffering, and confinement to his room for five months, his active and useful life came to a close, on the 13th of May, 1868. He died at the house of his son-in-law, Mr. McGowen, in Shelby county.

Dr. Burrow lost three sons in the course of the late cruel war. The oldest of the three was Rev. Aaron Burrow, a highly educated and very promising young man. His loss was deplored as a public calamity. I felt it very deeply myself. Of the others th writer knew nothing. A daughter has died since the death of her father. Five children still survive—two sons, and three daughters. One of the sons is a minister in the Cumberland Presbyterian Church.

In 1845, Dr. Burrow published a small volume on the subject of Baptism. He also had several public discussions with Baptist ministers on the vexed question. At Denmark, in Madison county, he had a discussion with the redoubtable Rev. J. R. Graves, now Rev. Dr. Graves, of Memphis; at McLemoresville, with Rev. J. M. Hurt, and in Mississippi, with Rev. Mr. Latimore. The account of my informant is, that "he vindicated Pedobaptist principles triumphantly." I suppose candid Baptists would have allowed that he was very strong upon the question of Baptism.

He was also an extensive contributor of the Theological Medium. He write largely for that work, upon the subject of Sanctification; also, upon other subjects of general doctrinal interest. Upon the doctrine of Sanctification he was understood to hold views slightly variant from the views of many of his brethren, and from the general Presbyterian view of the subject. No one, however, doubted his fidelity to what he regarded as the truth.

Dr Burrow and myself belonged to what I have been in the habit of regarding the third generation of Cumberland Presbyterian ministers. He was somewhat my senior in age, and about as much my junior in the great work of our lives. I saw him for the first time at the meeting of the old Cumberland Synod at Princeton, Kentucky, in 1825. We were for a year or two members of Hopewell Presbytery, in Western Tennessee, previous to my going to Kentucky in 1830. We were never intimately associated, yet I heard him preach often. He was unquestionably one of the strongest men in the pulpit that the Church ever produced. He was both intellectually and physically a powerful man. The reader will be able to form some idea of his capacity of physical endurance from his own account of his labors and trials in the preceding sketch. Nor did he spare that strength. Evidently it was always at the service of the Church. Through good report and evil report, he was always at his post.

> *Firm as an iron pillar strong,*
> *And steadfast as a wall of brass.*

Dr. Burrow and myself did not always agree in our views of Church polity, nor exactly in our modes or interpreting one or two points in theology. After the years 1852, we were placed, too, in unhappy relations to each other. Feelings which should never exist between Christian men laboring for a common great end may have sometimes grown out of these relations. If it were so, all such feelings are buried now, and I take the highest pleasure, here in my place, in bearing my unequivocal testimony to his great ministerial and personal worth.

Dr. Burrow was on three occasions Moderator of the General Assembly—in 1836, at Nashville, Tennessee; in 1840, at Elkton, Kentucky; and in 1850, at Clarksville, Tennessee. And on four several occasions he opened the Assembly with the customary sermon—at Lebanon, Tennessee, in 1838; at Owensboro, Kentucky, in 1841; at Pittsburgh, Pennsylvania, in 1851; and at Lebanon, Tennessee, in 1855. He has left a noble record. The young men of the Church may well profit by his example.

REV. THOMAS CALHOON
(1782-1855)

Sources: Manuscripts of Rev. D. Lowry, B. W. McDonnold, D.D., and Letter of Col. Smith.

Thomas Calhoon was born in Mecklenburg county, North Carolina, May 31, 1782. His parents, Samuel and Nancy Calhoon, were members of the Presbyterian Church, and were strict and thoughtful in the government of their children. He says himself of his father's family: "The children were taught to repeat the catechism every Sabbath evening. The Sabbath was observed with great particularity. No fruit was allowed to be gathered on the Lord's day; all was gathered on Saturday evening. This religious training has been of singular service to me through life."

The grandfather and grandmother of Mr. Calhoon emigrated from Ireland, and settled in Pennsylvania. They were there converted, under the preaching of Mr. Whitefield. From Pennsylvania they moved to North Carolina, and settled in Mecklenburg county. The old man, the grandfather, having been blind for a number of years, was led by the hand, on a certain occasion, to hear Mr. McGready. Whilst the sermon was in progress he became much excited, and declared that he was hearing another Whitefield. Mr. Calhoon says: "My old grandfather would call me into his room every day, and make me read a chapter in the Bible." The old couple would sing,

"Begone, unbelief, my Saviour is near," etc.

The grandfather, who was mighty in prayer, would then pray. "These influences, says he, "threw around me many restraints." His first religious impressions, however, seem to have been produced by the agency of his mother, when he was still very young. His father was from home, and the mother conducted family prayers. From some cause, the occurrence brought unusually serious thoughts to his mind. Some time, and it seems not long, after this, a minister who had married a relative visited the neighborhood and preached. At the close of his sermon, he invited all the young relatives of his wife to meet him at a particular house in the evening. All assembled, trembling, however, with fear of the preacher. The good minister took his seat in the room, and called up the children one by one, and gave them a tender religious talk; and said he, sixty years afterward, "if there was a dry cheek in the house, it is not now recollected." Such an occurrence could hardly fail of making a salutary impression. In those days of his early boyhood, he was accustomed to retire often for secret prayer. To use his own language, he thought that "this was all that anybody could do, and that it was the way to become good." It is not strange that a child should have reasoned thus. Older people have reasoned thus, both before and since his time.

In the fall of 1800 Mr. Calhoon's father moved with his family from North Carolina to Tennessee, and stopped first at Haysboro, a small village a few miles above Nashville. Here the family were under he ministry of Rev. Thomas Craighead. Mr. Craighead was an opposer of the revival, and of course there was but little religious interest in the congregation. In the spring of 1801 Thomas Calhoon came up to Wilson county, and with the help of a negro man that he brought with him, cleared some land, and made a crop near the Big Spring. In August of 1801 a camp-meeting was held at the Old Ridge Meeting-house, in

Sumner county. The family were to attend the meeting. I have before me a manuscript written, it would seem, some time before his death, in his own hand-writing, but now much mutilated, giving a very minute account of this meeting, and of his experience in it. He seems to have been with his father's family, in Davidson county, at the time. I take my sketch of the meeting, and of the religious interest excited in his mind, from this manuscript. Says the subject of the present sketch:

My early religious training threw around me a strong moral influence. My first serious impressions relative to the importance and necessity of religion were produced by a prayer of my mother, in the family, in the absence of my father. I remember she prayed most fervently and devotedly for her children. The same year my father emigrated to Tennessee, there was a camp-meeting at what was called the Ridge Meeting-house, in Sumner county. It was usual for families, on such occasions, to go fifty miles or more in wagons, and remain on the ground four days and nights. My father took his family to that meeting. I was then in my eighteenth year. The day before we set out, there was a dancing party in the neighborhood, and my sister and myself were invited to attend. Such parties were common in that day, and it was not thought wrong to attend them. Our preacher in North Carolina was in the habit of being present at such parties, particularly when they took place at weddings. Just before we were ready to set out to the party, my mother observed to met that we were going to the camp-meeting the next day, and it would not look well to go to the ball that evening. I paused for a moment, and then replied that I agreed with her. We declined going, and I never attended a dancing party afterward.

Our own family, with several other young people, started on Friday morning for the camp-meeting, and I suppose a company of young persons never felt more careless and playful on arriving at such a place. We stopped about a hundred yards from the pulpit, where the religious exercises were going on. Many sinners were on their knees, crying for mercy. I had never before heard such cries. A trembling at once seized my whole frame, so that it was with some difficulty I walked to the ground where they lay. Shortly after taking my seat, a sermon was delivered which seemed greatly to increase the work of my conviction. My sisters were weeping, and in much distress. There was a great shaking in the valley of dry bones. Several ministers from Kentucky were present. All seemed to partake of the excitement of the occasion. In the meantime, however, my own feelings had subsided, and my heart rose in opposition to the work. My first thought then was, to go into the congregation and bring my sisters away; but I had not courage to undertake it. I urged my mother to interfere; but when she went to them, instead of complying with my request, she began to pray for them This increased my opposition. I was furious. I would have put an end to the whole affair, if I could have done it. My corrupt nature seemed to have entire control. Some friend asked me to go into the crowd where my sisters were. I refused absolutely. I thought they had hopelessly disgraced themselves. My feelings were indescribable. In process of time, however, the evident distress of my sisters, their tears and cries and for mercy, overcame me in some degree; and a friend prevailed on me to go into the crowd where they were. William McGee and Samuel King were talking to them. Just as I took my seat, a proposition for prayer was made, but I refused to go upon my knees. Prayer was soon proposed again, and I bowed on one knee, but rose before the prayer was ended. Prayer was called for a third time, when I fell among the slain, overwhelmed with a sense of my sinfulness and rebellion against God. From that time to the close of the meeting no external object engaged my attention. The salvation of my soul was the engrossing concern. It pleased God to give me such a view of the spirituality of the divine law, of the justice and holiness of its requirement, and of the depth of my own depravity, that my heart sunk within me. I felt that there was not another sinner on earth who had sinned against so much light and knowledge. I was ready to despair, and continued in this state of mind until the meeting closed. I thought I could see in the plan of the gospel ground of hope for other sinners, but could not understand how a just and holy God could pardon and save such a rebel as myself. I was overwhelmed with a sense of my deeply rooted depravity, and the displeasure of Almighty God.

  The meeting closed on Tuesday morning. I was so overcome by my feelings, that my physical strength in a measure gave way. A sense of guilt, and of the probability of damnation, was like a mountain upon my heart. I had to be hauled home in the wagon. On reaching home, and looking at the house, I felt that I could never enter the door; that I was unworthy of a shelter or a place among Christian people. I walked to the grove, to make an undisturbed effort with God for mercy, if indeed any mercy remained for me but my heart appeared to grow harder and still harder, until it seemed that nothing short of Omnipotence could move it. I made my way back to the yard fence, and from there was conveyed into the house. A dreary night followed; my distress was indescribable. The next evening Mr. Craighead preached at my fathers's house, but the sermon afforded me no relief. Three or four weeks after this time, there was to be a camp-meeting at the Big Spring, in Wilson county-the neighborhood in which I have since lived for many years. In the intermediate time, I occasionally had some gleams of hope that God would bestow mercy at last. Still my bodily strength was very much reduced, and I was scarcely able for my customary duties on the farm. I visited Mr. Craighead, that he might instruct me in what I should do to be saved. He was very kind-encouraged me to hope; but my heart was not relieved. About this time I had a dream. I dreamed that God had pardoned my sins, and that I was a Christian. I awoke in great agitation, and for a moment could hardly realize that my experience was but a dream. During the moment I had some enjoyment; but as soon as reason resumed the throne, and reflection took place, all my fancied hopes fled. I felt myself an unpardoned sinner still.

During the three weeks which intervened between the meetings at the Ridge and at the Big Spring, I do not recollect that there was ever a smile upon my countenance. It was a matter of great astonishment to me to see professors of religion jest and laugh, whilst I, with thousands of others around them, was on the road to hell. The time of the meeting at the Big Spring arrived, and I reached there on Friday, with a heavy heart. The word was preached, but my unbelief and hardness of heart brought me to the brink of despair. I retired for the night under a deep impression that the day of God's merciful visitation had closed upon me, that I was a sinner undone for ever. My brother, older than myself, prayed with me and for me that night, though not a professor of religion himself. I arose in the morning and retired to the grove. I felt heavily burdened with the thought that my case, if not already decided against me, was to be decided for heaven or for hell that day. I spent several hours in earnest prayer, without any results except a deeper experience of my utter helplessness, and the impossibility of salvation in any other method than through the abounding grace of God. About nine o'clock in the morning I started back to where the congregation was assembling. About three hundred yards before I reached the place, I suddenly stopped. I hardly know why, but I stopped, looked up and around me with amazement. The glory of God appeared in every thing, and the very leaves of the trees seemed to be tinged with a Saviour's blood. I did not think at first of claiming this as a religious experience, but soon found that I was involuntarily ascribing glory to God for his unbounded goodness and mercy to helpless and perishing sinners. My burden of guilt and condemnation was gone, and hope soon sprang up in my mind that I had received the blessing which I had been so long seeking. Under this impression I turned to meet my brother, who I supposed was coming behind; but the thought immediately came into my mind that I ought to be well satisfied in regard to this matter before I disclosed my feelings to any person. I turned again, and started for the congregation, with a fixed purpose of keeping these things a profound secret until the meeting would close, thinking that I would be able after such an interval to settle the question of my conversion in favor of or against myself infallibly. When I reached the congregation, I was astonished to see the people so little impressed with a sense of the awful presence of Almighty God. I took my seat, and Mr. McGready rose in the pulpit. His appearance was fearfully solemn. A profound silence prevailed. He delivered one of his most impressive and stirring sermons. It was wholly experimental. He took the sinner up in his enmity against God and his hardness of heart. He followed him through all the steps of the process of his return to God. He pointed out many of the stratagems used by Satan in so critical a time, for the purpose of misleading and destroying. He finally brought the thoroughly subjugated sinner to the foot of the cross, and to the point of accepting and trusting in Christ, as his only hope of salvation. When he came to this point, I involuntarily spoke out in the congregation and said, 'If this is religion, I have experienced it.' So unexpected an occurrence produced an extraordinary excitement in the congregation. Many sinners wept aloud; others fell to the ground and cried for mercy.

I make no apology for introducing so long and so minute an account of a very interesting religious experience. It is a specimen of what a great many of the good men felt and suffered, who afterward became the fathers and founders of the Cumberland Presbyterian Church.

Somewhere about the time of his profession of religion at the Big Spring, his father moved with his family from Haysboro, and settled in that neighborhood. Shortly after his profession, his mind began to be exercised on the subject of preaching. As his religious experience presents us with a terrible spiritual struggle, in his call to the ministry we meet with much of the same kind. He was powerfully converted, and powerfully called to the great work of his life. He had been raised a Presbyterian, and with the highest degree of respect for Presbyterian usages. His education was very limited; so much so, that he thought the work of the ministry out of the question with him. He struggled against his feelings which seemed to point in that direction. I have some statements before me in manuscript; and I have often heard him express some of his early feelings on this subject. He at first thought of exhorting, but could not admit the idea of preaching. "The thought," says he, "of standing as a mouth for God, was on my mind day and night. I trembled in prospect of the responsibility. I spent nearly the third of a year in the woods. My agitation was so great that I became incapable of physical labor." At length, however, he yielded so far as to make an experiment. At the little log meeting-house near his father's, after a terrible spiritual struggle, he arose in the presence of the old people and said: "I will do what I can; and if I cannot utter a word, I will at least raise my hand on the Lord's side."

Under the influence of Mr. King, he attended the meeting of the Cumberland Presbytery, held at old Red River Meeting-house, in 1803. At the second session of this Presbytery he was licensed as an exhorter. This meeting was held at Shiloh, in 1804. It is not known at what time he was licensed to preach. He is represented, however, as a licensed preacher at the time of the meeting of the Commission of the Kentucky Synod. This meeting occurred in December of 1805. He was evidently ordained soon after the constitution of the Cumberland Presbytery as an independent organization, in 1810. There was a large number of young men who had acquired experience, and even reputation, as preachers, that had not been ordained up to that time. Some of them had not even been licensed to preach. The Council, as it was called, did not feel itself at liberty to license and ordain.

When Mr. Calhoon was licensed as an exhorter, he set off at once upon a circuit with David Foster, who was, by a year or two, his senior in the work. We have the following account from himself, of his feelings when he was leaving home:

"My oldest brother," says he, "was settling a place near my father's I went to tell him farewell, and found him splitting rails. I looked at him, and said in my heart, What an easy time you have! I felt like I would be willing to be obligated to make a hundred rails a day for life, in preference to the work in which I was then engaging. I left my father's house in tears, shuddering at the thought of what might be the consequences of an undertaking of such vast moment."

He was, however, now fairly committed to an experiment in the work. They were out about three months. Foster preached, and he followed every day with an exhortation. They had almost daily indications that the Spirit of God was with them. After preaching and dinner, their custom was to retire to the woods for reading, study, and prayer. They tolerated no levity in themselves. This is his own account. Although young men, they never allowed any thing to prevent their holding family prayers where they lodged.

After they had been out about three months, they came to the neighborhood of Franklin, Tennessee. They held meeting according to appointment, and went home with a friend. Something went wrong with him; his doubts and discouragements in regard to his course revived. He spent nearly the whole night in prayer, and in the morning determined to return home, marry, and bury himself in seclusion. The Providence and Spirit of God, however, ruled otherwise. He continued in the work.

Some time after this, Mr. Calhoon and Mr. Chapman made an excursion through what is now Rutherford county. They preached on Stewart's Creek, and went as far as Cane Ridge. There they met two Baptist ministers. One of them preached a sermon in which he took stringent ground in favor of the doctrine of predestination. His text was, "If ye be Christ's, then are ye Abraham's seed, and heirs according to the promise." The division was, the gift, the purchase, and the conquest. God gave some to his Son from eternity. Christ bought these with a price. He then finding them in fetters, rescued them. The illustration was taken from the purchase of a hand-cuffed negro in South Carolina. Mr. Calhoon did not relish the theology of the sermon, and immediately took ground in conflict with it. The meeting resulted well. That evening there was a powerful movement among the people, and many professions of religion occurred. He calls this his first theological battle. About the same time he assisted Rev. William Hodge in holding three camp-meetings in succession. He lived Mr. Hodge as what he calls "a gracious old man." They lodged one night with Dr. Yandle, on Goose Creek. The Doctor remonstrated with him, and urged him to greater moderation in public speaking. He said, "If you continue your present course, you will be dead in less than three years." Mr. Calhoon remarks, in giving an account of this conversation, "He has been dead twenty-five years, and I still live."

At an early time he and James B. Porter, Finis Ewing, and Ephraim McLean visited Livingston county, in Kentucky, and held a meeting at old Mr. Wheeler's. The record is, that the meeting was interesting. He was greatly embarrassed in his feelings, in having to preach before Ewing. He preached, however, with some freedom, from a favorite text: "For I determined not to know any thing among you, save Jesus Christ and him crucified." From this meeting he and Porter went to Piney Fork, and preached two or three days.

About the same time he formed a circuit extending through White and Warren counties, of his own State. The country was new, and as rough as it would well be. He had the usual adventures of an itinerant preacher of early times. One of these may be mentioned. After preaching on a certain occasion, he stayed all night with a prominent man. In the evening several gentlemen cam in on business. Their business detained them also through the night. Their hospitable host sent off and got a jug of whisky. All drank freely but the preacher. They ridiculed Saint Paul. One insisted that the apostle was drunk when he left his cloak at Troas. By bed-time they were in a poor condition for prayers. Still Mr. Calhoon proposed prayers. The old lady and four daughters cam in. Some of the men were on the floor drunk. No one kneeled with him except the old lady. The next morning the gentleman of the house proposed prayers himself. No one, however, kneeled with him, and yet, says he, "I lived to see all those young ladies members of the Church."

On the 16 of February, 1809, Mr. Calhoon was married to Miss Mary R. Johnson. He settled near his father, in the neighborhood of the Big Spring. In a short time he built the house in which he lived till he died, and which still stands, a monument of the olden time.

In the fall of 1810 he received a call to the pastorate of Cedar Creek Big Spring congregation. I have the original call before me. It is dated October 6, A.D. 1810, and signed in behalf of the congregation by Andrew Foster and John Calhoon, as trustees. The call is for one-third of his time, and the promise is, in order that he "may be measurably free from worldly cares and avocations," to pay him the "sum of forty-eight dollars and twenty-five cents, in regular yearly payments, for the one-third part of his labors, during the time of his being and continuing the regular pastor of this Church. Some of our present pastors would think this a small allowance for one-third of their ministerial and pastoral labors. They would be correct, too: God "hath ordained that they that preach the gospel, should live of the gospel." It was a small allowance for the times in which the transaction occurred; but the transaction itself is illustrative of the spirit of those times. Neither the congregations nor the preachers thought of what would now be a remunerative consideration for ministerial labor. The doctrine of the fathers was, to preach, with or without pay, and it was very easy for the congregations to imbibe the same spirit.

In the spring of 1819 he was called to the care of Smyrna congregation, in Jackson county. He engaged to give them one-fourth of his time. Smyrna was forty miles from his home, but he kept up his connection with that Church twenty-four years. It was at length dissolved on account of his advancing age and increasing infirmities. Col. Smith, a leading elder in the Church, says: "He was very punctual in meeting his appointments; there were many revivals of religion during his pastorate; many were brought into the Church; he was beloved by all who knew him." The attachment of the congregation was so great, that he made two or three applications for a dissolution of his connection with them, before they would consent. Mr. Calhoon himself says that, during his connection with Smyrna congregation, he never missed but one appointment, and on that occasion went half way, and was stopped by unusual weather.

Some time after the organization of the Church, he and Robert Donnell made a tour through East Tennessee. They were the first Cumberland Presbyterians who visited that country. They went as far as Maryville, and preached for Dr. Isaac Anderson, who, although an uncompromising Hopkinsian, received them kindly. In this excursion they became acquainted with Col. Campbell, of Campbell's Station, who afterward moved to Wilson county, and joined the Cumberland Presbyterian Church.

After this, he made a tour by himself through the more recently settled portions of East Tennessee. In this excursion he preached at Calhoon, a place named by the Indians for himself; at the house of a prominent Indian named Renfro, and at Pumpkintown, now Athens. He crossed Little Tennessee, and preached again at Campbell's Station. Thence he made his way through Kingston and the Wilderness, across Spencer's Hill, toward home. This excursion was undertaken at the urgent solicitation of John Miller, who was not then a professor of religion. Miller made the most of his appointments before him.

In 1813 Mr. Calhoon, in connection with Finis Ewing, William McGee, and Robert Donnell, was appointed by the Cumberland Synod to frame a Confession of Faith for the use of the Church. In that work he labored in conjunction with Mr. Ewing, but he himself ascribed the framing of the Confession and Book of Discipline mainly to Mr. Ewing.

In 1829 the first General Assembly of the Cumberland Presbyterian Church held its sessions at Princeton, Kentucky. Mr. Calhoon was the Moderator of that Assembly.

In 1845 the Board of Missions was established at Lebanon. He was the first President of the Board, and held the position till his death.

In his latter years Mr. Calhoon's health failed by degrees. In 1855, on the 13th day of April, he closed his active and stirring life, in his quiet home. His wife had died several years before. A brother minister had visited him a short time previous to his death, and was in the act of bidding him farewell. The dying preacher supposed it would be their last meeting on earth: he aroused himself from great prostration, pointed upward to heaven, and said, "We will meet there."

Mr. Calhoon left behind him four sons. One of these, Thomas P. Calhoon, had been in the ministry several years. In the fall of 1857 he moved to St. Cloud, Minnesota, and in the course of the winter of 1859 he was thrown from a bridge, and mortally wounded. He was a young man of promise. The other sons still live, and two of them are members of the Church.

I have a great many personal recollections of Mr. Calhoon. Some of these I could not overlook in such a sketch as this. His name was a household word in my father's family when I was growing up. I heard him preach in my early boyhood. He preached upon the balm, and the physician of Gilead, on Monday evening of the camp-meeting at which I professed religion, and but a few hours before that event of so great interest to myself. He was a member of the first Presbytery that I ever attended; he afterward officiated at the licensure of Robert Baker and myself. When I was ordained, although not then a member of the Presbytery, he was present, and was one of those who laid hands upon my head. I knew him onward to his death. I never considered myself a personal favorite with him, though I claimed him as a friend. Our habits of mind were different; yet I honored him, and still honor his memory.

In the summer of 1818 occurred the first camp-meeting which was ever held at the Dry Fork. The Dry Fork congregation was an offshoot of the old Shiloh congregation, of the Presbyterian Church. This latter congregation had been greatly favored in the revival of the early part of the century. The camp-meeting which I now mention was attended by Thomas Calhoon, Alexander Chapman, David Foster, David McLin, and other ministers. McLin, Chapman, and Calhoon preached on the Sabbath. Calhoon occupied the popular hour. The congregation was very large. He preached from a text in the 111th Psalm: "His work is honorable and glorious." He frequently preached from that text in those days. His object was to vindicate the Divine administration from the charge of being concerned actively, or by connivance, in the introduction of sin into the world. The controversy with the mother Church was still fresh in the minds of men. A great many of the good people of Shiloh were present. Some complained of the sermon, but it was a powerful effort in support of the doctrines of the Cumberland Presbyterian Church.

At the meeting of the Nashville Presbytery in the spring of 1819, great discouragement was felt, from the fact that so few young men were coming forward into the ministry, and a day was appointed for fasting and prayer that God would call men to the work. The fast day occurred in the following May. A camp-meeting was held at Fall Creek, including the fast, which occurred on Monday of the meeting. The people fasted and prayed, and Mr. Calhoon preached from the Saviour's command to his disciples: "Pray ye, therefore, the Lord of the harvest, that he will send forth laborers into his harvest." It was a day of great interest. Two young men, Robert Baker and Robert S. Donnell, were called out, and devoted themselves to the work. They afterward became honored and useful ministers.

In the spring of 1820 Mr. Calhoon made a tour round what was afterward called the Tennessee Circuit. That section of country had been but recently transferred from the Logan to the Nashville Presbytery, and it was thought proper to render special attention to it. Mr. Calhoon was sent, because he was considered one of the best preachers in the Presbytery. Foster had preceded him. The old counselors encouraged me to go with him as a sort of an assistant. I was then a candidate for the ministry. The first appointment was in the neighborhood of Nashville, at the house of Mr. Castleman. The next was on Harpeth; near the mouth of Dog Creek. From thence we went to old Mr. Mabin's-he lived at the head of a little branch of Yellow Creek; from thence to John Hutchison's; from thence to the neighborhood of William Clements, a man of great importance to the Church in his time-he was an educated Scotchman, and a ruling elder; from thence we went to Frank Smith's. John L. Smith was then an irreligious young man. Mr. Calhoon preached every day until we reached Reynoldsburg, on the bank of Tennessee River. His sermons were very strong, and highly popular. Several times he lectured on one of Dr. Watts' hymns, which he used in the worship:

> O, if my soul were formed for woe,
> How would I vent my sighs!
> Repentance should like rivers flow
> From both my weeping eyes.

The object of the lecture was to show that the poet could not possibly have implied any apprehension that his soul was created for the suffering of woe or damnation. His labors were useful and honorable to the Church. I made, however, but little improvement myself. I was constantly under an oppressive and embarrassing sense of the superior greatness of my mentor.

In 1821 the first camp-meeting was held on West Harpeth. Mr. Calhoon and John L. Dillard were the preachers. Robert Baker and myself were, as licentiates, to assist. Mr. Calhoon managed the meeting. On Sabbath he preached a favorite sermon, from the passage in the Lord's Prayer, "Deliver us from evil." In the evening he directed me to prepare to preach the next morning before breakfast. I arose early, and went off to the woods to make my preparation, but remained out rather too long. On my return, he met me with such a reproof as was characteristic of the times. It was too severe. But the boys in those days thought of nothing but unquestioning submission. From West Harpeth he, and Baker, and myself, went to Wells' Creek. The Wells' Creek meeting possesses some historical interest, from its being the occasion upon which Dr. Cossitt first became acquainted with Cumberland Presbyterians. He was brought and introduced there by Mr. Clements. Mr. Calhoon treated him with great respect, and he preached once at the meeting whilst he was still an Episcopalian. The next meeting was at Richland. Here James McKee, an obscure boy, professed religion. He afterward entered the ministry, and became very promising, but died young, at Trenton, Tennessee.

I might multiply these recollections much farther, but restrain myself. I dwell upon them with a melancholy interest. Mr. Calhoon was one of the most useful men of his time in the Church. His influence was not so extensive as that of Ewing, or King, or Robert Donnell; but where it prevailed, it was equally controlling. He was a great man, if not the great man of the country in which he lived. Personally, he was a man of expressive appearance; about six feet high. His form was athletic; his bearing that of a gentleman; his eyes were dark and piercing; his countenance, always solemn, sometimes in the pulpit was fearful. His voice was strong, but unlike any other voice that I ever heard. He was mighty in prayer. While he was yet a young man, a wicked fellow wanted to bet that he could out-pray Dr. Blackburn. This was a high encomium, as Dr. Blackburn could pray three-quarters of an hour, and be interesting throughout. Mr. Calhoon's prayers were not only interesting-they were sometimes overpowering. We have the following from a living witness: "On a certain occasion, a young man was to be set apart to the whole work of the ministry. Mr. Calhoon offered the ordaining prayer. The congregation was very large, and scattered over a large space. They were very thoughtless, and man of them engaged in conversation. As the prayer progressed, seriousness arose. Those nearest the preacher began to weep, and drop upon their knees. Others followed the example. The influence spread; and before the prayer was closed, the whole vast congregation, far and near, were on their knees, and weeping in sympathy with the good man who was leading them to the throne of grace."

His manner in the pulpit was impassioned, often powerful. On one occasion, a young man came to a meeting where he was to preach with the avowed intention of producing disturbance. He arose once while the sermon was in progress, with a view of carrying out his purpose, but the piercing eye and awful manner of the preacher were resistless. The young man fell a convicted sinner. He professed religion, and became a useful Cumberland Presbyterian minister.

Mr. Calhoon says himself, that for years after he took charge of the Big Spring congregation, he scarcely ever preached to them without indications of deep feeling on the part of the people. On almost any ordinary occasion he could have had mourners, if he had called for them. It was a sort of continued revival.

I heard him once, at a camp-meeting at the Ridge Meeting-house, preach on this text: "Rejoice, O young man, in thy youth, and let thy heart cheer thee in the days of thy youth; and walk in the ways of thine heart, and in the sight of thine eyes; but know that for all these things God will bring thee into judgment." He read the first part of the text, and then proceeded to tell the young men how to be worldly and wicked in good earnest. Everybody was astounded that he should have turned out to preaching, as it seemed, for the devil. After spending some time in this strain, and putting expectation on tip-toe, he paused and with a changed countenance, and an awful manner, proceeded to read the remaining part of his text; "but know thou that for all these things God will bring thee into judgment." The transition was terrible. It seemed hardly possible for a human heart to support itself. He frequently preached on that text, and usually with great effect. But few men could have sustained themselves through such an effort. There was something of the dramatic in it; but I suppose he never failed.

In the judicatures of the Church he was always in his place, unless there was a real providential hindrance. His own statement is, that he "never for any sort of circumstance omitted family religion in his whole life." He was always in earnest. I certainly never knew a more earnest man.

A word should in justice be added in regard to his secular life. We have seen that a great proportion of his time must have been given to the Church. He never traded-I mean, he never traded for purposes of gain; he never went in debt; still he educated his children well, and then left them sufficient property for an advantageous entrance upon the career of life. Altogether, he was an unusual man: he belonged to a past age. "There were giants" in that age.

REV. ALEXANDER CHAPMAN
(1776-1834)

Sources: Bird's **Life of Chapman**; Rev. David Lowry's Sketch.

Alexander Chapman was born in Bucks county, Pennsylvania, January 2, 1776. His parents were James and Martha Chapman. His mother's family name was Kirkpatrick. The Chapman family were of English origin. Alexander Chapman's grandfather, Philip Chapman, was born in London, or its neighborhood, and his great-grandfather, the father of Philip Chapman, was in his time a merchant of considerable wealth in that city.

The family, as far back as their lineage can be traced, were Protestants and Presbyterians. James Chapman was an officer of some prominence in the Revolutionary War, and, at its close, moved to Prince Edward county, in Virginia. Here he remained until 1797, when he removed again to Tennessee, and settled in what is now Sumner county. In December of that year he arrived at King's Station, about two miles from where Gallatin now stands. He lived a year or two near the head of Desha's Fork of Bedsoe's Creek, but, in 1800, bought land near King's Station, and settled there. He died the same year. He seems to have been a member and ruling elder in the Presbyterian Church. While he lived on Desha's Creek an afflicting providence was experienced in his family-the youngest daughter, when but a child, came to her death by falling into a vessel of boiling water.

Alexander Chapman was a farmer's son, and, of course, he was trained to such pursuits as are common on a farm. The country, too, was new, and the labor of opening a farm and of its early culture was very severe. His education was limited, as we would suppose from the circumstances of the country. He was but seven years old when his father settled in Virginia, and about twenty when the family came to Tennessee. There were but few educational advantages at that time in Virginia, and such a thing as a school was hardly known in the portion of Tennessee in which the family settled. Mr. Chapman was, in the strictest sense of the expression, a self-made man.

When the great revival began to develop itself in Tennessee, in 1800, he became deeply interested on the subject of religion. The Shiloh Congregation, within the bounds of which he lived, was one of the first congregations in the Cumberland country that shared in the blessings of that great work. He was, it seems, for some time troubled with doctrinal difficulties. To those indoctrinated as he had been, a common difficulty almost inevitably comes up in their first serious hours. There is a fear, at least, of the possibility of their having been proscribed by the decree of predestination. Mr. Chapman had his share of trouble from that source. Still he was an earnest seeker of salvation. His convictions were deep, and his conflict was terrible. The writer has heard him say more than once in the pulpit, in describing the struggles of his mind in his approaching the crisis of his spiritual experience, that, on a certain occasion, he became so intensely interested on the subject that he lifted up his hand before God, and bound himself under what he felt to be the solemnity of an oath, that he never would relax his efforts until he secured the pardon of his sins, or became satisfied that there was no pardon for him. Such earnestness of purpose was characteristic of the man. Says his biographer in describing his experience at that time:

> Late in the year 1800, he was riding along the road in great distress. Anguish, sorrow, and brokenness of heart had seized him. His soul was quaking between hope and despair. His grief became so great that he could not refrain from tears and prayers. When passing over a tract of land he had purchased, within half a mile of where his father had settled, such was the poignancy and burden of his grief he could no longer endure it without one honest effort to secure salvation through the blood of the cross. As he rode along he paused-he determined that he would make a full test of the matter whether there was any salvation for him. He dismounted and knelt beside a large stump, and commenced praying with the intention, as he afterward said to a friend, of seeking a final settlement of the great question then and there. He continued long in prayer. He was brought to see the worst of his condition before God. He saw and felt his utter helplessness. He had a fearful view of the magnitude of his sins before a just and holy God. He felt that there was no hope for him, but through the merits of Jesus Christ. With confidence his heart embraced him as the only Saviour, and just such a one as he needed.

This was a common Christian experience. With him, however, it was terribly intensified. Such was the habit of the times. God was working a strange work among the people. Furthermore, he was doubtless, in this case, preparing, by leading him through a dark valley, a chosen vessel for the fulfillment of a great mission among men.

He joined the Shiloh Congregation. Rev. William Hodge was, at that time, pastor of the congregation. He retained his membership here until he removed to Kentucky, which occurred in 1805. Soon after joining the Church, he was put forward in religious services: he conducted prayer-meetings, and exercised his gifts in exhortation. "He soon evinced such gifts, piety, and zeal, as gave the friends of the revival hopes of his being useful." In such labors he employed himself, with much agitation of mind and many misgivings in relation to the work of the ministry, until the fall meeting of the old Cumberland Presbytery in 1805. At this meeting he was received as a candidate for the ministry. The meeting was held at Red River Meeting-house in the month of October.

It will be recollected that the Commission of the Synod of Kentucky met in the following December, and from that time to the reorganization of the Cumberland Presbytery as an independent body, in 1810, the old Cumberland Presbytery intermitted the exercise of its Presbyterial functions. Mr. Chapman identified himself with the revival party in that unhappy conflict, and, of course, was really amongst those proscribed by the Commission. His name does not appear, however, for the reason, it is supposed, that he had not advanced so far in his trials as to be officially recognized.

At the meeting of the new Cumberland Presbytery, at the Big Spring, in Wilson county, Tennessee, in March, 1811, Mr. Chapman, after the customary trials and examination, was licensed as a probationer for the holy ministry. William

Harris and Robert Donnell were licensed at the same time.

At an intermediate meeting of the Presbytery in February, 1813, at Mount Moriah Meeting-house, in Logan county, Kentucky, Alexander Chapman and William Barnett were set apart to the whole work of the ministry. Rev. Thomas Calhoon preached the ordination-sermon, and Rev. Finis Ewing presided and gave the customary charge.

The 22d of October, 1805, Mr. Chapman was married to Miss Ann Dixon Carson, daughter of Thomas Carson, of what was then Logan, but afterward became Butler county, Kentucky. Mr. Carson was an emigrant from Virginia to Kentucky. The marriage proved to be a happy one. The wife was one of the women for the times. Whilst her husband was almost incessantly, and with great self-denial, from home, employed in promoting the interests of the Church, she labored as incessantly, and with equal self-denial, in keeping up the interests of his home. She made that home always a pleasant retreat from a varied and, in some respects, stormy life.

In 1805, he settled in Butler county, in the neighborhood of his father-in-law. His settlement here placed him in connection with Little Muddy Congregation. This continued to be his home as long as he lived.

In the division of the Cumberland Presbytery into three Presbyteries, with a view to the formation of the Cumberland Synod, Mr. Chapman became a member of the Logan Presbytery. Within the limits of that Presbytery the chief work of his life was performed. The territory of the Presbytery, however, extended into the great and almost limitless North-west, and into that country he made frequent missionary tours. We have the following report of one of his excursions into the State of Illinois in 1820. The mission was undertaken under the direction of the "Missionary Board for Western Missions of the Cumberland Presbyterian Church:"

> DEAR BRETHREN:—According to your instructions I commenced my tour to the State of Illinois, crossing the Ohio River at Shawneetown on the 17th day of December, passing through a part of Gallatin, White, Wayne, and Edwards counties, visiting, as far as possible, the most populous neighborhoods, and preaching to the people the word of eternal life, by day and by night, as often as my strength would permit. I administered baptism to one adult, and, to the praise of God be it said, two professed faith in the Lord Jesus Christ. I found in all that boundary only about one hundred and fifty-seven professors of religion who considered themselves attached to us, and but a few belonging to any denomination of Christians, except a few settlements which were almost entirely swept away by the schismatics.[15]
>
> According to your instructions I endeavored to ascertain whether the people were anxious for preaching from our body.

---

[15]The schismatics were the followers of Barton W. Stone, who made a figure in the early part of the revival of 1800. They were Unitarians.

This I ascertained sometimes by private inquiry of the most prominent characters, and sometimes in a more public way. Still their universal coming together to hear the gospel, the great attention to preaching, and the tears which bathed their cheeks were not only proof on this subject, but were sufficient to break the rocky heart into softness and to arouse every power of the Christian's soul into anxiety that they might have the word of eternal life declared unto them. Among those distressed settlements I spent one month. I crossed the Ohio River again at Shawneetown on the 17th of January, 1821. There were nine days in which I had no appointments. I preached thirty-two times.

ALEXANDER CHAPMAN.

This was, I suppose, about the commencement of the operations of the Cumberland Presbyterian Church in Illinois. The one hundred and fifty-seven have grown into a large body of Christian men and women. The little fire has kindled a great matter. Illinois now contains three Synods and a corresponding number of Presbyteries.

In answer to a call from some ministers and congregations in Western Pennsylvania, the General Assembly of the Cumberland Presbyterian Church sent, in the summer of 1831, several missionaries into that country. Mr. Chapman was one of these missionaries. He set off for Pennsylvania on the 28th of June, passed through upper Kentucky, Ohio, Western Virginia, on horseback, and reached Washington, Pennsylvania, on Friday, 22d of July. It will be observed that Mr. Chapman was now fifty-five years of age. He had reached a period of life when men usually begin to feel old. Still, in the heat of summer he performs this long journey of a month in the manner already mentioned. At Washington he met Messrs. Morgan and Bryan, who had preceded him a few days. He labored in Pennsylvania in connection with the other missionaries about two months, when he returned to Kentucky.

In October of 1831, the Green River Synod constituted the Pennsylvania Presbytery. As a matter of convenience Mr. Chapman was temporarily attached to the new Presbytery. This arrangement took him again to Pennsylvania in the spring of 1832. He attended the first meeting of the Pennsylvania Presbytery, and remained and labored in the country several weeks. His connection with this Presbytery continued about two years. Notwithstanding the distance, he attended the most of its meetings.

Mr. Chapman preached the opening-sermon of the Cumberland Synod at its last meeting, I suppose by request, as the Moderator of the preceding meeting was not present. The Synod that year met at Franklin, Tennessee. The Moderator of the preceding meeting was Rev. James S. Guthrie. Mr. Chapman was also Moderator of the General Assembly in 1831.

No man in the Cumberland Presbyterian Church lived a more active and useful life than Alexander Chapman. Owing to the difficulties growing out of the revival, and the transition state of what became at last the Cumberland Presbyterian Church, he was not licensed until 1811, nor ordained until 1813. Yet his real ministerial life commenced in 1805, when he became a candidate for the ministry. It has been stated that he was received as a candidate for the ministry in

October of this year, and that the meeting of the Commission of the Synod of Kentucky met in December of the same year. Although Mr. Chapman was not named in the proscribing act of the Commission, he was evidently included in it. And as it was supposed that his usefulness might be impaired by it, we have the following informal indorsement:

> We, the majority of Cumberland Presbytery, do conceive from the book of discipline that the power of licensing and ordaining belongs to Presbyteries; and that the Presbytery did legally license Alexander Chapman to exhort; and, although the Commission of Synod did forbid, we do believe that, upon the principle of discipline, they had no power to prohibit him where no charges of immoral conduct were brought against him; and as we conceive that it is the right of Presbytery to license or forbid, we, therefore, believe that said Alexander Chapman has a lawful and constitutional right to exercise his gifts in the bounds of the Cumberland Presbytery, or whereever God in his providence may call him. Given under our hand this eleventh day of December, 1805.
>
> WILLIAM HODGE,
> JAMES McGREADY,
> JOHN RANKIN,
> WILLIAM McGEE

The prohibition of the Commission of the Synod was promulgated on the 6th day of December, and this paper was given to Mr. Chapman, as it appears, on the 11th. A similar one was given to others at the same time. The object was, as far as possible, to break the force of the action of the Commission, and to keep open the way to the continued usefulness of the young men in the congregations, a great many of which, without their labors, would have been wholly unsupplied with the word and the ordinances of the gospel. This places the commencement of Mr. Chapman's active and real ministerial life in 1805.

For nearly thirty years, therefore, was he connected with the struggles of the early history of the Cumberland Presbyterian Church. His name is a household word in what was once called the Green River and Cumberland countries, and with the old people no name connected with the operations of the Church militant brings up more pleasant and hallowed recollections. He was the compeer, and on almost all extraordinary occasions the fellow-laborer, of Rev. William Harris. They were finely adapted to cooperation-in a striking sense, complements of one another.

On the 15th day of September, 1834, the useful life of this good man came to a close. He was far advanced in his fifty-ninth year. The funeral-sermon was preached by his old companion in the service, Rev. William Harris, from the very appropriate words: "For he was a good man, and full of the Holy Ghost and of faith; and much people was added to the Lord."

I quote the following sketch of Mr. Chapman from the Appendix to Smith's "History of the Cumberland Presbyterians:"

This eminently useful servant of the Lord Jesus Christ was born in the State of Pennsylvania, on the 2d day of January, 1776. His father emigrated to this country at an early period, and settled in Sumner county, Tennessee. About the commencement of the revival in the Cumberland country, he became deeply interested on the subject of the salvation of his soul. After remaining in this condition for a considerable time he obtained a clear and satisfactory evidence that his sins were pardoned, and his iniquities covered. Immediately after his conversion he felt it his duty to devote himself to the work of the ministry. By the first Cumberland Presbytery he was licensed to exhort and catechise, and, having given satisfactory evidence that he possessed an aptness to teach, he was received as a candidate for the ministry, and was one of the number who went through all the troubles, trials, and persecutions of the Cumberland body, when it was struggling for existence. He was licensed as a probationer, and ordained to the whole work of the ministry shortly after the constitution of the Cumberland Presbyterian Church, and, until the time of his death, he sustained the character of an eminently useful minister of Jesus Christ. He married and settled in Logan (now Butler) county, Kentucky, when he was very young, and had the happiness of seeing a large and flourishing society spring up around him as the first-fruits of his labors of love. But Mr. Chapman did not confine his labors to his own vicinity: he traveled extensively, and operated with great success in upper Kentucky, in Indiana, and Western Pennsylvania, and few men of any denomination have been more useful in promoting the cause of Christ in the West than Mr. Chapman. He died in the triumphs of faith, at his own residence, on the 15th of September, 1834, and left not only his family, but a whole denomination of Christians, in tears at his loss.

Mr. Chapman's temper was of the most meek and placid nature, which recommended him to the favor and friendship of all who became acquainted with him. From what we have learned of him when he was a young man, he treated the opinions and counsel of those who were more experienced in the ministry than himself with deference and respect, and many ministers now living can bear witness to his kind and affectionate conduct toward those who were his juniors. Indeed, to all the young man under the care of the Presbytery of which he was a member, he was a prudent counselor, an affectionate father; he took a deep interest in their temporal and spiritual welfare. He never lorded it over young men under his guidance, but by his winning affability he secured the affections of all, who loved him as a brother and revered him as a father.

He was not what the world would call a great man-but he was far better, he was emphatically a good man, and full of the Holy Ghost. His human learning was limited, but he was deeply versed in the Scriptures. His address was peculiarly pleasing, and, as his communion with God was almost constant, he rarely failed to reach the hearts of his hearers. The character of his discourses, especially when he addressed the followers of Christ, was generally of the most encouraging and consoling nature, but tot he self-deceiver he showed no quarters. He dwelt much upon the necessity of knowing where and when we are converted to God; 'upon the new views, new joys,' and new course of conduct of the true believer. His labors were blessed to the souls of thousands, who, through his instrumentality, were led to Jesus Christ; and we believe we are not mistaken when we say that scores are now in the gospel ministry who claim him as the honored instrument in bringing them from a state of sin to a knowledge of God and of his Son Jesus Christ. The last time we had the pleasure of seeing him was at the General Assembly of 1834, when he presided at the sacramental-service. He then appeared to have some forebodings that he would no more do this in remembrance of Christ with his brethren in the ministry. He dwelt much on the happiness of heaven. He alluded to his gray hairs, and mentioned the probability that in a short time he should leave the walls of Zion; his words fell upon the hearts of his brethren like rain upon the parched and thirsty ground. Little did we then think that he was addressing us for the last time, and that we should hear his voice no more until we heard it among the redeemed, crying with a loud voice: 'Worthy is the Lamb that was slain to receive riches, and power, and wisdom, and strength, and honor, and glory, and blessing.'

I quote also selections from a sketch of "Mr. Chapman's Life and Labors," written by Rev. David Lowry, and published in the Theological Medium of 1846.

Says Mr. Lowry: "The Rev. Alexander Chapman was the first preacher of the Cumberland Presbyterian Church the writer ever saw, and he delivered the first sermon he ever heard after he became old enough to distinguish the text from the discourse. During the first five years of my ministry his house was my home, where I often retreated from the toils of the circuit, sometimes sick, and found all that kindness and hospitality which my situation required.

"Personal recollection enables me to say that he was blessed with early religious training, but made no profession of religion till grown up to manhood. The precise date is not in the possession of the writer. It was, however, in the great revival which commenced about the beginning of the present century. He entered the ministry about the time the late Rev. William Harris did, and labored with him in much harmony and love till the day of his death. They generally attended camp-meetings together, and no preachers in the Church were more successful in winning souls to Christ."

In this sketch we have some specimens of Mr. Chapman's letters to his brethren, especially to Mr. Harris.

To Mr. Harris: "October 23, 1811. Dear Brother:—I desire to keep up a correspondence with you. I have not heard from you since we parted, but hope the

Lord will permit us to meet soon, and that we shall have good news to impart, not only of his dealings with our own souls, but the conversion of our neighbors."

In the same year he writes:

> I am now on my way from a sacramental-meeting at Salem, Livingston county, Kentucky, where the Lord was present in great power. There was little opposition. Christians were happy, and eight sinners professed religion.
>
> But O, brother, the harvest is great, and laborers few! There were persons at the meeting from Hendersonville, and above the mouth of Green River. They are anxious for preaching, and, after hearing their pressing solicitations, I gave them an appointment for a two-days' meeting, and hope it will be in your power to accompany me.

Now it is to be observed that Salem in Livingston county was more than a hundred miles from Mr. Chapman's home, yet he went all that distance to a sacramental-meeting.

I make another observation: there were people at that sacramental-meeting from Hendersonville and from above the mouth of Green River. Hendersonville and the mouth of Green River are near a hundred miles in another direction from the Salem in Livingston county where the meeting was held. We would think that these people were hungering for the word of life, and we should think correctly. They were hungering and thirsting. I was a feature of the times. The Spirit of God was abroad in the land.

We have another letter of 1811:

> I attended the camp-meeting in Christian county. Never have I seen a more glorious communion. Twenty-five professed religion. O that the Lord would revive his work all over the world! I hope to see you at my camp-meeting, commencing on next Friday. Influence as many as you can to come with you. May the Lord make it a happy season of his grace!

The Christian county meeting must have been seventy miles from Mr. Chapman's home, yet he went. His own camp-meeting was to commence, too, on the following Friday. It will be observed, however, that this was but the second year of the existence of the Church. It was a struggle for life. Says my authority very appositely: "Those were days that tried men's souls."

We have the following letter of May 5, 1819:

> It is by no means certain that I shall be able to attend the annual meeting of our Bible Society at Hopkinsville. I have to-day, from a fall, received an injury in my back, which threatens to be serious. If I think it safe, however, to attempt such a journey, I shall go. I wish, however, that you and the rest of the society would consent to erase my name from the Board of Directors, and permit me to remain as a private member.

Hopkinsville was near seventy miles from the residence of Mr. Chapman, and yet he made it a matter of conscience to travel that distance to sustain and promote the Bible cause.

In the same letter we have the following:

> I returned yesterday from a Methodist camp-meeting. We had a good meeting, About thirty professed religion, and many left the ground with broken hearts. Christians enjoyed much of the power of religion, and the utmost harmony prevailed. I enjoyed the meeting myself as well as any I have attended in a long time. O that the spirit of party were destroyed, and all the lovers of Christ bound together in the spirit of the gospel!

My informant responds a "most cordial amen to this prayer." Most Christians would doubtless render a similar response. Still the weakness of Christendom, and especially of Protestant Christendom, is that we pray for union one day, and quarrel the next. But a better day will come. We agree upon the character and value of the wheat now, but quarrel over the chaff. After awhile there will be such a thorough purging that the chaff will not be left, and we shall have no subject of quarrel.

I am indebted to Mr. Lowry for these extracts of letters. I call in his aid, furthermore, for a general summation of the characteristics of Mr. Chapman. No one could form a more correct estimate of the man.

"The subject of this memoir," says he, "was uniform and constant in attending the judicatures of the Church, and but few men exerted a stronger influence in counsel. He was distinguished for the purity of his motives. Nothing like double-dealing ever appeared in his conduct to gain a point. His apparent object was always his real one-his course always open and honorable.

"He was social in feeling, and a sweet companion, and his company was desired by all his brethren. No one could be with him long without feeling that he was 'the disciple whom Jesus loved.'

> His manner in the pulpit was universally admired, imperfect imitations of which are now seen in the actions of many of our young preachers. He was truly a natural orator. The dry rules of rhetoric had little to do with his gestures. They were natural and graceful, emanating from the feelings of his heart. His voice was full, melodious, and subduing. The Spirit of Christ was in him-it beamed from his eyes, and breathed from his lips. There was nothing far-fetched in his discourses-one universal air of seriousness pervaded them, and he seldom closed without leaving his congregation in tears.
>
> He dwelt much, and with great discrimination, upon the evidences of personal piety. This indeed was one of his peculiarities as a preacher, and a department in which he excelled.
>
> His private life fully corresponded with what he taught in the pulpit. No preacher ever enjoyed in a higher degree the

confidence of his neighbors. In his intercourse the gentleman, in the true sense of the word, was blended with the Christian; he was always ready to act on subject of general interest, and to advise and feel where religious sympathy was needed, yet sufficiently reserved to avoid the imputation of being a 'busybody in other men's matters.'

In his family much of the beauty and heavenly simplicity of religion appeared. Evening and morning the family, including servants, were convened for devotion, when a portion of Scripture was read, a hymn was sung, and prayer offered. The father was not a man of smiles and kindness abroad, and churlish, abrupt in speech, and cruel at home, but maintained a perfect correspondence between his public and domestic character.

He settled in the neighborhood in which he died previous to his being licensed to preach. He found that country a complete moral waste, but left it a beautiful garden of God.

Among the ministers remaining in the Church there may be those who surpass him in literary attainments, but in the varied knowledge necessary to the discharge of the ordinary duties of a preacher, so as to win souls to Christ, he has left but few equals behind him.

A few personal recollections will be added in concluding this sketch.

There was a relationship by marriage between Mr. Chapman and my father's family, and it might be supposed that I knew him intimately. I knew him, however, as preacher only, and as a member of the highest judicature of the Church. Still my impressions of him have been very distinct and abiding. He was not a man to be forgotten. My first recollection of him goes back to 1812. I mentioned in the sketch of Mr. Harris the camp-meetings of that year at the Ridge, and my father's living with his small family in a house, or cabin, in immediate connection with the camp-ground. Mr. Chapman attended the meeting with his wife. As she was a relation, they almost as a matter of course stopped at our house. I recollect a remark he made to my step-mother. "Do you," said he, "take care of Anna; I can take care of myself." His manner struck me as that of a cheerful and agreeable man. Strange as it may seem, my recollections of that meeting are very vivid. It was the first time I ever saw William Barnett. His lion-like appearance and trumpet-liek voice awakened my attention. It was the first time, too, in my life in which a direct, personal appeal was ever made to me on the subject of religion. The good man (Rev. David Foster) who made it has long since gone to his account. Should I ever get to a better world I have no doubt of finding him there. But I wander.

My next distinct recollection of Mr. Chapman is connected with the first camp-meeting which was ever held at the Dry Fork, in Sumner county, Tennessee. My father lived at that time on the Dry Fork. In the fall of 1817, myself and some other young persons of the neighborhood professed religion. From some families of old material, and the young converts, a congregation was organized in the following winter. In the spring we built a very common log meeting-house, and our zeal was so great that, although few in number and by no means strong otherwise, we determined upon a camp-meeting in August. The time arrived, and a number of preachers came to our help. Among the rest, Mr. Chapman reached the ground on Friday. He had ridden fifty miles to attend the meeting. It is to be observed that the Dry Fork Congregation was an outgrowth of old Shiloh, which had been so greatly favored in the revival. The old members of the new organization had been members of the congregation at Shiloh, but they had adhered to the revival party. Mr. Chapman himself had been a member of the Shiloh Congregation. He was, therefore, in the neighborhood of his old home. Two or three families of Shiloh that sympathized with use were camped at the camp-meeting. I do not recollect how Saturday of the meeting passed; but Sunday, David McLin, Mr. Chapman, and Thomas Calhoon preached to a great and well-ordered congregation. Mr. Chapman's text was from Job: "I know that my Redeemer liveth." It was a pleasant, precious sermon, and evidently left a fine impression. On Monday he preached again from a text in Proverbs, the call of wisdom: "Unto you, O men, I call; and my voice is to the sons of man." The very appearance of the preacher indicated that he was burdened with the wight of his message. The congregation was large. The people of Shiloh were there. Among them were many of his old acquaintances and friends. The sermon was one of the most powerful appeals that I ever heard. There were numerous allusions to Shiloh, to its past privileges, to its great distinction in the revival, and to its fall from its former high spiritual estate. Several times in the course of the sermon he apostrophized: "O Shiloh, Shiloh, exalted to heaven in point of privilege-thrust down to hell for disobedience!" It was a fearful philippic, and would have been intolerable under other circumstances; but the man, the obvious spirit which moved him, and, in addition to all, the experience of the people themselves, bearing testimony too faithfully to the truth of a great deal of what was uttered, subdued the spirit of opposition. They sat and stood at the roots of the trees and bore it all. I did not understand then so fully the relations of the sermon to the people, but after an experience of more than fifty years, I can very readily imagine that, rather than otherwise, it left an impression of increased respect for the earnestness and fidelity of the preacher.

In two or three years, Mr. Chapman attended a camp-meeting at the same place. He preached again on Monday from the words of Felix to Paul: "God thy way for this time; at a more convenient season I will call for thee." The sermon was, of course, an account of the experience of the unconverted in finding excuses for delay. It was an earnest, solemn, but tender sermon. At its close he called for mourners. There was a considerable number. Among them was a little girl, daughter of one of the leading men of Shiloh. Her case attracted unusual attention. Mr. Chapman himself seemed to take a special interest in her. She professed religion there before she left the congregation. Of course it was a cause of rejoicing. That little girl became a woman, and is now the esteemed wife of a Cumberland Presbyterian preacher. God has made her a needed helper of an honored, but partially disabled, husband.

In the fall of the same year of the first camp-meeting at the Dry Fork, I spent a night and part of two days at a camp-meeting in Robertson county,

Tennessee. Messrs. Harris, Lewis,[16] and Chapman were the preachers. Mr. Lewis preached on Monday, and was followed by Mr. Chapman. His text that day was from Romans: "But to Israel he saith, All day long have I stretched out my hands to a disobedient and gainsaying people." At this meeting I saw for the first time William C. Long[17] and David Lowry.[18] I believe they were then candidates for the ministry.

Mr. Chapman was present at the first meeting of the Synod which I ever attended. In the appointment of the committees it turned out that he and Rev. John L. Dillard and myself were appointed a committee upon the Minutes of some one of the Presbyteries. I was added to the committee, of course, merely to make up the customary number. Mr. Chapman and Mr. Dillard both sometimes relished a quiet joke. The Minutes of the Presbytery had been badly kept, and in making the report the committee descended to some rather ludicrous particularities which excited a little amusement in the Synod at the expense of the Presbytery. Mr. King

---

[16]Rev. Isaac Orrey Lewis was born June 7, 1777, in North Carolina. His father, Isaac Lewis, was a Welshman, and for many years a member of the Presbyterian Church. His mother was of Irish descent. Mr. Lewis, the son, married Miss Fannie Stone in North Carolina, and emigrated to Kentucky about the year 1800, and settled in Warren county. He was for years a man of the world, had a passion for horse-racing, and, at one time, came very near losing his life while training one of his horses. His experience on that occasion alarmed him, and he summarily renounced the practice. He afterward became terribly convicted under the preaching of Mr. McGready. In process of time he professed religion, and, although the father of a considerable family, turned his attention to the ministry. He was licensed and ordained by the Logan Presbytery. His education was of course imperfect. He was, however, a useful man, and highly esteemed "for his works' sake." He died July 20, 1850, having acquired the unusual weight of four hundred and fifty pounds.

[17]Rev. William C. Long was brought into the ministry by the Logan Presbytery. He was a preacher of medium ability, but of great zeal and spiritual worth. He labored a number of years acceptably and usefully in Kentucky, then in Missouri, and then again in Kentucky. He died some years ago.

[18]Rev. David Lowry was likewise brought into the ministry by the Logan Presbytery. He has labored with great ability and success in Kentucky, Tennessee, among the North-western Indians, and now lives and labors in Missouri, still bringing forth fruit in old age.

was the patriarch of the meeting, and took occasion to administer a severe rebuke to the committee for taxing the patience of the Synod with so small matters. I have always in such cases remembered that rebuke. Such reports result in a waste of time, and sometimes in an exposure of the weakness of Zion.

I was once in Mr. Chapman's neighborhood, and at his house, in the course of his life. It was a lovely community. It seemed to bear the impress of his own excellent spirit. The seed sown there is still developing itself. His generation has passed away. A second has followed, and the third is now taking up the burdens of their predecessors. Thus the work goes on, and thus it is that the influence of good men never dies. Alexander Chapman was one of the good men, and from south-western Kentucky, in the great day, hundreds and thousands will rise up with thanksgiving upon their lips that God ever sent such a messenger of mercy among them.

Two of Mr. Chapman's sons entered the ministry. Rev. A. H. Chapman was born September 13, 1813. He professed religion October 8, 1832; joined the Little Muddy Congregation on the twenty-first of the same month. He was then about nineteen years old. In process of time he joined the Logan Presbytery as a candidate for the ministry, was licensed and ordained in due course. After his ordination he devoted himself mainly to itinerant preaching in the upper portion of Logan Presbytery. He is said to have been a good English scholar, and to have read Latin well. His views of truth were clear and distinct, and he sometimes presented them with great power. He died August 22, 1849. Nothing is said of his death, but that it was calm and triumphant. He died at the house of Thomas Barnett, Esq., in Greene county of his native State.

Rev. B. C. Chapman was educated at Cumberland College, and at Cumberland University, or rather at what afterward became Cumberland University. He has spent most of his ministerial life in Middle Tennessee, but is now pastor of the Cumberland Presbyterian Church in Selma, Alabama.

Two of Mr. Chapman's grandsons are also engaged in the work of the ministry: one in Ohio, and the other in Pennsylvania. The most of his descendants are honored and useful members of the Church.

REV. EZEKIEL CLOYD
(1760-1851)

Ezekiel Cloyd was born on the 12 of February, 1760. His parents are supposed to have lived at the time in Montgomery county, Virginia. He was the son of John and Margaret Cloyd. His mother's name before her marriage was Scott. His parents emigrated from Ireland and settled in Virginia in 1758. They were, however, of Scotch origin. The name seems to have been originally Clyde. Of course the family were thoroughly Scotch. The parents were both members of the Presbyterian Church. I have in my possession the mother's certificate of Church-membership in Ireland. It is dated August 14, 1758, and given to Margaret Clyde, alias Scott.

In 1789 the parents of Mr. Cloyd, and himself with them, moved from Virginia to North Carolina. Some time previous to this removal he was married to Miss Rebecca Williamson. I have before me three certificates given by his friends and neighbors of Montgomery county, Virginia, upon the occasion of his removal to North Carolina. They all represent him as a "well-behaved person." a "good member of society," and one of them as a "patriot."

About the year 1800 he left North Carolina, and settled in Tennessee, it is supposed at the place where he spent the most of his remaining years, in the lower end of Wilson county.

In the year 1800 he professed religion at Shiloh Meeting-house, in Sumner county. He received his first deep religious impressions under the preaching of Rev. James McGready. One of the Virginia certificates, however, represents him and his wife as members of the Church in that State. Whatever may be true in this respect, it is certain that he made a profession of religion at Shiloh, and considered himself to have been converted there.

On his return home from the meeting at Shiloh, he immediately commenced the exercise of family prayers, which he kept up with strict punctuality for fifty years.

It was customary in those days for zealous and active men to be employed, whilst still private members of the Church, in holding prayer-meetings, and in exhortation. In this way Mr. Cloyd commenced his public labors. He was always unusually gifted and effective in exhortation and prayer.

At what time he was received as a candidate for the ministry it is not known, but he was probably received by the Cumberland Presbytery before its division. The first Presbyterial notice of him which we have been able to find, is a notice of his licensure, at the spring meeting of the Nashville Presbytery in 1814. The following is the record: "Mr. Ezekiel Cloyd delivered a written discourse from the second Epistle of St. Paul to the Corinthians, 8th chapter and 9th verse, which was sustained as a popular discourse, preparatory to his licensure." It will be seen that the record is very full. Those good old men were in the habit of doing their business carefully. There is an additional record of the same day, Wednesday, March 30, 1814: "Presbytery examined Messrs. Robert Guthrie and Ezekiel Cloyd on Divinity and English Grammar, which were sustained, and having obtained a good report of their moral character, Presbytery licensed them to preach the gospel in the bounds of this Presbytery, or wherever God in his providence may cast their lots." This meeting of the Presbytery was held at New Hope.

At an intermediate Presbytery held in July of 1822, at Sugg's Creek Meeting-house, Mr. Cloyd, in connection with James S. Guthrie, and the writer, then a very young man, was ordained. The transaction was a very impressive one, at least to myself. A camp-meeting was held at the same time, and a number of persons professed religion.

Previous to his ordination his wife, who had been in feeble health for a number of years, died. After a widowhood of some time, he married Mrs. Nancy White, of Wilson county. Mrs. White was the widow of Rev. John White, a Methodist minister. She was a woman of great worth, and contributed much to the comfort and happiness of his latter days. My correspondent says that "in the latter part of his life he was subject to much bodily infirmity and mental affliction, yet he staggered not at the promises of God through unbelief, but was strong in faith, giving glory to God." He died in Lebanon, in August, 1851. Mrs. Cloyd, his second wife, died also in Lebanon, April 17, 1854.

The whole ministry of Mr. Cloyd extended through a space of near forty years. He was always a zealous and earnest man. He made no pretensions to a high order of ability, or attainments; he rather underrated himself in these respects; but he was a useful man, and left a precious record behind him. He was especially effective in exhortation, and in his labors with mourners. After his ordination, although advanced in life, he traveled as a circuit-rider for a number of years. For a short time he served as pastor of Stoner's Creek congregation, in the bounds of which he spent the most of his life. Indeed, he was one of the fathers of the congregation, and preached to them occasionally during his whole ministry. His son-in-law, Benjamin Alexander, an elder in the congregation, who has been curious in recording such things, has a record of two hundred and ninety-two sermons preached by Mr. Cloyd to that congregation.

His example and presence were a standing reproof of wickedness and vice of every kind. On one occasion he was greatly troubled at what seemed to be the prospect of the introduction of dancing-parties into the neighborhood. An appointment was made, as he learned, for such a party at the house of an acquaintance on a particular evening. He determined upon an effort to arrest the progress of the evil in its commencement, remembering the wise injunction, "Obsta principiis: Resist wrong in its earliest stages." He went to the house about the time he supposed the dancing would commence, knocked at the door, and was ushered into the room. Of course the company were somewhat startled at such a movement. Without taking his seat, he at once proposed singing and prayer, gave out a hymn, and a negro of the neighborhood, who had some connection with the occasion, joined him in singing. The rest of the company, however, were too much taken by surprise to participate, even if they had been disposed otherwise to do so. After singing and prayer, he delivered an earnest exhortation, and left the company. The effort was successful. Some of the young gentlemen were very much incensed—threatened violence—but the dancing-parties died out. It is worthy of remark, too, that the negro who shared in the singing afterward professed religion, and lived and died an unusually consistent Christian.

Mr. Cloyd raised a large family. As far as I know, they all became members of the Church. His youngest son is now an elder in the congregation which his father contributed so much toward building up. His youngest daughter is the wife of Rev. John Beard, of Kansas. His grandson is now pastor of Stoner's Creek congregation.

Mr. Cloyd was a farmer as well as preacher. According to the custom of the times in which he lived, he labored on his farm during the week, and performed his ministerial service on the Sabbath. The principal portion of this service was a work of love. He received scarcely any pecuniary compensation. Still he lived comfortably, and was always able to minister a generous hospitality to his friends, especially to his brethren of the ministry. His house was a home to such. It is pleasant to remark, took that the same "house of cedar" still stands, a monument of patriarchal simplicity and economy.

The personal appearance and bearing of Mr. Cloyd were those of an unaffected gentleman of the old school. His dress was always neat, and his manners, without the slightest parade or pretension, were affable and kind. It is cheerful to linger amidst the recollections of such a man.

FRANCEWAY RANNA COSSITT
Francois René Cossitt
(1790-1863)

Franceway Ranna Cossitt was born at Claremont, New Hampshire, April 24, 1790. His family were Episcopalians. His maternal grandfather and an uncle were in succession pastors of the Episcopalian congregation at Claremont. I have received the impression from himself, that whilst his family were perhaps not bigoted, they were decided in their ecclesiastical preferences. They were of those who had sympathized with the king in his conflicts with the parliament—a series of conflicts which resulted in the overthrow and death of the king, and the establishment of Cromwell in the Protectorate. Of course his ancestors could hardly have been genuine Puritans.

At the age of fourteen Mr. Cossitt commenced his preparation for college, and after the usual embarrassments and delays in such cases, entered Middlebury College, in Vermont. In 1813 he graduated. His standing was high in a large class. After leaving college he spent two years in teaching, at Morristown, in New Jersey. It was customary, in those days, for men, after having completed their collegiate studies, to spend some time in teaching before entering upon the study of those things relating more immediately to their chosen profession. From Morristown he went to North Carolina, and took charge of Vine Hill Academy, on Roanoke River.

From North Carolina he returned to New England deeply impressed with the necessity of personal religion. What particular circumstance awakened his attention to that subject is not now known to his friends. After using the ordinary means, and passing through many discouragements, his mind at length found relief. In his own self-distrusting account of this occurrence, he says: "If I ever embraced Jesus Christ as he is offered in the gospel, it was near the bank of the Connecticut River. I had tied my horse to a sappling in a thicket, whither I had retired to pray for mercy." In such a manner a man of his temperament was more likely to settle the great question to his satisfaction. The pressure of a crowd who are encouraging and exhorting may be the best for some, but it is not the best for all.

Mr. Cossitt's original purpose was to engage in the legal profession, but with his spiritual change came a change of purpose. He resolved to devote himself to the Christian ministry. He studied theology at New Haven, in what has since become the General Episcopal Seminary of New York—the institution having been removed. Bishop Brownell, of Connecticut, gave him license as a "lay reader" in the Episcopal Church.

He then directed his course to Tennessee, and established a school at a little place on Cumberland River, called in its day New York, a few miles below Clarksville. A number of his Carolina friends had moved and settled there. They were wealthy, and desired to educate their children. With a view to this object, they urged his settlement among them. In addition, the opening and improving condition of the country presented a fine prospect to men engaged in the work of education. His school became in process of time, amongst other things, a sort of theological seminary. A number of young men preparing for the ministry resorted thither for the purpose of receiving instruction.

While he was engaged at New York I first became acquainted with Mr.

Cossitt. In the fall of 1821 he came to a camp-meeting held on Wells's Creek, in Stewart county. He was accompanied to the meeting by William Clements, an educated gentleman and an elder in the Church, who had previously become acquainted with him. An introduction by such a man as Mr. Clements was a recommendation. They arrived at the meeting on Saturday. The ministers in attendance, besides myself, were Thomas Calhoon, Robert Baker, and Robert S. Donnell. Mr. Cossitt preached on Saturday evening, although still an Episcopalian. His text was, "If they hear not Moses and the prophets, neither will they be persuaded, though one rose from the dead." The sermon was a respectable argument in support of the truth of the Christian Scriptures. This was his introduction to Cumberland Presbyterians. Mr. Calhoon was the manager of the meeting, and treated him with great attention and respect.

In 1822 he was set apart to the whole work of the ministry in the Cumberland Presbyterian Church, and became a member of the Anderson Presbytery. On the 19th of February, of the same year, he was married to Miss Lucinda Blair, of Montgomery county, a lady of unusual personal attractions. Her father was a prominent member of the Church. Of course Mr. Cossitt was now fairly identified with the Cumberland Presbyterians.

Shortly after his marriage he issued a prospectus with a view to the publication of a paper, which he proposed to call the Western Star. For some reason the publication was never commenced. I suppose the reason to have been an insufficiency of encouragement on the score of patronage. The movement was in advance of the times. After spending two or three years at New York, he moved to Elkton, Kentucky, and established a school there. His associations at Elkton were unusually pleasant. He always spoke of them with interest.

At the sessions of the Cumberland Synod at Princeton, in 1825, the plan of Cumberland College was projected, and commissioners were appointed to examine particular points, and make the location. Another set of commissioners was appointed to procure a charter for the proposed Institution from the Legislature of Kentucky. It was to have been called the Cumberland Presbyterian College. The gentlemen who visited the Legislature for the purpose of procuring a charter, were advised to drop the "Presbyterian" from the proposed name, as it might arouse sectarian opposition among the members and their friends, and thus cause the application to be rejected. Accordingly the application was made for a charter of Cumberland College. The change was displeasing to some leading members of the Church, and was perhaps the first step in producing a series of embarrassments which in process of time became very numerous and great—so much that in a few years the existence of the Institution was placed in jeopardy.

Princeton and Elkton were rivals in their efforts for the location. The Institution was located in the vicinity of Princeton; a farm was bought about a mile from the town. It was to be a manual labor school, and arrangements were made accordingly. Mt. Cossitt was chosen President, and opened the College for the reception of students in March, 1826.

Cumberland College was an experiment. The country was comparatively new. The Cumberland Presbyterian Church had been chiefly devoted to the more immediate work of saving sinners, and collecting congregations. The itinerant plan of preaching, and yearly camp-meetings, constituted a large part of their machinery. The establishment of denominational schools and of colleges had been overlooked. The lessons necessary to conducting such enterprises with success had to be learned from experience. A practical man would have expected blunders and a probable failure. Again, the plan of the Institution was a novelty. It was a generous conception. Almost any reasoner would have decided that it was suitable to the wants and genius of a plain, practical people. It looked to the education of young men, and especially of young men preparing for the ministry, who had not the means of supporting themselves at more expensive institutions of learning. Rugged young men, who had been first trained at the plow, and who had vigor of body, were to be converted into scholars, and statesmen, and pulpit orators. This was the theory, and it was a theory worthy of a trial. The students were to occupy dormitories provided for them, to use straw-beds, and furniture of the plainest and cheapest king, and to board at a common boarding-house. The fare was to be healthful, but plain and cheap. All luxuries were proscribed. The students were to work two hours each day except the Sabbath, and to pay sixty dollars a year into the College treasury.

Upon the opening of the College, Mr. Cossitt collected around him some of the best young men in the land. A large log-building was constructed for College purposes, and the students who were educated there during ten of the first years of the Institution "rubbed their backs against wooden walls." Notwithstanding what would now be considered the grimness and severity of the system, the number of the students was large. In the spring and summer of 1830 it reached one hundred and twenty-five.

At the meeting of the General Assembly in 1830 it was thought necessary to raise the charges in money from sixty to eighty dollars. Experience had shown that the expenditures of the establishment were greater than its friends had anticipated. The circumstance operated unfavorably, of course, upon the patronage of the Institution; still its patronage was respectable. Pecuniary difficulties, however, rather increased than diminished. Money had been borrowed to pay for the farm, and other debts had been contracted, and the interest was an eating cancer.

In 1831 the General Assembly leased the College to Rev. John Barnett and Rev. Aaron Shelby for a term of years. The pecuniary difficulties of the Institution had become very great. The Church had become in some degree alienated; confidence in the final success of the enterprise was failing. Messrs. Barnett and Shelby were to have all the proceeds of the College after paying the necessary expenditures—to support a sufficient number of instructors, to keep up the boarding-house, and pay the debts of the College. They were considered men of great energy and perseverance, of respectable financial ability, and devoted friends of the Church. Mr. Shelby continued his connection with the Institution till the summer or fall of 1833, when he sold his interest to Mr. Harvey Young. In the summer of 1834 Mr. Young died, and the entire management of the financial affairs of the College fell into the hands of Mr. Barnett. In the summer of 1834 the cholera visited the town. A number of persons fell victims to the terrible disease. The College, however, did not disband. But the cholera was followed by a malignant fever, which extended to the College community, and spread over the country. The condition of things became so bad at the College, that a temporary suspension of operations was found absolutely necessary. The manager of the farm and boarding-house died; one of the professors was finally prostrated, one of the students died, and a number in addition were sick. It was a terrible blow upon the Institution. It rallied, however, and the fall session commenced with favorable prospects. Still there were financial troubles. The Church, too, began to complain of Mr. Barnett. Some thought he managed badly; others thought he managed wholly with a view to his own selfish ends; others went so far as to impeach his integrity as a man of business and a Christian. A change became necessary.

Accordingly, at the General Assembly in 1837, which met at Princeton, Cumberland College Association was formed. Mr. Barnett's interest was transferred to the Association. It was a joint-stock company. It was pledged to carry on the operations of the Institution under the direction and control of the General Assembly. A number of the most respectable and wealthy citizens of Princeton and the neighborhood entered into the Association. Prospects seemed to brighten, and hope was restored once more. The Association entered upon their with vigor and energy. Still, after a temporary revival of interest and confidence, another cloud arose. An impression was made upon the minds of those in the neighborhood of the College that the Church had deserted it, and that neither contributions nor patronage were to be expected from that quarter. It was believed that busy persons, with selfish designs, contributed to that impression. The subject of transferring the Institution to the control of the Episcopalians of Kentucky was seriously considered. How far Episcopalians of Kentucky may have been answerable themselves for the state of feeling which existed, the writer has no means of knowing, but some of Dr. Cossitt's friends thought that they were not inactive. It was natural enough that they should have felt an interest in a measure which would have contributed greatly to their success and establishment in Lower Kentucky.

The result of this condition of things was a great effort on the part of Dr. Cossitt to arouse the Church once more to an interest in behalf of the College. He and Rev. F. C. Usher, who was connected with him in the department of instruction, published a circular letter, in which earnest appeals were made to the ministers and members of the Church. I append also a private letter, written about the same time, and on the same subject, to one of the fathers of the Church. I suppose he may have written twenty or thirty such letters.

CUMBERLAND COLLEGE, Feb. 3, 1840.

DEAR BROTHER IN CHRIST:—By this time probably you have received a printed circular signed by myself and Brother Usher. By that you will see that we are in trouble—I have not dared to show how much. To tell you that mine are days of sadness, and nights of waking—to say that my eyes stream with tears, and my heart bleeds with agony, would be to tell you of what your knowledge of me, and your perusal of the circular, must already have informed you. I will not attempt to describe the shame, mortification, and anguish of spirit which I feel; but will devote this sheet to the reasons why I thus feel at present. Surely I may be permitted to show the wounds of my spirit to sympathizing brethren.

I have devoted the best years of my life to the College. I have done it for the Church. The Church must and will sustain it, in justice to herself, if not to me. For all that I have done, sacrificed, and suffered, I ask nothing for myself—not even thanks; but I ask that she may not suffer the fruits of her own labors, as well as mine, to go to swell the triumphs of another denomination, and to fix the indelible stain of ignorance, supineness, and covetousness upon our names and memories.

When I compare what other denominations are doing in behalf of ministerial education with what we are doing, I must confess I am alarmed, not that I envy or wish to impede their success, but because I tremble for our own. I have at great pains obtained the following statistics, which may be relied on as correct: The Episcopalians have seven colleges and four theological seminaries in the United States. The Presbyterians have fifty colleges and nine theological seminaries. The Congregationalists, nine colleges and five theological seminaries. The Methodists, eight colleges. The Baptists, seven colleges and five theological seminaries. The Catholics, six colleges and five theological seminaries. There are forty-nine colleges and twelve theological seminaries West of the Alleghany Mountains, and I believe every one of them much better endowed than our own; yet but very few of them hold an equal standing. Thirty-seven colleges and ten theological seminaries have been established since ours, and nearly all the colleges and twelve theological seminaries, on the West of the Alleghanies. And now, my brother, shall the only Cumberland Presbyterian College pass to another denomination? The whole world would cry out, 'Shame! Shame!' Our very name would become a by-word and a reproach for ages to come. I am not a prophet, but, my dear brother, permit me to make a prediction. This College may die, or go into other hands, but its epitaph will be written in the everlasting disgrace of that body which founded, but did not appreciate and sustain it. It is better for us to hear this plain, but unpleasant truth, now while the remedy is in our power, than for posterity to hear it when the time has passed for effacing the stain from the escutcheon of the Church of their ancestors. Should the Church in future ages mourn over the supineness and negligence of the present generation of ministers and members of our branch? Should future generations of men regard us as too weak to appreciate the blessings and manifold mercies wherewith an indulgent Heaven has favored us, or too covetous to extend and perpetuate them as a rich legacy to our spiritual descendants, whose reputation would be most likely to suffer? The name and memory of him whose afflicted heart now communes with you in these lines, will probably be overlooked in the crowd of those more conspicuous; or if remembered at all, will at least be known as an advocate for education. Should posterity fix the broad seal of condemnation on our Church for suffering our College to pass into other hands for the want of aid, who, I ask, will bear this load of censure? Rely upon this fact: the more conspicuous any one may have been in founding and building up the Church, the more conspicuous must he be in the history of the loss of the College to that Church of which he was a minister. Do you think I fear for my own reputation, in such an event? How is it possible to entertain such a fear? I can fear nothing, while faithful records are preserved. The body proposing to take the College would, I doubt not, render it a splendid Institution in a very few years. They say so, and it is known that they are fully able. Their colleges are all splendid—some of them the most so in the world. Did I wish to get myself a great name as the founder of a splendid College, at the expense of duty, conscience, and the interests of the Cumberland Presbyterian Church, together with the reputation of its ministers and members, the readiest way to accomplish this end would be to let the Episcopalians have it. But Providence has cast my lot with you; my sympathies are with you, and I wish to live and die a member of your Church, which has adopted me as a son, and honored me as a minister. I trust I feel for the honor of the Church. And while my heart is torn with agony under existing prospects, permit me, with humble deference, to say my heart assures me we all ought to raise our voices and wield our pens; we ought to sound the tocsin of alarm; stir up every minister and member; traverse the whole length and breadth of our bounds; visit every Church and every family from the palace to the cot, and invite and urge all to contribute to a fund for the education of a future ministry. I verily believe our doctrines are the truth as taught in the word of God. I also believe they are taught in the writings of the fathers of the Christian Church, up to the time of Augustine, who was the first teacher of the system now called Calvinism. The doctrines of our Church are much older than the Westminster Confession, and just as old as the Bible. This I have intended to show at some time in a little book on the subject. Now if our doctrines are the truth, ought we not to give the world the benefit of them? And how can we do this without some men at least of extensive learning? Believe me, if any Church under heaven needs an educated ministry, that Church is our own. If so many colleges and theological seminaries are employed in educating men to disseminate error, ought we not to have one employed in the cause of God's own truth? Resolve upon it, and it shall be so. I, for one, have embarked in the cause of education, as auxiliary to the diffusion of the gospel. I have had many discouragements, and have often been censured and condemned. I may be again, but hope is still my anchor. I have put my hand to the plow—I cannot turn back. It is true, at the beginning I did not count the cost in regard to my sufferings in feeling, but be them what they may, I am now prepared to endure them until every prospect has vanished, and hope's last lingering ray has given place to the gloom of utter despair.

You are at liberty to show this to as many brethren as you judge to be faithful and true. Let me hear from you, if you please, as soon as possible. Could you not write something, and publish it in the paper, in favor of sustaining the College? And I hope you will come up to the next Assembly determined to sustain it, and prepared for prompt and efficient measures.

In great affliction, but with hope for my consolation, I remain your in Christ,

F. R. Cossitt.

These efforts were continued to the meeting of the General Assembly, which occurred in May following, Its sessions were held at Elkton, Kentucky. When the Assembly met, it appeared that the Church had been fully awakened to the importance and danger of the crisis. A magnificent scheme was formed. If it had been carried into effective operation, it would have relieved the College from debt, and rendered it permanent, if not prosperous. It was proposed to raise one hundred thousand dollars for educational purposes. Fifty-five thousand dollars of that sum was to serve as a perpetual endowment of Cumberland College; thirty thousand was to be used in Pennsylvania, in the endowment of a college there; and the remaining fifteen thousand dollars was to constitute a sort of floating capital, to be used as circumstances might suggest. Several of the most popular young men in the Church were engaged as agents; the people were not illiberal in their subscriptions, and every thing seemed to promise well. Dr. Cossitt confidently believed that the College would be endowed, and that the most liberal provision would be made for the education of candidates for the ministry. This last was always a controlling thought with him, as it has been with all the earnest educators in our Church. This thought originated the impulse which led to the establishment of Cumberland College at first, and afterward to the establishment of Cumberland University. As an evidence that he was sanguine in his hopes, I offer the following extract from a letter written to myself a few weeks before the meeting of the Assembly in 1840. He had received the impressions from his correspondence which developed themselves at the Assembly. The letter indicates great hopefulness:

PRINCETON, April 8, 1840.

DEAR BROTHER BEARD:—It is now near midnight, I suppose. I have been in bed, but cannot sleep, and have arisen to write a few lines to you. I suppose you have received my printed circular, also the first number of the Banner of Peace. You will see our prospects, in part only, of the endowment of the College, I tell you it will be endowed. If for years 'we have sat down by the rivers of Babylon and wept when we remembered Zion,' the redeeming spirit which is abroad leads us to say, now 'is our mouth filled with laughter and our tongue with singing.' Even I, who have been so long brooding over my hard fortune, like one shorn of his strength and bereft of his energies, feel my native energies rising within me, and the promptings to action, which I could scarcely suppress, if I would. Our Church is to awake from her apathy, depend upon it. 'The Lord hath not forgotten to be gracious—he will not always chide.' An impetus is to be given to ministerial education. Were you here, you could judge of the signs of the times as well as I—especially after reading the many letters which I have received. I and my family have written during the winter about fifty letters, in some respects like the one I sent you some short time since, notwithstanding my labors are much more arduous in College than when you were here. You would be astonished at the amount of labor of all kinds I now perform. I am astonished at it myself. I am complaining of a cold, but Mrs. Cossitt says mental efforts agree with my health.

 I am writing, and expect to write, much on the subject of ministerial education. I hope to give the subject some of my best strokes before I have done with it. Brother Usher is doing well. Mr. P. is too fractious; but we have harmony in the Faculty. I have given him some plain and faithful talks, by which Brother Usher thinks he has profited. * * * Good-night.

F. R. Cossitt.

I present an extract from another letter, received ten months after the action of the Assembly in 1840:

PRINCETON, March 27, 1841.

 BELOVED BROTHER:—* * * Your letter convinces me that you are somewhat behind the times with respect to the present feelings and sentiments of the Church. Perhaps you are yet incredulous. I do not know that I ought to wonder at it, considering the past. I for years was just where you are. But I tell you, the Church is getting awake on two important subjects—The means of education for candidates for the ministry; and, The means of support for laborious ministers, together with a general plan of operations. I am sure I could convince you of this in a short conversation. Do not smile, and say, 'Brother Cossitt is sanguine.' Let me smile, rather, and say, 'Brother Beard is skeptical." Trust me, for once: I cannot be mistaken. * * * With some, learning is useful, NECESSARY, for INDISPENSABLE; with other, it is popular and praiseworthy. The people are almost universally in favor of it, as you know. Who shall dare to oppose it? I tell you, the day for open opposition has passed. * * * The spirit of the age is onward; and this spirit has at last entered our Church. I could, if time and paper would allow, give you many evidences. * * * The College will be endowed. We cannot doubt it. You must give up your incredulity—you will be compelled to yield it. * * * I am overwhelmed with cares and business. My labors in

the College are not at all lessened. * * * Sometimes I think I have business enough for two or three men. I have to write much, while others sleep. But they say I fatten on it. I feel that I can do much with a prospect of success, but very little without it. I do hope and pray that I may never again sink into that state of listlessness and despondency in which I was for some years of our acquaintance.
Yours in the gospel,

F. R. COSSITT."

It will be perceived that this letter was written but a few weeks before the meeting of the General Assembly of 1841. At that Assembly things seemed to be going forward smoothly. The friends of the College were still hopeful, and even buoyant. I have letters in my possession, written by Dr. Cossitt several months after the Assembly of 1841, in which the same hopeful and confident spirit is expressed. My persistent incredulity had been almost overcome. The reader will then judge of the revulsion which the public mind must have experienced when it was announced at the General Assembly of 1842, that Cumberland College was still hopelessly in debt, that its property was under execution, and liable to be placed under the sheriff's hammer any day. None but those, however, who knew Dr. Cossitt intimately can appreciate the shock which his feelings must have suffered as the true condition of things became known, and its inevitable results were developed.. The writer makes this statement with a full knowledge of many, if not of most, of the circumstances connected with the dark cloud which spread itself over the prospects of the College. And however Dr. Cossitt may have felt compelled to follow the lead of a train of circumstances which he could not control, the troubles of Cumberland College, of which we now speak, threw a shadow over his path which continued to his dying day. The happiest hours of his life were those in which he was struggling—often against fearful odds—for the prosperity, or to maintain the existence, of the Institution. It was, from its inception, a darling enterprise-it was that through which he became known to the world. It was the enterprise through which he expected his name to be handed down to posterity, if it should reach posterity at all. It was an enterprise of his own selection. His Banner of Peace was pressed upon him by the force of circumstances. He felt that his work in the College was the great work of his life. This is evident from his private and most earnest letters.

As we would have expected, when the condition of the College became known to the Assembly, the revulsion of feeling and the disappointment were so great that steps were immediately taken toward the removal of the Institution. A commission of gentlemen, all prominent members of the Church, was appointed to consider the matter, and take some action upon it. The commission met in Nashville, on the first day of the following July, 1842, and determined to establish Cumberland College at Lebanon, Tennessee. Dr. Cossitt was elected to the presidency of the new College, and accepted the appointment, and of course the Commencement of the College at Princeton, in 1842, terminated his connection with that Institution. The friends of the old Institution, however, rallied, sold its useless property, paid its debts, and continued its operations with respectable success, and, I trust I may be allowed to say, with usefulness, for a number of years.

But the question will naturally present itself to my reader, What was the cause of all the troubles in Cumberland College, and especially of those which developed themselves so disastrously in 1842? It is not my purpose to enter into an investigation of this subject. I have often thought and said, that if the history of the Cumberland Presbyterian Church should ever be written, the history of the old College would constitute its darkest chapter. I have no disposition to extend this chapter farther than I have already done. But a few words may, and perhaps should, be added in justice to the living, and to the memory of the dead. And first, Mr. Barnett was not the cause of the trouble. It was once fashionable to ascribe at least a great deal of it to him. But there were troubles and discouragements before he and Shelby became connected with it. There were troubles after it fell into the hands of the Association. These troubles culminated in 1842, five years after Mr. Barnett's connection with the Institution had ceased. Furthermore, before his connection with the College, he was a successful farmer in the country, was understood to be very practical and skillful in the management of his business, and had acquired a respectable property. When he left the Institution, he was an insolvent debtor. He was never able to extricate himself from his financial difficulties, and died under the cloud which those difficulties brought over him. He spent his last years under a deep impression that he had been injured and cruelly mistreated by the Church. Under that impression his spirits were at length broken, and he sunk in sorrow to the grave. Mr. Young, who was connected with him for some time, had prospered in his quiet home, and was making a good living for his family. After an experiment of a year at the College, he left them in a great measure penniless. Mr. Barnett and Dr. Cossitt did not always agree in judgment; they became at length estranged in feeling, but they were both honest; they meant well, and were both unyielding in their devotion to the Church. I knew those good men well; they served their generation, and their estrangements have been forgotten in the quietude of the grave.

Secondly. The people of Princeton were not the cause. The Church sometimes complained that they did not feel as much interest in the College as they ought to feel. This may have been true to some extent. There are men in every community who would sell any public enterprise for a mess of pottage, if they could appropriate the price to the satisfying of their own hunger. Still the people of Princeton would have kept up the College, if they could have done it. They have given the best possible evidence of this for twenty-five years past. They are not more selfish or sectarian than other people.

Thirdly. Dr. Cossitt was not the cause. He never controlled the financial affairs of the College. Furthermore, the number of young men of very high order that he kept around him in the College, and their high regard for him as a man and as an instructor, furnish sufficient evidence of the influence which he was capable of exerting upon the youthful and aspiring mind. He labored with great earnestness, and a portion of the time, at least, with great self-denial, in trying to support the Institution. It was opened in 1826, and it was understood at the General Assembly in 1829, three years afterward, that the financial difficulties had commenced, and that the existence of the College was already in peril. From that time to 1842 the struggle was continued and unremitting between hope and despair, and the wonder is, that a man with feeble health and sensitive feelings should have lived and labored so long under such circumstances.

Beyond these negatives I shall not go, farther than to say that there was unquestionably a combination of causes which operated in producing the results that we have been considering. The enterprise was new. As it has been already said, it was an experiment. Its partial failure can be accounted for without bringing reproach upon the Church or any of its individual members. Still Cumberland College, although it has now ceased to exist, fulfilled a useful and an honored mission. It has a noble record. Its alumni are known, and their power is felt in high places. Notwithstanding its financial troubles, and its partial failure in 1842, and its entire failure since, no member of the Church needs be ashamed of its contributions to the educational interests of the country. I must be allowed to include in these statements its whole history, from 1826 to its final failure. Trace the footsteps of its sons, and you will find the most of those who survive where men are wont to be.

In 1829 Mr. Cossitt made an excursion through some of the Middle and Southern States. He spent some time in Washington City, and while there published and circulated a pamphlet, setting forth the character and claims of the College. He preached in several of the churches of the city, and received some donations. He preached also in Baltimore and Philadelphia, receiving very respectful attention in both cities. In Baltimore especially, his preaching seems to have made considerable impression. He brought one young man from Baltimore, and two or three from Eastern Virginia, to the Institution. Two of these young men remained until they graduated. They became useful and honored men.

Early in 1830 the leading men connected with the College commenced the publication of the Religious and Literary Intelligencer, at Princeton. It was the first periodical of the Church. Mr. Cossitt was identified with it for a few months, and a principal contributor to its columns. The Assembly of 1830, however, transferred the editorial control of the paper to Rev. David Lowry. It afterward became the Revivalist, and finally the Cumberland Presbyterian, in Nashville.

In 1833 Mr. Cossitt lost his wife and the mother of his children. She endured a long illness, and died in the triumphs of faith. On the 19th of January, 1834, he was married a second time, to Miss Matilda Edwards, of Elkton, Kentucky. The respected widow still lives. In 1839 he received the Doctorate of Divinity from Middlebury College, and also from the Trustees of Cumberland College, with which he was then connected.

In March, 1840, he commenced the publication of the Banner of Peace. It was at first a monthly periodical. He continued it a year under this form. In December of 1841 the publication was renewed. It was changed, however, from a monthly to a small weekly. The following letter will serve as an illustration of the feelings with which he undertook the publication of a weekly paper. It brings us back once more into the region of trouble:

PRINCETON, June 5, 1841.

DEAR BROTHER:—I received your letter, but could not find time to answer it before the General Assembly. I now write in haste, on another subject.

You have probably heard of the proceedings of the late Assembly. While I rejoice at what that body did for the College, I mourn over the loss of a weekly paper. I was strongly solicited to undertake a weekly on a plan similar to the one I am about to propose; but not knowing what arrangements I could make at home, I declined, and concluded to continue my little monthly. I could doubtless obtain a large list of subscribers.

But, Brother Beard, shall it be said that the Cumberland Presbyterian Church has not supported, and cannot support, one weekly paper? Shall truth and falsehood be so blended together and presented to the public, as to make the following impression: that a patriotic individual, at great personal sacrifices, sustained a respectable weekly at Nashville, for the benefit of a Church which had not the gratitude, nor the liberality, nor the justice to sustain his laudable efforts, until he finally became the victim of his own zeal for the cause of the Church, and of the indifference of the Church to her own welfare; and that now three little pitiful monthlies have sprung up, each struggling for a bare existence, and contending for a moiety of that poor patronage which was so grudgingly bestowed upon, or rather withheld from, the late Cumberland Presbyterian?

I have no desire to be an editor. It is not consonant with my interest or inclination. But I cannot, I CANNOT, I CANNOT let things continue in their present situation, without an honest effort, at least, to better them. When I left the Assembly, I thought I could bear the reproach and live; but when questioned on my way, and after my return home, by our own members, those of other churches, and people of the world, and after hearing their remarks, etc., etc., I do feel myself destitute of that moral courage, or rather indifference to the respectability of the Church, which will enable me to bear the cross, despising the shame of a policy which must and will be regarded by very many as groveling, niggardly, and ridiculous, and which is calculated to discourage our friends and rejoice our enemies.

What must be done? Who will make the sacrifice, and get up a weekly paper for the edification and comfort of the whole Church, and the propagation of our excellent doctrines abroad? Any one who will do it shall have all the assistance I can afford. I feel much like shrinking from the task, and would rather bid God speed to another than undertake it myself.

But I do feel I shall have to try it, because no other will. I give you my plan. Brother McPherson, you know, writes well, and has had some experience as an editor. I shall associate him with me, and commence a weekly paper as soon as we can get one thousand advance-paying subscribers, which will about cover expenses, we working for nothing and finding ourselves. We will associate with us as editors (they consenting,) Brothers Ewing, Donnell, Beard, Burrow, Reed, and Anderson, who will incur no pecuniary liabilities, and have not profits, (there cannot be much, if any,) give us the influence of their names, the benefit of their counsel, the assistance of their patronage, and write for the paper as much as time and other circumstances will permit. It is important that the Church should be united. By having these prominent men associated, even though some of them do not write much, they will be more free to make suggestions, give counsel, and guard us against faults and errors. Most men feel to shrink from reproving a brother. Associate editors will feel it a duty, if we err; and we will feel bound to receive admonitions with docility and thankfulness. The contributions of each for the paper will be signed by his initials, unless he direct otherwise. Their names will give us influence—they and their friends will afford to us patronage.

We will be able to publish Brother Donnell's new lectures entire, (which he is now preparing, and which would twice fill a monthly,) Ewing's revised and much enlarged lectures, and, I hope many things worthy of perusal and preservation, from the pens of other editors. We will issue our prospectus as soon as we obtain the consent of the above-named to become associate editors. There is now in the Church manuscript enough to fill all the three proposed, monthlies, for the present year—verily, much more. Your humble servant wishes to say a few things on some theological subjects-if for nothing else, just to let folks know that his head contains something more than the adventures of 'INEBRIATES,' and 'DANCING MANIACS.' Please to consent to my proposition, and return me a speedy answer, that I may issue our prospectus before I go to the East to lay in a stock of books. Excuse all mistakes. Love to Sister Beard and children. Wife and daughter join me.

Yours, in the best bonds,

F. R. COSSITT.

Early in the year 1843 Dr. Cossitt moved to Lebanon, and took charge of Cumberland College at that place. In a short time the Institution became what is now Cumberland University. He continued in the presidency of the College till the fall of 1844, when he resigned, and was succeeded by Rev. T. C. Anderson. He now gave himself up to the management of his paper, enlarging, and otherwise improving it, as he was able. He continued the publication of the Banner of Peace to the close of 1849. His editorial valedictory is contained in the number of the 24th December, 1849. The paper was transferred to Rev. W. D. Chadick and Mr. W. L. Berry. Mr. Chadick assumed control of the editorial department. After the expiration of eighteen years, it will doubtless be a matter of interest to many of the old readers of the Banner to read again the valedictory of its first editor. I therefore embody it in this sketch:

OUR FAREWELL

Our labors as editor of the Banner of Peace are now

concluded. This is the last number which will be issued under our supervision. The paper has been transferred to others, who have assumed the labors and responsibilities of conducting if according to our contract with its patrons. The 27th number will be issued in a few weeks, perhaps during the first week in January. This short delay is occasioned by the intervening holidays and late changes. The proprietor of the Religious Ark is about to remove to Lebanon; and the list of that paper will be added to the list of the Banner. The skill, industry, and experience of Mr. Berry, as a printer, are well known and appreciated.

It is expected that Rev. David Lowry will remove to Lebanon, and become associated with Rev. Wm. D. Chadick, as pastor of the Church in this place, and that these two brethren will henceforth conduct the Banner of Peace. With this expectation, we have transferred to Brother Chadick the editorial honors and pecuniary responsibilities of the paper, with full confidence that he and his associate will be able to conduct it with an ability which will do credit to themselves, and confer lasting benefits on the Church. We commend the Banner of Peace and its editors to all our friends, and hope they will lend their influence and aid in extending its circulation throughout the length and breadth of our beloved Zion. We believe it is destined for good. God has blessed it, and will yet bless it. Let it go forth, preaching peace on earth and good-will toward men.

In bidding our readers farewell, we have many favors to acknowledge—many blessed memories to treasure up, as a fund for future consolation to a heart that can never cease to be grateful. And to correspondents we would say, if we no more exchange thoughts and tokens of affection on earth, we may address the same Divine throne in each other's behalf, and when life's labors are over, greet each other in a purer, holier clime. We think we have honestly labored for the welfare of our patrons, the Church, and the community. So far as we may have succeeded, we would take no glory to ourselves; so far as we may have failed, we crave charity and forgiveness. Peaceful be our parting. Could the richest heavenly blessings accompany the word, we would feel less regret than we now do in saying farewell.

F. R. COSSITT.

In 1853 Dr. Cossitt published his Life and Times of Finis Ewing. The literary execution of this work would be creditable to any denomination of Christians.

In the same year he was elected by the Trustees Professor Systematic Theology in Cumberland University. This appointment he declined, on account of his age and increasing infirmities.

The last decade of his life he devoted to the management of his own domestic concerns, and no doubt to a more earnest and prayerful preparation for that great change which for years had seemed to be at the door. He had seen his family melt away around him. In addition to the wife of his youth, he had buried a daughter at Princeton. Two others, both young wives, and one of them a young mother, had been taken from him after he came to Lebanon. He had committed to the grave also in Lebanon, an only son and a son-in-law. He had drunk deeply of the cup of sorrow. He had lived an active and laborious life; he had served his generation. The evening of his life was what we would desire after the day which had preceded. It had been in many respects a cloudy day, but its close was calm. In the quietude of his own pleasant home he found time and opportunity for rest, for intellectual refreshment, for meditation and prayer. His sun went gently down.

A few weeks before his death he became unusually ill. For more than two weeks he was closely confined. He endured his affliction as we would have expected, like a Christian; and on the morning of the third of February, 1863, between four and five o'clock, without a struggle, and without a groan, he sunk into the arms of death. Not a muscle of the face was changed in the conflict with the last enemy.

At the spring meeting of the Lebanon Presbytery, in 1863, the following minute was adopted, expressive of the feelings of the Presbytery in relation to the death of Dr. Cossitt:

> The Committee appointed to draft a minute in relation to the death of Dr. Cossitt, beg leave to make the following report:
>
> Dr. Cossitt had been for more than forty years a member of the Cumberland Presbyterian Church. A large portion of that time he had occupied conspicuous positions in the Church. He was especially a pioneer in the work of liberal education among us. The Church always regarded him as one of her ablest and most useful ministers. His pious and consecrated life as a Christian and Christian minister was an illustration of the purity and power of our holy religion, to which we expect always to look back with pleasure, and we hope with profit. He has finished his work. On the 3d day of February, 1863, after an illness of about twenty days, he died quietly and peacefully, and in full hope of the resurrection of the just. His health had been feeble for many years—so much so that for years past he had seldom met with us in the judicatories of the Church. He bore his last, as all his previous afflictions, with the patience and gentleness of a Christian. In view of so solemn and impressive a dispensation, the following resolutions are presented to the Presbytery for adoption:
>
> Resolved, That we hereby express our deep sense of the great worth of Dr. Cossitt, and of the bereavement of the Church in his death.
>
> Resolved, That whilst we feel an unfeigned sympathy with his surviving family and friends, and the Church at large, we will still submit with quietude and humility to the will of Him who orders all such dispensations aright.
>
> Resolved, That we feel ourselves called upon, and that we will endeavor to obey the call, to consecrate ourselves as presbyters, and as Christian ministers, more fully to the great

work which God in his providence has committed to us, seeing that we too may soon be called hence, as our fathers and brethren have been before us.

The Middle Tennessee Synod bore a similar testimony to the worth of Dr. Cossitt, which we find in the following extract from their Minutes:

> Rev. Franceway R. Cossitt, D.D., was raised and entered the ministry in another Church. Near forty years ago he attached himself to the Cumberland Presbyterian Church. He often remarked that he was led to this step by a full conviction of the truth of its doctrines, and especially by his sympathy with the earnest and devout spirit manifested by its ministry and membership, in promoting the great object of the organization of a Church in this world—the glory of God and the salvation of men. He was a pioneer in the work of education among us. His connection with Cumberland College, Cumberland University, and the Banner of Peace, gave him the means of great influence and usefulness in the Church. The committee take great pleasure in bearing their testimony to the fidelity with which he used these means. For some years before his death he had been unable for active service. He bore repeated attacks of sickness, and the gradual decline of life, with great patience, and died full of hope and faith. May his mantle fall upon many of those who are following in his footsteps!

My acquaintance with Dr. Cossitt was very intimate during thirty-three years. I knew him better than most men in the Church knew him. Two years and a half he was my instructor. Six years we were colleagues in the department of instruction in Cumberland College. I was his confidant when he was laboring under the sickening and blighting influence of disappointed hope. In the early operations of Cumberland College he had great difficulty in governing the students. Vicious young men had to be dismissed, and sometimes expelled. He showed me a letter once, while I was a student, in which his life was threatened. I learned from him that such letters were not uncommon. Whilst these troubles existed within, there were dark clouds over the prospects of the Institution. He felt that the Church was tired of it, and sometimes was almost ready to feel that they were tired of him. It was a pioneer work.

After our separation at Cumberland College we were constant correspondents, until I became his neighbor a second time, in 1854. We did not always agree in matters of Church policy, and once or twice in the course of his life an estrangement seemed to be threatened. It is a reflection, however, in which I certainly take great interest now, that what might have been almost expected from the frailty of human nature, and the stormy scenes of more than thirty years, never occurred. I have letters in my possession, containing expressions to myself, and in relation to myself, which delicacy would forbid my making public. He was a great and good man, and has gone to his rest. The Cumberland Presbyterian Church owes his memory a debt of gratitude, especially as an educator, which it will never be able to pay.

In concluding this sketch, I cannot express myself more appropriately than in an outline of the character of Dr. Cossitt which has already been given to the public. I present its substance here:

In contemplating the prominent characteristics of Dr. Cossitt, we consider him—

1. As an educator. Although a minister of religion, he was chiefly known as an instructor. The providence of God threw him amongst us for the fulfillment of a great mission in this respect. The character of his pupils is the best illustration of the character of the teacher. His principal work as an instructor was performed at Cumberland College. During seventeen years he labored in that Institution under disadvantages which could hardly be appreciated now. It was literally for several years a 'log college'—as rough in its exterior as an ordinary barn. Its interior fitness was by no means superior to its outward appearance. The dormitories of the students were coarse cabins, furnished with straw-beds. Other means of comfort were of a similar kind. There was an indifferent library. No apparatus was used for some years. Still, under all these disadvantages, and scores of others which might be mentioned, he collected around him, for year to year, some of the best young men in the land. I take it upon myself, too, to say that a collection of nobler men, or more generous scholars, have left no institution of learning in the South-west, than Cumberland College sent forth in those days. Many of them have passed away, but they have left their mark upon the age in which they lived. Others still survive, stirring actors in the conflict of life. In the pulpit and at the bar their voice is heard; at the bedside of the sick and dying their kind ministrations are imparted; and—it is a tender thought—on the field of battle their blood has been shed.

2. As a Christian minister. Although disease had enfeebled him many years before his death, and old age came upon him prematurely, in which he was able to render but little active service, his early ministrations were effective and popular. They were attended with frequent revivals of religion, and many of the old people of Kentucky still speak of his labors forty years ago with interest and delight. He was not eloquent, in the popular sense of the term. His manner was calm and quiet; but when he was aroused, it was earnest and impressive. His preaching in Baltimore and Philadelphia, in his visit to these cities in 1829, was spoken of in very high terms. He would have been a more popular preacher farther North than in this country.

3. As a public journalist, he was kind, respectful, and dignified. He engaged in no petty strifes—he indulged in no personal abuse. He was no mere sectarian tool. His paper was the Banner of Peace, as well as the Cumberland Presbyterian Advocate. Whilst he was not backward in defending the doctrines

and order of his own Church, he provoked no quarrels. He sought to promote peace; he endeavored to allay strife, both in his own Communion and between his own Communion and others. He maintained his opinions with no intolerant or arrogant spirit.

4. Dr. Cossitt was a catholic Christian. Whilst his fidelity and earnest devotion to the Church of his adoption were unquestionable, he was not a narrow-minded bigot. His incessant labors, his editorials in the Banner of Peace, and especially his 'Life and Times of Finis Ewing,' are monuments of his fidelity to Cumberland Presbyterians. His whole life was an illustration of his catholic spirit.

5. In his intercourse with society he was, in a very high sense of the expression, a Christian gentleman. No man ever witnessed in him a rude act, or heard a rude or uncivil expression from his lips. He respected the feelings of others, and labored to promote the happiness of all around him. There might be differences of opinion between him and his brethren, or his neighbors; but on his part, at least, they were attended by no unkind feelings or harsh words. There was charity enough to cover a multitude of sins, if there were sins to be covered. He was a chastened, thoughtful, and courteous Christian minister.

Dr. Cossitt's youngest daughter survives him. At his death, she and a granddaughter were his only living descendants.

REV. CLAIBORNE ALBERT DAVIS
(1825-1867)

Sources: Mrs. Anna Davis; Rev. Hugh R. Smith; **Banner of Peace**; **Memphis Bulletin**; **Memphis Avalanche**; **Memphis Christian Advocate**.

Claiborne Albert Davis was born in Hardin county, Tennessee, November 8, 1825. He was the son of Chesley B. and Hannah Davis, and the youngest of seven children, four daughters and three sons. When he was quite young his parents moved to Illinois. A short time after reaching Illinois his father died, and the mother with her children moved to St. Louis county, Missouri, where they lived until 1841. The sisters all having married, and three of them having settled in Platte county, the mother with her two youngest children, Claiborne and William, followed them.

It was while Mr. Davis, then a youth of sixteen years, was living with her brother-in-law, Mr. John Stokes, that he was first brought in contact with Cumberland Presbyterians. He professed religion at one of their camp-meetings held in the neighborhood. This occurred in September of 1842. In August of the following year he united with the Cumberland Presbyterian Church. In October of 1845, he was received as a candidate for the ministry by the Platte Presbytery. By the same Presbytery, in April of 1846, he was licensed as a probationer for the holy ministry. At a meeting of the Presbytery in the fall of the same year, an order was passed directing him to prepare for ordination at the next regular meeting of the Presbytery. At the next meeting, which embraced the first Sabbath in April, 1847, after the customary examination, he was set apart to the whole work of the ministry. The occasion is said to have been one of peculiar interest and solemnity. The late Rev. Hugh R. Smith seems to have been his principal instructor in his studies preparatory to the ministry. Mr. Smith gave direction to his English studies and also to his studies in theology. He made in addition some progress in the study of Latin.

The first six months after his ordination he devoted to missionary work, chiefly in the cities of St. Joseph and Platte. In the fall, however, of 1847, he took up his residence in Platte City, and this became his first permanent charge. While there he determined to spend some time in Chapel Hill College, an institution of learning at that time under the direction and control of Missouri Synod. He felt the necessity of an extension of his education, but the experiment did not work well. His health failed, and he went back to Platte City.

In 1850, Mr. Davis was married to Miss Rebecca Robinson, of Clay county, Missouri. She lived, however, but a few months. In 1851, he was called to the charge of Lexington Congregation, also in Missouri. His labors there are said to have been very great. In addition to his principal work in the city, he was instrumental in building up a good congregation at Mount Hebron, twelve miles from Lexington, where he preached once a month. He performed a great deal of labor in holding protracted-meetings in the country around. Says my informant: "I can give you no idea of how much labor he performed. He went through heat and cold, and was sent for from places far and near to hold meetings, and raise funds for other congregations."

In December of 1852, he was married a second time, to Mrs. Anna Digges, of Lexington. She still lives a respected widow, struggling with a meek and quiet spirit, and as a "widow indeed" under the burden which God in his mysterious providence has caused to be left upon her solitary hands. Mr. Davis remained in Lexington till 1859. In the fall or early winter of that year he was called to the pastoral care of the Memphis Congregation, as the successor of Rev. Dr. A. M. Bryan. Previous to his call to Memphis he had been called by the congregation of Lebanon, Tennessee. A deep interest was felt by the Lebanon Congregation in procuring his services. This call, however, he had declined.

Mr. Davis had from the beginning of his ministerial work been regarded as a man of unusual interest and promise, but he never developed himself fully until he came to Memphis. He found himself there in a situation well calculated to bring out his whole strength, intellectual and spiritual, and he seemed at once to expand forth to the fullness of the demands of his new circumstances. He soon stood in public estimation in the front rank of an able ministry of a great and growing city. The congregation had four years previously lost a pastor by death, whom they loved almost to idolatry, and who was certainly one of the most promising young men in the Church, or in any of the Churches of the country; they had just previously lost a pastor of eminent worth and ability by his removal to a former charge; but now their losses all seemed made up to them. As an evidence of the promising condition of things, the house of worship was soon found to be too small for the accommodation of the large assemblages that attended on the customary ministrations of the new pastor. The necessity of enlargement was forced upon the attention of the congregation. Steps were taken in that direction, but the war came on, and everything was thrown into confusion. The walls of the building, however, were put up and roofed, and the lecture-room finished for use. The whole work was consummated in the spring of 1867. It is a magnificent building, and a monument of his energy, perseverance, and influence with his people.

In the course of the war and toward its close, he received a call to the pastorate of the Pine Street Presbyterian Congregation in St. Louis, as the successor of Rev. Dr. McPheeters. He visited the congregation, and preached a few times, but the call was declined.

In May of 1866, Mr. Davis was appointed by the General Assembly of his own Church as a delegate to the General Assembly of the Presbyterian Church, South, which was to meet in Memphis in the following December. He accordingly attended the meeting of the Assembly to which he was appointed, and in the course of his address on that occasion he brought up the subject of a union of the Presbyterian Church, South, and the Cumberland Presbyterian Church. The suggestion seemed to be, and no doubt was, received with great favor by the Presbyterian Assembly, and a committee was appointed by that body to meet a similar committee which it was supposed would be appointed by the General Assembly of the Cumberland Presbyterian Church, that they might jointly consider the question of a union of the two denominations. A committee was appointed by the Cumberland Presbyterian Assembly at its meeting also in Memphis, in May of 1867. The joint-committee met in August of the same year, in Memphis. The subject was very frankly and kindly discussed during a meeting continued by adjournment from day to day for several days, but the union was not consummated. The spirit which prevailed, however, throughout the consideration of the delicate question, was creditable to both parties.

In 1866, the degree of Doctor of Divinity was conferred upon Mr. Davis by the Trustees and Faculty of Cumberland University. Rev. A. J. Baird, pastor of the First Cumberland Presbyterian Church in Nashville, received the degree at the same time.

I have in possession some memoranda of the early religious life and ministerial labors of Dr. Davis, furnished by the Rev. Hugh R. Smith, who, it will have been observed, was his early religious counselor and instructor. I introduce these substantially in the words of the writer. They give the best insight into his early and true character:

RECOLLECTIONS OF REV. C. A. DAVIS, D.D.
BY REV. H. R. SMITH

Rev. Claiborne A. Davis, D.D., professed religion at a camp-meeting held by Cumberland Presbyterians at the Bee Creek Camp-ground, in Platte county, Missouri. The meeting embraced the second Sabbath in September, 1842. At that time he was living with his brother-in-law, Mr. John Stokes, in Platte county, near the little town of Barry, situated on the line between Platte and Clay counties. I learned his name, and that he had professed religion, from some friends with whom I was intimately associated, and who also were acquainted with him, and had knowledge of the interesting step which he had taken. In the course of the spring and summer of 1843, my ministerial duties required me to pass frequently through the neighborhood of Mr. Stokes, with whom he, his mother, and two brother, made their home. Sometimes I stopped at Mr. Stokes's house. These visits, and my meeting with Claiborne at some of my appointments for preaching, afforded me an opportunity of becoming intimately acquainted with him, and laid the foundation of that strong attachment which ever existed between us, and of the high estimate which I placed upon his piety, zeal, and ability for usefulness. This estimate I continued to entertain to the end of his life. It increased with his increasing years.

At a camp-meeting at Lebanon Meeting-house, in the western part of clay county, embracing the fourth Sabbath in August, 1843, Claiborne united with the Cumberland Presbyterian Church. I was invited by the Church session to assist them in conducting the meeting, and to officiate as their Moderator during the occasion. Of course I was present when he made application for membership, and attended to the examination on experimental religion. It occurred on Sabbath-morning of the meeting. The examination being approved on the same morning at the commencement of the public service, he stood up in the presence of the large congregation and received the ordinance of baptism. Never shall I forget the deep and solemn impression made upon my mind when the tall and slender figure of youthful manhood arose and stood before me, receiving the seal of God's covenant and making the vow of unceasing devotion to his service-a vow which he so faithfully kept to the end of his life.

After that meeting I occasionally met with Brother Davis as I passed through the neighborhood, or at some of the meetings which I held in it, and he always met me with indication of regard and esteem which I fully reciprocated as long as he lived. Our mutual attachment seemed to strengthen with each meeting. This was at least my own experience toward him. At one of my meetings Brother Stokes observed to me that something unusual was evidently resting with great weight upon Claiborne's mind; that he never participated in the amusements of the young people with whom he associated; that, on the other hand, he was commonly silent, and rather sought solitude; that when at work he often appeared so absorbed in subjects of thought, that he was scarcely capable of attending to business; and that every moment of respite from business he devoted to reading his Bible. I suggested to his brother-in-law that perhaps Claiborne was laboring under the impression of a call to the ministry; that the matter ought to be inquired into; and if that was the burden which was resting on his heart, he ought to be encouraged to go forward, and that himself and his other friends must afford him assistance.

In the month of June, 1845, while I was sitting in my study at home one day, Brother Davis unexpectedly called on me. He appeared to be agitated, and in a great hurry. I asked him for an explanation. He replied that his mind was deeply impressed with the conviction that it was his duty to preach, and he had come to me for counsel; that he had no education, and had not the means of obtaining it; that his friends were poor and unable to help him, and he knew not what to do. As he uttered these words his countenance and manner indicated intense agitation of mind, and a deep sense of the responsibility of the work toward which his attention was directed. I told him he must content himself and remain with me till morning, and then I would give him such counsel as I should consider adapted to his case. He consented to do so. I then entered into conversation with him upon the exercises of his mind. He gave me a clear, and what seemed to be, a candid account of his thoughts, and feelings, and discouragements, in relation to the subject which was before his mind. I felt perfectly satisfied of the line of duty to which the Spirit and providence of God were calling him.

The next morning, after I had myself sought divine direction, I advised him to enter immediately upon a course of preparation for the ministry; if an opening should present itself for obtaining a classical education, to accept it without hesitation; but for the present to go and associate himself with Brother John A. Prather, who was at that time preaching as a missionary in the northern portion of Platte county; to exercise himself in exhortation as often as opportunity offered; to read the Bible every day; to study English Grammar under the guidance of Brother Prather, who I knew was capable of instructing him; to write a sermon on some text of Scripture which he might select; and at the next meeting of Platte Presbytery to offer himself as a candidate for the ministry, after which I would give him farther advice. He yielded to my counsels, and started immediately to join Brother Prather.

In the course of the summer he visited me, in company with Brother Prather. Indeed, they considered my house their home. I examined him on English Grammar and theology, and found that he was making commendable progress. I also received many favorable reports concerning him from the different portions of the district in which he was laboring in connection with Brother Prather. All accounts were favorable in relation to his piety, zeal, and promise in every respect. He was with me at some protracted and camp-meetings at which I witnessed his performances in public prayer, exhortation, and instruction of mourners, which I thought fully justified the favorable reports which I had received concerning him.

Before the close of the summer he had made so favorable an impression upon the minds of the people that he received considerable assistance in contributions of money and clothing. As the time for the meeting of Platte Presbytery drew on, and no opening presented itself for his entering a good school, having consulted my family and also his brother-in-law in relation to his case, I determined to take him to my own house, and give him such instruction as he needed, it being understood that his relatives and other friends should furnish some provisions in consideration of his boarding, and needful clothing, whilst otherwise his board and instruction should be gratuitous.

At the meeting of the Platte Presbytery, embracing the first Sabbath in October, 1845, Brother Davis was received as a candidate for the ministry. At the close of the Presbyterial-meeting I made known to him the arrangement which had been made for his board and instruction, with which he seemed highly pleased. Soon after this, he and Brother Prather came to my house and entered upon a course of study. We fitted up a little room for them apart from my family-room, and furnished it with other conveniences in addition to my library. The plan of instruction was the following; Scripture readings in the morning, recitations in their scientific pursuits at noon, and again at night, and a lecture on theology one night in every week. On Sabbath the young men held religious meetings in the country around, sometimes together, and sometimes separately. The progress of Brother Davis in English Grammar was also greatly facilitated by attending a lecture on that subject from a competent teacher one day in each week during the winter.

At the meeting of the Presbytery in the spring, embracing the first Sabbath in April, Brother Davis having read a discourse, and undergone the customary examinations with approval, was licensed to preach the gospel as a probationer, and appointed to preach in the southern portion of the Presbytery as a missionary. Before he commenced his labors I gave him some instructions on the subject of the proper method of pursuing his studies, both literary and theological, in connection with his itinerant preaching. In the course of the spring and summer he visited me every two weeks. I of course had an opportunity of ascertaining his progress, and adding such instruction and counsel as I thought he needed. He was often with me at protracted and camp-meetings. I heard him preach frequently, and always wondered at his soundness in doctrine, his correctness in the expositions of the Scriptures, and the power of his pulpit performances. He was greatly admired everywhere as a young man of unusual promise. He knew he was popular, but he seemed never to be puffed up with pride or self-conceit. Piety, zeal, humility, and devotion to his Master's cause appeared always to be the leading characteristics of his giant mind.

At the fall session of the Presbytery, embracing the first Sabbath in October, an order was passed for his ordination, to take place at the next regular meeting of the Presbytery. He immediately returned to my house, and entered upon his studies preparatory to ordination. He prosecuted them with great interest and ardor, intent on coming fully up tot he requirements of the Form of Government. During the winter he also preached regularly at Platte City, and occasionally elsewhere, with increasing popularity.

The Presbytery met on Thursday preceding the first Sabbath in April. Brother Davis was examined on the parts of trial preparatory to ordination, and the examinations being eminently satisfactory, he was set apart to the whole work of the ministry. It was one of the most solemn and impressive ordinations that I ever witnessed. The tall figure of the youthful probationer bowed low in the dust before God, with his head inclined downward to receive the imposition of the hands of the presbyters, and the weightier burden of the obligations which those hands imposed, was an impressive sight. The probationer wept. The voice of the presiding minister faltered as he offered the ordination-prayer. The ministers, while they stood around with hands imposed upon the head of the youthful candidate, in like manner-wept. It was evident that God was there, and we felt that the act was approved. He was again appointed to preach as a missionary in the southern portion of the Presbytery, as far north as St. Joseph, and, by the request of the members of our Church in that and Platte City, he agreed to preach one Sabbath in the month in each place. He visited me occasionally for the purpose of receiving additional instruction, particularly in some difficult points in theology.

In the fall of 1847, Brother Davis made Platte City his place of residence, and the people there made a contribution of means for his support at Chapel Hill College, with a view to enabling him to take a full collegiate course. He went to the institution, and spent some time there, but perceiving that his health was likely to fail, he returned to Platte City, and commenced preaching regularly there and at St. Joseph. He labored at these points and in the country around until the fall of 1850, when a portion of the Platte Presbytery was detached from it, and attached to the Barnett Presbytery. By this arrangement Brother Davis was thrown into the latter, and we were thus partially separated in our ministerial labors. In the fall of 1851, he was called to the charge of the congregation in Lexington. While he was there I assisted him at three sacramental-meetings, and in a protracted-meeting at Wellington, in Lafayette county. We met at the meetings of the Missouri Synod, and sometimes on other occasions. I found him at all times the same humble, earnest, devoted Christian minister that I had been accustomed to consider him from the beginning. He was always popular, and was fully aware of his popularity, yet the sanctifying grace of God seemed to keep in subjection his naturally lofty spirit and large heart, and to direct all to the promotion of one great object-the interests of the Redeemer's kingdom on earth.

In the autumn of 1867, the yellow fever visited Memphis. In the summer preceding, Dr. Davis's session had allowed him a short vacation, which he spent at one of the watering places in Kentucky. He returned to his charge greatly invigorate, and, as it would have seemed, prepared for the labors of a long life. The epidemic, however, soon developed itself. It appeared to be especially violent in the part of the city in which he resided. He girded himself for the responsibilities of the terrible visitation. He visited the sick; he stood as a comforter at the bedside of the dying; he followed the bodies of the dead to their last resting-places. He preached, and talked, and prayed. He was far from confining his labors to the members of his own immediate congregation. He went wherever the voice of suffering and sorrow called him. Many a sinking spirit was strengthened and comforted by the strong and earnest manner in which he presented the truths and promises of our holy religion. His presence was felt as an angel of mercy. On Sabbath, the 13th of October, he preached to his congregation on the following words, than which one could have been more appropriate to their circumstances: "Be careful for nothing, but in all things with prayer and supplication make your requests known unto God." His health still seemed to be good, but that night he had unfavorable symptoms. These, with slight alternations, grew more and more discouraging, until it became evident that the epidemic was upon him in a violent form, and that he must die. The circumstances attending his sickness and death were such as seldom fall to the lot of mortals. It was a triumph, something like a departure in a chariot of fire. Others, however, shall give the details of this afflicting, but nevertheless glorious occasion. I quote from the Banner of Peace the first announcement of his death to his friends at a distance. The number is under date of October 24, 1867:

> With a sad and sorrowful heart we announce the death of Rev. Dr. C. A. Davis, of Memphis, Tennessee. He died of yellow fever at his residence in that city on the 19th instant.
> Believing, as we sincerely do, that he was one of the most powerful pulpit orators in America, we consider his loss one of the saddest bereavements the Cumberland Presbyterian Church has ever been called upon to suffer. The melancholy intelligence did not reach us until our paper was ready to go to press, hence we defer a more extended notice for our next issue; besides, we feel that tears are more appropriate now than words, and with a stricken heart we weep for him whom we loved with all the tenderness of a brother."

From the Banner of Peace of October 31 I copy a more extended notice:

> With melancholy pleasure we yield our columns this week to the testimonials obtained from various sources in relation to the death of Rev. Dr. C. A. Davis, of Memphis, Tennessee, who died of yellow fever at his residence on the 19th instant, at twenty minutes past four o'clock P.M.
> Though we were in daily communication with him through mutual friends by telegraph, and notwithstanding each successive dispatch became more and more sad and alarming, thereby tending to prepare us for the worst, yet when the telegram came on Saturday afternoon, 'Dr. Davis is dying,' we in a moment felt that our mind and heart had not been adjusted to the dreadful stroke. And even now, though the sad event occurred several days ago, we find it exceedingly difficult to yield without a murmur to the afflictive dispensation. This, however, is wrong, and we would, though our very soul is smitten with grief, bow in humble submission, and say, 'The Lord gave, and the Lord hath taken away; blessed be the name of the Lord.'
> In the death of Dr. Davis not only the Cumberland Presbyterian Church, but the whole Christian world sustains a loss; for, without doubt, he was one of the brightest stars that adorned the firmament of the American pulpit. Deprived at an early age of his father, he was thrown upon his own efforts and resources. The difficulties with which he had to contend would have crushed an ordinary spirit, for he has often rehearsed them to us; but by persevering industry and untiring efforts, the unlettered youth arose from one position to another until he became one of the leading spirits of the age.
> How mysterious to us are the ways of Providence in permitting such a man to be snatched from the work which he so dearly loved while yet in the prime and vigor of manhood! Truly his loss is a calamity to society, and we cannot avoid weeping when inexorable death places his extinguisher on lights so brilliant;

especially when, to all human appearances, they have not burned half way down to their sockets.

We have said, and we sincerely believe, that he was one of the most powerful pulpit orators of the age. The truth is, God made him great, a man of most commanding and graceful appearance, fine form, and piercing eye; yet he was a mild and gentle as a child. It is true he was not remarkable for what the world calls the graces of elocution; for he was above the formularies and trammels prescribed by the books. His was the eloquence of truth and earnestness-an eloquence bold, fervid, vigorous, like the great gospel he preached-an eloquence which, as a mighty tornado, prostrated every thing before it. But he is gone! His career was brief, but it was a success. He lived to some purpose, and the heritage of such a life consecrated to God is a rich legacy to the Church which will stimulate others to like deeds of Christian heroism.

He was a model pastor as well as a powerful preacher. Vast multitudes, both of the living and the dead, can testify that 'Christ, and him crucified' was the Alpha and Omega of all his efforts. Never was a pastor more beloved by a people, and never a people more beloved by a pastor. As an evidence of this, his Church has resolved to continue his salary to his family until next May;and, aside from his wife and children, his flock lay next to his heart.

We have stated before that his life was a success-a brilliant success. He entered the ministry at an early age, and with a singular unity of purpose he consecrated his whole life to the great work-never engaged for a single day in any secular avocation; yet no man was more liberally provided for. What a commentary on the truth of the Bible, and what a rebuke to his surviving brethren in the ministry who are holding to the cross with one hand and to the world with the other! And hear him, even in his last interview with his family; turning to them, he said: 'To God and the Church I commit you.' He leaves a wife and five children to mourn his loss; to mourn only as such a wife and children can mourn such a husband and father. May God's grace sustain them, and may the mantle of the father fall upon the sons that he leaves behind!

We forbear farther comment on the dying scenes of this great and good man; for with us it is a matter of too much tenderness. With weeping eyes and a sorrowful heart, therefore, we leave the subject and present to our readers a brief account of the closing scenes of one of the most triumphant deaths which history records.

The following is from the **Memphis Bulletin** of October 20:

The religious community were profoundly impressed

yesterday by the announcement of the death of Rev. Dr. C. A. Davis, the beloved and regretted pastor of the Cumberland Presbyterian Church. At twenty minutes past four o'clock yesterday afternoon, full of faith, and with a hope of a glorious resurrection, his spotless spirit passed away from earth. Only a few days ago he was laid on a bed of sickness which ultimately proved a bed of death. His death-bed was, however, one of triumph, and made one ready to exclaim, 'O that I might die like the righteous, and that my last end might be like his!' During his last illness Dr. Davis had full possession of his mental faculties, and had for each one who approached his bedside a kind and cheering word. He frequently talked of all that the Saviour had done for him, and few that visited him in his last sickness will ever forget the angelic words which he uttered. Each day he lay languishing on the bed from which he was never to rise produced its series of sermons, so to speak; for he was ever full of good counsel, and spoke to his clerical and lay brethren almost like one inspired. He was perfectly calm and of tranquil mind on the morning of his death. He felt that his end was approaching; that he had fought the good fight; that he had completed his Master's work on earth, and was about to be called to receive his reward in those bright realms beyond the grave, and to hear the Master he had served so faithfully on earth say to him, 'Well done, good and faithful servant, enter thou into the joy of thy Lord!' Death had no terrors for him, for he frequently expressed himself satisfied with the will of God in thus taking him away so early from the field of labor, and in the fervency of his joy he exclaimed, just before his spirit passed away, 'O, is it possible that in a short time I will be with Christ and his apostles?' He then called his beloved wife and children around his bedside and delivered to them a brief parting address, in which he told them to be of good cheer; that although he was about to be taken from them, the separation would soon come to an end, and that in a short time they would all be reunited in heaven, where there was no sin or sorrow, and where they would meet to part no more. As these heaven-like words passed from his lips, he gently closed his eyes and fell asleep in Jesus. Thus died a truly Christian minister, one who was not only honored and respected by the clergy and laity of his own denomination, but also by many Christian virtues had endeared himself to many of the citizens of Memphis. He leaves a widow and family to lament the loss of him who was the kindest of husbands and tenderest of fathers.

During his last illness the deceased was daily attended by Rev. Dr. Steadman, Rev. Mr. Graves, Rev. Mr. McPherson, Rev. Mr. Johnson, Rev. T. D. Witherspoon, and other clergymen, with many of the members of his congregation, both male and female.

The attending physicians were Drs. Snyder, Avent, Chandler, and Mallory, all of whom did everything in their power, or which medical skill could suggest, but it was unhappily of no avail.

I quote also from the **Memphis Bulletin** of October 21, in relation to the funeral-services:

Few deaths have occurred in Memphis for a lengthened period which have caused so profound sorrow as that of Rev. Dr C. A. Davis, whose demise, after a short illness, on Saturday afternoon, was referred to in the Bulletin of yesterday. The funeral-services took place yesterday forenoon at eleven o'clock, in the Cumberland Presbyterian Church, and were largely attended, the sacred edifice being crowded to its utmost capacity. Eleven o'clock was announced as the hour at which the funeral-services would commence, but long before that hour the pews were occupied by the sorrowing members of the congregation who had come to pay the last mark of respect to the remains of him whom they had so much loved and respected, and under whose ministrations they had sat with so much profit while he preached to them the glad tidings of salvation. At the hour above mentioned the coffin, containing all that was mortal of the esteemed divine, was borne into the church and placed in front of the altar. As the coffin, on which were several wreaths of beautiful flowers, was borne up the aisle, audible sobs could be heard arising on every side, while many strong men were observed to shed tears at the great loss all have sustained. The church was appropriately draped in habiliments of mourning. Behind the pulpit festoons of black cloth were pendant from the pilasters. The pulpit, reading-desk, altar, chairs, and gasaliers, were all covered with the same material, while wreaths were pendant from the chandeliers, and from the front of the chair-gallery. On the pulpit platform were the following clergymen: Rev. Dr. Steadman, Rev. Dr. Ford, Rev. Dr. Guilford Jones, Rev. Mr. Graves, Rev. Mr. Sample, and Rev. Mr. McPherson.

The funeral-services were conducted by Rev. Mr. McPherson, of the Cumberland Presbyterian Church, and Rev. Drs. Steadman, of the Presbyterian, and Ford, of the Baptist Church. The two latter made appropriate and impressive addresses. I quote a passage from the address of Dr. Ford. It is an account of the exercises of Dr. Davis the last day, and a few of the last hours of his life:

"On Saturday morning," said Dr. Ford, "his physician called upon him. He asked him: 'Is there any hope for me? Do you think I am going to die?' The answer was silence, accompanied with tears. Rev. Dr. Steadman, Rev. Mr. Witherspoon, and Rev. Mr. Graves, had now arrived. He told them he was going to die, and repeated aloud the whole of the twenty-third Psalm. Prayer was then offered, and he joined in it with a calm resignation. This was about ten A.M. Through the lingering hours of the day he frequently asked the time, and to each one who entered addressed himself with calmness, recommending the religion he had preached to them, and exhorting them to meet him in heaven. 'Tell your people,' said he to Rev. Mr. Graves and myself, 'that I die in this faith-faith in Jesus.' 'It may seem singular,' said he, 'to some people, that a professor religion and a minister of the gospel, dying, should express himself as I feel, that I am a poor sinner deserving nothing; but this is a part of religion. Religion may be said to have two halves to it: one half to know and feel yourself a sinner, the other half to know that Christ is your Saviour.' He repeated with touching emphasis the fifty-first Psalm: 'Have mercy on me, O God, according to thy loving kindness;' and when his memory failed in repeating it, he called on me to read the remainder, while he made remarks most striking and affecting on almost every verse. I then turned to the twenty-seventh Psalm, and read down to the words, 'Wait upon the Lord and be of good courage,' when he interrupted me, saying, 'Now let us wait-wait upon the Lord. Lord, I wait for thee; I shall soon be in glory.' He requested, naming the page in a hymn-book from memory, that a favorite song with him should be sung. I asked him what tune. He answered, 'Mear;' and said, '

I will start it.' He did so, with a calm and steady voice, and we joined with him in singing it. In the course of the evening Rev. Mr. Graves read to him the eighth chapter of Romans. He anticipated the reading, repeating much of it himself. When the fifteenth verse was reached, 'For ye have not received the spirit of bondage again unto fear, but ye have received the Spirit of adoption, whereby we cry, Abba, Father,' he exclaimed, 'I would not give that glorious doctrine for worlds!' He soon after complained of darkness; his sight and hearing began to fail; but he retained his memory and general consciousness clear until four o'clock P.M. At fifteen minutes after four he turned himself, and seemed to be in great agony. We all prayed in deep anguish that he might be relieved from the agony, and might be permitted to die without a struggle. Our prayer was answered; he breathed calmly, and evidently without pain, and in entire silence for about ten minutes, and then, without a struggle, and apparently without a pang, he sweetly fell asleep in Jesus. 'Blessed are the dead that die in the Lord.'"

At the risk of seeming tedious, I must be allowed to make two more extracts. In the **Memphis Avalanche** of October 22 we have the following, so truthful that it must not be overlooked:

> Death discloses the human estimate of character. The weeping crowd at the Cumberland Presbyterian Church on Sunday last, the festoons of mourning, the sad pageant which wended its way through our streets, clad in the habiliments of grief, with the learned, the noble, and the good mingling in the train, were but the honest tribute of hearts that loved and respected the Rev. Dr. C. A. Davis. We have already announced in these columns the death of this eminent divine-a death which has spread a general gloom over the public mind. We join in the universal grief which pervades the community, and feel unwilling to let this good and talented citizen pass away without a brief but heart-felt expression of our appreciation and admiration of his character. The death of a private citizen, endowed largely with all the attributes which adorn life, and possessed of a pure and lofty nature, is regarded as a great loss; but when these qualities are

united with useful talents, with experience in Christian labors, with a temper suited to successful execution, and an ardor of industry in promoting the welfare and happiness of the people, their possessor becomes a public property, and his death is a public as well as a private calamity. These were some of the elements of the character of Rev. C. A. Davis, and hence his funeral was one of the largest that has ever taken place in this city, and hence the general grief to which we have alluded. . . . It is almost useless for us to speak of the character of Mr. Davis. He was certainly an eloquent, learned, and upright Christian. He was beloved by all who knew him. His grave and stern dignity of character, his want of deceit and palaver, and his detestation of hypocrisy and humbuggery, did not make him a favorite on a casual acquaintance. But he had the nobility of character, the solid worth, the steadfastness of mind, which fixed the admiration and bound his friends to him with hooks of steel. The characteristic of his great mind was solidity. He cared nothing for the meteoric flashes of oratory, and there was more of strength and energy in his style of speaking than of eloquence. He had that energy which always indicated honest sincerity, and hence he forced the assent of his hearers, instead of stealing their admiration. There was no subject beyond the grasp of his powerful intellect, and no theme, however complicated, that he could not unravel by his analytical powers. He possessed the reasoning faculty, in its practical application, in an eminent degree. As he thundered great and eternal truths in the ears of sinners, his stern and solemn accents seemed tolling the knell of immortal souls. He talked plainly, like a fearless man, confident of the truth of what he was saying, and ready to stake his life on the issue. . . . In the moral qualities which constitute firmness and decision of character, he had no superior among all his contemporaries. He never sacrificed the true to the expedient, right to policy. . . . His name ought to be inscribed in the magnificent church which was erected through his energy and piety in letters as imperishable as his greatness is fadeless. Like a true soldier, Mr. Davis died at his post. His nodding plume never led a column into victorious battle, but he blazed out a hero in the vanguard of the world's grand march to eternity. If not mighty in arms, if not invincible in battle, he girded himself for a far nobler struggle, and won upon the vast field of religion and humanity the proudest triumphs. How appropriate to the sublime heroism of his glorious life the truthful language of Milton:

Peace hath its victories,
No less renowned than war.

From the **Memphis Christian Advocate**:

      His dying hours were full of trust, peace, joy, and victory, and while with others we stood by his bed listening to his eloquent expressions of faith and hope, we felt the truth of what Dr. Steadman then said to the dying servant of God: 'You are to-day preaching the greatest sermon of your life.' That sermon will stir the souls of the preachers who heard it to their latest day. The funeral-services were held Sabbath-morning, in the Cumberland Presbyterian Church-Presbyterians, Methodists, and Baptists suspending services, and joining a sister Church in a sincere tribute of esteem, love, and tears, for a beloved pastor and able minister of Christ. The services were conducted chiefly by Dr. Steadman, of the Presbyterian Church, and Dr. Ford, of the Baptist Church, and the occasion was exceedingly impressive and mournful-a season of deep grief for the loss of a prince in Israel. As we write lying on a sick-bed, we cannot say all we would, and will only add, that in the death of Dr. Davis our city has lost a representative man, and the Church of Christ, a strong, noble, useful, and faithful preacher.

    I have chosen to let others speak thus far of Dr. Davis rather than to speak myself. I add, however, a few words to what has preceded. My acquaintance with him was limited. Our fields of labor were distant from each other, and our ages were different by something more than a quarter of a century.

    The first time I ever saw him was at the General Assembly of 1850, at Clarksville, Tennessee. He was a member of that Assembly from Platte Presbytery. Nothing unusual occurred to attract attention to him on that occasion. He had a youthful appearance; his bearing was rather lofty than otherwise-not, however, by means, offensively so. He was spoken of as a young man of promise. I met him at the Assembly of 1852, at Nashville. On that occasion he preached, perhaps more than once. In the course of the proceedings of the Assembly he made a short but appropriate speech in favor of the establishment of the Theological School which now exists at Lebanon. I saw him at the Assembly at Huntsville, Alabama, in 1858. His preaching there attracted unusual attention, and most probably led to his being called in the course of the following summer or fall both to Lebanon and Memphis, and to his settlement in Memphis in the fall or early winter of that year. He was a member of the Assembly of 1860, and had come to be considered one of the most prominent preachers in the denomination. On that occasion he preached on Sabbath in the First Presbyterian Church a strong, earnest sermon on the "witness of the Spirit." In the meantime he had assisted the pastor of the Lebanon Congregation in a protracted-meeting of several days' continuance. I was surprised at his pulpit performances. They were strong, spiritual, and powerful. His preaching was greatly admired. The war came up, and men from the Southern section of the Church were practically excluded from attendance upon the General Assembly.

    In 1866, I met Mr. Davis for the first time after the meeting in 1860. The meeting at Owensboro was a memorable meeting. I have always since regarded it as the crisis of the Church. It was so regarded at the time by all serious men. Mr. Davis was one of the leading actors in the trying scenes of that occasion. There were honest and very decided differences of opinion upon one or two important questions, not only of ecclesiastical polity, but of moral principle. All those then present who may have survived, and may read this, will recollect his great speech upon these vexed questions. I have called it "his great speech." I so denominate it thoughtfully. It was one of the finest efforts of the kind that I ever witnessed in a deliberative assembly. The ability displayed would have been creditable to any man in any of the high places of the country. I should have so said, and felt, in relation to the merits of the production on whatever side of the troublesome questions under discussion I may have stood. It was afterward published, but the printed copy fell far short of the interest and power of the original.

  I never saw Dr. Davis after that meeting. In a year and a few short months a mysterious Providence removed him under such circumstances as have been described from his post of great usefulness. He was great by nature, and greater by grace. In the prime of life; in the vigor of strong manhood; in the midst of a people regarding him with a feeling kindred to idolatry, the earnest pastor, the husband, the father, is cut down. Resolutions of condolence came up from all sides, but these, however well meant and proper in their place, were but a feeble and unsuccessful effort at filling up the terrible space which had been made vacant by his death. Our last and only true consolation in all such cases is, a trustful conviction that God reigns.

REV. SILAS NEWTON DAVIS
(1808-1854)

Sources: Minutes of the Anderson Presbytery; Mrs. Ella Coffman; Rev. W. G. L. Quaite; and Rev. Drs. A. Freeman and B. H. Pierson.

The parents of Mr. Davis, David and Mary Suter Davis, were married in Abbeville District, South Carolina, June 8, 1770. His mother was born and raised in Pennsylvania, but both her parents were members of the Presbyterian Church. From South Carolina they moved to Greene county, Georgia, where they remained till they had seven children, when they moved to South-western Kentucky, and settled in Livingston county. Here the subject of this sketch was born, May 28, 1808. The parents had ten children, of whom Silas was the ninth. He was baptized by the Rev. Mr. Dickey, pastor of the congregation to which his parents belonged, and it is said that his mother, on the occasion of his baptism, dedicated him to God for the ministry in the Presbyterian Church. We admire the devotion of such mothers to the interests of the Church and the kingdom of Christ, and the kingdom of Christ, and wish we had more of them now. Being dedicated to the Church, he was called Silas, from the name of Paul's companion. His second name was, of course, derived from that of England's great natural philosopher.

In 1825, the family moved still farther south-west, into what was then called, in the language of the times, Jackson's Purchase. They were still, however, in Kentucky. The same year the Anderson Presbytery sent Revs. B. H. Pierson (the present Rev. Dr. Pierson, of Arkansas), and Adley Boyd, as missionaries for twelve months into that section of country. The Presbyterians in that portion of Kentucky were sheep without a shepherd, and David Davis and his family received the young missionaries with cordiality, and connected themselves with the Cumberland Presbyterian Church, and he was made a Ruling Elder in a congregation which was soon organized in his neighborhood. His house became a home for the preachers, when the writer knows, from a sufficient experience, that good homes were not very numerous in that country. A considerable revival soon developed itself under the labors of the missionaries, and among the converts was Silas N. Davis. According to my information, he professed religion in his sixteenth year. There is some difficulty in reconciling other dates to that age; but I suppose it may be safely stated that in his sixteenth or seventeenth year he took that important step. He was, at least, very young. He made profession at Mobley's Camp-ground, in Hickman county.

In 1827, November 14, he was received as a candidate for the ministry by the Anderson Presbytery. The sessions of the Presbytery were held that fall at Elkton, Kentucky. Late in the same fall, or early in the winter, he entered a school which was conducted by the writer at McLemoresville, Tennessee. He was connected there with William A. Bryan, John McKee, and James McKee, who were considerably older, but were preparing for the ministry at the same time. My impression is that Bryan and James McKee were preparing for ordination. It was a very interesting school—something like a theological school in embryo. It was sometimes jocularly called a college, but it had no pretensions of that sort.

Mr. Davis was licensed as a probationer for the ministry September 11, 1828. In the spring of 1829, he was appointed to ride and preach in what was called the Livingston District. The time of his ordination cannot be exactly determined, as some of the Presbyterial records are lost or mislaid, and among them those which relate to this subject. The probability is that he was ordained in the fall of 1830, as he spent the summer of that year at Cumberland College, it seems most likely, preparing for ordination.

He spent the early years of his ministry, from 1828 to 1834, almost entirely in the itinerant work. A good deal of the time he was very closely connected in his labors with Rev. Hugh B. Hill, somewhat the senior of Mr. Davis, a minister of great worth and usefulness, and a fine model for a younger man. The field of their labors extended through Jackson's Purchase, and Christian, Todd, and Logan counties, and some of the adjoining portions of Tennessee.

Mr. Davis was married October 9, 1834, to Miss Elizabeth A. McLean, youngest child of George Brevard and Pamelia Davidson McLean, of Todd county, Kentucky. Mrs. McLean was a descendant of General Davidson, of North Carolina, who fell in one of the conflicts of the Revolution. Mr. Davis himself was, in the line of his father, of Welsh descent, and the original name was Davies. The proper orthography is generally given in the name of Colonel Joseph H. Davies, who fell at the battle of Tippecanoe, and who was a distant relative of our subject.

Mr. Davis was what is called a doctrinal preacher. He studied very carefully, and understood well, the system of doctrines taught by the Cumberland Presbyterian Church. My informant says, that "he was often called upon by persons of other denominations to explain the theology of his Church in a public manner, and that the results were, frequent changes of views to those which he presented, and sometimes changes of Church relations." He certainly had a very intelligent apprehension, as I have mentioned already, of the doctrines of the Church. The baptismal controversy has absorbed to a great extent the religious mind of the country in which he operated for many years. He investigated that subject very thoroughly. All Pedobaptist ministers throughout the South-west have been compelled to the same course, in order to maintain any degree of self-respect, and to keeping their congregations together. Mr. Davis understood that subject, and expounded it very effectively. He never became, however, a regular theological pugilist. He kept a sort of ministerial diary, in which he was accustomed to record all marriages which he solemnized, funeral-services rendered, and sermons delivered upon particular subjects and occasions. He delighted in the work of the ministry. His secular affairs were never allowed to interfere with the demands of duties which he considered to be of immeasurably higher importance. His worldly interests sometimes suffered; still he seemed never to allow himself to think of losses from such a cause. His heart and soul were devoted to higher interests.

After his marriage, Mr. Davis spent the most of his time for a number of years in Todd county. By this is meant that Todd county was the home of his family. He himself traveled a great deal in attending meetings in the adjoining counties. For some years, too, he had the pastoral charge of the Elkton Congregation. He also lived some time in Henderson county.

In 1850, he removed from Todd county, and settled at Cumberland College. His object in this change was the education of his children with greater convenience and less expense. Of course his membership was transferred from the Anderson to the Princeton Presbytery. Here he continued, spending his time in his customary manner, till his death. He preached often and extensively in the congregations around, always with acceptance and usefulness. Here he died, on the 26th day of September, 1854. His death was no doubt hastened, if not caused, by excessive ministerial labors during an unusually hot summer. A relation by marriage, and a fellow-presbyter and near neighbor, Rev. George D. McLean, had fallen in his work a short time before. Another member of the Presbytery, a beloved young man, Rev. J. J. Wilson, had also died in the course of the summer. Mr. Wilson was a student of Cumberland College, but was growing rapidly into usefulness and importance. These successive blows fell very heavily upon Mr. Davis. He felt that additional responsibility was accumulating upon himself in sustaining the interests of the Church in the community around him. There is no doubt that he fell a victim to an oppressive sense of this increasing responsibility. It impelled him to efforts which his physical system was not able to bear. It is mournful to see men who are willing to labor—to spend and be spent for Christ and his cause, men who are so much needed—cut down in the midst of their years and their usefulness. Still it is often the way of a mysterious Providence. He works behind a cloud. We cannot understand what he does, yet we are assured that "righteousness and Judgment are the habitation of his throne." He may call off the shepherd, but he still cares for the flock. Mr Davis died in his forty-seventh year, in the prime of his life, and in the full strength of his manhood. He left a widow and four children, a son and three daughters. Two of his daughters are the wives of beloved young ministers in the Cumberland Presbyterian Church, Rev. James L. Payne, of Tennessee, and Rev. John W. Campbell, of Arkansas. The husband of the other daughter, Mrs. Coffman, is an efficient member of the Church. To Mrs. Coffman herself I am mainly indebted for the materials of this sketch. The son died in 1868. The widow still lives. Mr. Davis was greatly respected and beloved by his family. His influence over them was almost unbounded. He sowed good seed there, too, which developed itself into an early maturity.

There is an incident connected with the life of Mr. Davis too remarkable to be overlooked in such a sketch as this. The authority for it is unquestionable. He had an older brother who professed religion before Silas made a profession. This brother felt it to be his duty to preach the gospel, but shrunk from what seemed to him to be the call made upon him. The younger brother in process of time made a profession, joined the Church, and soon began to turn his attention to the ministry. It is said that the older brother had made it a matter of prayer that Silas might be called to preach, and himself excused. He regarded the apparent call of his brother, when it developed itself, as an answer to his prayers, and turned his attention wholly to other pursuits. Matters stood thus until the death of the subject of this sketch, a space of twenty-six years. When the younger brother was called to his reward, the older felt that the old woe was renewed against him if he failed to preach the gospel. He immediately yielded to what he considered a call of duty, and at the age of fifty-six gave himself up to the work of the ministry. Says my informant:

> Notwithstanding his age, he advanced far enough to be licensed. I heard him preach several times, and was greatly surprised that he succeeded so well, commencing as he did so late in life. I could almost imagine sometimes that I was hearing my own dear, sainted father.

I append here a communication to the Watchman and Evangelist, at that time published in Louisville, by Rev. Milton Bird. The communication was written by Rev. A. Freeman, now Rev. Dr. Freeman, of Greenville, Kentucky:

CUMBERLAND COLLEGE, PRINCETON, KENTUCKY

September 30, 1854.

BROTHER BIRD—My Dear Sir:—The death of our dear Brother McLean has already been announced, and now, after three short months, we are called upon to make a similar report in relation to Rev. Silas N. Davis. And as it was said of the former, it may as truly be said of the latter, 'he died in the midst of his years and of his usefulness, at his post and with his armor on.' Brother Davis was a good man, an efficient preacher, and a wise counselor. In Presbytery or Synod, he was sure to be present, unless prevented by circumstances strictly providential. Indeed, he always looked forward with interest to such meetings, and made his arrangements to attend them, and his advice in all ecclesiastical measures were earnestly sought, and almost universally followed. As a speaker he was argumentative and vehement, abounding in forcible appeals to the judgment and the conscience. He was a vigorous defender of the doctrines of the gospel as set forth in the Cumberland Presbyterian Confession of Faith.

Often, indeed generally, he preached to weak congregations, which were in a great measure destitute of the means of grace, and which would otherwise have perished for the lack of knowledge, discipline, and the comforts of the gospel. He went into the highways and hedges, where there was no earthly prospect of remuneration, and compelled the poor and neglected to come to the gospel-feast. He looked for a reward which was not long delayed. He preached his last sermon to a feeble congregation in Canton, some thirty miles from his home, whither he had gone according to a monthly engagement to break to them the bread of life. He came home sick, and, after two weeks of suffering, he went to another, an everlasting home, where those who have turned many to righteousness shall shine as the stars forever and ever. It was good to see him calmly and triumphantly meet the last enemy. To the writer, who had the mournful pleasure of waiting around his dying bed, and cooling his fevered brow, he said: 'Brother, all these plans will fail, but, blessed be God! the Christian has plans that cannot fail. This is my joy. This is my consolation.' The preceding is a sample of many similar expressions used by him when aroused from the stupor induced by the typhoid fever.

The funeral-sermon of Brother Davis was preached by Rev. W. C. McGeehee, and was one of the most appropriate I ever heard. The remains were borne to their last resting place by the Masonic Fraternity, and buried with the impressive ceremonies of the Order. 'Earth to earth; ashes to ashes; dust to dust; looking for a general resurrection in the last day, when the earth and the sea shall give up their dead.' 'Let me die the death of the righteous; let my last end be like his.'

Brother Davis has left a wife and four children, who feel deeply the bitterness and desolation of widowhood and orphanage. Though they sorrow not as those who have no hope, they need the prayers and sympathies of the Church.

But what is to become of the Princeton Presbytery, bereft in so short a time of its most valued and most useful ministers? Since the last regular meeting of the Presbytery, J. J. Wilson, George D. McLean, and Silas N. Davis, have rested from their labors. The Lord send us help! The Lord send us faithful laborers to take the places of those who have gone to their reward on high!

AZEL FREEMAN.

I append to this sketch two letters written at the request of the family of Mr. Davis, from Rev. Dr. B. H. Pierson, of Arkansas, and Rev. W. G. L. Quaite, of Texas. Dr. Pierson was regarded by Mr. Davis as his spiritual father, and Mr. Quaite was long a fellow-laborer and particular friend. They both knew him well, and no testimony could be more trustworthy than theirs.

The following is the letter from Mr. Quaite, of Texas:

SISTER DAVIS:—It affords me great pleasure to bear my testimony to the worth of such a man as Brother Davis. The lives and labors of men like him are a rich legacy to the Church, and should be preserved. I could write pages in illustration of his character. I knew him long, and loved him much. But others will bear similar testimony, and I will be brief.

The first time I ever saw Brother Davis, he was in attendance upon the sessions of Anderson Presbytery. The meeting was held in Hopkinsville, in the native State of both of us. He was a young man then, and I was a boy not yet out of my teens. I heard him preach an excellent sermon, as I thought. I know it was so regarded by the people generally. The impression prevailed that he was a young man of unusual promise. Two or three years afterward, he and Rev. Thomas Bone came to my father's house. I was not then a member of the Church, but I formed an attachment for him that continued and increased through life. He was at the camp-meeting at which I professed religion, and preached every day with an earnestness and power which carried conviction to many a poor sinner's heart. On Monday evening we retired into the grove together. He talked with me and prayed for me with a tenderness which will never be forgotten. Two hours afterward light, life, and joy indescribable, sprung up in my heart. He was present when I became a candidate for the ministry. At my ordination, he preached the ordination-sermon. He treated the young preachers with so much tenderness that they could but love him. I have labored with him a great deal. The first year of my ministry I rode what was then called the Henderson Circuit. He then lived in Henderson county. In the course of the summer of 1839, we attended a number of meetings together, at every one of which there was a large ingathering. His religion was of a scriptural character. His sermons were always well arranged, and well delivered. And, whilst he was no bigoted sectarian, he loved his Church, and was always ready to defend its doctrines, and he could do it with great ability. He was neither ashamed of the gospel, nor a reproach to it; always in his place in the judicatures of the Church; taking a deep interest in all the business of the body. In all his intercourse with his brethren he was kind, courteous, respectful, and showed a Christian spirit, and many will rise up in the great day of God Almighty and call him blessed.

W. G. L. QUAITE.

The following letter is from Rev. Dr. B. H. Pierson, of Arkansas:

MY DEAR SISTER DAVIS:—Your letter requesting from me something on the subject of the early history of your worthy departed husband, the Rev. Silas N. Davis, was duly received, and I take pleasure in complying with your request, especially as you intimate that I was more familiar with his character and first labors in the ministry than any other person.

In the spring of A.D. 1826, I was ordered by the Anderson Presbytery of the Cumberland Presbyterian Church to travel and preach in what was then called 'the Kentucky portion of Jackson's Purchase,' included in the then recently organized counties of McCracken, Graves, Hickman, and Obion, a field of labor that had been preoccupied by Rev. R. Beard, the present Rev. Dr. Beard, of Lebanon, Tennessee, and John B. McKinney, but which had been abandoned by the Hopewell Presbytery for some time, as included in a Presbytery to which these young men did not belong.

In connection with my much-loved brother, Rev. Adley Boyd, I entered this field, in which there was not a Cumberland Presbyterian minister, or, so far as I remember, an organized congregation. Notwithstanding our great lack of literary and other qualifications for the work, our labors were so blessed that in the brief space of five months the converts numbered more than one hundred. Among them was Silas N. Davis, at that time, I think, about seventeen years old. He had had the advantage of religious training by parents who had belonged to the Presbyterian Church, but who joined the Cumberland Presbyterians with their son Silas.

At the fall session of the Presbytery, Brother Boyd and I were remanded to the same work for the following six months. Soon after I returned to it I was informed by his parents that Silas was impressed to preach. But his age, his almost entire want of education, the entire destitution of schools in that but recently settled region, and the fact that his parents were poor, and consequently unable to send him abroad to be educated, all seemed to present insuperable barriers in the way of his entering the ministry. We were unable, at once, to determine as to the best course to pursue. I proposed to take him with me on the circuit, and teach him, as I might have opportunity, English Grammar and other things that I deemed important, and that, on becoming a candidate for the ministry, I knew the Presbytery would require him to know.

Although the circumstances that attended him in his early youth were very unfavorable to his mental development, I soon learned that he possessed a mind of no ordinary character. His memory, especially, was above ordinary. I will give an illustration: One evening we were going to a night appointment in a neighborhood where a beginner would have but little to fear from the size or intelligence of the congregation, and I proposed to him to exhort and pray. He replied that he knew nothing to say. I proposed to furnish the outlines of a religious talk, and did so by alluding to the parable of the 'Supper' as a suitable representation of the blessings of the gospel—their fullness, their freeness, their adaptation to the situation, circumstances, and wants of the human family—giving the points of a discourse, the clothing of which with such thoughts as I supposed they would suggest to his mind, and the delivery of which might require fifteen or twenty minutes, which was agreed to. The time came. The congregation were present. He lined a hymn; we sang it. He offered a prayer, every word of which seemed to be necessary and in its proper place. He arose from kneeling, commenced where I began, proceeded as I had done, expressing the same thoughts that I had expressed, and in the same order, so far as I could remember, and stopped where I did, without adding a single word or syllable, so far as I could recollect. Although the effort showed his great lack of information, it demonstrated his capacity of learning.

In the following spring (1827), he went with me to Presbytery, and presented himself as a candidate for the ministry. But his awkward appearance, his illiterateness, and (shall I say) his homely costume, all conspired to make the Presbytery reject him, notwithstanding all my efforts to persuade the Presbytery that he had merit. All the encouragement he received was to write a piece on a subject of his own selecting, and be at the next meeting of the Presbytery, in the hope that he might then be received. And to show the liability of the wisest and best man to err in determining as to who should preach the gospel, as well as still farther to demonstrate that his native ability was extraordinary, I will say that three years from that time, at Bethlehem camp-meeting, within six miles of Cumberland College, at 11 o'clock on the Sabbath, and in the presence of Dr. Cossitt, Rev. D. Lowry, and others of like prominence in the Church, he delivered a sermon which was creditable to himself and to the occasion. About this time I became a pioneer in Arkansas, and it was my privilege after that to meet him but rarely; never, except my duties called me nearer to the heart of the Church to attend its highest judicature.

In conclusion, it is but justice to the memory of Brother Davis that I should say he was always affable and pleasant. None that I ever assisted into the ministry gave me less anxiety or trouble.

In Christian kindness your,

B. H. PIERSON.

My own personal acquaintance with Mr. Davis extended over his whole ministerial life. Our intimacy, however, was confined chiefly to its last few years. As I have already mentioned, in the fall of 1827 he came to McLemoresville, for the purpose of entering a school which I was then teaching at that place. He had a youthful and country-like appearance. I had begun to learn a little then of what I have learned a great deal since, that such exteriors often conceal abilities and worth which only want time and means for development. He passed through the school in a quiet manner, attending to his duties and making the usual progress. As I have mentioned before, there were several young men in the school—two or three of them preparing for ordination. A weekly prayer-meeting was kept up, and it was customary for some one of the young men to conduct the meeting. After having been there a few weeks, he was appointed to take his part in that way. Although it seemed a necessary extension of courtesy and encouragement to make the appointment, all were afraid it would not work well, he being so young, and seeming so utterly destitute of experience. He did not hesitate, however, but took his place, opened the exercises with the customary hymn and prayer, and then, instead of carrying the prayer-meeting directly forward, quietly slipped into a text, and gave us a very respectable little sermon of about twenty minutes' length. It took every one by surprise, but satisfied us that time and experience, and the grace of God, would make him a preacher.

He spent some months, and then returned to Kentucky. In the spring of 1830, I met him at Cumberland College. He spent the summer there, but our courses of study were different, and of course we were not very intimately associated.

After my return from Mississippi, in 1843, and when the Green River Synod resolved to make an effort for the reestablishment of Cumberland College, he became deeply interested in that enterprise, and in 1850, as it has been said, bought a home and settled near to the institution. The property which he bought was a part of the old College farm. We lived in adjoining yards until the early part of 1854. He was one of the best preachers of any denomination within the bounds of his operations. His education was not of the highest order, but what he read and heard he used to great advantage. Dr. Pierson has given an illustration of his aptitude in the use of material with which he became furnished from whatever source. This aptitude, perhaps rather improved than otherwise, followed him through life. He never preached a sermon which did not embody a greater or less amount of substantial doctrinal truth. On one occasion, two or three years before his death, he preached in the progress of a revival in Princeton. It was at a night-service, and the house was crowded. An intelligent hearer remarked at the close of the sermon, with earnest significance, that it contained truth enough to lead every hearer in the congregation to the kingdom of God, if it were rightly improved.

The loss of Mr. Davis was a heavy blow upon that portion of the Church with which he was more immediately connected. He was highly regarded both as a preacher and a counselor. As a tribute of respect to his memory, the Presbytery by which he was both licensed and ordained having been divided not long after his death, the new Presbytery received and still bears the name of the Davis Presbytery.

At the time of his death he was President of the Board of Trustees of Cumberland College. He was engaged with others in a vigorous effort to maintain and elevate the institution which had been a clustering point of so much care and labor. He was an earnest man, and in the most exalted work committed to human hands fulfilled an honored and useful mission. His memory is dear to many, and especially to his bereaved family, who loved and honored him almost to idolatry.

REV. GEORGE DONNELL
(1801-1845)

Sources: President Anderson's *Life of Rev. George Donnell*. **Banner of Peace**.

George Donnell was born on the 9th of August, 1801, in Guilford county, North Carolina. He was the son of George and Isabella Donnell. The maiden name of his mother was Kerr. George Donnell, senior, the father, was a ruling elder in Alamance congregation, which was under the pastoral care of Rev. David Caldwell, D.D. Dr. Caldwell was for near sixty years pastor of Alamance congregation. George was the third son and seventh child of a family of twelve children. His parents were of Scotch-Irish descent. He was baptized in his infancy by Dr. Caldwell.

In the fall of 1804 George Donnell, senior, with his family, moved from North Carolina, and settled in Spring Creek congregation, in Wilson county, Tennessee. The Spring Creek congregation was then, and for many years continued to be, under the pastoral care of Rev. Samuel Donnell.

Nothing seems to have occurred in the boyhood and early youth of George Donnell to indicate that he would ever arrive at distinction. His parents attended church with punctuality, and took their children with them. This was a Presbyterian usage in those days. They otherwise instructed and trained their children with care.

When the son was six years of age the mother died. Such a loss is almost always irreparable, and young George seems to have felt the blow in his case very sensibly. After two years of widowhood his father married a second time, but the affections and respect of the son had lost their natural object. Still, he is represented as having been obedient and respectful to his second mother.

He acquired his early education at the school of Rev. Samuel Donnell, pastor of the congregation. In this school he is said to have acquired rapidly the rudiments of an English education. He was also a fine companion, "prominent in every sport, expert at every game, full of hilarity, humor, and wit; ever pleasant and affectionate, the favorite of all his companions." One of his companions says of him, that he "was a warm-hearted, manly, honorable boy; mischievous and wild, but he never did a mean thing; was never profane; and always abhorred a lie."

His father was a farmer; but as the son grew up he exhibited some mechanical tact, and was accordingly placed under the care of a wheelwright in the neighborhood, for the purpose of learning the trade of wheel-making. This, by the way, was a very important business at that time, when all families manufactured their own clothing. About this time, too, he received his first abiding religious impressions. The immediate occasion, however, of those impressions is not known. But his convictions were deep and earnest. They impaired his health, depressed his spirits, and changed his former buoyancy and liveliness into thoughtfulness, melancholy, and gloominess.

At a camp-meeting at Sugg's Creek, in Wilson county, Tennessee, held in August of 1819, he professed religion. He had had a long and painful struggle of mind. His friends had feared derangement. The struggle was succeeded by corresponding peace and joy. "The height of his joy was proportionate to the depth of his despair. His convictions had been agonizing—his transport was rapturous; darkness had long enveloped his mind—the light of the glory of God, in the face of Jesus, shone upon his heart. Though prostrate upon the ground, he seemed to be at the gate of heaven."

By permission of his father, he attached himself to Bethesda congregation, which had originated in a secession of some persons who favored the old revival of 1800, from the Spring Creek congregation, of which his father was an elder.

He immediately became very active and efficient in his neighborhood in promoting prayer-meetings, in exhortation, and in various ways endeavoring to promote the salvation of his friends and neighbors. He was an excellent singer, and became at once altogether useful.

On the 5th of April, 1821, Mr. Donnell was received as a candidate for the ministry by the Nashville Presbytery. The sessions of the Presbytery were held at Moriah Meeting-house, in Wilson county. Soon after becoming a candidate for the ministry he reentered the school of his uncle, Rev. Samuel Donnell, where he studied those branches of science required by the Cumberland Presbyterian Church preparatory to licensure and ordination.While at school he kept up prayer-meetings one or more nights in every week; prayed, exhorted, and labored otherwise for the promotion of religion in the neighborhood. In the fall of 1821 he accompanied some old ministers to what was called the "Mountain District," to aid them in holding camp-meetings. The following winter was passed at school.

In October, 1822, he was licensed to preach at Bethesda Meeting-house, by the Lebanon Presbytery, which had previously been stricken off from the Nashville Presbytery. He was appointed to ride the Lebanon Circuit, in conjunction with Rev. Robert Baker. His labors were greatly blessed. The next twelve months he spent on the Overton Circuit—"the Mountain District."

In the spring of 1824 he was sent, in company with another licentiate, Samuel M. Aston, to East Tennessee. Here he encountered Old School theologians, of the strictest sort, together with Hopkinsianism in full maturity. He labored principally in East Tennessee for twelve months. A good deal of opposition, many trials, but great success, attended his labors.

At the spring sessions of the Presbytery in 1825, at Big Spring Meeting-house, in Wilson county, Mr. Donnell, in company with Abner W. Lansden and Samuel M. Aston, was set apart to the whole work of the ministry, Rev. Samuel McSpadden preaching the ordination-sermon, and Rev. Thomas Calhoon presiding and giving the charge. The following year he spent in East Tennessee. Shortly after the spring sessions of the Presbytery in 1826, by the appointment of the Synod, he visited the Charity Hall Missionary School, located among the Choctaws, then residing in Mississippi. His colleague in that visit was Rev. David Foster. Mr. Foster was much the older minister of the two, and was considered the principal in the appointment. The following was also spent in East Tennessee.

Early in the summer of 1827 Mr. Donnell was married to Miss Elizabeth E. McMurray, eldest daughter of Mr. David McMurray, of Big Spring congregation. The union was in all respects a suitable and happy one.

About the beginning of the year 1829 he commenced his labors in Lebanon. His work here proved to be the great work of his life. When he commenced his labors there was but one house of worship in the place—that belonged to the Methodists. There was also a regularly organized Methodist Society. There was no other organized Christian congregation in the place. He commenced his labors in the court-house. He encountered the usual discouragements, embarrassments, and opposition, from wicked men and sectarian influence, but at length succeeded in collecting and organizing a congregation of seven members—all of these were females. A house of worship was also built in due time. The congregation increased from year to year, gracious revivals were enjoyed, and the good man saw the pleasure of the Lord prosper in his hands. At the time of his death, it was the largest and most influential congregation in the denomination to which it belonged.

In the year 1820 Mr. Donnell commenced preaching to the New Hope congregation, situated about nine miles from Lebanon. He labored here a number of years, in connection with his labors in the Lebanon congregation.

The General Assembly of 1838 was dissolved according to order, and another Assembly appointed to meet in 1840. Of course there was no Assembly in 1839. In the intermediate time between the two Assemblies, however, it appeared that the Cumberland Presbyterian, the weekly organ of the Church, was about to be suspended. The result was, the meeting of a convention in Nashville, in May of 1839, for the purpose of considering the question of a Church paper. A plan was adopted for the publication of a paper, and Mr. Donnell was assigned prospectively to the editorial department. For reasons which need not be mentioned here, the plan was not carried into execution, and the paper was not published.

He continued his labors in the Lebanon congregation up to 1845. His health, however, had become impaired, by insensible degrees, until the early part of that year, when, after severe labor at a protracted meeting in Columbia, and a fatiguing ride home, he was prostrated. At first no serious apprehensions were felt, but his disease soon developed itself in a threatening form. After lingering for some time, on Saturday night, March 22, 1845, he closed his earthly career. His afflictions were borne with patience and quietness. His mind was at peace, "occasionally rising to a rapturous transport that made him long to soar away to visions of God." On the following day, "Sabbath, Dr. Cossitt preached a funeral-sermon to a Church and community overwhelmed with grief; and on Monday his remains were committed to the silent tomb, there to repose till the dead in Christ shall arise to appear with him in glory."

The following is the testimonial of the session of the congregation to the worth of their departed pastor. The preamble and resolutions were adopted on the 25th of March, three days after his death:

> Whereas, it hath pleased Almighty God, since the last meeting of the session, to remove from earth to heaven our much-beloved pastor, Rev. George Donnell; to this inscrutable decree of Providence we mournfully bow with Christian submission, knowing that the great Head of the Church can do no wrong. Yet, as the session of the Lebanon Church, of which he was the spiritual father, we cannot refrain from placing upon the records of our Church an expression of our estimation, as well as that of the members whom we represent, of the great, if not irreparable loss, which we have sustained in this afflictive dispensation of Providence.
>
> He whose death we now so deeply deplore was the

founder of our Church in this place, and has sustained to it the endearing relation of pastor since its organization in the year 1830. By him its members, every one, were received into the Church, and all of its elders ordained. By his fostering care, and efficient instrumentality under God, it has grown up from infancy to its present size and condition. He had watched over its growth and progress with a solicitude and interest which could only be equaled by that of a good and tender father toward his children. During the fifteen years he has occupied the pastoral relation to our Church, he has been the first and only choice of its members. At no time would they have willingly submitted to a change. He was indeed a good shepherd, loved by his flock, and respected by all. As a minister, he was able, zealous, and devoted, occupying his position upon the walls of Zion with dignity, efficiency, and untiring perseverance. As a Christian, he was ever seeking to do good, pouring the balm of consolation into every wounded heart, and illustrating by his walk and conversation the beauties of the Christian character. As a member of society, he was lovely and pleasant; his wife was blameless, and his conduct beyond reproach. This session do therefore resolve—

First. That in the death of the lamented Donnell, the widow has lost a husband, the orphans a father, society one of its most valuable and exemplary members, the Church one of the best of pastors, the ministry one of its brightest ornaments, and the Christian cause one of its most efficient champions and vigilant watchmen.

Secondly. That a copy of this preamble and these resolutions be furnished by the clerk to the widow of the deceased, and to the editor of the Banner of Peace for publication.

Dr. Cossitt thus testifies, in the **Banner of Peace**, of March 28, 1845:

It becomes our duty in this number to communicate to the Church and public an event which will fill many hearts with mourning and many eyes with tears. Rev. George Donnell, pastor of the Cumberland Presbyterian Church in Lebanon, has rested from his labors. * * * The Church for whose interests he has devoted the best years of his life, which has flourished almost beyond example under his pastoral labors, and for which he seemed only to live and labor, will no more hear his instructive voice. The unconverted will no more hear his affectionate warnings, nor the mourning penitent enjoy his faithful guidance to the Lamb of God which taketh away the sin of the world. The people of Lebanon will no more have the benefit of his fervent pleadings in their behalf, nor will his closet longer be a Bethel sacred to the remembrance of their spiritual interests and the conversion of the world. The bower of prayer near his country residence will no longer witness his heart's agony and his spirit's groanings for those who despise God's law. * * *

During his sickness he seemed entirely to trust his all with the Saviour whom he loved, and most strikingly exemplified the power of sustaining grace under the severest trials. The blessed gospel which he preached to others was his consolation when earthly comforts failed, and at times filled him with exceeding great joy and rapturous emotion. He expressed his resignation to the Divine will, whether to live or to die.

When we remember his career of surpassing usefulness, the confidence with which all who knew him regarded him, the tender affection with which his people loved him—when we reflect that he had arrived only to his forty-fourth year, and was filling one of the most important stations in his own Church, or perhaps of any other in the South-west, it seems to be a mysterious providence which has removed him. Well are we assured that our loss is his gain. But we are led in inquire, Why was such a father called from a most interesting family, when his continuance with them seemed to mortal minds so necessary and desirable? Why was a pastor so able, faithful, and successful, called from so wide a field of usefulness? Why was the Presbytery and Church to which he belonged deprived of a counselor so valuable—one whose mind was sufficiently capacious to pass beyond mere local interests, comprehend all the parts of a great whole, and regard with equal interest all members of our body? Why was this community to lose one of its brightest ornaments, and this generation a burning and shining light?

The following is an extract from the records of the Chapman Presbytery, which met in April, 1845:

Whereas, it hath pleased the great Head of the Church, since our last session of Presbytery, to remove from earth to his rest in heaven our much-esteemed brother, George Donnell; to this most afflicting and inscrutable stroke of Divine Providence we mournfully bow with trembling submission, knowing that the Judge of all the earth will do right. * * *

The deceased was, in all the relations of life, most eminently qualified to impart comfort, and to aid those with whom he stood connected; able in counsel, eloquent in the pulpit, animating in the social circle, and soothing in the chambers of sorrow and affliction. Truly, he was a 'good man, and full of the Holy Ghost and of faith, and much people was added unto the Lord' through his agency and indefatigable labors.

Resolved, That this Presbytery most tenderly sympathize with the widow of the deceased in her irreparable loss, and her children, who have lost a most tender and kind father.

And be it farther resolved, That this Presbytery, in the

death of this esteemed brother, has lost one of its ablest counselors, the Church at Lebanon a faithful pastor, society one of its brightest ornaments, and the world a brilliant example of religion and patriotism.

As a farther testimony of their regard for their late pastor, the congregation at Lebanon erected to his memory a beautiful monument, which still covers his remains in the quiet cemetery of the town. On the face of the monument is a suitable inscription.
In 1849 Mrs. Donnell herself died, and was laid by the side of her husband. On the side of the monument next to her resting-place, in addition to the ordinary inscription, we find the following: "They were lovely and pleasant in their lives; and in death they are not divided."
Mr. Donnell left five children. One of them died soon after his mother; the others still live, and are all members of the Cumberland Presbyterian Church. The eldest, David M. Donnell, has been for some years President of Cumberland Female College, at McMinnville, Tennessee.
Mr. Donnell published two sermons in the **Cumberland Presbyterian Pulpit**: one in 1833, upon "The Gospel Feast;" the second in 1834, upon "The Nativity of Christ."
Of his personal appearance and habits, his biographer gives the following sketch:

> In person he was of about medium stature, slender, and slightly stooped; his head rather under medium size, his hair black and glossy; face rather small and pointed; features delicate; complexion ruddy; eyes clear blue, and ever lighted up with a mild luster; general expression pleasant, but not striking. His bearing modest, retiring, and unpretentious. In society he was easy, affable, and agreeable. Ever cheerful, and abounding in humor and wit, he was the life and soul of the social circle, without seeming to be conscious of his influence. To the young and the old, the gay and the gloomy, he was alike companionable. In the palace of the wealthy, or the cottage of the poor, he was alike at home. His social powers were unsurpassed, and yet he never made an effort to be interesting, or to engross attention.
> In the pulpit, to a stranger, his appearance was not commanding or prepossessing, yet his voice was mellow, and its tones peculiarly tender; and when he commenced speaking, he invariably attracted attention, and as he advanced, he held it enchained. Through the first few sentences his manner was subdued, but soon the heart warmed, and the fire burned, and then, though not vehement or boisterous, his earnestness grew into an agony of spirit while he wrestled for souls, and though he shed not a tear, yet his eyes seemed as liquid as if dissolving in tenderness and sympathy. Or if he discoursed of heaven, or the glories of the Saviour, his whole countenance lighted up with a brilliancy that seemed to be the reflection of the glory he was

contemplating. He conquered and subdued, not by the force of popular eloquence, but by a happy mingling of persuasive tenderness and constraining earnestness. He penetrated the hearts of his audience and subdued them, ere they were aware of his design.

In the preparation of his discourses, he reflected more than he read—relied more upon evolving thoughts from the depths of his own creative mind than upon culling and collecting ideas from books. He kept a good library, and read much when he had leisure; but when he engaged in framing a sermon, he made but little use of books. He used a text as a nucleus around which he grouped his own thoughts, gathered from reflection, experience, and observation. He relied more upon the preparation of the heart, and the elevation of his spirit and feelings to the proper degree of interest and solicitude, than upon the matter of his sermon. And yet his discourses were always fresh and interesting; they came welling up from the inner fountains of thought and feeling, the gushings of a warm heart dissolving with sympathy for souls.

I may add to the preceding personal sketch that the printed sermons of Mr. Donnell are not fair specimens of his abilities and effectiveness as a preacher. He was a natural as well as a practiced preacher, but not a practiced writer; and even if he had been a writer of sermons, there were an aptness, and a facility, and a directness in his style in the pulpit which could never have been represented in print. This is the case with all natural preachers: they can preach better than they can write.

This naturalness of which I have spoken developed itself largely, too, in what might be called tact. Mr. Donnell had a great deal of pulpit tact. It showed itself in his style of expression, in his prayers, in his addresses to serious persons, in his selection of songs in a revival. The right word always seemed to be in the right place, the right song was sung at the right time, the right illustration came up precisely where it was needed.

In short, he presented both publicly and privately such a character and such habits of life and labor as we love to contemplate. We linger upon such memories with delight, and should cherish them as an imperishable treasure to the Church.

This brief sketch must not be concluded without two or three practical remarks which it suggests. And,

First. We see what an amount of good can be accomplished by a man of ordinary abilities and ordinary attainments, devoted to a single object. Five years were spent in missionary labor. No doubt during all that time he was receiving souls for his hire. It has been said, however, that his great work was his work in Lebanon. In the course of the fifteen years of his pastorate there, according to the record, he added two hundred and thirty-six members to his congregation. The session say that "its members, every one, were received into the Church, and all of its elders were ordained by him." The most, if not all, of those members and elders, if not his spiritual children, acknowledged his aid and guidance in the great work of their personal salvation. It should be added, too, that many of these additions were from the most intelligent and influential portion of the community. These were no ordinary results. Few men can show such a record.

Secondly. When Mr. Donnell commenced his labors in Lebanon, he had not even the nucleus of an organized congregation as a basis. He did not, he could not, build upon another man's foundation, because no foundation had been laid. There was material, but nothing more. Still he went to work upon that material; he soon collected and organized a congregation of seven members, all of them being females. To a man of the world this would have seemed a small beginning. Yet earnestness, perseverance, fidelity, and the grace of God carried him forward, and this unpromising beginning became the nucleus of one of the largest and most respectable congregations in the land. There are scores of young men in the Cumberland Presbyterian Church who are standing all the day idle, because no man hath hired them. Why do they not thus go into the vineyard and seek their own hire? The field is wide; openings are numerous; the Lord of the harvest will employ them, and give them wages if they will enter earnestly into the work. Why do they not make the experiment?

Thirdly. The labors and success of Mr. Donnell are an illustration of the importance of the pastoral work as a means of doing good. One who is truly a pastor will live with his people; will see them at their homes; will visit their sick; will bury their dead; will be their counselor and friend in all the exigencies of life. Such a pastorate by an earnest and faithful man will not fail of success. It may be added, too, that such a pastorate is the main reliance of a Christian congregation. It is especially so of a congregation of Presbyterians. Nothing else will serve as a substitute. Mr. Donnell was an earnest and devoted pastor. The impressions which he made still remain. Since his death the congregation have had the services of the best and the ablest men in the Church, and yet after the expiration of near twenty years, when the old members speak of a man after their own heart, they always speak of George Donnell.

Fourthly. I cannot close without an additional remark. The interesting case which we have been considering illustrates another principle. When Mr. Donnell commenced his labors in Lebanon, he had no assurance of a temporal support, or even, I suppose, of the smallest compensation. Yet he entered upon the work; God opened the hearts of the people, and the laborer received even his temporal hire. We have proof enough that in similar circumstances this will always be so. If an earnest and faithful man of respectable ability will give himself up to God and the people, he will receive his reward. The mouth of the ox that treadeth out the corn will not be muzzled. Let our young men who are doing nothing, and waiting for assurances, make the experiment. "Trust in the Lord, and do good; so shalt thou dwell in the land, and verily thou shalt be fed."

REV. ROBERT DONNELL
(1784-1855)

Sources: **Sketch of the Life, etc., of Rev. Robert Donnell**, by Rev. G. W. Mitchell. Manuscript by Rev. Dr. Cossitt. **Life and Times of Ewing.**

    The parents of Robert Donnell were of Scotch descent, but their ancestors had settled in Ireland previous to the year 1688. The family being Presbyterians, participated in the conflict between James the Second and William of Orange. This was a conflict not merely of persons but of principles—between Protestantism and the Papacy—for the ascendancy in England, Scotland, and Ireland. The family subsequently emigrated to this country, and settled in North Carolina.

    Robert Donnell was the son of William and Mary Bell Donnell, who were married about the year 1760, and settled in Guilford county, where their son Robert was born, in April, 1784. The day of the month is not known, owing to the destruction of the family records by the Indians, in the removal of the family to the West. William Donnell, the father, was a soldier of the Revolution, and shared in the battle at Guilford-Court-house, in 1781.

    The Donnell family seem to have been originally Seceders, but some time previous to 1794 joined the Presbyterian Church. It also seems likely that William and Mary Bell Donnell were members of Dr. Caldwell's congregation, as Dr. Caldwell is represented as having baptized their son Robert in his infancy.

    In October, 1789, William Donnell started with his family for what was then called the Cumberland Country, expecting to join another emigrating party near Abingdon, Virginia. It seems, however, that they were too late to effect the junction, and remained in the neighborhood of Abingdon until the following year, when with other emigrants they made their way to what is now Sumner county, Tennessee, and settled at Bell's Fort, on Drake's Creek, near where the little town of Hendersonville now stands. Some time in 1792 the family moved, and settled in Wilson county, on Spring Creek, about eight miles from what is now Lebanon. Here Robert Donnell grew up to his manhood. In the manuscript which is one of my guides in this sketch, it is stated that the whole of his school education consisted of what he acquired in nine months, and that he acquired this before he was thirteen years of age. The account is not improbable, owing to the condition of the country at that time. Flavel's "Husbandry Spiritualized," his father's Bible, and Russell's "Seven Sermons," were his text-books in learning to read, and these were packed over the Cumberland Mountains when the family came to Tennessee.

    When Robert Donnell was thirteen years of age, his father died, and the management of the farm and family interests, as well as the care of his mother and two sisters, devolved on him. The testimony is that he was faithful to his important trust, doing every thing which could have been expected of an affectionate brother and a dutiful son to promote their interest and happiness.

    At the age of sixteen he planned and constructed a horse-mill for grinding corn, which proved a great convenience to the neighborhood, as mills were then very scarce. The writer of this sketch, too, once heard a gentleman, who grew up in the same neighborhood with Mr. Donnell, remark that it was understood that Robert Donnell could split more rails in a day than any man in the country around. Those who have known him personally will hardly question the truth of the statement, as he must have been a man of great physical power in his early life. It is said, also, that in those day of dram-drinking, he took a stand against the practice, and argued strenuously for entire abstinence from all intoxicating liquors. It will be observed that there were then no temperance societies, that he himself had not reached maturity, had not yet become a member of the Church, and that the practice of drinking spirits was not only tolerated, but approved generally by good people. It was an early development of the practical good sense which characterized him throughout a long and useful life.

In the year 1800, when he was in his seventeenth year, Mr. Donnell professed religion. His own account of his religious experience, communicated to his wife, is substantially the following: "I had been," said he, "for some time in great distress of soul on account of my sins, and after having spent several hours late one afternoon in the secret grove, seeking rest and finding none, I returned to my mother's house; and just as I was setting my feet on the threshold, I was enabled to put the rope around my own neck, to prostrate myself before the cross divested of all self-dependence, and to rely alone upon the merits of Jesus Christ." This account is characteristic. He soon became an efficient helper in holding prayer-meetings, and in otherwise promoting the interests of religion in his neighborhood. He would often exhort his friends and neighbors "with melting heart and streaming eyes" "to flee the wrath to come."

He seems to have entertained the idea from very early life that he was to be a preacher of the gospel—even before he professed religion. Such cases are not uncommon. The impressions are probably derived from outward circumstances: they may, too, be specially providential, directing the youthful mind into the channel in which the Spirit of God intends to lead it. Why should it not be so? At least, in process of time, after he professed religion, he felt that he was called of God to preach the Gospel of Christ to a perishing world, and in 1806 presented himself before what was then called the Council, for advice and instruction on that subject. The Council did not feel at liberty to transact Presbyterial business, but advised him to labor in a more public capacity than that in which he had been laboring, as an exhorter and catechist. With this authority he entered upon his work, and soon became practically and really an efficient preacher, although he had received no formal license.

In 1809 he penetrated into Northern Alabama, and commenced the work of collecting, and, as far as he felt himself authorized, of organizing congregations in what was then a new, but rapidly opening country. He was in this country when he received intelligence of the reorganization of the Cumberland Presbytery, in 1810. The following is his own account of his labors, fears, and hopes:

"I was traveling," says he, "in Alabama Territory when I heard of the constitution of the first Cumberland Presbytery, by Messrs. McAdow, Ewing, and King. If I ever was free from sectarian feelings, it was at that period. I often thought, For what am I laboring? I am connected with no constituted Church, and know not that I ever shall be. For what, then, do I labor, If I cannot build up a Church? The reply was, Only for the glory of God, and the salvation of precious souls. But what will become of the few so strongly united in the bonds of love? This could only be solved by the great Head of the Church. Of Him I often sought for an answer, and I am persuaded he did answer; as, some time before the Presbytery was constituted, I became quite calm on the subject, under the firm persuasion that the

Lord would open a way for us. I was in this frame when the intelligence reached me which caused me to feel truly thankful to God who had thus opened a door for a feeble handful of his followers to become more extensively useful."[19]

The date of Mr. Donnell's licensure is not known. At the first meeting of the Cumberland Presbytery, after its constitution on the 4th of February, 1810, his name appears on the record as a candidate for the ministry. This meeting was held at the Ridge Meeting-house, in the following month, March, 1810. In October of the following year, 1811, he was set apart to the whole work of the ministry.

On the 17th of March, 1817, he was married to Miss Ann E. Smith, daughter of Col. James Webb Smith, of Jackson county, Tennessee. Several children were the fruit of this marriage, all of whom died in infancy, except the eldest son, James W. S. Donnell, who still survives.

Previous to his marriage Mr. Donnell labored chiefly as an itinerant minister. He traveled extensively, especially over the southern portion of the Church, and I suppose the labors of no man in any of the denominations have been more signally blessed. He possessed vigorous health, a fine constitution, and in all his labors a feeling was manifest that he belonged to God.

After his marriage he settled first in Madison county, Alabama, where he lived about two years, and then removed to the adjoining county of Limestone, and settled about ten miles from Athens. He now became a farmer, but still continued, I suppose, the most active and laborious minister in the Cumberland Presbyterian Church. Many congregation were collected through his agency in Tennessee and Alabama. A number of these are still flourishing, yielding fruit from the precious seed sown by his ministry.

While he resided in Limestone his wife died. She seems to have been a most estimable and pious lady. The record is that she died full of faith and hope. Her death occurred on the 3rd of November, 1828.

The General Assembly of 1831 appointed, in conformity with several petitions from that country, five missionaries to Western Pennsylvania, of whom Mr. Donnell was one. Their mission was eminently successful, his labors with the others being greatly blessed.

On the 21st of June, 1832, he was married a second time, to Miss Clara W. Lindley, daughter of Rev. Jacob Lindley, of Pennsylvania. Miss Lindley had, however, been some time in the South, engaged as an instructress. In 1835 Mr. Donnell settled his white family in the village of Mooresville, a few miles from his farm. After about two years he returned to his former home. During these years, from the period of his first settlement in Madison county, his labors were chiefly confined to the counties of Madison and Limestone.

Some time about the year 1830 he commenced a series of efforts in the city of Nashville. The result was, the introduction of Cumberland Presbyterianism into that city. As fruits of the seed thus sown, two houses of worship have been built, and two respectable congregations collected.

In 1845 he went to Memphis, for the purpose of organizing a congregation, and aiding in building a house of worship. After spending some months there, and accomplishing the object of his visit, he returned home, and in a short time was

---

[19]**Life and Times of Finis Ewing**.

called to the pastorate of the congregation of Lebanon, Tennessee, as the successor of Rev. George Donnell, who had recently died in that place. He remained in Lebanon until February, 1849, when he moved to Athens, Alabama, which became, as he expected, his last earthly home. He had now passed half through the seventh decade of life—a period when serious men begin to think seriously of setting their house in order. He built a comfortable mansion, rather then otherwise, as a home for his family, and from this mansion he entered into his rest.

On the second Sabbath in August, 1853, he preached at the camp-meeting at Bethlehem, near Huntsville, to an immense congregation. In order to being heard by the multitude present, great physical effort was necessary. He endeavored to accommodate himself to the circumstances, and in his extraordinary exertions laid the foundation for a protracted illness, which resulted in death. Still, although partially prostrated, he continued to labor as he could.

On the second Sabbath in October of the same year he preached twice in Athens, the place of his residence. His text for the morning was 2 Peter i. 13-15. It was called by many of those who heard it his own funeral-sermon. Still he labored on. On the first Sabbath in November he preached the dedication-sermon of a new church in Huntsville, and on the third Sabbath in the same month attended the funeral of three aged Christians a few miles from his residence. His text for the occasion was, "These all died in faith." This was his last sermon. He lingered to the 24th of May, 1855, when he died. The circumstances of his affliction and death were such as would have been expected from such a life. His pastor gives the following account, which deserves a permanent record:

> During all his afflictions, religion was his theme. He admonished all who visited him in regard to that subject. During his whole confinement he manifested, in a preeminent degree, the graces of a Christian. He made no complaint of his lot. Daily would he express his gratitude for kind attentions, and the comforts with which he was surrounded. He was ever calm, submissive, happy, and frequently in ecstasies of joy. His mind seemed never to be in the least beclouded, but was always rational. His conversation were often intensely interesting, and many might be related of a thrilling character. He often said: 'Heaven is not far off; it is'—pointing with his finger—'just there.' Again, he would say: 'I do not know, but it seems to me that the soul might be so filled with the presence and glory of God that it would just leap out, and leave the body a lifeless lump. I feel sometimes like I am almost carried away.'
>
> On one occasion last winter he had a hemorrhage, and was for some minutes in a state of suspended animation; yet he said, 'I was perfectly conscious of all that was going on. I could see my lifeless body lying there, while my soul seemed like the bird just let loose from its cage, which, instead of at once flying away, was circling round and round its former habitation; and I thought, If this is death, how pleasant a thing it is to die!'
>
> On the morning before his death he was asked by a

brother what were his prospects now, when so near the end of his course. To which he replied, 'That business has long since been settled with me, and it is too late now to call it is question. I can say, Whether I live, I live unto the Lord; or whether I die, I die unto the Lord. Whether I live, therefore, or die, I am the Lord's.'

The day before his death he sunk into a profound a sweet sleep, from which he only awoke when aroused by some one. In the latter part of the night his wife aroused him, and offered him some medicine. He replied in a soft and beseeching tone, 'Please do not make me take it; do not trouble me now, for I never felt better in my life,' and immediately fell asleep again, and spoke no more, nor awoke, until he awoke to the glorious realities of heavenly bliss.

Thus he came to his grave in a "good old age," like a ripe shock of corn gathered in its season. He died in his seventy-second year.

Mr. Donnell left but one child, James W. S. Donnell, who still lives a respected planter in Alabama. His widow also still lives, an honor to the memory of both a sainted husband and a sainted father.

The funeral services took place on the Sabbath after his death, in the Cumberland Presbyterian Church in Athens. They were attended by a large congregation, by the ministry generally of the town and surrounding country, and the venerable Dr. Lindley, the father of Mrs. Donnell. The second chapter of first Thessalonians was read; the beautiful hymn was sung, of which the first stanza is,

> How blest the righteous when he dies!
> When sinks a weary soul to rest,
> How mildly beam the closing eyes,
> How gently heaves the expiring breast!

A sermon was then delivered by Rev. George W. Mitchell, pastor of the congregation, from Rom. xiv. 8. The whole occasion is represented to have been, as we would have expected it to be, deeply interesting and impressive. At the close of the sermon the hymn was sung, commencing with the stanza,

> *And let this feeble body frail,*
> *And let it faint and die,*
> *My soul shall quit this mournful vale,*
> *And soar to worlds on high.*

Prayer was then offered by Rev. Mr. Finley, of the Methodist Church.

Some time subsequent to his death the members of the Tennessee Presbytery erected a beautiful monument to the memory of Mr. Donnell.

At the time of his death he was the oldest Vice-President of the American Tract Society. He had been for years a devoted friend and promoter of the interests of the American Bible Society. His views upon the Temperance question have already been noticed. He was a temperance man in principle and practice before there was a temperance society.

Mr. Donnell was unquestionably one of the most laborious and useful ministers that ever labored in this country. Says the writer of the sketch to which I am indebted for most of the facts mentioned here:

> He was, perhaps, instrumental in the conversion of as many sinners, organized as many churches, assisted in building as many houses of worship, and brought as many young men into the ministry, as any contemporary minister of his own, or any other denomination of Christians."

This is no doubt a faithful testimony.

After his first marriage, Mr. Donnell was considered rather wealthy. In the management of his business, however, he never lost sight of the great end of providential blessings of every kind. These blessings made "his house the abode of peace, cheerfulness, and contentment. There hospitality dwelt unrestrained as if in her native home. The humble poor no less than the opulent were welcome visitors at his house, and sharers of his friendship."

Mr. Donnell published two sermons—one in 1833, occasioned by the death of Rev. William McGee; the sermon was, however, first delivered in 1817; the other in 1835, upon the Christian Profession. He also published in the latter part of his life a small volume under the modest title of "Thoughts." The pulpit was his stronghold: he never wrote much. Raised, and spending the first years of his ministry in the wilderness, he was trained to action rather than to the use of the pen.

Mr. Donnell's personal and family religion were of the most exemplary kind. Mrs. Donnell says, that during her whole married life of twenty-three years, she never saw her husband manifest or betray in any single instance a spirit or temper inconsistent with the Christian character, or do what she considered a wrong or inconsistent thing. He evidently lived in great watchfulness, and in the habit of daily prayer. He uniformly kept up domestic worship morning and evening. The account we have is, that he was unusually punctual in this respect. On such occasions he brought all his family around him, including his servants. These were not allowed to leave the house in the morning for their daily toil until after family prayers. The dining-room was used for the purpose, and it came to be considered rather a sacred place in the estimation of the negroes. On a certain occasion, when the white family were absent, some young men came in, and one of them taking the liberty of crossing the room in the manner of a person dancing, an old female servant felt so much scandalized at the unseemly levity of the young man, and the desecration of the place, that she exclaimed, "I shall tell my master as soon as he comes home about your dancing in his religious dining-room."

It was his custom also in the morning at the breakfast-table, immediately after the blessing, to repeat a passage of scripture, and to require the same of all present, even his visitors. On a certain occasion he observed his wife to be in some trouble about some domestic matters, in which she supposed she had failed to come up to his views or taste. The next morning his passage for the breakfast-table was, "Many daughters have done virtuously, but thou excellest them all." He emphasized the pronoun "thou." Of course she was at once relieved from all anxiety in regard to the matter which had troubled her. This is given as an illustration of the kindness and tact with which he administered his household affairs.

Mr. Donnell preached the opening sermon at the meeting of the first General Assembly. The meeting was held at Princeton, Kentucky, in 1829. His text for the occasion was 1 Kings iii.5-9. The subject was Solomon's choice of wisdom and understanding, that he might be able to judge the people of God, and go out and in before them in a becoming manner. The sermon was characteristic. Of course the General Assembly was Solomon, a little child, placed in the midst of a large people, acknowledging its insufficiency for the great work before it, and asking wisdom, and strength, and grace from God. In 1837 he was Moderator of the General Assembly. Its sessions were also held in Princeton that year.

From the time of Mr. Donnell's maturity in the ministry, he was regarded as the leader of the Southern portion of the Church. No other man contributed so much toward directing its theological inquiries or its practical policy. For thirty years he was the highest authority in these matters. He was a great natural man. Furthermore, by extraordinary application and industry in his early ministry, he had made himself a respectable scholar. It used to be said that he carried his English Grammar and other elementary books in his saddlebags on his circuits, and studied them on horseback between his appointments. I expect what was said was true, as it was the custom of those days. He possessed fine administrative abilities, and could not well have been otherwise than a leader. At the same time it is to be remarked that no man seemed less anxious to be a leader. If he was ambitious, the world never knew it.

Personally, he was a man to be observed any where. His figure was commanding. He was something over six feet in height. His usual weight in later life was about two hundred and twenty. He was always neatly dressed—stood erect in the pulpit, delivering his message in an unusually solemn and impressive manner. He never descended to what is called the arts of elocution. Nature had done enough for him in this respect. His voice was like the voice of a trumpet: he never lacked words, and notwithstanding the defects of his early education, his words were always well selected. His thoughts were very clear, and his method of utterance unusually distinct. No man needed misunderstand him. Above all, there were a spirituality and an unction in his performances which subdued, while his mind and manner led. I have heard him often when he seemed to be absolutely overwhelming. He was not always so, it is true, but was always interesting. Mr. Donnell belonged to a race of men that has passed away. We may not see their like again. I never expect to see it myself. Let their memory be cherished. It is a sacred legacy to the Church. Their mantle has fallen: let us see to it that such a mantle be never desecrated; that it be worn by men at least worthy of them, if not their equals.

I saw Mr. Donnell for the first time in my early boyhood. He called at my grandfather's, with whom I then lived. He was accompanied by his mother, an aged lady of serious and quiet appearance. They had been on a visit to one of his sisters. But one thing occurred in this visit which made any impression on my mind. My grandfather had a large family Bible which he had packed over the mountains from Virginia to this country. This, with the Hymn-book, Confession of Faith, and the Travels of True Godliness, made up the principal part of his library. Mr. Donnell, in walking over the house, found the Confession of Faith, and made some jocular remark about it. The controversy was then raging which gave rise to the Cumberland Presbyterian Church. My grandfather replied in an equally jocular, but characteristic manner, that the Confession of Faith was a very good book, but that Mr. Donnell and his party were trying to disembowel it, and that such treatment was very cruel. This occurred whilst the revival party were struggling in the capacity of a Council.

In 1817 he delivered the sermon occasioned by the death of Mr. McGee, at a camp-meeting at the Beech Meeting-house, in Sumner county. Mr. McGee had once lived in that neighborhood, and been pastor of the congregation. My recollection is that it was an exceedingly tender occasion. The preacher himself wept freely, and but few eyes in the great congregation were dry. I was then a very young Christian.

In 1820 he preached at the same Beech Campground. It was late in October, and the weather was unusually cold for the season. He was then in the prime of life, and was certainly a noble specimen of humanity. He preached in the open air. It was cold; there was no shelter, and snow was falling during most of the time of the sermon. But the large concourse of people kept their places, and heard apparently with intense interest. The text was, "That as sin hath reigned unto death, even so might grace reign through righteousness unto eternal life, by Jesus Christ our Lord." I had been licensed to preach but a few days before, and was, perhaps, in a good frame of mind for hearing. It is certain that I never heard a sermon with more intellectual interest. "Sin has reigned unto death"—in throwing darkness into the understanding; in perverting the judgment; in controlling the will; in impairing the memory; in depraving the affections; in subjecting the body to the power of disease and death. Grace reigns in enlightening the understanding; in correcting the errors of the judgment; in persuading the enabling the will; in rendering the memory more tenacious of what is good; in renewing the affections; and finally, in restoring the body to life and immortality in the resurrection of the just. This is an outline of the sermon which was delivered that cold day. My recollection of it is distinct and vivid after the expiration of forty-six years. It was almost the only sermon of another that I ever tried to make my own, and to use as such.

In 1823 the Cumberland Synod met at Russellville, Kentucky. At the close of the sessions of the Synod, a camp-meeting was held at a place about four miles from town. I believe the name of the place was Moriah. Mr. Donnell preached on Saturday evening. The text was, "I speak as unto wise men; judge ye what I say." The sermon consisted of an exposition and vindication of the doctrines of his Church. On one topic he gave a direction to my thoughts which they have still kept. I had entertained a confused motion that regeneration was a sort of physical change. The sermon of that evening relieved my mind on that subject. It seems to me now that he was very distinct and satisfactory, and the wonder is, that with the means of information which Cumberland Presbyterians then had, he could have been so much so. The next day he preached the funeral-sermon of Judge Ewing.[20] It was a massive discourse.

It has been stated already that he preached the opening sermon of the first

---

[20] An uncle of the later Judge Ephraim M. Ewing.

General Assembly. In 1843 he delivered a sermon at the General Assembly at Owensboro, Kentucky, upon the life, character, and death of Rev. Samuel King. In his latter years he showed in his performances in the pulpit something of the effects of age. He was always heard, however, with interest. He continued to preach, too, while he had physical strength for his work. Both nature and grace had formed and fitted him for the pulpit. It was his forte and his throne. He loved its labors, and would have stood in the front rank of preachers in any Christian communion.

REV. ALEXANDER DOWNEY
(1799-1848)

Sources: Manuscript letter of Rev. Hiram A. Hunter.

Alexander Downey was born in the upper part of Kentucky, it is believed, in 1798. He was a cabinet-maker by trade. He professed religion in vicinity of Russellville, Kentucky, in the winter of 1817.

The next year he was received as a candidate for the ministry, under the care of the Logan Presbytery. He was licensed to preach in the fall of 1820, at the same time with Revs. Hiram McDaniel and James Y. Barnett, who have passed away, and Hiram A. Hunter, who still survives. The Presbytery held its sessions at the time at Old Red River Meeting-house. Rev. William Harris propounded the constitutional questions, and offered the prayer. He was ordained in Russellville, in 1822 or 1823. Rev. William Barnett performed the ordination services.

Mr. Downey was married to Ann P. Taylor, in Ohio county, Kentucky. The time of his marriage, however, is not known to the writer. The marriage service was performed by his friend and fellow-laborer, Rev. Hiram A. Hunter.

He spent his early ministerial life in Kentucky, but died in Belleville, Indiana, in 1837 or 1838. His death is represented as a most triumphant one.

Says the contributor to whom I am indebted for most of these facts:

> When I visited him two weeks before his death, he recounted some of the fruits of his ministerial labor. About one hundred persons had professed religion at his own meetings. He had a presentiment that he would die in two weeks from the night which I spent with him, requested me to preach his funeral-sermon, and appointed the time and place for the service. At his request, the citizens of the village were invited in that night, and I preached to them. When the sermon was closed, he asked to be propped up in his bed, and in that position exhorted the congregation to prepare to meet him in heaven. The whole assembly were bathed in tears. He told them that he would die in two weeks from that time, that death to him was no terror, that he was rather pleased with the prospect, since it would introduce him into heaven.

Whatever we may think of presentiments, Mr. Downey died two weeks from the interesting night here described. He died, as we would suppose, in the full hope of a glorious immortality. Says the respected authority already quoted:

"He was a good man, much devoted to his work, and few men have done more for the Church and the world than he did."

Mr. Downey entered the ministry about the same time with the writer, but in a different part of the Church. My acquaintance with him was of a public kind altogether. I met him several times at the meetings of the Old Cumberland Synod—but I believe nowhere else. He had the reputation of being an earnest, warm-hearted, and efficient man. His countenance was pale, and not very expressive. He had the appearance of a man of feeble health. I imagine his health was feeble. This, in connection with his earnest and devoted labors, will probably account for his death when he should have been in the prime of life. Indeed, in his day men were not taught to take care of themselves. They hardly thought it a duty.

Mr. Downey was a revivalist in his time—not, however, in the sense in which that term is now used. It has become at present rather technical. But he had revivals on his circuits, and wherever he labored. He expected them as common results. Doubtless his record is on high. It is good to go back and make an estimate, if we can, of the labors of such a man.

With but a limited education, with but few personal advantages, in his sphere he made his impression upon society. May not that impression have been far deeper and more permanent than the impression of many who have occupied higher places? A man who in heaven wears a crown of rejoicing containing so many stars, deserves to be remembered on earth.

Mr. Downey, at his death, left a widow, but no children.

FINIS EWING
(1773 - 1841)

Finis Ewing was born on the 10th of July, 1773, in Bedford county, Virginia. His father and an uncle had settled there on their emigration from Ireland to this country, a number of years previous to the American Revolution. The two brothers seem to have ranked among the most respectable and prosperous farmers of the county. The older of the two, Robert Ewing, was for many years Clerk of Bedford County Court, and an elder in the Presbyterian Church. He married Miss Mary Baker. They had twelve children—nine sons and three daughters. The subject of this sketch was their twelfth and last child, and from his being the last, his parents gave him the fanciful name of Finis—the end.

Both the parents are said to have been pious, and to have trained their children in an exemplary manner. The subsequent lives of the children gave evidence of their correct training. All the sons who lived to maturity became prominent, engaged deeply in the business of the world, but still, I believe, maintained Christian characters.

Of Mr. Ewing's early history but little is known. He seems to have been fond of books, and acquired what was considered in his day a respectable education. He studied Latin somewhat extensively, and Greek to some extent, together with some of the more common branches of science. Where he obtained his education, is a matter of some doubt—perhaps at Spring Hill Seminary, in Davidson county, Tennessee, under the instruction of Rev. Mr. Brooks. His parents had died in Virginia, and the family had moved and settled in Davidson county, near Spring Hill. Nashville, the county seat of Davidson county, and now the capital of the State, was then a poor village, hardly worth notice. The country was new, and had just passed through the horrors of an Indian war.

On the 15th of January, 1793, Mr. Ewing was united in matrimony with Peggy Davidson, daughter of Gen. William Davidson, formerly of North Carolina. Gen. Davidson was one of the heroes of the Revolution, and lost his life on the Catawba River, in endeavoring to oppose the advance of the British army under Lord Cornwallis. The Legislature of North Carolina consecrated his name, by giving it to one of the first counties organized in the Cumberland country. At the time of their marriage, Mr. Ewing, says his biographer, was in his twenty-first year, and his wife in her nineteenth.

Soon after their marriage, they both joined the Presbyterian Church, in their neighborhood, under the pastoral ministrations of Rev. Thomas Craighead. It seems, however, that at this time neither of them had any spiritual knowledge of religion.

After the birth of their first child, they removed from Davidson county, and settled in Logan county, Kentucky, about eight miles from Russellville, near the old Red River Meeting-house. Mr. McGready ministered to the congregation here. His ministrations were very different from those of Mr. Craighead. Mr. McGready was a preacher of great earnestness and power. They heard the new preacher with interest, and the result was that both soon became uneasy in relation to their spiritual condition. After some time spent in inquiry, prayer, and deep anxiety of mind, one morning, while engaged in family prayer, Mr. Ewing received an evidence of his acceptance. He was filled with peace and joy in believing. This he considered his conversion, and from this point he regarded his spiritual life to have begun. In a few days his wife was relieved in a similar manner.

A new path of duty was now opened up, in the providence of God, before Mr. Ewing. A history of the difficult times upon which we enter at this point has been written more than once. It is not the purpose of the writer of the present sketch to dwell upon them. Let it suffice to be said, that from the extensive spread of the revival, and the enlargement and multiplication of congregations, a great want of ministerial labor soon began to be felt. Another thing is be said, which may as well be said plainly: A considerable portion of the Presbyterian ministry were not adapted in their spirit and habits to the wants of the people. This statement is not made for the purpose of stirring up an old strife, which was certainly bitter enough in its day; but for the purpose of presenting those facts with which history should always deal. The prevailing religious preference, in the West, was Presbyterian. Presbyterian agencies were mainly employed in the revival. The new congregations wished chiefly to become and to remain Presbyterians; but there were not Presbyterian ministers enough, who sympathized with the new condition of things, to supply them with the word and ordinances.

In this exigency, one of the oldest ministers in Kentucky, Rev. David Rice, advised the encouragement of a few young men of promise and unquestionable piety, to direct their attention to the work of the ministry, with such literary qualifications as they might have been able to acquire. Mr. Ewing was one of the young men so encouraged. In the fall of 1801 he, together with Alexander Anderson and Samuel King, presented himself before the Transylvania Presbytery, with a written discourse. The other two were similarly prepared. They were permitted to read their discourses privately to Mr. Rice. Mr. Anderson was received as a candidate for the ministry; Mr. Ewing and Mr. King were encouraged, but not received as candidates. In the fall, however, of 1802, the three were licensed as probationers for the holy ministry.

At the session of the Presbytery in October, 1803, petitions were presented from the congregations of Spring Creek, McAdow, and Clarksville, for the ordination of Mr. Ewing. The Presbytery accordingly met on Friday before the third Sabbath in the following month, for his ordination, and he was duly set apart to the whole work of the ministry, Rev. William McGee preaching the ordination sermon, and Rev. James McGready presiding and giving the charge.

In December, 1805, the celebrated Commission of the Synod of Kentucky met at Gaspar Meeting-house, in Logan county, Kentucky, for the purpose of conferring with the members of Cumberland Presbytery, which had in the meantime been formed from a part of Transylvania Presbytery, and adjudicating upon their Presbyterial proceedings. The result of the conference and adjudication was, that all the "young men," as they were then called, from Mr. Ewing, down to those who had been most recently licensed, were declared to have been irregularly ordained to the ministry, and were solemnly prohibited from exhorting, preaching, and administering the ordinances, in consequence of any authority which they had received from the Cumberland Presbytery, until they submitted to the jurisdiction of the Commission, and underwent the requisite examination. The Presbytery had declined the jurisdiction of the Commission, for the very best of reasons, that a Presbytery alone has the right to "examine and license candidates for the holy ministry; to ordain, install, remove, and judge ministers." The act of the Commission of Synod was an act of great ecclesiastical violence, and it is not a matter of surprise that it defeated its own end. The young men exhorted, preached, and administered the ordinances, as before. A council was formed for mutual conference and encouragement, but no Presbyterial business was transacted. During the four years of the continuance of the council, it is not too much to say, that Mr. Ewing was its guiding and controlling spirit.

On the 4th day of February, 1810, the Cumberland Presbytery, which had been dissolved in 1806, by the Synod of Kentucky, was reorganized as an independent Presbytery, by Revs. Messrs. Finis Ewing, Samuel King, and Samuel McAdow. This act was performed at the house of Mr. McAdow, in Dixon county, Tennessee. I have seen the house, and, I believe, I preached in it once in my early ministry. From this important transaction originated the Cumberland Presbyterian Church. There is no probability that the actors anticipated such results as have followed. Still, it is not the first time, in the providence of God, in which a little fire has kindled a great matter. Nor is it the first time in which men who have been traduced, oppressed, and outlawed, have been made the instruments of an great and good work.

The new Presbytery proceeded immediately to the ordination of Mr. Ephraim McLean, who had accompanied Mr. Ewing to Tennessee. Of his feelings in connection with the ordination, Mr. Ewing gives the following account: "During the whole preceding transactions," says he, "I felt an indescribable awe, solemnity, and even timidity. My judgment was clear, that it was duty to constitute the Presbytery; but I feared that I had no immediate, special, and overpowering evidence, direct from God, that we were about to do right. But being appointed to preside in the ordination, it became my duty to pray. I distinctly recollect, that with one hand on the head of the preacher, and the other lifted to heaven, upon the utterance of the first sentence, the immediate presence and power of God were most sensibly felt by me, and I believe by all engaged in the transaction; and such were my feelings, that every doubt concerning the propriety of what we had done was entirely banished."

Mr. Ewing and his fellow-laborers had now commenced a stormy career. It was to be expected that they would have their share of misunderstanding on the part of the public, of misrepresentation and abuse. Nor was it unnatural that the Presbyterian Church especially should misunderstand them. It would be too much to say, that all who questioned their motives and criticised their course, were wholly selfish and dishonest. There was an earnest conflict; the opposition was persistent and violent; but these good men held on their way.

In October, 1813, Cumberland Synod was constituted. At the first session of the Synod a committee was appointed to prepare a Confession of Faith, Catechism, and Discipline. The committee consisted of Revs. Messrs. William McGee, Finis Ewing, Robert Donnell, and Thomas Calhoon. The committee divided itself into two sections; the one consisting of Messrs. McGee and Donnell; the other, of Messrs. Ewing and Calhoon. From some cause, but it is supposed, mainly from the self-distrust and diffidence of Mr. McGee, his section of the committee accomplished but little. Mr. Calhoon was a young man, and the principal labor of the other section devolved upon Mr. Ewing. I have myself heard Mr. Calhoon speak of the intense interest and prayerful spirit with which Mr. Ewing carried forward that work.

Some time previous to the war of 1812, Mr. Ewing was invited to join a military expedition to the north of the Ohio River, against the Indians, in the capacity of chaplain. He accepted the invitation, with the understanding that he was to be permitted to carry his rifle, and act in the twofold capacity of chaplain and common soldier. There was something belligerent in his composition.

In May of 1820 Mr. Ewing moved from Kentucky, and settled in Cooper county, Missouri. He soon organized a congregation in what was then the "far West," and called it New Lebanon. His congregation in Kentucky had been "Lebanon" congregation. While here, he established a Theological School, in which he gave gratuitous instruction, and to a considerable extent, gratuitous support to a number of candidates for the ministry. This was the first movement toward a Theological School in the Cumberland Presbyterian Church, and, I suppose, west of the Mississippi River.

In the fall of 1825 Mr. Ewing attended the meeting of the Cumberland Synod, at Princeton, Kentucky. He opened the meeting with a sermon from the heroic language of the Apostle to the elders of the Ephesian Church: "But none of these things move me, neither count I my life dear unto myself, so that I might finish my course with joy, and the ministry which I have received of the Lord Jesus, to testify the gospel of the grace of God." It was an exceedingly impressive sermon. The old courthouse was densely filled with ministers, and delegates to the Synod, and citizens. Certainly there were but few who did not feel that the preacher entered into the spirit of his text.

At this meeting of the Synod incipient measures were adopted for the establishment of Cumberland College. It was intended to be called Cumberland Presbyterian College, but the "Presbyterian" was stricken off by the delegation appointed by the Synod to the Legislature of Kentucky, for the purpose of procuring a charter. The change was made from considerations of policy, and was perhaps the first error which was committed in the management of that ill-fated institution.

At these sessions of the Synod another subject of deep interest to the Church was discussed for the first time. This was the formation of a General Assembly. In this discussion Mr. Ewing too, of course, a prominent part. Two plans were before the Synod. One was for the division of the Synod, and the formation of a General Assembly after the manner of the Presbyterian Church. The other was for the formation of what was called a "delegated Synod"-a Synod not composed of all the ordained ministers in the Church, but of a few delegates from each Presbytery, after the manner of the present General Assembly. Had this plan been adopted, there would have been Church Sessions, Presbyteries, a delegated Synod or General Assembly. The present Synods would never have existed. Mr. Ewing took a decided stand in favor of a delegated Synod. He seemed to have matured the subject, and certainly understood it well. I went myself to the Synod in favor of the other plan, but his arguments seemed to me conclusive and overwhelming. I yielded to them, and have believed from that to the present day, that for the Cumberland Presbyterian Church, at least, a delegated Synod would have been preferable to a General Assembly.

Mr. Ewing attended the General Assembly at Princeton, Kentucky, in 1830. He also opened that meeting with the customary sermon. It was a good sermon, but not equal to the one of 1825. He was five years older. This may have been one of the reasons. I believe he never attended another Assembly.

In 1836 Mr. Ewing took up his residence in Lexington, Missouri. He there organized a considerable congregation, to which he ministered till his death. The immediate occasion of his settlement in Lexington seems to have been, that he had been appointed by the United States' Government Register of the Land Office. No doubt some good men thought that he ought not to have encumbered himself with such an office. Still even good men ought to consider, that the very highest authority has said that "the laborer is worthy of his hire." The writer of this sketch is one of the last men to encourage the mingling of ministerial and secular pursuits. But Mr. Ewing was now an old man. He had given the labors of his life to the service of the Church, and his compensation had, I suppose, been meager. If the laborer does not receive his hire from the proper source, is he culpable if he accepts it from other sources which are neither unlawful nor dishonorable? The culpability in these cases is not in the earnest and faithful minister, but in the churches.

It is said that Mr. Ewing kept up his habits of study, and improved intellectually while he lived. He died July 4, 1841, in the sixty-eighth year of his age. Says his biographer: "His death was calm and peaceful. His hopes were in heaven. He left the world trusting in the merits of that Saviour whom he loved, and whom he had served."

Mr. Ewing had thirteen children-seven sons and six daughters. Of his sons who lived to maturity, the most, if not all, have become prominent men. His eldest son, now deceased, was for some time a United States' Senator from Illinois. As far as the writer knows, his children who still live are members and supporters of that Church which their father had so prominent and active an agency in establishing and rearing up to its present respectability and usefulness.

He left a handsome bequest to the Lexington Presbytery, of which he was a member at the time of his death, and also a bequest of three hundred dollars to Cumberland College. This latter bequest his biographer has omitted to mention. It was made, however, and duly paid over to the Cumberland College Association.

At some period in Mr. Ewing's life, but the precise period is not known, his mind became exercised on the subject of slavery. In 1835 he published a sermon in the **Cumberland Presbyterian Pulpit**, in which he took strong ground against at least some of the evils of slavery. The public mind was not so easily inflamed on the subject at that time as it has been since, and he expressed himself, to what has since been denominated a slave-holding Church, with great freedom. In the progress of the sermon he gives the following as his own experience and purposes in relation to his slaves:

"Lest some of my readers," says he, "should say, 'Physician, heal thyself,' I think it proper to state in this place, that after a long, painful, and prayerful investigation of the subject, I have determined. not to hold, nor to give, nor to sell, nor to buy any slave for life, mainly from the influence of that passage of God's word which says, 'Masters, give unto your servants that which is just and equal.'"

The result of his experience and resolution was, that at his death all his servants were emancipated.

In 1814 Mr. Ewing published a Sermon on National Affairs. This sermon was delivered soon after the fall of Bonaparte, and published by request.

In 1827 he published a "Series of Lectures on the most important subjects in Divinity." This work reached a second or third edition, enlarged. It was one of the fruits of his Theological School.

In addition to these, he furnished sermons from time to time for the **Cumberland Presbyterian Pulpit**, published years ago in Nashville-A Sermon on Faith, published in 1833; A Sermon on the Atonement, published in 1834; A Sermon on the Duty of the Church, published in 1835; A Sermon on Christian Union, published in 1835; A Sermon on the Reason why the Prayers of the Church are not Answered, published in 1835.

Also, a short time after the reorganization of the Cumberland Presbytery, in 1810, a Pastoral Letter was addressed by the West Tennessee Presbytery to the Churches under its care, warning them against the ministers of the Cumberland Presbytery. To this letter an anonymous reply was published. It was supposed to have been written by Mr. Ewing. The reply was a strong, and very severe production. The severity was provoked, and at least partially justified, by the character of the Pastoral Letter.

A few remarks upon some of the personal characteristics of Mr. Ewing, will close this brief sketch. And

First. He was unquestionably a man of a high order of talents. The immense work which he performed, and the great personal influence which he exercised over the men of his time, afford ample proof of this. Although he wrote and published to some extent, as we have seen, yet his greatest power was exhibited in the pulpit, and in the judicatures of the Church. As a preacher he was not eloquent, in the popular acceptation of the term; but he was argumentative, impressive, forcible, and when fully aroused, overwhelming. He never resorted to rhetorical arts, or to empty declamation. He sought the judgment and the heart of those whom he addressed. It was sometimes said that he was fond of politics. He would have distinguished himself as a politician, had he devoted himself to those pursuits.

Secondly. Boldness was a prominent characteristic. In the pursuit of truth, and in search for the path of duty, he "conferred not with flesh and blood." He may not always have reached both truth and duty; but if he did not, his failure arose from no shrinking produced by fear. His relation to the Cumberland Presbyterian Church would of course render him prominent in defending both its doctrines and measures. When called out in this way, he shrank from no responsibility. Whilst, however, all this is true, he was no blustering, intermeddling disorganizer. He never threw down the gauntlet; but when it was thrown down, and he thought it necessary, he took it up. He was a man of war, but his wars were always defensive, not offensive. I believe this statement is true of him universally, in every controversy of his life.

Thirdly. Mr. Ewing was a good man, a Christian. If I had no other evidence of this but his private letters to his friends and brethren, published by his biographer, these would satisfy me on this subject. These letters were written under the impulse of circumstances, with no expectation of their being seen by other eyes that the eyes of those to whom they were addressed. They express the feelings of a man who loved and feared God, and whose soul was deeply interested for the salvation of his fellow men. But in addition to these, we have the testimony of a long and consecrated life. Imperfections there may have been in that life; otherwise, it would have been a superhuman life. Still, making every allowance for human frailty, we look upon it as a life consecrated to God and the great interests of humanity. These are the fruits of a spiritual tree.

Fourthly. His patriotism is not to be overlooked in an estimate of his character. He was a descendant of Virginia, one of the first, if not the very first, of the Colonies in which the fires of the Revolution were kindled. The labors, the struggles, and the sacrifices of that revolution were fresh events in the memory of the generation in which he passed his childhood and youth. That they should have made a deep impression upon his mind, is not surprising. He loved America and her institutions. He was an uncompromising enemy of tyrants and tyranny. His first published sermon was upon the inestimable value of civil and religious freedom. His intimate acquaintances knew well how deeply the sentiments of the sermon had taken hold upon his mind. He never lost his interest in the subject.

Fifthly. It may be remarked in conclusion, that the temperament, habits, and general character of Mr. Ewing fitted him for the position which, in the providence of God, he was called to occupy. He was constituted for a leader, and the men with whom he was associated needed a leader. He occupied his space, and occupied it well. He never faltered in the management of the high trust providentially committed to him. His published sermons, up to his old age, show clearly enough that the purity and prosperity of the Church, especially of the Cumberland Presbyterian branch of the Church, together with the salvation of the world, were the great objects of his thoughts, labors, and prayers.

Rev. David Foster
(1780-1833)

David Foster was born on the 4th of May, 1780, in Rowan county, North Carolina. His parents were William and Nancy Foster. They were poor, but respectable, and distinguished for their earnest piety. His father and mother were careful to instruct him in the principles and precepts of our holy religion. Their labor seems not to have been in vain, for when a boy, he was remarkable for his morality and seriousness of deportment, and for his respect to the worship of God. His deportment was so exemplary, that when quite young, he was admitted to the communion of the Presbyterian Church, in a congregation under the pastoral care of Dr. McCorcle.

In the fall of 1797, William Foster removed to Tennessee, and settled in Sumner county, within the bounds of Shiloh congregation. This congregation was then under the pastoral care of Rev. William McGee. In the following year the parents and the son presented their certificates of Church-membership to Mr. McGee, and applied for membership in his congregation. They were all examined on the subject of experimental religion, and the parents were received, but David was discouraged, and admonished to examine the ground of his hopes more carefully. This circumstance made a deep impression upon his mind, and he immediately commenced a course of prayer and self-examination. The result was, a conviction that he was destitute of religion. He, however, became a penitent, and soon found the pearl of great price. He is said to have experienced the great change at home, in that still and quiet way which is pleasing to many, and which is perhaps the most promising of permanent results.

When the revival of 1800 commenced, under the ministrations of Mr. McGready and others, he immediately fell in with it, and became on of its most active promoters. From his zeal, and promise otherwise, he was encouraged to direct his attention to the work of the ministry, and was accordingly licensed to preach the gospel by the original Cumberland Presbytery, on the 2d of October, 1805, at Old Red River Meeting-house. For some time previous to his licensure, he had been authorized to travel in the character of an exhorter, for the purpose of supplying, as well as possible, some of the scattered and destitute congregations.

Mr. Foster was of course one of the "young men" who were called before the Commission of the Synod of Kentucky, in December of 1805. He shared with the others the proscription by that body. He still, however, continued his probationary labor, under the direction of the Council, the organization of which followed the dissolution of the Cumberland Presbytery. Some of his most useful and effective services were rendered during those years of darkness and trouble.

In the summer of 1806 he was married to Miss Ann Beard, of Sumner county. His wife outlived him, and during her whole married life was "a help-meet" to him in the highest sense in which a wife could be such to a Christian minister. She was deeply and devotedly pious; and although a woman of modest and retiring habits, it was sometimes said that under the influence of high religious excitement she surpassed her husband in exhortation. In the quietude of home, it would be difficult to conceive of a higher degree of diligence, self-denial, and devotion to the interest of a family, than an observer would have found in her.

After Mr. Foster's marriage, he procured a home for his family near his father's, in Sumner county, but spent the most of his time in traveling and preaching, as before. Indeed, this was the only means of supplying the destitute portions of the Church, which would otherwise have been entirely without the means of grace.

In the fall of 1808 he moved to Wilson county, and settled in Sugg's Creek congregation. On the 27th of July, 1810, he was set apart to the whole work of the ministry at Sugg's Creek Meeting-house, and installed the regular pastor of that congregation. He also preached regularly during his whole pastorate in his regular congregation, to Stoner's Creek congregation, and to Fall Creek congregation, until 1824. A large proportion, however, of every summer and fall season, was appropriated to attending camp-meetings in different, and especially remote, parts of the Presbytery to which he belonged. This was the custom of pastors in those days. At the fall session of the Nashville Presbytery, in 1824, he was released from his connection with the Fall Creek congregation, the Presbytery having been divided, and this congregation having fallen within the bounds of the new Presbytery. As specimens of the labors performed by Mr. Foster in remote parts of his Presbytery, I quote the following:

Minutes of the Fall Sessions of the Nashville Presbytery, 1814.—"Ordered that Revs. David Foster, Robert Guthrie, Benjamin Lockhart, and Samuel McSpadden, attend the sacramental meetings appointed in White and Warren counties; also the meeting in Sequatchie Valley." These meetings were from fifty to a hundred miles from the homes of Messrs. Foster and Guthrie, and they both had large and dependent families.

Minutes of the Spring Sessions of the Nashville Presbytery, 1815.—"The Presbytery revived the itinerant plan of preaching, and directed David Foster to ride and preach in the eastern bounds of the Presbytery, embracing what was formerly called the Upper Circuit, and to extend his labors into East Tennessee."

Minutes of the Spring Sessions of the Nashville Presbytery, 1819.—"The Board of Female Missions petitioned the Presbytery for a Missionary for two months, or more: the petition was granted, and Mr. David Foster was appointed."

Minutes of the Spring Sessions of the Nashville Presbytery, 1820.—"Ordered that David Foster ride twice round the Tennessee Circuit, before our next Presbytery." A large portion of this circuit was a hundred miles from Mr. Foster's home. These are presented as specimens of what was expected of him and such men in their day. And those of us who have any recollection of the usages of those days, will readily suppose that all such orders were fulfilled, as no indulgence was tolerated, except from considerations strictly providential.

The subject of slavery was not agitated in Mr. Foster's days. At least, if there was agitation, it was not such as it has been since; but both he and his wife were antislavery in their feelings. From this, and perhaps other considerations, in the fall of 1827 he moved to Illinois, and made a temporary settlement in Sangamon county. In 1829 he made what he considered a permanent settlement, in Macon county. Here he organized two or three congregations, which he ultimately left in a promising condition.

I have mentioned Mr. Foster's antislavery feelings. He was a moderate and good man, and would never have been a violent proscriptionist. He loved the Church, and loved all its good men, whatever their relations to property and to general society might be. In illustration of his views on the subject of slavery, I mention the following incident in his history. Some time after he settled in Wilson county, from considerations which I do not now recollect, he was induced to buy a negro man. The negro had but one arm, but would otherwise have been considered valuable. The purchase was made, however, with the distinct understanding, that when the negro's services should have been considered a fair equivalent to the purchase-money, he was to have his freedom. The pledge of the buyer was redeemed, and at the expiration of four or five years the negro was made free. The laws of Tennessee at that time gave the privilege to the master of emancipating his slaves. The arrangement, however, proved unfortunate for the negro. He was inefficient when left to himself; his family were worthless. He fell into difficulties, and died in the midst of them. I do not mention this circumstance as an illustration of what may be expected in the case of colored men thrown upon their own resources, but simply as a historical fact connected with the life of a good man. Mr. Foster intended to give to his servant what was just and equal.

A year or two after Mr. Foster's last settlement in Macon county, he entered into the service of the American Tract Society. It seems that one of his objects in undertaking this agency was to enable him to preach more extensively. The country was new—his congregations had been but recently organized. He derived from that source, therefore, a very slender support. He expected the customary compensation from the Tract Society, and, in addition to the circulation of books, to be able in some degree to supply the destitutions of the country with the means of grace. On the 7th of May, 1833, he visited St. Louis, to obtain an additional supply of books for his agency. The next day, on his return homeward, he was attacked with the cholera, and on the 9th of May, 1833, about seventeen miles north-east of Edwardsville, closed his mortal career. The following extract of a letter from a respected brother in the ministry to the afflicted and bereaved family, contains some particulars respecting his death:

> My dear Friend:—It becomes my painful duty to communicate to you heavy tidings. I saw your father last Wednesday, on his return from St. Louis. He was apparently in good health. He proceeded about five miles that afternoon toward home. Thursday morning he traveled about twelve miles, was unwell, but still proceeded about two miles farther, when he stopped. His complaint soon discovered itself to be malignant cholera. There was no physician nearer than ten or twelve miles. A man was dispatched to obtain medical aid, and in the meantime camphor, opium, calomel, and warm bathing were resorted to by those about him, but all to no purpose. The cramp came on very soon in his feet, hands, legs, and body. He suffered severely about six hours, when death came to relieve him from pain, and remove his soul to the bosom of that God and Saviour in whom he believed, whom he loved and preached to a fallen world. He expressed a wish to see me. A man came to let me know. He came in the night. I arrived at the place at seven o'clock on Friday morning. I found the lifeless clay, but the lovely spirit had taken its flight from our sinful world. He died about nine o'clock on

Thursday evening.

Brother Foster spoke but little, but expressed himself resigned to the Divine will. His confidence in God, and his hope of future felicity, were firm and unwavering. His wish was to have been at home; but as the Lord had ordained otherwise, he was submissive. He retained his senses perfectly to the last, and in the closing scene was entirely calm, and for some time appeared to be sinking into a quiet sleep. Not a feature was discomposed.

Mr. Foster was the friend and counselor, and, in many respects, the guide of my early ministry. My recollections of him and his sainted wife are very tender and very sacred. Still I do not suppose that my estimate of his character is extravagant. I intend that my record shall be faithful. As a preacher, though not the leading man, he was one of the leading men of his time in the portion of the Church in which he labored. His preaching was unequal. Sometimes his manner was smooth, unembarrassed, entirely free; at other times, he labored in the expression of his thoughts, his manner was cramped, and he seemed dull. When in his better moods, he was exceedingly tender and impressive, and occasionally overwhelming. In the summer of 1817 he preached at the former residence of his father-in-law, my own grandfather. There was no house of worship in the neighborhood then, and private houses were used for the purpose. The congregation was large, and the preaching was powerful. A favorite young lady of the neighborhood was deeply convicted. It was a rare occurrence. In the course of a few months this young lady, with some of her associates, professed religion at a camp-meeting a few miles distant. It was the commencement of a revival in the vicinity. A house of worship was soon built; camp-meetings were introduced; a Church was organized, which still exists. It is not a large, but a model congregation.

He once preached at Smyrna, in Rutherford county, upon the occasion of a Presbyterian camp-meeting. His text was, "Knowing, therefore, the terror of the Lord, we persuade men." The sermon made an unusual impression. He sometimes spoke of it afterward himself. The old people remembered it a long time. It was a terrible appeal to the judgments and hearts of unconverted men.

In one of his camp-meeting excursions, he attended a meeting in Overton county. Old Mr. McDonald, father of the Rev. Philip McDonald, one of the brightest lights of the early Cumberland Presbyterian Church, lived in the neighborhood. The son had finished his brilliant career, but the father had lived to be an old sinner. Mr. Foster preached on a favorite text: "And whosoever shall fall on this stone shall be broken; but on whomsoever it shall fall, it will grind him to powder." At the close of the sermon the old man was among the mourners. In giving an account of his experience afterward, he described his feelings as being awful. "But," said he, using his Scotch-Irish brogue, "I thought I would cast mysel' on that stone." The old man obtained a good hope.

I once heard him at Wells' Creek, at a camp-meeting, upon the benevolence of God. At that time I was unacquainted with Dr. Paley's argument on that subject. Mr. Foster's argument was constructed very much after the manner of Paley's. The whole discussion was new to me, and seemed at the time the most interesting one which I had ever heard.

Mr. Foster's pastorate at Sugg's Creek was his principal work. He had a most interesting and devoted congregation. The Board of Elders consisted of Hugh Telford, James Law, John Roach, and John Currey. They were a noble band. I hardly expect ever to see another such generation of men. Whilst they did not neglect their worldly interests, religion was with them the absorbing interest. They confided in their preacher, and cooperated with him. On one occasion, at the commencement of their camp-meeting, on Friday, Mr. Foster preached rather a searching sermon upon the address of Eliphaz to Job: "Are the consolations of God small with three? Is there any secret thing with thee?" After the sermon, some of the older brethren were discussing its merits. One or two novel, but rather striking points, had been presented. Brother Roach was called on for his opinion in regard to them, but somehow he had missed them. The brethren rather chided him for hearing so inattentively, since a preacher might advance unsound opinions and he would not notice them. "Aye," said he, "but I never think it necessary to watch Davy, for I take it for granted that he is always right."

I have mentioned that Mr. Foster was sometimes embarrassed and dull in his delivery. On some occasions this defect was striking, and rather painful. I was once conversing about it with old John Currey. He remarked to me, that he could always tell on Sunday morning, before preaching, whether Davy would have liberty in preaching that day. Said he, "I always pray for him on Sunday morning, and if I have an evidence that my prayers are answered, I take it for granted that he will have liberty." These are specimens of the interest which these good people felt in their preacher, and of the confidence which they reposed in him.

In his private relations, Mr. Foster was one of the best of men. His religion was strictly practical. He believed in Divine direction, and made every thing a subject of prayer. If he plowed or sowed his field, he prayed for the blessing of God upon his labors. If he started upon a journey, he prayed for guidance and protection and for the safe keeping of those at home. He lived in the fear of God, and looked for a reward in heaven. I conclude this sketch with some characteristics, written by myself, and published in the Revivalist shortly after his death.

> 1. He was a good man. His qualities, though not of the most shining, were nevertheless of the most scriptural and useful kind. He always praised and cultivated the virtues of the heart more than those of the head. However, with regard to the latter, he was by no means indifferent." He loved knowledge, and sought it for its own sake, as well as a means of usefulness. "The writer of this article knew him well. He has been in habits of closest personal intimacy with him, has seen him in his family, and also before the people, and in the judicatories of the Church; and has always found him the same. In principle and in practice he was an upright, conscientious, and good man.
>
> 2. He was a plain, honest, and practical preacher. He hated pomp and show in the pulpit, as well as elsewhere. His sermons were of the practical and useful kind. A favorite topic with him was experimental religion. Sometimes in his pulpit exhibitions his manner was rather feeble, and his mind seemed not with interest to pursue his subject; but at others he appeared to have

the tenderness of the sweet singer of Israel, and the strength of Samson. Every thing melted and trembled around him. Many will regard him in heaven as their spiritual father, guide, and friend.

3. He was an industrious preacher—industrious in the preparation of his sermons, as well as in his more general ministerial labors. "He labored in the preparation of his sermons. He considered it a shame to impose words upon his hearers instead of thoughts. He studied his sermons well. He prayed for Divine assistance, and expected it; but was not willing to serve God and the souls of men with that which cost him nothing. He studied to show himself approved unto God—a workman rightly dividing the word of truth. He gave himself to reading as much as possible. He was industrious in the discharge of all his ministerial duties. He lived a life of labor and effort. He preached regularly, and with great punctuality, to the several congregations of which he had the oversight on the Sabbath, and again and again on other occasions, improving every opportunity of doing good. He was instant in season and out of season, reproving, exhorting, admonishing, and encouraging, as necessity might require. Although poor, he spent much time in riding and preaching to the needy and destitute.

4. He was enlarged and liberal in his feelings. He considered the world as the field. He felt, and longed, and prayed, for the conversion of the nations.

Who does not love to cherish the memory of such a man? He has finished his work; he had borne his testimony; his sun has gone down, but long, long will he live in the hearts of many. He had recently settled in a destitute frontier. Much was expected from his labors, and much did they seem to be needed; but how little does man know! In the midst of usefulness, surrounded by pressing calls for the bread of life, he is cut off in a day, and the fond hopes of many are disappointed. But it is right. The Lord hath done it, and who will murmur? He fell where every man should fall— at his post. He did not desert it, terrified by the raging pestilence. Trusting in God, at whose bidding the shafts of disease and death were flying around him, he went forward. God was well pleased, and took him to himself.

Mr. Foster left six children—three sons and three daughters. Two of his sons and two of his daughters died several years ago. One of his deceased daughters became the wife of Rev. Daniel Traughber, of Illinois, and lived some years after her marriage. His oldest son, and one of the daughters, still live. The son lives on Sugg's Creek, where the father spent the best years of his ministry; the daughter somewhere in Illinois.

Mr. Foster published a sermon in the **Cumberland Presbyterian Pulpit**, for August, 1823, on "The Redeemer's Kingdom."

Rev. James Smith Guthrie
(1793-1856)

James Smith Guthrie was born May 12, 1793, either in Orange county, North Carolina, or on Holston River, in what is now East Tennessee. His father was in an unsettled state at that time, and the family record is lost. It is consequently not known whether James was born in North Carolina or Tennessee. He was the eldest son of Rev. Robert Guthrie. In his baptism he received the name of James, simply, but after he grew to manhood, and before he became known to the public, he added the name of Smith to the original, to distinguish himself from a cousin who lived near his father, and whose name was also James Guthrie. He derived his middle name from his mother's family. Her family name was Smith.

Mr. Guthrie was not only the eldest son, but the oldest of five brothers, two of whom, in addition to himself, entered the ministry. He was born purblind, and was considered in his early life rather a dull boy. His dullness, however, was evidently apparent only, as his subsequent life proved; and the appearance no doubt arose in a measure from his near-sightedness, which gave him an awkward and dull aspect, especially in his early life. He was remarkable for morality and industry. Indeed, industry was a distinguishing characteristic through his whole life. After he grew up to manhood, and before he entered the ministry, he performed more farm-labor than any ordinary man.

When about seventeen years of age he became concerned on the subject of religion. His convictions were deep, and his distress of mind was great. This distress continued three or four years, almost without intermission. It is said by a correspondent, that often during the time, "the dead hours of night witnessed his supplications for mercy." When at meetings where any interest was excited he was a habitual mourner, and, as a general thing, was first and last at the "mourner's bench," or rather, in the mourner's place—the mourner's bench had not been introduced in those days. An anecdote is told of him in connection with these scenes. He was in attendance at a camp-meeting, and as usual was a mourner. He was dressed in clothing of rather a light color. While the meeting was in progress it rained, and the seats and ground were all rendered very unsuitable for clothing of such a color; but he was still a mourner, and down upon the bare earth. His friends remonstrated, and tried to induce him to change his position, telling him among other things that unless he did he would ruin his clothes. His reply was characteristic: "I would rather ruin my clothes than ruin my soul."

In the year 1816 Mr. Guthrie went to live with old William Foster, in the character of a cropper. Mr. Foster was a religious patriarch in those days. His house was the abode of a consecrated piety. There was no house of worship in the neighborhood, and Mr. Foster's house was used for that purpose. When the preachers passed through the country they preached there. Every influence was salutary. In the course of that year Mr. Guthrie professed religion. On a Sabbath evening, while the family were engaged in singing, he obtained the first evidence of his acceptance. He believed, however, that he had experienced a change some time before, while engaged in secret prayer.

After such an experience of conviction, and such a spiritual struggle, there could be no doubt of the stand which he would take on the subject of religion. It was a very bold and decided. He joined the "Old Ridge congregation," and soon commenced the exercise of public prayer and exhortation. His mind seemed at once to turn to the ministry. He spent some time (the writer does not know how long) under the instruction of Rev. Hugh Kirkpatrick. His early education had been defective, but no man ever made a more diligent use of time. The public impression was, however, that he was a poor prospect for the ministry. He was near-sighted, his education was indifferent, his whole exterior was rather unimposing and unimpressive; but he was zealous, and no one doubted his piety. We have another anecdote of him while he was in the stage of his progress which I am now describing. A union meeting was held at Shiloh in 1817, under the superintendence of Rev. William Hodge, pastor of the congregation. Rev. Dr. Blackburn, of the Presbyterian Church; Rev. James Gwynn, of the Methodist Church; and two or three Cumberland Presbyterian ministers, were in attendance. William Barnett preached on Monday night, on the Shortness of Time, and there was a good deal of interest. Several mourners presented themselves at the close of the sermon. James Guthrie was then a zealous exhorter, and of course was among the mourners trying to instruct and encourage them. Some one called the attention of Dr. Blackburn to him, and remarked that "the Cumberland Presbyterians were trying to make a preacher out of that young man." The Doctor, with many others, thought that it was a hopeless case. Said he, "I would as soon think of making a preacher out of any stump in the yard." His incredulity was excusable, but time proved that he was greatly mistaken. A few years after that occurrence James S. Guthrie preached in the same house, and to the same people, with an acceptance and power seldom equaled there.

In the spring of 1818 Mr. Guthrie was received as a candidate for the ministry by the Nashville Presbytery. The meeting was held at old Mother Landsden's, on Bradley's Creek, in Wilson county, Tennessee. He had attended the preceding meeting of the Presbytery, and laid his case before them. He was not discouraged by the Presbytery, but still was not received as a candidate. Presbyteries were thoughtful and careful in their action in those days. But on application at this Presbytery, he was received. On the 14th of October, 1819, he was licensed at Big Spring, and "ordered to ride all his time on the Upper Circuit," until the next meeting of the Presbytery. At the next meeting of the Presbytery, in April, 1820, he is again "ordered to ride the Upper Circuit." At the meeting of the Presbytery in October, 1821, it was "ordered that James S. Guthrie spend the whole of his time on the Hiwassee Circuit, until the next meeting of the Presbytery." The Hiwassee Circuit had been formed by an extension of what had been called the Upper Circuit. These circuits lay in the mountain region between East and Middle Tennessee. It was a rough region, but his labors were greatly blessed.

In July, 1822, in connection with the writer and Mr. Ezekiel Cloyd, Mr. Guthrie was set apart to the whole work of the gospel ministry. This occurred at an intermediate meeting of the Nashville Presbytery. The meeting was held at Sugg's Creek. Immediately after ordination, as Mr. Guthrie and myself were single men, we were sent off to attend the more remote camp-meetings. We held camp-meetings at West Harpeth, Wells's Creek, and Richland, and sacramental-meetings at Adley Alexander's, on the North Fork of the Forked Deer, and also on Clear Creek, in Carroll county. Western Tennessee was then a new country. At the meeting on Forked Deer we had the assistance of Mr. Francis Johnson. In a history in manuscript of the Nashville Presbytery, I find the following in relation to the fall meeting of 1822: "James S. Guthrie and Richard Beard were sent to the more distant parts of the Presbytery, to plant new societies, and water those already planted." Mr. Guthrie went into East Tennessee.

From this time to 1826 he labored as an itinerant preacher in Tennessee. His labors were divided between the three divisions of the State. In the fall of 1826 he went to Alabama, and about a year from that time, in the fall of 1827, he was married to Miss Lethe Burns, of Alabama.

He remained in Alabama some years; then moved to the northern part of Mississippi, and finally to Texas. Soon after he reached Texas his wife died. He continued to devote himself to the work of the ministry, sometimes as a pastor, but more generally as an evangelist. Whilst the Religious Ark was published at Memphis, he is said to have been a frequent contributor to its columns. The writer thinks also that he projected, if he did not carry into partial execution, after he reached Texas, a monthly publication, designed for his own control. It was filled, or intended to be filled, chiefly with sermons—a sort of monthly preacher.

Some years before his death he had an attack of severe sickness, which resulted in the formation of an abscess on his side, accompanied by a distressing cough. Under the influence of these afflictions he wasted away. About a year before his death he attended the meetings of his Presbytery and Synod. From the Synod he was not able to return home, but remained with his friends and brethren until the time came for his removal by death. Some time before his death he wrote, or rather dictated, as the writer supposes from the hand-writing, a short letter to Rev. David Lowry, from which the following extract is taken:

> Such have been my afflictions since 1853, that I have been unable to write or preach any of consequence. I have a running abscess in my side, accompanied by a constant cough, which renders my life a burden, and yet I cannot die. I have no hope of being better in this life, but, thank God! heaven is a healthy clime. O for patience to wait, and willingness to suffer, 'till my change come.' Dear brother, pray for me and mine! The idea of lingering out an unpleasant existence here, unable to do any good, is gloomy indeed; but I must bear it as best I can.

In his last letter to his brother, Robert W. Guthrie, of Tennessee, he says: "You need not write any more. Farewell, till I meet you in heaven!"

These extracts indicate the feelings of a good man under great and protracted sufferings, and in the prospect of death.

Mr. Guthrie left four children—a son and three daughters. They are said to be all members of the Church. It is understood, too, that he left a considerable amount of manuscript, which might be of some interest to posterity if it could be collected and published. He was a strong, if not a polished writer. He published two sermons in the **Cumberland Presbyterian Pulpit**—the first, in the number for March,[21] 1833, on the Obligations of Christians; the second, in the number for August, 1833, on Looking to Christ. This latter sermon was made a subject of

---

[21]**Sic**: January.

severe animadversion by Rev. Finis Ewing. The position was impliedly taken in the sermon that the suffering and death of Christ upon the cross were not necessary to the atonement, but that Christ could have suffered sufficiently otherwise to accomplish the object. Mr. Ewing thought the position very objectionable, and assailed it with severity.

I have a great many personal recollections of Mr. Guthrie which are very interesting to myself, whatever they might be to others. I should be ashamed if they were not interesting to myself. He was several years older than myself, but we were school-fellows together, in my father's old-fashioned school at the Ridge school-house. He was the first person who ever made a direct and personal appeal to me on the subject of religion, after I began to approach maturity. He was with me when I engaged earnestly in the work of seeking my salvation, and I suppose did not leave me many minutes at a time during the whole struggle. He first encouraged me to look to the ministry, and was my companion in my first attendance at the Presbytery. After he was licensed, and whilst I was still a candidate for the ministry, I traveled with him once round what was called the Upper Circuit. We were ordained at the same time, and immediately sent off together to attend some remote meetings. He was on many accounts a remarkable man—an excellent preacher, never below mediocrity, and often far, very far above it. He was sometimes austere, sometimes even rough in his manners. His reproofs, when he administered them, were often terrible. His passions were strong, and his prejudices were almost invincible. In one of my last conversations with him, he remarked to me in reference to a minister who stood high in the Church, and had done so far many years, that "he had no confidence in him, and never had any." Still, no man was kinder and gentler in his treatment of those in whom his confidence was entire.

When he first attended the Cumberland Synod, he went there under the impression that there were two or three men belonging to the body who were disposed to dictate to it, and rather act the part of "lords over God's heritage." His impressions were strengthened by what he thought he saw, and he had the boldness at once to throw himself in their way. They thought it an unpardonable assurance in him to take such a stand, but he took and held it. They were good men—rugged like himself, but good men. They respected him, but felt his weight while they lived. The meeting of the Synod to which I allude was held at the Beech Meeting-house, in Sumner county.

In 1827 Mr. Guthrie was Moderator of the Synod. This was previous to the organization of the General Assembly, and the position was of course considered an important one. I suppose the appointment had never before been conferred on so young a man. He was also a delegate to the first General Assembly, which held its sessions at Princeton, in 1829.

A more distinct notice of a few of the characteristics of Mr. Guthrie, will bring this sketch to a close. It may be remarked, too, that this part of my task is not difficult—I mean that the notice of them will not be difficult, however I may fail in setting them forth in a suitable manner. His characteristics were distinctly marked. The most casual observer would detect them. Their outlines could hardly be mistaken.

1. In a letter from a friend, to which I am indebted for a number of the facts heretofore stated, it is mentioned that "he was remarkable, even in early life, for

fixedness of purpose." This trait of character he carried through life. If he took a stand upon any question, he was immovable. This may sometimes be a vice, as well as a virtue. If he formed a prejudice against a brother, it could hardly be eradicated. I have already alluded to this subject. Still, in all his prejudices he was honest. If he believed a brother upright and conscientious, he stood by him, whether the many or the few stood with him. If he made up his mind to pursue a particular course, he pursued it, whatever difficulties and obstructions might be in his way. Had it not been for this characteristic, deeply rooted, he could never have reached the ministry—at least, he could not have reached the eminence which he did reach. One or two anecdotes will afford some illustration.

Some time rather early in his ministry, he was traveling in East Tennessee, as an evangelist. He had an appointment in some one of the towns for a particular night. When he reached the place, he learned that another meeting was in progress, and he received the impression that some pains had been taken to supersede him in his appointment. The worship was to be held in the court-house. As soon as the house was lighted, he walked in and took his seat on the judge's bench, laid out his books, and thus gave a significant notice of his purpose. After a while the representative of the other meeting came in and took his seat near him. Mr. Guthrie spoke to the stranger, and told him that he himself had an appointment for that hour, and expected to fulfill it. Whether right or wrong, he executed his purpose. He thought he was right. He thought, furthermore, that it was the intention of the other parties to do him wrong.

The writer witnessed a similar occurrence when once in his company. In a town in Western Tennessee, three ministers had appointments for preaching at the same hour. Mr. Guthrie was one of the three. There was but one house of worship, and the people would hear but two sermons in succession. From some cause, the first place was yielded to one of the others; he, however, asserted and maintained his right to the second. Of course the third brother was excluded.

In making an estimate of such developments of character, we must take into account the circumstances which surround the actors. Forty years ago young Cumberland Presbyterian ministers were considered rather a small matter, and it was considered no great breach of propriety to set them aside when the convenience of others required it. Mr. Guthrie, however, had energy enough to maintain his own rights, when he considered them invaded or threatened.

2. The boldness with which he defined and carried out his theological opinions, and his opinions in regard to Church-order, deserves to be noticed. This sometimes led him to extremes. When he assumed a position, he had no dread of carrying it to its ultimatum. In his early ministry he took and pressed the position that "mercy is not an attribute of God." It has already been mentioned, that in 1833, in a published sermon, he impliedly denied that the "sufferings of Christ upon the cross were necessary to the atonement." It is easy for a man accustomed to theological difficulties to account for his taking both positions. They were the results of correct principles carried to extremes. Mr. Ewing assailed the latter position with considerable severity, in a sermon subsequently published.

In the General Assembly of 1846 he took a violent stand in opposition to our sending delegates to the "World's Christian Convention," which was appointed to be held, in the course of the following autumn, in London. We thought his opposition the opposition of an extremist; but he sincerely looked upon the whole matter as a great humbug. It must be confessed, too, that time has done something toward vindicating his opinions on that subject. At least, it was soon found that the doors of Exeter Hall were too narrow for the admittance of Southern Christians.

3. The characteristics of his preaching were earnestness, originality, and power. The earnestness and fervency of his early ministrations were remarkable. He felt deeply, and his whole soul was expressed in his public addresses. Many will carry the impressions received from his powerful appeals into eternity. Such a manner rendered him eminently useful. His bold and independent originality was unusual. As a model, he acknowledged the authority of no mortal man. He thought, spoke, and acted for himself. The last sermon which the writer ever heard him deliver was preached at the Assembly of 1846. Years and disease had taken something from him, but there was still a remnant of his former self. A great many of his early sermons were very powerful. On many occasions he excelled himself. There is a tradition of his preaching a sermon at a camp-meeting held by another denomination of Christians, near Jackson, in Western Tennessee. The account is that the meeting seemed to drag heavily. Some of the outsiders made application at some time near its close, to those who managed the meeting, that Mr. Guthrie, who was present, might be permitted to preach. The request was granted, not with very great apparent cheerfulness, but still it was granted. He preached on Monday, from the passage in Zachariah, "Who art thou, O great mountain? Before Zerubbabel thou shalt become a plain," etc. The sermon was represented as one of extraordinary interest and power. For years there were references to it in that country. Many similar occurrences might be mentioned. Another is remembered. It has been stated that in the fall after ordination, Mr. Guthrie and the writer, with the assistance of Francis Johnson, held a sacramental-meeting at Adley Alexander's, in the Western District. On Sunday he preached from James's description of "Pure Religion." It was a very strong and impressive sermon. At some distance behind the preacher's stand, a man sat by himself on a stump. The truth reached his heart. He wept freely. He had been raised by Christian parents—had married and become the head of a family. He had wandered far from the home and from the ways of his fathers. In a few years that man professed religion, entered the ministry, and is now an old and much-respected preacher.

4. Mr. Guthrie's exterior was rough, but as years multiplied and he developed himself, it became impressive. His deportment was thoughtful and serious—a striking rebuke to the unseasonable levity sometimes found among good men. His kindness to young men entering the ministry in whom he had confidence was very great. If there was a want of confidence, however, he showed but little favor. Of his kindness and sympathy the writer speaks from experience. Often when he would have sunk under the discouragements and trials of an early ministry, the words of encouragement, and the undoubted sympathy of the friend of his youth, kept him up. Others no doubt had a similar experience. These are pleasant recollections. Perhaps they ought to be cherished with more tenderness than we often feel for them.

I have said that his exterior was rough. Sometimes in the pulpit, to a stranger, it was at first unpromising. I am furnished with the following anecdote: In one of the years while he was living in Alabama, he had made an excursion of some extent into Tennessee and Kentucky, and perhaps farther northward. On his return home he called at Winchester, Tennessee, and found a sacramental-meeting in progress. The evening after his arrival, by invitation, he occupied the pulpit. His clothes had become more than threadbare—they needed patching. He was a stranger in Winchester. When he commenced the service, the elders and leading men hung down their heads. They thought the prospect hopeless. But before the sermon closed, their heads were up, and they were drinking in the word of life. All were delighted with the sermon. The next morning a rally was made, a new suit was furnished to the stranger, and he left with the benedictions of the congregation.

5. Mr. Guthrie's piety was deep, sincere, and earnest. It had a rugged nature to subdue, but the subjugation was effected. He felt himself from the beginning to be a consecrated man. His call to the ministry was of the old-fashioned kind. It stirred up the very depths of his soul. "O that my head were waters, and mine eyes a fountain of tears, that I might weep day and night for the slain of the daughter of my people!" "My bowels, my bowels! I am pained at my very heart; my heart maketh a noise in me; I cannot hold my peace, because thou hast heard, O my soul, the sound of the trumpet, the alarm of war!" Such exclamations were common with him in his early struggles for the salvation of his friends, and of others around him; and no one who heard them doubted that they expressed the feelings of his inmost heart. His respected father once remarked of him in the early part of his work, that "James seemed to him more like a soul maturing for glory than any thing else." His devotion in those days was ardent and intense.

6. His preaching was distinguished by plainness and boldness. If sin in any particular form needed reprehension in his estimation, it received what he considered its due without measure or mercy. He made no compromise with it. Such a manner would of course arouse opposition. He would have enemies. Still, if such persons became his enemies for the truth's sake, it was a small matter with him: he went forward in his fearless course. He was one of the men for his times. God will always have such.

7. Perhaps I ought to add, as I am writing history, and not discussing opinions, that although Mr. Guthrie never owned a slave, except for a few years after his marriage, and I suppose never preached what is called a political sermon in his life, still he was intensely southern and democratic in his social and political sympathies. Some of his friends thought him too much so. In these, however, as in other things, he thought for himself. God, in his good providence, took him away before those principles and their opposites developed themselves in so fearful and violent a form as they have since done. He has met men from all parts of the land, and of all sorts of social and political sympathies in heaven—I mean, of course, such sympathies and opinions as are common among us. It is good to think that there is a land in which the sword will never be drawn, the arm of violence will never be lifted, and the tongue of vituperation will be stilled for ever.

REV. ROBERT GUTHRIE
(1770-1843)

Robert Guthrie was born near the city of Baltimore, on the 12th of November, 1770. While he was still a boy, his father moved to North Carolina, and settled near Hillsboro. He used to relate to his children, that he heard the sound of the cannon on the memorable day of the battle at Guilford Court-house. Of course he was in his eleventh year. It is supposed that his parents were members of the Presbyterian Church. It is at least evident that he was reared under a Presbyterian influence.

In 1791 he was united in marriage with Mary Smith, of Orange county, North Carolina. It would be difficult to conceive of a more congenial union. It lasted about fifty years, attended by all the trials incident to the settlement of a new country, and the rearing and education of a large family; but the writer believes it was a union of more than ordinary interest and affection. The wife was "a help-meet" in the scriptural sense of the expression.

In 1792 Mr. Guthrie left North Carolina for the West, and spent one year in East Tennessee, near Jonesboro. The next year he left East Tennessee, and after spending some time in the neighborhood in which Gallatin, Middle Tennessee, now stands, settled finally on the Ridge, near the Old Ridge Meeting-house. One of his sons has now in his possession a letter of dismission and recommendation granted to Mr. Guthrie and his wife by the session of the Presbyterian congregation of which they were members in North Carolina, and signed by the pastor, Rev. James Bowman. It appears from this letter that both he and his wife were members of the Presbyterian Church previous to their settlement in the West. Subsequent examination, however, satisfied them that they were destitute of religion. Soon after their settlement in this country, the great religious movement began to develop itself which resulted in the revival of 1800. Mr. Guthrie was attracted to one of Mr. McGready's early meetings, and there became convinced, for the first time, that he had never experienced a change of heart. With Luther we recollect that "justification by faith" was the great truth which instrumentally wrought the Reformation. This truth seems first to have been deeply wrought into the Reformer's own heart. Its out-working shook the papal throne. With Mr. McGready and his fellow-laborers the new birth, as a deep and powerful experience, seems to have occupied a similar place. In the preaching which preceded and attended the revival it overshadowed all other truths. The new birth, as an earnest reality, was emphatically the doctrine of the revival. Mr. Guthrie returned home from this meeting, and some time afterward experienced the change which he felt to be necessary, or at least received the evidence of it, while engaged in family prayer. It is believed that both he and his wife made their second profession of religion previous to the full development of the revival, and of course were among its first-fruits. As we would suppose, he entered heartily into the new and great work. He was, however, no enthusiast. In what he did, he followed the convictions of a sober, thoughtful, yet decided mind.

It is not known at what time Mr. Guthrie began to exercise his gifts as a public speaker, but we find from the record that he was a licensed exhorter and candidate for the ministry in 1805, at the time of the meeting of the Commission of Kentucky Synod, and that he was included in the sweeping resolution of that body which prohibited the "young men" who had been before the Commission "from exhorting, preaching, and administering the ordinances, in consequence of any authority which they had obtained from Cumberland Presbytery."

The action of the Synod's Commission resulted in the formation of what, in Cumberland Presbyterian history, is known as the "Council." After the organization, or rather the reorganization, of the Cumberland Presbytery, in 1810, he was licensed and ordained by the Nashville Presbytery. In addition to the parts of trial which had preceded, at the meeting of the Nashville Presbytery, at New Hope, March 30, 1814, having been examined on "English Grammar and Divinity," in connection with Ezekiel Cloyd he received licensure. At this same Presbytery it was "ordered that Messrs. Guthrie and Cloyd ride each three months on the upper circuit." It will be recollected that "Messrs. Guthrie and Cloyd" were at that time poor men, and had large families dependent upon them for support, and that the upper circuit was at least a hundred miles from their homes. Upon the minutes of the fall session of the Presbytery, in the same year, we find the following resolution: "Resolved, that all the licentiates under our care prepare to stand an examination from time to time on such branches of science as Presbytery may direct." In conformity with this resolution, Mr. Guthrie was ordered to prepare for an examination on Natural and Moral Philosophy at the next regular meeting of the Presbytery. At the same time he was furnished, from the Presbyterial library, with "Ferguson's Astronomy and the Plates," for additional study.

The next particular notice of him which we find in the Presbyterial records is an order upon the fall minutes of 1819 for his ordination. He was accordingly ordained the following spring, at Stoner's Creek, April 6, 1820, Rev. Thomas Calhoon preaching the ordination-sermon, and Rev. David Foster presiding and giving the charge. The record is that he was previously examined "on experiential religion, his internal call to the work of the ministry, his knowledge of Natural and Revealed Theology, of Philosophy, Astronomy, Geography, English Grammar, and Ecclesiastical History; also as to his knowledge of the Constitution and Rules of the Church, and the principles of its Government."

It will be perceived from this brief sketch, that previous to his entrance upon the work of the ministry, he had charge of a family. It had grown to some size. He was the father of several children. He had commenced the world with but limited means, and had added but little to the original stock. He was a poor man, and his education was limited. He nevertheless labored to prepare himself for ordination in conformity not only with the letter, but the spirit, of our form of Church-government. If the record has been faithful, and his examinations were not a mockery, his preparation was very respectable. The writer has heard him speak more than once of his trials in this respect. He was compelled to labor closely for the support of his family; and when at his daily toil, his custom was to carry his English Grammar in his pocket, and improve the intervals which might occur, in preparing for his examinations before the Presbytery. In the summer, while his horse rested from the plow, he would snatch the moments for necessary study. In the next generation these things will seem almost fabulous, but they were the works of a generation of men who have just passed before us. Men who are now beckoned to the halls of our Colleges, instructed gratuitously, and in many instances greatly favored otherwise; men at whose feet the treasures of knowledge are poured in profusion, can never appreciate fully the trials and the necessary self-denial of their fathers.

But while the young minister is laboring to fulfill his obligations to his Presbytery, he must also labor to fulfill his mission to the people. Mr. Guthrie was a laborious preacher. A portion of his early ministry was employed upon the circuit. The necessities, however, of a large family required his attention at home; his preaching was therefore mainly local. A portion of each summer and fall was devoted to attending camp-meetings. This was expected of all the preachers. It was additional to their ordinary local preaching. In this latter service, too, he was indefatigable, considering his circumstances. The writer has a personal knowledge of his having ministered for a long time to two congregations, at a distance of ten and fifteen miles from home. In preaching to the nearest congregation, he usually went and preached and returned the same day. It will be recollected that this occurred after a week of hard work upon the farm. To the neighborhood of the other congregation he usually went on Saturday evening, returning on Sabbath evening after preaching. This was considered necessary, and was perhaps unavoidable, in order to meet his obligations at home.

It may not be improper to say something here of his compensation for his pulpit services. It will present an illustration of his patient self-denial, as well as of the habits of the times. Of the liberality of one of the congregations we are not so well informed; but in the other there lived two men—one a member of the Church, the other a man of the world—whose regular contribution was a silver dollar each a year. It is believed that this was his entire salary from that congregation. This, however, was considered as certain as if it had been annually collected by law. The time, too, when the contribution would be made was generally known in the family of the preacher, and was considered a matter of sufficient interest to be made the subject of a family talk. These worthy men were far richer then the preacher, but they seemed to think themselves doing well, and the preacher seemed to think them doing well, when they contributed annually each a silver dollar. The other congregation was a little more numerous, and perhaps their measure, according to the degree in which God had prospered them, was a little larger. They were good people, but poor, and unable to contribute much. The preacher was, therefore, but poorly compensated.

In 1831 Mr. Guthrie moved to the State of Missouri, and settled near Keytesville. In the course of the next year he joined the McGee Presbytery, the sessions of which he afterward attended as long as he was able. He had, however, become enfeebled by age and previous exertion, and was not able to preach much. Although a talented man, his lungs were never strong. In the new country in which he now lived his house became the home of the wayfaring minister, and a sanctuary in which himself, when able, and others ministered the word of life. In 1836 he assisted in organizing a Church in Keytesville, which was named, by his request, Ebenezer.

In September, 1843, he closed his earthly career. In relation to the occurrence I quote from a letter of youngest son, Rev. A.W. Guthrie, who was with him at the time:

"After an absence of several weeks, I returned home late in the evening, and learned that father had had two chills. This was a little alarming, from the fact that he was advanced in life, and his constitution was becoming infirm and his strength declining. I spent most of the next day with him. This day he had no chill, sat up most of the time, was able to walk about the house, conversed as usual on ordinary topics, spoke of the crops, which by the blessing of Providence were likely to be very good, although at one time he had almost despaired of a crop in consequence of the wet weather. He enlarged on the sinfulness of distrusting the good providence of God. None of us thought of any immediate danger. If he did himself, he did not mention it. He, however, remarked that, according to the course of nature, his time was near—that he felt that he could not live long—that he was ready at any time to depart and be with Christ; expressed a firm assurance of acceptance with god through a Redeemer's blood.

"I left in the evening, and returned next morning at the time the chill was expected. Found him sitting up, and his mind in the same composed and happy frame as on the day before; stayed with him till the hour had passed at which the chill was expected, supposed it would not return, and left. In about an hour a messenger came for me. I returned, and found him in a hopeless state of congestion. He did not speak after my return, seemed to suffer very much, and in about an hour expired."

Thus died a good man, near the close of his seventy-third year. It may with great truthfulness be said that, as he died full of years, so he died full of faith. His last conversation was upon "the sinfulness of distrusting God," and an expression of his remaining confidence "of acceptance through a Redeemer's blood." In his life, to those who knew him most intimately, he presented, as nearly as we could expect here, a realization of what was doubtless Solomon's idea of a perfect and an upright man; but in his death we have, if possible, a still sweeter realization of the peaceful end of such a man: "Mark the perfect man, and behold the upright; for the end of that man is peace."

This brief sketch may be closed with some general remarks upon the character of Mr. Guthrie. If biography is worth any thing, it is in presenting to us such characteristics as are worthy of imitation.

We find, then, in him, a specimen of the class of men who founded the Cumberland Presbyterian Church. They were laborious, patient, self-denying, prayerful men. In the three first of these characteristics history is doing them justice. In the last they were known, and could only be known, to those in intimate relations with them. But they were eminently men of prayer. Those of us who in age have followed close upon their footsteps, have had many proofs of this. Mr. Guthrie was a man of prayer; and when I say this, I do not mean that he was so in the ordinary sense of that expression, but that he was deeply imbued with the spirit of prayer. It was his daily life. The writer speaks thus from personal knowledge. A stranger would soon have felt in his presence that there was a spiritual atmosphere around him. He was not noisy, or obtrusive; but calm, thoughtful, serious. I was an inmate in his family some time, and had a close acquaintance with him for many years; and although he was habitually cheerful, I do not know that I ever heard him say, or knew him do, a foolish thing. In this respect I have always considered him a model, far above many who attracted more attention and excited more interest in his time. And I confess that in this respect, as well as in many others, his memory commands a degree of respect with me which the memory of many of his cotemporaries, who made much more noise in the Church, has failed to command. I remember him as a kind, cheerful, (but at the same time thoughtful,) and serious old man—as a man conscientious in his intercourse with men, and in fulfilling his obligations to God. He loved and feared God, and loved those in like manner who loved him.

Again: I have known no man who realized in the government and management of his family more fully my idea of the patriarchal manner than he. He raised a large family. There was no apparent effort in the exercise of authority, yet the authority of the father was complete. In the course of our acquaintance of many years, I never saw it treated with disrespect. When the writer was an inmate of his family four of his sons were grown, and the oldest, who afterward became a prominent preacher, Rev. James S. Guthrie, was preparing for the ministry. The three others, with myself, had but recently professed religion. The religious exercises of the family were regularly kept up. At night the "boys," as we were called, officiated alternately—in the morning the patriarch himself was leader. On Sunday evening, if we were not at meeting, there was a theological examination, generally founded on the Catechism. I recollect, on two occasions I was assisted in answering difficult questions by a whisper from the old lady. One of the questions was: "Why can there be but one God?" I was a young theologian, and hesitated. She was sitting at my elbow, and whispered in my ear, "Because one fills immensity." The other question was upon a matter of history, and ignorance was a little more inexcusable—still I was ignorant: "Who was the father of Moses and Aaron?" I could not answer; but Mother Guthrie relieved me again by whispering, "Amram." This mode of religious administration will assist us in understanding why two of those sons became prominent and effective ministers of the gospel as well as acute and practical theologians, whilst the other two, though not ministers, are nevertheless pillars in the house of God. A third son also entered the ministry, and still lives an efficient and laborious preacher. He was, however, but a lad when the things occurred of which I write. Of the elder brothers who entered the ministry one preceded, and the other has since followed, the father to the grave. It is pleasant to believe that many works will follow them both. They made their mark in their day.

Still again: the case of Mr. Guthrie, like many others which history ought to record, presents great encouragement to pioneer labor in the ministry. The congregations to which he ministered in Tennessee were small, and scarcely organized. It is believed that he did not receive twenty dollars a year for his services; yet he cast his bread upon the waters. In one of these congregations, a few years after he left it, there was a powerful revival of religion. It is still small, however, but for years past has paid two hundred dollars annually for half the time of a young preacher. Of the congregation which he organized in Missouri, and which at first was composed chiefly of his own family, it is said that "it now has a respectable membership, and a house of worship creditable to any people." It is thus that the hardy pioneer clears the ground, breaks it up, sows the seed from which others may have the honor and the joy of reaping. This would seem a very unequal distribution of things, were there no future reward to be measured out to him whose patient and self-denying labors and sufferings God alone can appreciate. How many are now laboring in different parts of the great West and South-west as pioneers? Let them not be discouraged, but still hold on to their self-denying work. God watches the seed which they are sowing in perhaps poorly prepared soil, and will cause it to spring up in an abundant harvest when they themselves are in the grave. Let them remember, too, that the day is coming which will reveal the full value of their works, and bring them an adequate reward. Scores of noiseless, unpretending ministers, are performing a work upon the frontiers of our vast country which God will acknowledge. Hold on, valued brethren! He that appointeth you, and in his providence assigns you your field of labor, has said, "Behold, I come quickly; and my reward is with me, to give every man according as his work shall be."

I feel inclined to give expression to another thought which this brief notice suggests. Mr. Guthrie raised five sons: three of these entered the ministry. Two of them have finished a useful work; the other is still a laboring minister. Two sons of his oldest daughter and child are likewise now respected and useful preachers. These may all be supposed to have received their first impressions from a common source—I mean such impressions as tuition, discipline, counsel, and example, are calculated to make. A great many families grow up in the Church. Some of them are numerous. The sons of these families are promising, and apparently pious, but they turn their attention to other pursuits. Is there not a reason? And may not the reason in many cases be found in the character of our family religion? I am far from believing that this is the only reason. Surrounding circumstances may be so unfavorable as to counteract the influence of precept, counsel, and example at home. Still I press the question which I have propounded: Are we not to find in many cases the reasons for the fact that the sons of the Church are not brought more directly forward to her assistance, in the character of the religion of our own firesides? It is true that God calls men to this work; but he may have a reason when he calls. God knew Abraham, that he would command his children and his household after him, that they should keep the way of the Lord, to do justice and judgment, and therefore God made each of his sons a great nation. Do such providences teach nothing? A great many families of promising sons afford the Church no ministerial strength. May not a reason be, that the subject of religion is not properly presented at home? Are the obligations of these sons to God and to the Church explained and enforced? God calls men from sin to holiness by the use of means. Why should he not use means in calling them to the work of the ministry? If ministers and Christian friends should from the pulpit and in social and domestic intercourse inculcate a worldly spirit, and direct attention to worldly pursuits as the great business of life, it is very plain that but few men would become Christians. Is it not as plain, that if parents and Christian friends encourage a worldly spirit and worldly pursuits in the young men of the Church, very few of them will ever seek the self-denying work of the ministry? I know one of the largest and most influential congregations in the Cumberland Presbyterian Church; it has been organized more than thirty years, has enjoyed revival after revival, has done much, even nobly, in promoting the interests of the Church and the general kingdom of Christ, and still has never furnished a single candidate for the ministry. Is there not a reason? We do not believe that God calls men irresistibly to Christ: why should we believe that he calls them irresistibly to the ministry? He does not do it. I conclude by stating, and pressing—if I could but press it—what is with me a full conviction, that if we had more families really, practically, and intelligently pious, we should find more young men consecrating themselves to the self-denying but noble work of the Christian ministry. God accepted Samuel at the hands of his mother, and made him a Prophet and a Judge in Israel. god also accepted Samuel Davies at the hands of a pious mother, and made him the greatest of American preachers. Why should he not accept such offerings at the hands of Christian parents now, and honor their children by making them useful ministers of his most precious word?

REV. WILLIAM M. HARRIS
(1772-1845)

William Harris was born in 1772. His father was a Revolutionary veteran, and a member of the Presbyterian Church. Very little is known of his early life, except what would be expected from the character of his father; he was religiously educated. It is not known that he manifested any particular interest on the subject of religion himself, until the opening of the revival of 1800. His locality would bring him into early contact with this great work. He became deeply convicted soon after the revival began to develop itself. He was, however, much perplexed with the doctrine of predestination, as it was taught by the Church of his fathers. This was a very common experience in those days: it is not an unusual experience now. At a certain time, when on his way to a camp-meeting, he stopped for the night at Russellville. Russellville is situated in that portion of Kentucky in which the religious movement commenced. In the course of the evening or night, while engaged in prayer, to use his own language, "the Lord broke into his soul; he saw a fullness in Christ for the whole world." His mind was at once relieved of some of his doctrinal difficulties. On those subjects, it is supposed, he never faltered afterward, to the day of his death.

"A short time after he professed religion, Mr. Harris began to feel that it was his duty to preach the unsearchable riches of Christ to a dying world, and his powerful exhortations and great usefulness at prayer-meetings soon satisfied his brethren that he was not mistaken in his feelings." In consequence of the troubles which grew up in the Presbyterian Church, in connection with the licensure and ordination of what were called the young men, he was not advanced to the ministry until after the constitution of the Cumberland Presbytery in 1810. He had, however, been encouraged to exercise his gifts in exhortation, and during the stormy period which preceded the constitution of the Presbytery for several years, he was one of the most efficient laborers in the country, in the capacity of an exhorter. The Council, during the four years of its existence, abstained from all Presbyterial acts. This accounts for his not being licensed to preach. In these days, says my authority, while some of his more timid brethren declined holding meetings, he labored with great zeal and success. "In his own neighborhood, so powerful was the work of God through his instrumentality, that meetings would continue all night. His widow relates that on one occasion, after being up all night, he came home about daylight for some refreshments, and then returned and continued the meeting through the day." It will be observed that this was an ordinary neighborhood meeting.

At the first regular meeting of the Cumberland Presbytery, Mr. Harris was received as a candidate for the ministry. This meeting was held at the Ridge Meeting-house, in March of 1810. Several others were received at the same time—Robert Donnell, William Barnett, William Bumpass, Robert McCorkle, and David McLin. It is an interesting catalogue. In 1811 he was licensed. In the following year he was ordained. I have in my possession the records of the meeting of an intermediate Presbytery, which had been appointed for the ordination. As a matter of special historical interest these records entire are inserted here:

Agreeably to the order of our last Presbytery, the

Intermediate Presbytery met in Dunham's settlement on the 14th of February, 1812, to attend to the trials of William Harris, preparatory to ordination. Preachers present, Messrs. Finis Ewing, Foster, and Kirkpatrick. Mr. Ewing was chosen Moderator, and Mr. Kirkpatrick was chosen Clerk. Constituted with prayer. A sermon was delivered from Rom. v.9, which was unanimously sustained. Examinations were attended to upon the different branches of literature, pointed out in our circular-letter, which were sustained. Presbytery adjourned to meet to-morrow morning at ten o'clock. Concluded with prayer. Saturday morning, Presbytery met according to adjournment; opened with prayer. The Moderator proceeded to preach the ordination-sermon from 2 Tim. iv.2, first clause. After sermon, the necessary questions in our Confession of Faith being proposed to Mr. Harris, according to the custom of the Presbytery, and being answered in the affirmative, the Presbytery, by the imposition of hands and solemn prayer, set him apart to the whole work of the ministry. Afterward a solemn charge was given with respect to his duty, likewise with respect to the duty of the congregation; and the whole was concluded with prayer. This 15th of February, 1812.
FINIS EWING, Mod.
HUGH KIRKPATRICK, Clerk.

The trial-sermon on this occasion is said to have produced a powerful effect. The members were so interested that they forgot the customary criticisms, and rather united with the preacher "in shouting forth the praises of God." There must have been a good deal of spirituality in the ordination.

Mr. Harris, when he became a candidate for the ministry, was poor; his education was limited; in addition, he had the charge of a considerable family. His efforts for the cultivation of his mind were very great, and afford ample proof of what vigorous and persevering application may accomplish under the most appalling discouragements. "When at work on his farm, he carried his book in his pocket, and employed the moments of respite from labor in study. Frequently, after a hard day's work, he would ride several miles to recite to a gentleman of his neighborhood. His proficiency and success in mental improvement may be inferred from the fact that, after entering the ministry, he was frequently asked at what college he obtained his education."[22]

Mr. Harris was as incessant in his labors, after entering upon them, as he was in preparing for them. No ordinary weather was allowed to prevent him from attending his appointments for preaching. When friends expostulated with him upon the necessity of care of himself, and remonstrated against what they considered his imprudence in exposing himself to all sorts of weather, his general reply was, "I have nothing to do with the weather." He preached to Marrow-bone Congregation, in Cumberland county, seventy-five miles from his home, once a month, for twenty years, and it is not remembered that he ever missed but one

---

[22]Mr. Lowry's Sketch.

appointment in all that time on account of bad weather. The trip on that occasion would have called him out on the cold Friday, and he very wisely shrunk from it. It is worthy of mention, too, that he rode on horseback, crossed creeks and rivers which were mainly unbridged, and received for his labors, upon an average, about seventy-five dollars a year. Still he collected and kept together a congregation from which several others afterward sprung up as offshoots from this common stock. The old congregation in Cumberland county is said now to be represented in many of the congregations of the North and West. And wherever such representatives are found, the name of the earnest old preacher is a household word. "In the whole course of his ministerial career, his Presbyterial books show no mark of absence. He has been heard to say that he was often sick before and after Presbytery, but never during the sessions. With all the infirmities of age, and in the incipient stage of his last illness, he attended the Presbytery preceding his death, but was unable to remain to the close of the sessions."

"Nearly one-fourth of every year of his life, from the commencement of his ministry, was literally spent encamped in the woods, at camp-meetings. The writer (Rev. David Lowry) has heard him avow it as his belief, from the pulpit, that a camp-meeting was the best place on this side of heaven. It was not unusual for him to preach once or twice going to, and returning from, those meetings."

This statement will create no surprise with the old people who read it. Such was the custom of the times. "In season and out of season," was the motto.

"His favorite topics in the pulpit were the fall of man, the atonement of Christ, and experimental and practical religion. He never attempted those nice and intricate distinctions in theology which, like the lines of the spider's web, are invisible to all eyes except those of the speaker, and, if seen by others, would still be, like the lines of the spider's web, of no possible use to man. His sermons, being filled with rich thought, striking illustrations, and solemn appeals, rarely failed to interest and affect the audience. His talent for argumentation, both in and out of the pulpit, was above what is ordinary, and his quickness of mind in apprehending and presenting truth, gave him great advantage in controversy. The following may serve as a specimen of his manner: He was discussing, on one occasion, in a friendly conversation with a clergyman of another denomination, the moral of infants. 'We believe,' said his opponent, 'that infants come into the world justified.' 'We believe,' replied Mr. Harris, 'that they go out of the world justified.' There the controversy ended, for as both believed that infants dying in infancy were saved, there was nothing worth contending about."

We have the following account of one of his visits to the sick. It is contained in a letter from himself to Rev. Finis Ewing, written in 1816:

"I received a request on Tuesday last to visit an old lady at the point of death. She wished me to preach and administer the sacrament in the room where she lay. On my arrival I found her very low, and under the operation of medicine. But she still urged me to preach and administer the Supper to herself and as many of her friends as were present who loved the Lord Jesus. My text was, 'My departure is at hand,' etc. Her physician would not permit any except a few friends to remain in the room during the sermon. The congregation were seated in the yard, and I stood in the door. The Lord helped, and the people felt. Just as I was about the administer the sacrament, the doctor and the people were forced into the house by a heavy shower of rain. During the celebration of the ordinance God poured out his Spirit, and the doctor and many of the irreligious wept much. Two of the old lady's sons were powerfully convicted. The communicants, in addition to herself, were five daughters of the afflicted mother, one daughter-in-law, and two granddaughters, and all appeared to feel the powers of the world to come. The poor old lady's faith became strong, through which she had a most charming view of her heavenly inheritance, and in that situation I left her."

In 1817, the Green River Bible Society was organized, and Mr. Harris was elected President. It is said that "the society derived much aid from his indefatigable labors." This is almost certain, as his heart would be in such a work as was contemplated by the American Bible Society in all its branches. The society at that time was in the second year of its existence. I allude to the American Bible Society. He was also one of the first who engaged in the distribution of tracts in the section of country in which he lived. In this work he seems to have anticipated the operations of the American Tract Society itself.

At the close of the war of 1812, the great Northwest was opened up for settlement to the American white population. It is meant by this statement that the Indians were dispossessed, and the country came under the control of the United States, and that the people of the United States were permitted to settle there. A great many emigrated from various States, but the emigration from Kentucky was especially large. As a matter of course, some families belonging to the Church would be among the emigrants. Such families soon felt very sorely the want of the Christian privileges of which they were deprived by their removal. They would very naturally turn their attention to the Churches which they had left behind for help. The following letter to Mr. Harris was written, in June of 1812, on this subject, by Mrs. Lindsey, a Christian lady, who had moved from Kentucky to Indiana:

"Dear Brother:—Great alarm prevails in this country, both on account of the shaking of the earth and danger apprehended from the Indians. The people have generally gone into forts.

"Shall we see you and Brother Chapman this fall? We still remain at home, and do not feel in much danger.

"The situation of the people here gives me great pain. We have had but one sermon since your visit to this country. One Sabbath after another comes, but all is silent—the glad news of salvation is not heard. I have great confidence that you and Brother Chapman will do something for us at Presbytery. Tell your young preachers to come and preach the gospel for us in this destitute part of God's vineyard."

The same lady writes to him again in September of 1819. The following is an extract:

> Dear Brother:—What entreaties can I use to induce you to send more preachers to Indiana? The State is filling up, and thousands are destitute of preaching. It would be gratifying news should it be consistent for you to send back Brother Lowry to this part of the State.

Such appeals made their impression. The Logan Presbytery appointed a day of fasting and prayer that God would call more laborers into the vineyard. The preachers were directed generally to preach to their congregations on a call to the ministry. The result was, that at the next meeting of the Presbytery eleven young men were received as candidates for the ministry. The hearts of both preachers and people were deeply stirred.

"The next spring," says my informant,[23] "I heard Father Harris preach to the Presbytery in session at Lebanon, Christian county, Kentucky. In portraying the moral condition of our country, especially of the frontier, and the great demand for preachers, he became so much affected that he ceased to speak, and fell in the pulpit, apparently giving utterance to the feelings of the prophet when he exclaimed: 'O that my head were waters, and mine eyes a fountain of tears, that I might weep day and night for the slain of the daughter of my people.' Several more young men became candidates for the ministry at this Presbytery, among whom was the late Rev. Joseph McDowell."[24]

These indications made it evident that the providence and Spirit of God were calling out the men, and that they would soon be prepared for their great work. But another inquiry began to present itself to the Church. The frontier wanted missionaries, but it had no means—at most, very limited means—of supporting them. How were they to be supported? How were they to procure means for even an outfit for their work? A female missionary society was organized to meet the exigency. Mr. Harris was a leading spirit in this work. The following is a part of the preamble to the constitution:

"This day a number of ladies met in the town of Russellville, at the house of Mrs. E. Hunter, for the purpose of forming themselves into a society to be denominated the Russellville Female Missionary Society. The meeting was opened by prayer, and an affectionate and appropriate address was delivered by Rev. William Harris."

Mr. Harris was elected secretary of the society, and appointed traveling agent to promote its interests and objects. He was likewise requested and authorized by its Board to receive donations for the Green River Female Missionary Society.

Several missionaries were immediately appointed by the Logan Presbytery to labor in the settlements of Indiana, Illinois, and Missouri. Among these were Rev. Alexander Chapman and Rev. Robert D. Morrow. As a specimen of the conduct and spirit enjoined upon the missionaries, the following is presented. It is an extract from the copy of a letter of instruction from Mr. Harris, Secretary and General Agent of the Missionary Society, to Rev. Alexander Chapman:

"Dear Brother:—The Missionary Board of the Cumberland Presbyterian Church have nominated and appointed you to labor as missionary in the State of Illinois. They advise that you preach as often as your health will permit; that you organize Churches, ordain elders, administer baptisms, etc. Also, that you encourage the people to expect preaching from our denomination so far as our missionary funds and claims elsewhere will permit.

"It is enjoined that you attend in your administrations to the simplicity of the

---

[23] Rev. D. Lowry.

[24] Rev. Joseph McDowell was a promising young man, but died early.

gospel, and cultivate feelings of friendship with other Churches holding the radical doctrines of our holy religion. The Board also entreat you to endeavor to cultivate at all times the Spirit of your Master."

This letter is dated October 24, 1820. It will be observed that these good men and women were making the gigantic efforts which have been mentioned here—and I call them gigantic for the best of reasons—for evangelizing and saving the opening country, when the Cumberland Presbyterian Church was yet but ten years old.

The records of the Board of Missions show also that Mr. Harris had been sent as a missionary to Indiana in the winter of 1820. In his journal of this mission we find the following expressive entry: "A missionary in this country needs warm clothes, warm friends, and a warm heart."

I add two or three paragraphs from the sermon delivered upon the occasion of the death of this good man by Rev. David Lowry, one of his sons in the ministry:

"The sphere of usefulness in which Father Harris labored for upward of forty years was the work of the ministry. The efforts of but few preachers in the Church to which he belonged have been attended with equal success. He commenced with extraordinary zeal, and so continued through the whole course of his useful life. Some men set out well in the ministry, and labor apparently with much zeal for a time, but relax and become cold. The Church marks it with regret, and they themselves occasionally mourn over their declension, but the grace and power of earlier efforts never return. The deceased escaped this evil, and continued the zeal of his first love in the pulpit till dismissed from the walls of Zion. He loved to preach.

> The world has no arithmetic to calculate the value and influence of such a man, since its honors are reserved for men of another description. Our cities are named after the warrior and statesman, and bonfires celebrate their deeds, while the humble and devoted minister of the gospel is overlooked, and sometimes treated with contempt. 'His record, however, is on high,' and he has, too, goodly record below. The Churches planted by his toil, and watered by his care, will long preserve his memory, and society will feel the benefit of his labor ages after he shall cease to move and speak on earth. Most of our legislators and able politicians, as well as men of science, have sprung from religious families, and were reared up under the preaching of the gospel; and all, or nearly all, the great men of our nation were educated at schools or colleges indebted to ministerial effort for their existence, and to the superintendence of preachers for their standing in the country.
>
> Am I reminded of the noise, and nonsense, and quirks, and cant of the pulpit, and of the petty sectarianism of the preachers? I admit it all, and have lamented over it. But point me to a profession which has not been abused and perverted. The history of preaching, like all other history, is liable tot he reproach of folly and crime. The ministry is not what it ought to be, and

might be, still it has no substitute. What but preaching overthrew ancient Rome, and broke the chains of modern Rome, and added the islands of the sea to Christendom? Parental instruction, Sabbath-schools, and religious books have done wonders. But through whose instrumentality were the parents converted? By whom were the books written and Sabbath-schools organized? All are indebted to the Christian ministry.

The feelings to which our venerable father gave utterance on his dying-bed in relation to the future success of the Church for whose benefit he had labored so long, were similar to those expressed by Joseph in his last moments for the prosperity of Israel: 'I die, but God shall surely visit you, and bring you up out of this land to the land which he swore to Abraham, to Isaac, and to Jacob.'

Perhaps no congregation lay nearer his heart than Pilot Knob. Here he has preached for more than forty years. Some of you have friends in heaven converted through his instrumentality. He officiated at the sacred altar when many of your were consecrated to God in the ordinance of baptism. Here he has left the wife of his youth, and many of his children, grandchildren, and even great-grandchildren. That God would visit you, and prosper you, and bring you at last to heaven, the antitype of the promised land, was doubtless among the last prayers of your departed minister.

Mr. Harris raised a large family, and lived to see his seed to the fourth generation. Five of his sons became ministers of the gospel, and two of his grandsons had become candidates for the ministry when his funeral-sermon was delivered. "He lived to see the Church to which he belonged increase from a Council to sixty-five Presbyteries, twenty Synods, and a General Assembly. But 'in a full age, like as a shock of corn cometh in his season,' and after a life of great usefulness, he went down to his grave in peace. There was nothing unusual in the last exercises of his mind. He expressed unshaken confidence in the truth of the doctrine he had preached, conversed frequently and calmly on the subject of death, and exclaimed shortly before he departed, 'Thank God, I am not afraid to die!'"

He died on the 8th of July, 1845, in the seventy-third year of his age.

An account of the following incidents in the life of Mr. Harris has been furnished upon the most reliable authority. It is supposed to be correct, and it contributes greatly to an insight into the character of the man. Some of the incidents indicate an approach to a degree of eccentricity which we would hardly expect from one so serious and earnest. They are, however, striking and interesting, and the account will be read with pleasure, and in some of the cases, at least, with profit. His old friends especially, who survive, will feel an interest in them.

Mention has already been made of his ministering to the Marrow-bone Congregation for twenty years. It is said that many of the young men of the congregation under his influence doubtless entered the ministry. Some of them still live as blessings to the Church. At one time he took his son, Chatham, then a young preacher, with him to Marrow-bone. After they were seated in the pulpit, he turned to the young man, without having given him any previous notice, and said: "Chatham, you must preach to-day. I have an appointment to preach to the colored people at three o'clock, and you have too much sense to preach to them; you must preach to the white people." Of course, Chatham was thunder-struck. He had never before preached in the presence of his father, and it would naturally have been a great trial had he even been well prepared. The authority carries the account no farther, but it is supposed that Chatham yielded, as the young men were taught, in those days, obedience to the fathers. We may imagine, however, that it was a severe ordeal.

At a certain time, while making a tour through the country for the purpose of preaching, he stopped at Glasgow on Saturday evening, intending to improve the Sabbath there. He met there, however, a Mr. Davis, who had once been a Cumberland Presbyterian, and afterward a Baptist, and at the time mentioned was a follower of Mr. Campbell. Mr. Davis had an appointment for Saturday night. Mr. Harris went to hear him; and when he was through, he announced appointments for himself for the next day at eleven o'clock, at three, and at night. Of course he expected to absorb all the time. Mr. Harris arose, and remarked that, as there was but one house of worship in the town, and all the customary hours for public service were to be occupied, he could not preach at any of those hours, but stated that, if the people would meet him, he would preach to them the next morning at sunrise. Sunrise of the next morning came, and the house was crowded. The good old man preached with power and with the Spirit. Mr. Davis was present. He had become a little more liberal, and asked Mr. Harris to preach at eleven. The latter replied that he was satisfied, that he had delivered his message, and declined the invitation. They dined together, however, that day. In the course of the conversation at dinner, Mr. Davis remarked that he believed that Mr. Campbell was a great light sent from heaven to enlighten and bless the world. Mr. Harris replied that the only evidence he had that Mr. Campbell was from heaven was, that his back, as it seemed to him, was then turned to heaven.

At a subsequent time he met in Glasgow another of the inevitable Campbellites, Rev. William Jordan. Mr. Jordan had brought up against the Cumberland Presbyterian and the Westminster Confessions of Faith the old charge of teaching that the ministry had power to forgive sins. Mr. Harris denounced the charge, and told the people that if Mr. Jordan would repent, and confess that he had misrepresented our Confession of Faith, he would himself forgive him, and he would furthermore give assurance, that if he would take the same steps in relation to the Westminster Confession, the Mother Church would do the same thing. In that case his friend would have an illustration of the extent to which we professed to exercise the power of forgiving sins.

About the year 1814, Mr. Harris was very sick with what was called, at that time, the winter-fever. It was thought he would die. Both himself and his friends came to the conclusion that his work was done. He called his wife and children together, and, while they stood weeping around his bed, he turned his face toward the wall, as King Hezekiah did on a like occasion, and lay for some time in silence. At length he turned back, and said to his wife; "Nancy, weep not; the Lord has assured me that I shall recover, and yet preach the gospel to a dying world." From that time he began to improve, and lived and labored still thirty years.

Something more remarkable still is connected with this occurrence. Mr. Chapman had heard of the dangerous illness of Mr. Harris, and had called together his congregation of Little Muddy for the purpose of praying for the restoration of his afflicted fellow-laborer. In the course of the meeting Mr. Chapman arose and stated that he felt satisfied that their prayers were answered, and that Mr. Harris would survive, and still be a blessing to the world. It turned out upon inquiry that the meeting for prayer coincided with the day and hour in which Mr. Harris himself seemed to acquire the assurance of his own recovery.

Perhaps our cold-hearted skepticism will revolt at these accounts. I have nothing to say in relation to them, except that they seem very well authenticated. I am writing history, and not attempting to explain all the methods of God's providence in his dealings with good men. But, in conflict with all our skepticism, what does the apostle say? "Is any sick among you? Let him call for the elders of the Church, and let them pray over him, anointing him with oil in the name of the Lord; and the prayer of faith shall save the sick, and the Lord shall raise him up; and if he have committed sins, they shall be forgiven him."

After his recovery from this illness he spent one whole night in prayer for his children, that they might be converted and saved in heaven. In the morning he came in from his night's wrestling with God, and told his wife, with rejoicing, that he was satisfied his prayers had been heard, and in due time would be answered. He lived to see all his children members of the Cumberland Presbyterian Church.

Mr. Harris always assisted Mr. Chapman at his camp-meetings. In the course of one of his meeting, Mr. Chapman seems to have been particularly impressed with the condition of three of his brothers-in-law. They were good citizens, upright and moral men, but were considered to be unbelievers in the technical sense of the term. Indeed, infidelity seemed to be gaining a foothold, especially among the young people. He communicated his feelings to Mr. Harris, and, under the guidance of what seemed to be a sort of premonition, asked him to preach, at some suitable hour, in the progress of the meeting, upon the following text: "Thy word is truth." Mr. Harris entered fully into the spirit of the request, asked time for reflection and prayer, and finally agreed to preach in full view of all the responsibilities of the occasion. On Monday of the meeting, he delivered his sermon. It was like bearding the lion in his den. The brothers were all hearers, and at the close of the sermon were in the altar of prayer. Two of them professed religion at the meeting, and the other subsequently; and all became pillars of strength in the congregation. Mr. Harris remarked afterward that he never felt before so fully the significance of the words of the prophet when he spoke of the word as a burning fire shut up in his bones. It was a deathblow to infidelity in the neighborhood.

A few days before Mr. Harris's death he asked that a little grandson, David Madison Harris, might be brought and placed near him upon the bed. When the little boy was brought, the old man laid his hands upon the child's head, lifting up his eyes to heaven, as if in silent prayer. We do not know what the import of the prayer was, but that little boy is now a minister of the gospel, and holds a prominent place in one of our principal literary institutions. To say the least, it is an interesting matter to connect together two such events.

In 1838, his son, Rev. D. R. Harris, was teaching in Springfield,

Tennessee. He wished to combine, as far as possible, the work of the ministry with that of teaching, and occasionally obtained the use of a house of worship in town. In the progress of things, however, this accommodation was refused. He then went to the court-house, but the civil authorities excluded him from this. He then appointed a protracted-meeting to be held in the Academy in which he was teaching. He sent for his father to assist him. The father came, and the meeting was held. About one hundred persons professed religion. A Church of seventy-five persons was organized, and a subscription of about two thousand dollars secured toward the building of a house of worship. The house was built, and, in 1842, Mr. Harris and five of his sons, all ministers, held another very successful meeting in the new church. Many more were added to the congregation. A meeting held by a father and five sons, all ministers, would be an unusual occurrence anywhere, and in any age.

Incidents of this kind might be multiplied, making up a history of the life of a laborious, and honored, and useful man. Enough, however, has been recorded to give us some idea of his active labors, and of what is perhaps more interesting, his interior life. He was a good man—he emphatically walked with God. He was more—he was both intellectually and physically a man of great vigor. It was an unpolished strength, it is admitted, but still it was the strength of a true manhood. Such a vigor enabled him to perform the unwonted labor of his times. Providentially, he lived in the right time and in the right place. God made him a burning and a shining light. He belonged to a race of men whose like we shall not see again. We linger upon their memory as it begins to fade from us, and thank God that he gave them to the Church in its great necessities in this country.

I have a few personal recollections of Mr. Harris, which I take some interest in leaving upon record. My first distinct recollection of him goes back to a camp-meeting held at the old Ridge Camp-ground in 1812. I was, of course, then but a boy, about as old as the century. I recollect him there in connection with one service only. In the course of the meeting he ordained an elder. This is a common occurrence. But what made the vivid impression upon my mind was, that the officiating minister and the person taking upon him the vows of the eldership, and the whole congregation, seemed to be in tears. I never witnessed so much solemnity and tenderness upon such an occasion. It is impressive even at this distance of time to think of it. The Church was then but two years and a half old. All its public and official acts were probably regarded in the light of experiments. This circumstance, no doubt, accounts in part, at least, for the deep interest which was evidently felt upon this solemn occasion. It is a fit occasion to mention, too, and the mention is to be made with profound gratitude to God, that three of the grandsons of the elder ordained that day are now rendering a noble service to the Church of their fathers.

I suppose that Mr. Harris was Moderator of Cumberland Synod in 1821. At all events he delivered the opening-sermon of the sessions of 1822. This was the first Synod which I ever attended. It was held at the Beech Meeting-house, in Sumner county, Tennessee. The Synod met in the old meeting-house. It was a log building, presenting but little more neatness and taste than would be presented by a common log barn. It has been long since, however, displaced by a tasteful and well-furnished stone building. The opening-sermon did not equal my expectations. It was said that the preacher was not in one of his best moods. It was, nevertheless, a good sermon.

In the fall of 1826, Rev. John Beard and myself were to pass from a visit to some friends in Butler county, Kentucky, to Sumner county, Tennessee. Mr. Harris had knowledge of the visit, and kindly invited us to spend a night with him on the way. According to the custom of the times, it was also arranged that we must hold meeting at his house the night which we were to spend there. Between sundown and dark of the day appointed we came in sight of his habitation. Some distance before we reached the house we found himself walking to and fro, awaiting our coming, evidently feeling a deep interest in the meeting which was expected. I was the older of the two, and preached. But I was worn, and not much in the spirit otherwise, and the preaching was dry. John Beard exhorted, and he and Father Harris sang a good song, and went among the people, shaking their hands in the old-fashioned way, and we had, in the end, a very good time. I never saw him at home, except on that occasion. Two or three things made an impression upon my mind which the changes of forty-six years have not effaced. One was the interest which he evidently felt in a common night-meeting made up of his near neighbors only. It is no wonder that a man who thus felt under such circumstances was useful in the country in which he lived. Then, again, the consideration with which he treated us. We were young men, unimportant, and, in a great measure, unknown in the Church. Yet we were treated with as much apparent attention as if we had been leaders in the denomination. Taking that case as a specimen, it is inferred that Mr. Harris taught his family that it was no inconsiderable matter to be a Cumberland Presbyterian preacher. This, too, perhaps, enables us to account for the fact that so many of his sons were encouraged to enter the ministry. They were taught by precept and example to estimate the office at something like its value and importance.

Mr. Harris published the first selection of hymns which was ever published for the use of the Cumberland Presbyterian Church. The book was published in 1824. It was a good selection, and was in general use in the Church a number of years.

In 1797, he was married in Green county, Kentucky, to Miss Nancy Highsmith. They raised a large family. A few brief extracts from a recent letter from his youngest son, Rev. C. H. D. Harris, must close this sketch:

> My father remarked in his last affliction that in all his pulpit efforts he had uniformly tried to hold up the cross, and had claimed the world for Christ—that he had never intentionally gone around the truth—the plain, simple, and unvarnished truth. In relation to the Church he said:
>
> 'Her path is clear, her progress pleasant, and her end will be glorious. This gives me great consolation now that I am about to lay down my cross and receive my crown.'
>
> He was full of sublime intelligence, and had an imperishable hope. He performed an immense amount of labor. Every year, as far back as I can remember, he left home on a

preaching tour, about the first of August, and was gone two or three months, attending camp-meetings, and sometimes performing funeral-services. A few months before he went to his reward, he rode on horseback over a hundred miles into Marion county to dedicate a church.

In the fall of 1864, in company with my wife, I made a visit to my dear mother. The cruel war was upon us, and times were perilous, but I felt that I must see her once more. We found her in ordinary health, though feeble. I preached for her; she was very happy, filled with God's love. A holy radiance shone in her countenance. Who can estimate the value of a pious mother? Her presence is a benediction. On the 28th of October, I bade her farewell, assured that our next meeting would be in the General Assembly and Church of the first-born. She gave me her blessing, and on the 2d of November died suddenly. My memory comes up freighted with the past.

Two or three additional statements make up the sum of this letter so full of filial recollections. In one of them the writer makes kind mention of my own visit to his father's home in 1826, when he was himself as yet a little boy. I now close this sketch of William Harris. For years to come, however, his name will be a household word in many families in the Green River portion of Kentucky.

It has been mentioned that five of Mr. Harris's sons entered the ministry. One of them, David Rice Harris, was one of the earliest students of Cumberland College. After completing his education, he established a school in the neighborhood in which he settled. This school soon acquired considerable reputation. The business of teaching was thus connected with that of preaching for several years. In an evil hour he connected himself with Rev. James Smith, who was then conducting the Cumberland Presbyterian which had been published eight or ten years at Nashville, Tennessee. In the failure of Mr. Smith, which occurred soon after the connection, Mr. Harris was understood to have lost the principal part of his hard and economical earnings. He still bore himself, however, as a Christian and a Christian minister. His death occurred some years ago. He married in early life a Miss McCutcheon of the section of country in which he had been raised up, and in which he lived and labored until his death. Mr. Harris was a man of excellent ability and great moral worth, and was useful, but the Church had not learned in his time to make men as useful as such a man as he might have been made. We appreciate blessings when they are gone. D. R. Harris became a candidate for the ministry October 9, 1822; was licensed October 13, 1824; and ordained October 8, 1829.

REV. HUGH BONE HILL
(1801-1866)

Hugh B. Hill was born in 4th day of December, 1801. His parents, James Hill and Jane Bone, were born in North Carolina, and reached maturity about the close of the Revolutionary War. In early life they were both admitted to membership in a Presbyterian congregation under the care at the time of Rev. James Hall, D.D. Dr. Hall officiated at their marriage. He was for a number of years one of the leading ministers in North Carolina. He had distinguished himself not only as a faithful chaplain, but as a brave and vigorous soldier in the troubles of the Revolution.

James Hill and his wife were of Scotch-Irish descent, and had inherited their religious and Presbyterian proclivities from a long line of pious ancestors. John McWilliams, a remote ancestor, was a widower with two daughters. He devoted himself with great assiduity to their religious education. He seems to have taken Abraham for his model, although the two cases were by no means parallel in every respect. Abraham, while yet childless, received and believed the promise that he was to be the father of a numerous race. John McWilliams, while watching over his two motherless daughters, was steadfast in the faith that he was to be the father of a "numerous seed." His faith went farther. "He was often heard to say that it was his abiding conviction that he was to have a numerous progeny, and that not one of them would fail to enter the kingdom with him."

Whether the faith of this good man has failed in any particular instance, of course it would be difficult to determine, but it is certain, if tradition is reliable, that his descendants were numerous and generally pious. Hugh B. Hill was one of those descendants. He was the fourth son of his parents.

In the fall of 1802, Mr. James Hill moved with his family to Tennessee, and settled in Wilson county, on the head-waters of Caney Fork. The subject of this sketch was, of course, then an infant. Of James Hill, my authority says that he "was a man possessed of a strong natural mind, cheerful and uniform in his disposition. His piety was deep, and his devotion to the fulfillment of religious obligation a daily business. Every thing else was made to yield to the claims of religious duty."

Of Jane Hill, the wife, he says, she "was a woman of extraordinary mind, a constant reader of the Bible, and other books of a religious and literary character. This course of life raised her far above mediocrity among her sex. Her piety was bold and independent. She prayed invariably in her family twice a day in the absence of her husband. Her authority in the family was positive. The moral training of her children was never neglected; her influence never ceased to be felt." Such were the parents of Mr. Hill. They brought up their children "in the nurture and admonition of the Lord." These all embraced religion in early life.

The father of our subject was a farmer, and his sons were brought up as the sons of farmers generally were, upon the farm. There were but limited means of education. Boys went to school during the winter, to such schools as the country furnished, but their labor was needed at home during the summer.

When young Hill was in his eighteenth year, his father moved to Kentucky, and settled in Hopkins county. The settlement was made in the woods, and for two years the labor of all the sons was needed in opening a farm and in the construction of necessary buildings. Several other families of the connection settled with them, and they established a sort of colony upon Rose Creek. They applied to the Logan Presbytery for preaching, and were soon visited by Alexander Chapman, William Harris, and otheres. A congregation was organized, regular preaching was introduced, and the young people began to attend the camp-meetings around. Religious impressions were made upon their minds, and some professed religion. Mr. Hill was among the serious. The following is the account of his conversion, slightly condensed:

"In the course of the summer, a camp-meeting was held at 'Good Providence,' in Union county. Thither about thirty of the young peole of Rose Creek neighborhood went, nearly forty miles, all of whom were unconverted, but serious on the subject of religion. Among them was Hugh B. Hill. No one of the company was more deeply concerned than he. Indeed, it was his express object in going to the meeting to endeavor to find peace with God. The result showed that his efforts were not in vain. On Saturday night of the meeting, Rev. Aaron Shelby preached, and at the close of the sermon made the customary call for the anxious to the place of prayer for encouragement and instruction. Hugh B. Hill was among the first who rushed forward in answer to the call. For about two hours he lay prostrate on the ground in prayer and in intense agony. At last he was enabled to cast himself unreservedly upon the mercy of God through Christ, the crucified Redeemer, whom he found to be able and ready to save to the uttermost. He rose to his feet; his face reflected the peace and joy of his heart."

The next morning he presented himself to the session, was received into Christian communion; and in the course of the day shared in the symbols of redeeming love. It is a little remarkable that the whole company of thirty or forty from Rose Creek professed religion at that meeting.

Mr. Hill became at once an active and efficient laborer at camp-meetings, and in all revival seasons. He was particularly successful in the instruction and guidance of serious inquirers. Indeed, he excelled in this through life. If a man was seriously inquiring, and would talk to him, and thoughtfully set forth his difficulties, he scarcely ever failed of finding relief, and of being enabled to settle the great question of his salvation in an intelligent and satisfactory manner. Our friend never screamed into the ears of his subjects, telling them what to do, without telling them how to do. He talked to them as a friend to friends, and, as it were, taking them by the hand he led them gently to the foot of the cross.

In process of time his mind, almost as a matter of course, began to go farther in its thoughts than to these mere common exercises. In considering the question of the ministry, he had the customary difficulties of young men who have any thing like a proper appreciation of that work. His education was limited; there were no schools; and, if schools had been abundant, there was a want of means at home sufficient to keep him up at a good school. Besides, a young man raised and taught as he had been, would have some idea of the importance and responsibility of the work itself. He seems to have had a strange early impression on this subject. Says my informant: "Hugh B. Hill has been often heard to say that when a boy he strongly felt the impression that he would some day be a preacher. Indeed, it was a facorite amusement with him, when quite a little boy, to construct a pulpit of sticks and clapboards, and 'hold forth' from it to such auditors as a boy could collect. This impression seems to have been renewed in real force soon after he professed religion."

The result was, that ont he 15th day of October, 1823, at Liberty Meeting-house, in Muhlenburg county, Kentucky, he put himself under the care of the Anderson Presbytery, as a candidate for the ministry. He was now twenty-two years of age, and his education was scarcely rudimental. To meet the exigency, and, for the convenience of his own children and others, Dr. Johnson, pastor of the congregation, established a school in the neighborhood. The teacher admitted young Hill and another young man into his school and his family. His kitchen was the school-room, and the bed-room of the two young men. The condition of things was rather primitive, but the times themselves were primitive.

After spending some time at this school, Mr. Hill was received into the family of Rev. Henry F. Delaney who lived near Morganfield, and entered the school of a Mr. William H. Thomas, said to have been "an able scholar and Christian gentleman." In this family and school he was associated with Joseph A. Copp, afterward Rev. Dr. Copp, who died a few years ago in Chelsea, a suburb of Boston. It seems that Mr. Delaney, gave them something like informal lectures occasionally upon theology.

He afterward spent some time at a high-school kept at Greenville by Rev. Isaac Bard, a Presbyterian minister. Theology is said to have been his favorite study, and to this he devoted much the larger portion of his time. And in the investigation of its truths he was aided not a little by an old uncle whose name he bore, and who at all times took a deep interest in instructing him. We have the following passing notice of this uncle:

> It will not, it is hoped, be considered as going too far out of the way to pay a passing tribute to the memory of this 'uncle,' who, for the times in which he lived, and the limited education he had been able to acquire, enjoyed a high reputation as a theologian and an expounder of the Scriptures. In addition to his reputation in these respects, by his unaffected humility, and consistently pious life, he exerted in favor of religion a wide influence. He had never aspired to the ministry, and was not, therefore, a preacher in the technical sense of the term, but in the absence of the more regular exercises of the house of God, he would give public exposition of some appropriate passage of Scripture for the edification of his neighbors and friends, in what he modestly denominated his 'little talks.'

I hope I may take the liberty of saying here, that the foregoing quotation is evidently a filial tribute, which might be made much stronger, of a son to the memory of one of the best of fathers. That "old uncle" of Mr. Hill was he who, fifty years ago, was known all over this country as "Uncle Hugh Bone," the father of Rev. M. H. Bone, of Winchester, Tennessee. Old Uncle Hugh Bone—his memory is fragrant—understood the science of the theology and of scriptural interpretation more thoroughly, and was a better preacher, although not technically a preacher at all, than a large proportion of the expounders and preachers whom he heard from year to year. This is a short episode. It is hoped the reader will pardon.

At the fall sessions of the Anderson Presbytery in 1825, Mr. Hill was licensed as a probationer for the holy ministry. The meeting of the Presbytery was held at Princeton, Indiana. For the following six months he was assigned to the Princeton Circuit, in the southern part of that State. Says my authority:

> In the course of these six months of missionary work in Southern Indiana, Hugh B. Hill succeeded in accomplishing much good for the cause of his Master and his Church; numbers were led to a knowledge of the truth; Churches were edified and strengthened; and Hill himself much improved in his knowledge of Systematic Theology and sermonizing.

His next six months were spent upon the Henderson Circuit. This was in Kentucky, embracing the counties of Henderson, Hopkins, Muhlenburg, and Union. The report is that he fulfilled his mission on the Henderson Circuit with fidelity, but that his compensation was meager. Occasionally there was a special present of a pair of socks, or jeans pantaloons, or leather enough for a pair of shoes. The sum in cash was about sufficient to enable him to keep his horse shod, and possibly to pay the postage on an occasional letter from his mother. He followed the example, however, of his contemporaries, and of some who preceded him a few years; he bore all and kept to the work.

His labors for the next six months were divided between the Henderson and Christian Circuits; the following six months he supplied the Christian Circuit. His success in this latter half-year is said not to have equaled his hopes. Of course the disappointment was a matter of "deep regret and great self-abasement. He took all the reproach to himself."

In the fall of 1827, he was sent to the Southwestern District of Kentucky. The country was new and rough, and the traveling-preacher found but few of the comforts of life. The present writer preceded him in that country, and has a very distinct recollection of some of its characteristics; but there were scattered over it some good people, who received the word gladly. But the preacher had to swim creeks, to encounter deep mud, to endure the customary snow-storms, to preach, and often to lodge, in open houses, and in the spring and summer seasons to bear the torments of musquitoes innumerable. Still faithful men labored there, and collected congregations which have grown into strength and respectability. Mr. Hill labored on that circuit a year. Says my authority:

> It may readily be conceived what remuneration he received for the twelve months of toil, and privation, and hardship. A good conscience, frequent communion with God, the favor of the people, together with the well-founded satisfaction of having accomplished something for the kingdom of Christ, were his reward.

I do not put the case of the want of remuneration in quite so strong a light as does my authority. I know what the situation of the country was at that time, and am not surprised at the meagerness of the pecuniary results. Still, "the poor have the gospel preached unto them;" and it is well for the world that there have always been such men as the subject of our sketch who were willing to preach to the poor, even if the pecuniary returns were small.

At Piney Fork Meeting-house, in what was then Livingston county, Kentucky, Mr. Hill was set apart to the work of the ministry, on the 9th of April, 1829. He still continued in the itinerant work, some times under distinct directions, and at others under general directions, being allowed the exercise of an extended discretion.

In 1829, Dr. Cossitt undertook an extensive tour through the country, in behalf of Cumberland College, and at his solicitation Mr. Hill became the companion of his travels. They preached generally wherever they went, and Dr. Cossitt on his return is said to have made a most favorable report of the labors and promise of his fellow-traveler.

In the fall of 1830, Mr. Hill and Rev. M. H. Bone united in a protracted-meeting at Elkton, Kentucky. The meeting continued, with occasional intermissions, during six months, whilst the revival was uninterrupted through the whole time. More than a hundred professions of religion took place. A large number of the cases were of the most respectable citizens of the town and neighborhood. About eighty persons united with the Cumberland Presbyterian Church. Of these, about half were grown men, who immediately became helpers in the great work. It is remarkable, too, that out of so large a number there were but one ot two who fell back. This was one of the most interesting revivals of religion that ever appeared in that portion of Kentucky.

In the summer of 1832, Mr. Hill received a call to preach to a community in Cairo and its vicinity, in Sumner County, Tennessee. He accepted this call, and thereby found himself, by rather a strange providence, in a new field, and, as it turned out, the field in which he certainly accomplished the great work of his life. The southern portion of Sumner county, the portion in which Mr. Hill settled, is one of the richest and most interesting portions of Tennessee. When I speak of its richness, I allude to its soil, and in speaking of its interest, I intend to describe its population. The country was settled, and is still settled, with prosperous farmers. In one portion of the county Shiloh had, at an early time, exerted a powerful influence. It had been a favored spot in the old revival. In another and more obscure portion, the Dry Fork Congregation had been for a number of years doing a good work. In various parts of the county there were prosperous Methodist and Baptist congregations, but the particular section of the county to which Mr. Hill was called, whilst the population were civil, and moral, and orderly, had hardly ever been reached by a strong and stirring religious influence. God in his providence seems undoubtedly to have used the agency of a few good men in directing the steps of Mr. Hill to this field. He commenced his labors there, boarding with a worthy member of his little congregation.

In process of time, October 22, 1835, he married Miss Mary Reed, daughter of Captain William Reed, one of the principal citizens of the community in which he had located. Previous to his marriage, however, he had, in company with Rev. M. H. Bone, made an excursion into the State of Ohio. The young preachers visited Lebanon, in that State, and spent some time in preaching there. They were invited to the pulpits of the city generally, and by their earnest and evangelical ministrations seem to have made a fine impression. Mr. Bone remained some time, but Mr. Hill soon returned to his own proper field in Tennessee.

In describing the labors of Mr. Hill in Cairo and its vicinity during his principal years there, I cannot do better than to extract almost literally a few pages from the manuscript by which I am permitted to be mainly guided in this brief sketch. The letters which I shall copy are from men who were intimately mingled with the transactions which they describe, and their authority is unquestionable. No man can read them but with the most intense interest. I commence with chapter sixteenth, headed with,

SOME OF HIS WORKS

The ministerial labors of Mr. Hill were not confined alone to Cairo. Though the regular pastor of the Chruch here, he found time during the week to ride and preach must all over the surrounding country. There was not a school-house in all that region which was not made a place of assemblage to receive the messages of truth which he must needs deliver to the people. Frequently he would take excursions abroad, and would be absent for several weeks, preaching funeral-sermons and ministering to the more destitute portions of the country, and all at his own expense. His services were much sought after, both by ministers of his own and other denominations. Whenever it was all all in his power, he delighted to comply with these invitations. Lebanon, Tennessee, just across the Cumberland River, was one of his favorite places of resort. Rev. George Donnell was then the pastor of the Church there, and would frequently invite Mr. Hill to assist him upon sacramental occasions. On one of these, a revival of religion sprang up, which proved to be a most gracious time of ingathering of souls to Christ. It lasted some considerable time, during which many of the most prominent and leading citizens of the town professed a saving faith in the Lord Jesus, and were added to Mr. Donnell's congregation. Hill labored most indefatigably in this revival, and by his assiduous and patient efforts to win them to Christ, endeared himself to the good people of Lebanon ever afterward during his life.

About this time Middle Tennessee had become literally the land of camp-meetings; scarcely a neighborhood was without its organization, either Methodist or Cumberland Presbyterian, sometimes both; and each people had its regular time and place of holding camp-meetings. The summer and fall of 1837 was particularly noted for the many meetings of this character held all over the country. But the little Church at Cairo had never yet had a camp-meeting. The matter was talked about; a public meeting on the subject was called; and it was resolved by the members and friends in attendance to have one. But it was now late in the season; camps and a shelter had to be built; those who would contract to build the one had no time to work on the others. What was to be done about it? At length some one, more enterprising than the rest, got up and said, 'All those who intend to build tents form into line out here.' A goodly number promptly stepped out, and, what is remarkable, nine of this party were non-professors of religion, and so were all their families. 'Now,' said the speaker, 'do you go and build your tents, and the rest of us will be responsible for the shelter.' The time of the meeting was agreed upon; the place a beautiful oak grove some two miles east of Cairo. All went to work with a will, and by the time appointed every thing had been arranged; comfortable tents built; spacious shelter erected; and preachers enough in attendance to carry on the meeting. Rev. T. C. Anderson preached the opening-sermon; much good attention was rendered, and some serious feeling manifested. Exercises went on day and night; great crowds attended; every day the interest increased; many came forward to the altar; the work of God's Spirit became deep and general; conversions began to multiply; the news spread through the country; vast multitudes came flocking to the scene, until the shelter could no longer accommodate them. Exercises then spread out all over the woods, and every log became a mourner's-bench and every stump a pulpit. Like some mighty conflagration, the first of God's Spirit seemed to kindle up in the hearts of the vast multitude, and burned on, uncontrollable, to the utter consumption of every thing sensual, devilish, and wicked. Except those strange bodily exercises which characterized the revivals of 1800, this one, from all accounts, must have greatly resembled them.

Col. J. J. Hibbitts, Ruling Elder of the little organization at Cairo, and tent-holder at this meeting, gives the following account:

The first visit of Hugh B. Hill to Sumner county, I think, was in the fall of 1832. He was so well received that Brothers John Parsons, Thomas H. Essex, Jacob Greenhatch, and others, prevailed on him to organize a Church at Cairo, and remain with them and preach in that section of country, which he did, with wonderful effect. The Church at its organization consisted of about fifteen members. He continued to add to the little bank until 1837. He prevailed upon his little flock to build camps at Oak Grove, in the vicinity of Cairo. The meeting commenced the Saturday before the first Sabbath in October, and continued two weeks. The ministers in attendance were T. C. Anderson, George Donnell, J. M. McMurry, Francis Johnston, Robert Bell, H. B. Hill, and M. H. Bone. My recollection is, that there were about two hundred and fifty hopeful conversions as the results of that meeting; in fact, the revival continued that fall and winter. He preached nearly every Sabbath in the bounds of its influence, which extended from Gallatin to Hartsville, a distance of sixteen miles, and over a portion of Wilson county. I suppose there must have been fifty conversions at these meetings. There were more old men and women, in proportion to the number of converts, than I ever knew at any revival; some old persons sixty, seventy, and seventy-five years of age, sought and obtained religion, who have since died in faith. Some who were non-professors of religion built camps, and they and their wives professed and joined the Church. Some five or six days after the meeting commenced, the interest seemed to subside. One of the elders told Brother Hill he must preach that day. He hesitated, but the elder insisted. He finally consented. He went into the stand. His prayer was fervent, importunate. He announced his text—the eighteenth verse of the fourth chapter of 1st Peter: 'And if the righteous scarcely be saved, where shall the ungodly and the sinner appear!' and such a sermon I never before, nor since, heard fall from the lips of man. There was a solemn awe on the congregation, and a stillness like death. I recollect when the invitation was given for the anxious, old Captain William Reed, his father-in-law, and General Hall, came tottering to the altar of prayer, the first time they had ever started for Zion. They both professed religion shortly after. After that sermon of Hill's, the work went on with ease; in fact, every member and every convert was preaching.

At this meeting we added about one hundred and fifty members to the little flock. The Methodist, Baptist, and Presbyterian Churches, too, were greatly built up.

REMINISCENCE BY T. C. ANDERSON, D.D.

I first made Hugh B. Hill's acquaintance in the course of the sessions of Synod in Gallatin, in the fall of 1830. He and Rev. Alfred Bryan went home with me, and we soon became closely united companions. As I had promised Dr. Cossitt to visit Princeton, with reference to accepting a situation in the College there, I concluded to accompany Hill and Bryan on their return from Synod. We spent a night with Bryan, at his mother's, and the next day Hill and I went to Elkton. I 'fell in love' with both the young brethren, but Hill was my favorite. I have never known a more genial traveling companion.

During the two years I remained at Princeton, I saw but little of Hill, except that he attended a Synod and General Assembly there, and he was still my favorite.

In May, 1832, I settled in Nashville, and about the same time Hill took charge of a small Church in Cairo, Sumner county; but, as we were in different Presbyteries, we seldom met except at Synod.

In 1834 or 1835, we met at a camp-meeting on 'Goose Creek,' in the vicinity of Hartsville. He did most of the preaching, as I then had but little experience in the ministry. On Monday morning I was ordered to preach at 9 o'clock. Before I closed the excitement became so great that I could not proceed. Hill told me to 'call mourners.' The call was made, and the altar was filled. Hill then made an exhortation, and proclaimed that all the seats under the shelter would be devoted to the mourners, and those who declined to join the mourning band were invited to retire from the shelter, while those who were willing to mourn were invited to kneel. More than half of the congregation knelt. I had never witnessed so many mourners on their knees pleading for mercy. There was no more preaching that day; the congregation never dispersed, nor were exercises suspended till late in the evening. Hill labored incessantly, not less than six hours, and about fifty persons professed that day and night. When Brother Hill took charge of the society in Cairo and vicinity, they had no house in town or country. He preached in the Academy at Cairo, and in a Baptist church in the country. He soon began to gather members at each place, and in 1837 they concluded to have a camp-meeting. A site was selected two or three miles east of Cairo, and a shelter and camps were erected. As I was then residing at Lebanon, I attended the meeting, and preached the first sermon. Mourners were invited; a number came, and several professed during that first service; and at every service after that there were mourners and professions. I was compelled to leave Sunday evening, and did not return until the next Friday evening. There had been an unusually large number of professions during the week; but the altar was still crowded with mourners, and professions occurring every hour during the day and night, some in the altar, others in the woods and tents.

On the second Sabbath Rev. M. H. Bone preached for the benefit of those who had been waiting the Lord's good time. He endeavored to convince them that the Lord was willing at all times, and that whenever they became willing to have salvation upon the Lord's terms, he would convert them. At the close of the sermon the invitation was given to the anxious to come into the altar. I was engaged clearing the aisles, that the anxious might have free access to the altar. Having just cleared them, I saw seven large old ladies come tottering down one aisle toward the altar. Not thoroughly comprehending their purpose, I stepped aside to await the development. All walked into the altar and kneeled at the same bench. In about one half-hour, one of them cried out, 'Well, bless the Lord! I have been waiting his good time these thirty years. When the preacher told me it had come I did not believe it, but I thought I would come and see, and, bless the Lord! it has come, and he has converted my soul. O, bless the Lord!' The last one of those seven old ladies professed religion before the meeting closed.

After continuing eleven or twelve days the meeting adjourned. Some two hundred and fifty or three hundred persons professed faith in Christ, including all ages and grades of society.

Brother Hill collected a respectable congregation at Cairo, and a large one in the country, and, had they sustained him as they might and should have done, he doubtless would have remained with them till death.

Shortly after the Cairo meeting I removed to Winchester, and consequently seldom saw Brother Hill till I returned to Lebanon, in 1843, and, as my affliction prevented me from preaching, I have not been his fellow-laborer since that meeting; but I have seen him labor with great success in several revivals in this (Lebanon) place. But memory is treacherous, and I cannot call up incidents. Thus much I know, when a revival was needed we generally sent for Brother Hill.   T. C. ANDERSON.

One expression in the close of this letter brings up a painful subject. Mr. Hill, after a few years, changed his field of labor from Cairo, where he had been so eminently useful, and was evidently so greatly beloved. What was the reason? The old answer is the true one: "They did not support him." They admired the preacher; they loved the man; but, with what sorrow do we say it! they left him, in a great measure, to take care of himself, his wife, and his little ones. And yet these people were mainly prosperous farmers. They lived in the midst of abundance; they were able to educate their children, and start them favorably in the world. Why did they not retain a good and useful preacher, and thus, with the blessing of God, contribute to collecting and keeping together a good and useful congregation of earnest Christian people? Instead of this, the candlestick has been removed, and Cairo, and the neighborhood of the great camp-meeting of 1837, are to-day a spiritual desolation. Such evils, however, are not to be corrected by the use of hard words. They are, nevertheless, deplorable. When will men learn to be wise to do good? When will congregations learn to appreciate the truth of the divine ordination, that "they who preach the gospel shall live of the gospel"?

From Cairo Mr. Hill removed, and settled in the neighborhood of Cane Ridge Congregation, engaging to divide his time between Cane Ridge and "Ewing Chapel," in Rutherford county. Shortly after settling in this community he lost two of his children in quick succession. Of course it was a great trial.

In 1853, he commenced preaching once a month at the "Brick Meeting-house," between Nashville and Nolensville. His labors there were greatly blessed, and resulted in the organization of a large and flourishing congregation. Still he found the same remissness on the part of the people in the matter of support.

His next settlement was on Stewart's Creek, in the neighborhood of Old Jefferson, in Rutherford county. Here he bought a choice little farm, at a high price, but with a promising prospect of being able to pay for it in the course of time. The war came on, however, and blasted all his prospects in that connection. In the meantime he entered upon the pastorate of Jerusalem Congregation.

He was not a blustering, nor even a talking politician, but his political proclivities were very decided, and generally known. This circumstance, it is supposed, subjected him to greater hardships during the war. They were, at least, very great. He was unable to pay for his little farm. His creditor, however, was kind enough to cancel the obligation, and he was thus relieved from a burdensome debt. He renewed his ministerial work with his accustomed earnestness and vigor, but it was soon finished. About the middle of February, 1866, while engaged in some domestic labors, he was exposed to unusual cold, and seemed to be unusually affected by it. In a few days the affection developed itself into erysipelas; and on February 26, 1866, his active and earnest life came to an end. He died as such a man would be expected to die, with quietness, calmness, and resignation. His remains were deposited in a cemetery near what had been his home. A suitable monument was prepared through the liberality of his friends, and in the course of the sessions of the Middle Tennessee Synod, in 1867, it was set up by the Synod in its official capacity, in connection with representatives from several Lodges of the Masonic Fraternity belonging to the surrounding country. Thesolemnities of the occasion were imposing and impressive, and the monument stands as a memorial of the acknowledged worth of a laborious, unselfish, and devoted Christian minister. His most enduring monument, however, will be found in those whom he has turned to righteousness. They shall shine as stars in his crown of rejoicing forever.

I have a few words to add for the consideration of many who will perhaps read this sketch. During thirty-seven years Mr. Hill was an active, laborious, and devoted minister. His labors were for the most of that time bestowed upon what the world calls prosperous and thrifty communities—some of them were even wealthy. He was not himself a thoughtless and wasteful man in his expenditures. There was no frivolous and reckless extravagances in the economy of his household; and yet Mr. Hill, after all these years of labor, left his family without a home, or the means of procuring one. Surely a great wrong existed somewhere. I do not wish to press this subject, and have already said that wrongs, evils such as this must have been, are not to be corrected by hard words. But still, we are making history, and I am writing history, and the truth ought to be told. Let congregations consider these things. God exercised a special care of the priests and the prophets under the old dispensation. He feels just as deep an interest in an earnest and faithful ministry now. For idlers I have no word to say; but for the laborer I have to repeat what the very highest authority has said, that he is worthy of his hire, and if that is withheld we know where the wrong lies, and where the penalty must fall.

REV. JAMES JOHNSON
(1785-1837)

Sources: Manuscripts of Dr. J. M. Johnson, Hon. J. L. Johnson, and Minutes of Logan Presbytery.

James Johnson was born the 15th of June, 1785, in Prince Edward county, Virginia. In 1790 his father emigrated to Kentucky, and settled in Scott county. Subsequently, however, he moved to Barren county, and became the owner of the land upon which Glasgow now stands. In 1802 James Johnson, the son, left his father's house for the purpose of seeking his fortune in the wide world. He was then seventeen years of age. His leaving home does not seem to have been produced by any domestic difficulties or dissatisfaction, but from an anxious desire to take his part in the stirring scenes of life. The country was new, and there were many openings to active and aspiring young men. He made his way to Louisville, then a mere trading village and military post. He there became acquainted with General Clarke, whose confidence he seems to have soon acquired. He was sent by General Clarke on several perilous missions through the North-western Territory, then inhabited by Indians, with a few French settlements interspersed. In one of these agencies he landed his canoe at the mouth of Hurricane Creek, in what is now Crittenden county, Kentucky, and made his way to Centerville, then the seat of justice of Livingston county. Here he became acquainted with John Gray, then a prominent citizen of Lower Kentucky, and Mr. Woods, afterward of the house of Yeatman and Woods, of Nashville. He engaged himself as a clerk in the store of Mr. Woods. He continued in this position, however, but a short time, as we find that when he was but about eighteen years of age, through the influence of several prominent men, he was appointed sheriff of Livingston county. He held this office six years, and at the expiration of that time commenced the study of medicine with Dr. Stewart, who is represented to have been a physician of eminence and ability. He is said also to have enjoyed the friendship and esteem of Drs. Griffin and Delany, both, like himself, Virginians, and both men of education and refinement.

In 1806 Mr. Johnson was married to Miss Jane Leeper, of Livingston county. In process of time, he commenced the practice of medicine. The country was new, and thinly settled: he was a popular physician, and of course his practice was very laborious.

In 1808 he made profession of religion, and joined the Cumberland Presbyterian Church. About a year afterward his wife also professed religion, and seems to have become an unusually pious woman. I have in my possession a long and interesting account of her Christian profession, her life, and her death. She was awakened to the necessity of religion by the death of a younger sister. Says the writer: "On the fourth day of July, in the town of Salem, whilst the large majority of its citizens were engaged in the usual manner of celebrating the anniversary of American Independence in a public dinner, ball, and similar amusements, Mrs. Johnson now awakened to a sense of the danger of living without God in the world, as also of the depravity of her nature and corruption of her heart, in her garden was engaged at a throne of divine grace for that mercy and grace which she felt she so greatly needed. Whilst thus engaged, her mind was relieved: God shed abroad his love in her heart. She lived in the faithful discharge of religious duties. In the absence of her husband, she made it a matter of conscience to convene her children and servants for family prayer."

Such a wife could not be otherwise than a great helper to a good man.

In the war of 1812 he entered the public service as a volunteer, and was made assistant surgeon of his regiment. He also served in the campaign of General Hopkins against the North-western Indians. Finis Ewing was a chaplain in this expedition, or rather, served in the two-fold capacity of a private soldier and chaplain. The times were trying.

On the 11th day of December, 1818, Dr. Johnson lost his excellent wife. Her death seems to have been an unusual Christian triumph. Having joined her friends in a sweet song, she exhorted all around her to seek the salvation of their souls. Her friends thought that supernatural strength had been imparted to her. After addressing her relatives very earnestly for two, or two and a half hours, says my authority, "She ceased not to praise God, and express her views of heaven, which appeared just in prospect, in such language as the following: 'What is this I see—is it Pisgah's view? No, it is heaven itself! Glory, glory, glory!'" Such a death as this was well calculated to make an impression upon the mind of the surviving husband. He had already turned his attention to the Christian ministry. The circumstances were well calculated to strengthen his purposes in that direction. On the 8th day of April, 1818, he was received as a candidate for the ministry by the Logan Presbytery. Its sessions were held at Lebanon Academy, in Christian county, Kentucky. The first text assigned him for a trial sermon was Eph. ii. 8. At the fall sessions of the same Presbytery in 1819, on the 18th day of November, at Antioch Meeting-house, in Christian county, he and Woods M. Hamilton, John M. Berry, William C. Lang, and Joseph McDowell, were licensed. The text of Mr. Johnson's popular discourse, preparatory to licensure, was John iii. 16. On the 2d day of April, 1822, he and Woods M. Hamilton were set apart to the whole work of the ministry by the Logan Presbytery, at Rose Creek Meeting-house, in Hopkins county. Rev. Aaron Shelby preached the ordination-sermon, and Rev. John Barnett presided and gave the charge.

When Mr. Johnson was licensed, he was directed to spend two months of the time intervening between that and the next Presbytery on the Christian and Montgomery Districts as a missionary, and at the spring sessions of the Presbytery, in 1820, he was directed to spend the whole of his time on the Christian District. The record is that all these appointments were fulfilled. It will be recollected that at this time Dr. Johnson had a family of several motherless children.

After Dr. Johnson's ordination, according to the custom of those days, his missionary services were sometimes called into requisition. I quote from one of the manuscripts in my possession: "When ordered by his Presbytery to travel as a missionary through Indiana, Illinois, Missouri, or Arkansas, he went cheerfully to the work, carrying a bell and hobble for his horse, preaching in the wilderness, under the shade of a tree, often to half-a-dozen of poor hunters; still, however, erecting the standard of the cross whenever and wherever the opportunity offered itself. He was a zealous man in every thing he undertook; he never yielded to discouragements; dashed all obstacles aside, and moved directly on to the accomplishment of his purposes. His greatest efficiency was in exhortation and prayer. His sermons, however, were always good—sometimes excellent. In private life, he was kind and exemplary. He loved the Church, loved the ministry, loved the brethren. In his temperament he was cheerful, and always hopeful."

In 1820 or 1821 Dr. Johnson was married a second time, to Mrs. Louisa Harman, of Tennessee. Mrs. Harman's family name was Brigham. Some of her brothers and their families were amongst my earliest acquaintances and friends after I entered the ministry. I recollect them with deep interest.

After the death of his second wife, he was married again, to a Mrs. Jarratt, of Livingston county, Kentucky. He survived this marriage, however, but a few weeks. His last affliction was of short duration. On the 18th day of December, 1837, his laborious and active life came to an end. I recollect it was said at the time that his death was rather a triumphant scene. My informant says: "His mind was perfectly composed; his trust in the Saviour of the world was unfaltering. He died exhorting his children to meet him in heaven."

My personal knowledge of Dr. Johnson was limited to seven or eight of the last years of his life. The most of that time we were co-presbyters. He was genial, cheerful, and social in his habits. If he had dark days, I never happened to meet him in one of them. He had a very interesting family growing up around him. The most of them have since become honored men and women. His home was the abode of hospitality. It is intimated in one of the manuscripts which I have used, and I know it to have been true, that there was always a special welcome to the ministerial brother. He kept up the practice of medicine to some extent, I suppose, from the time he entered the profession to his death.

He had a large family, and received but little remuneration for his ministerial labor. Still he maintained the character of an earnest and laborious preacher. His sons says: "He never passed a Sabbath without religious exercises of some kind." When I knew him, the prospects of the Church were dark in the section of country in which he lived. We had discouragements. For some years three of us constituted the whole available strength of the Presbytery. Still he never faltered in his fidelity to the Church, or to his ministerial vocation.

Dr. Johnson had mingled more with men of the world then most ministers. His habits of life as a physician kept him in constant contact with such men. Such relations to society are not always the most useful to the ministry. They sometimes become a snare. Still, to a thoughtful and dignified man, they open new avenues to usefulness. Men of the world are better understood by those who mingle with them. They can be approached more advantageously by such men. The subject of this sketch never lost by his contact with men. It increased, rather than diminished, his influence over them. They thought the more of Christianity from the exemplification of it which they found in him. He was a gentleman, as well as a Christian and a Christian minister.

He was free from professional envy. Whilst he did not make the highest ministerial pretensions, he certainly never looked with a spirit of rivalry upon those who may have stood somewhat above him in public estimation. He would rather have strengthened than weakened the influence of such men.

He was a bold and fearless expounder of his religious opinions. He had been trained in a hardy and rugged school. It gave him independence. Some of his neighbors were unbelievers, and bitter opposers. He never turned his course to avoid them. He gave them his mind plainly—they understood him. The line between them was distinctly marked—he met them with no spirit of compromise.

His son says: "He never feared the face of man." I expect this is true. If he had seen an honest and upright man oppressed, he would have resisted the oppressor, if he had stood alone in his resistance. Such men are invaluable in any community.

    Dr. Johnson left ten children. Some of these still live: Dr. John M. Johnson, of Atlanta, Georgia; Hon. James L. Johnson, of Owensboro, Kentucky; and Major-General R. W. Johnson, of the U.S. Army—are three of them. Alfred B. Johnson, his youngest son, graduated at Cumberland College in 1848, studied law, and settled in Owensboro, Kentucky. he was an earnest member of the Church, became a ruling elder in his congregation, was a delegate to the General Assembly in 1857, but died in early life. He was a young man of fine promise.

REV. FRANCIS JOHNSTON
(1790-1856)

Francis Johnston was born in Iredell county, North Carolina, September 12, 1790. His parents were moral and upright persons, and his mother was, at the time of his birth, a member of Bethany congregation of the Presbyterian Church. The congregation was under the care of Rev. Dr. Hall. Dr. Hall baptized the subject of this sketch.

About the year 1795 Mr. Johnston's parents moved to what was then called West Tennessee, and settled in Sumner county. The county was then a wilderness, in more senses than one. It was very sparsely populated, and almost wholly destitute of the means of grace. Mrs. Johnston, the mother, however, soon united herself with Shiloh congregation, then under the care of Rev. William McGee. Mr. McGee was succeeded by Rev. William Hodge. The first camp-meeting that ever was held in Sumner county, was held at Blythe's place, on Desha's Creek, in the bounds of Shiloh congregation. This meeting occurred in the spring of 1800. Mr. Johnston attended the meeting with his father's family. He was then in his tenth year. He tells us, in a sketch of his own life, that although so young, "he was old enough to feel that he ought to have religion."

In 1803, in his thirteenth year, he professed religion at home, under the guidance of his mother and a sister younger than himself, who had made a profession a short time before. He joined the Shiloh congregation in connection with his mother and sister. His father, in a year or two, in like manner united himself with the same congregation.

From 1806 to 1810 his mind was variously exercised on the subject of preaching the gospel. He laid his case before Mr. Hodge, but was not much encouraged. Mr. Hodge, however, advised him to travel on the circuit a while, with one of the circuit-riders, and make an experiment of his ability to teach. He accordingly spent a month with Rev. David Foster, and also a month with Rev. James Farr on the circuit, but with little satisfaction to himself. His education was indifferent, and his father was poor. He thought that a minister ought to be an educated man. In 1808 or 1809 a good school was opened in an adjoining neighborhood. He determined, notwithstanding his poverty, to avail himself of its advantages, entered, and attended a few days; but his father fell sick, and he was obliged to desist. Upon the recovery of his father, having become discouraged in regard to the matter of education, he resolved to learn the blacksmith's trade, and devote himself to the business for life. He learned the trade in his father's shop, and commenced business, but still felt doubtful whether he ought not to preach.

To add to his embarrassments, on the 24th of September, 1812, he married Miss Caty Foster, Sister of Rev. David Foster. The marriage seemed untimely; still, his wife was a most estimable woman, and throughout life was an earnest helper in every good work. To embarrass himself still farther, in December of the same year he joined the army as a volunteer for twelve months—a strange race for a man to run who was feeling all the while that he ought to preach the gospel. The reader will recollect, however, that Mr. Johnston's entrance into the army was early in the last war of this country with Great Britain, when the pressure of public sentiment upon young men was very powerful. He served six months of his term, and then hired a substitute. In 1813 he bought a little farm, and determined to devote himself to farming and his trade, and to renounce all thoughts of the ministry. His own record is the following:

> I went in debt for my farm, commenced farming, and determined to look no higher than to the position of a private Christian. But this was not to be my lot. Adverse providences met me on every corner. My former impressions returned. I found farming a slow way of making money. I commenced the blacksmith's business again, and promised the Lord that if he would give me the means of putting me out of debt, I would try to do what I believed to be his will. I labored hard, made money, and paid my debts; but still there were many difficulties in my way. My wife was weakly, and a family of children was growing up around me, to be raised and educated. We were poor. I was ignorant, and opposed by friends and neighbors. This was hard to bear. I had one friend, however, who never forsook me: that friend was my wife. Though she sometimes felt that her lot was hard—and so it was—yet she murmured not, but bore all patiently.

After all these difficulties and struggles, in 1818 Mr. Johnston attended a meeting of the Nashville Presbytery, and disclosed his feelings on the subject of preaching. The Presbytery did not receive him as a candidate for the ministry at that time, but advised him to exhort in prayer-meetings, and from some text of Scripture of his own selection to write a sermon for a subsequent meeting of the Presbytery, as a specimen of his ability to sermonize. He went home discouraged, of course. The next Presbytery he did not attend; but in the fall of 1819 he presented himself again before the Presbytery. He also brought his written discourse, and was received as a candidate on the 14th day of October. The session of the Presbytery was held at Big Spring Meeting-house.

On the 5th day of April, 1821, he was licensed to preach the gospel at Moriah Meeting-house, in Wilson county, Tennessee. The following summer he spent on the Overton Circuit. In the fall minutes of the Nashville Presbytery for 1821 I also find the following order: "That Francis Johnston and Robert Tate spend each half of his time on the Overton Circuit." The Overton Circuit was about four weeks in length, and lay from fifty to a hundred and fifty miles from Mr. Johnston's home. He left behind him, when from home, a weakly wife and several little children to be cared for.

In 1823 the subject of his ordination was agitated, but he begged longer time, from a consciousness that he could not fulfill the requirements of the discipline. In the spring of 1825 the subject was brought up again, and he was ordered to prepare for ordination at the fall meeting. In order to enable him to make preparation, a wealthy member of the Church, in whose neighborhood there was a good school, offered him gratuitous boarding. The school was twenty or twenty-five miles from his home. He, however, accepted the offer, and spent the summer in study. He saw his family but three times from the first of May to the first of October. On the 10th of October of that year, 1825, he was set apart to the whole work of the ministry, at the Beech Meeting-house.

From 1825 to 1837 he was the stated supply of Dry Fork and Mount

Moriah congregations. He performed all the labors of a pastor in these congregations, in the meantime traveling annually, according to his own record, from three to four months, attending camp-meetings and protracted meetings.

In November of 1839 Mr. Johnston moved from Dry Fork, the neighborhood in which he had been raised and had hitherto lived, to Simpson county, Kentucky. From that time he became a member of the Logan Presbytery. His labors were still abundant, various, and useful. He had temporary connection with several congregations, the nature and length of which are, however, unknown to the writer. On the 16th of December, 1856, after a painful illness of two weeks, he died at the house of his son-in-law, Thomas Dickson Beard, in the sixty-seventh year of his age. His death was what might have been expected from the fidelity and devotion of his life—calm, quiet, and peaceful.

Mr. Johnston was not a great preacher—he made no such pretensions; but he was what was far better—a spiritual and useful preacher. His forte was in exhortation, and in the application of his sermons. In these he sometimes wholly surpassed himself. He had an iron-like bodily frame, and a voice like a trumpet, and when properly aroused, he was powerful. Sinners whom stronger men, intellectually, could not reach, often trembled beneath his terrible appeals. At a camp-meeting, among mourners, when the interest was beginning to flag, he excelled in arousing his fellow-Christians and mourners themselves to additional efforts. Often, in his earlier years, at least, he would thus labor through a whole night, and sometimes nights in succession, stirring up and kindling afresh the embers which were likely to die out.

I have spoken of what we called his exhortations at the close of his sermons. I recollect particularly one instance. In 1822 Rev. James S. Guthrie and myself, assisted by Brother Johnston, held the first sacramental-meeting that ever was held by Cumberland Presbyterians in what is now Western Tennessee. The meetings was held on Forked Deer, in a bottom near Adley Alexander's. We had no camps, no shelter; a few logs, however, for seats, and a coarsely constructed pulpit. The meeting was held about two months after the ordination of myself and Guthrie. Mr. Johnston was still a licentiate. We were all young men. The meeting was interesting from the beginning. When Monday came around, a brother of another denomination called in and preached. But little impression, however, seemed to be made. Mr. Johnston followed. He appeared to be, as we familiarly said in those days, in the brush for a while, but in the closing up of his sermon he became exceedingly aroused, the fetters fell off, and his appeals were stirring and effective in a very high degree. At the close, a few young persons of precious memory assembled around the pulpit as mourners. The most of them professed religion that day. It may be remarked, too, by the way, that these were the first professions ever made under Cumberland Presbyterian ministrations in a section of the country where the membership is, I believe, now numbered by thousands. I have witnessed many seasons of religious interest, but recollect few days of my life with greater pleasure than the Monday of that meeting. It was a day to be remembered.

Mr. Johnston is one of the men upon whose early career the writer looks with a tender personal interest. May not such an interest be indulged? He was my senior by a number of years, was the head of a family when I was but a boy; still, we grew up in the same neighborhood, were struggling in our preparations for the ministry about the same time, plowed several years in adjoining fields, often meeting at the partition fence and talking our troubles over; met once a week at prayer-meeting where one or both tried to exhort, suffered the same discouragements—even persecutions—from heartless, unappreciating neighbors and friends; with our own hands assisted in building the first meeting-house which was ever built in the neighborhood in which we lived—a very common log building, which still stands, a venerable landmark of former times. Many things conspire to create such an interest as I have suggested. I mention one more. I have always looked upon Mr. Johnston as a true man. Our habits of mind were very different. After a few years of our early ministry we pursued very different courses; still I think to the last meeting in life—and I recollect that meeting well—he was the same man that he was when we labored in our little prayer-meetings together. With many painful experiences of a different kind, I linger with a hallowed pleasure upon the memory of such a man.

Mr. Johnston had two sons who entered the ministry. Both were promising—the elder unusually so. The other died young. Both, however, preceded him to the grave. His widow survived him several years, shedding around her the sanctifying influence of an old age made honorable by a life of devoted, but unostentatious, piety and consecration to God.

The life of Francis Johnston suggests some practical thoughts which are too important to be overlooked in a work intended for usefulness.

We learn from his case, as well as from many others, something of the difficulty of our older men in reaching the ministry. Mr. Johnston thought an education important as a preparation for this work, but we had no colleges, no academies, or high-schools. The means of an education were not within his reach. I know what his sentiments were, however, for I have heard him express them a score of times. He thought preachers, if possible, ought to be educated men.

When the subject of ordination was pressed upon him, it was a matter of conscience with him to be as well prepared for it as possible. Instead of quarreling with the Book of Discipline and his Presbytery for requiring too much, he applied himself in such a way as few men would have done in order to meet these requisitions. At thirty-five years of age he left his family for five months, seeing them but three times in the course of those months, and went to school, for the purpose of enabling himself, as far as possible, to come up to the standard of order prescribed by the Church which he honored and loved. This seemed to indicate the spirit of an earnest man.

He commenced the ministry poor and encumbered with a family. He labored upon his farm; he labored in his shop—its traces still remain—but still he labored for God and the Church, spending, for years in succession, annually three or four months outside of his more immediate ministerial charge. He was a hard-working man everywhere. Many will rise up in heaven and call him blessed. It may be observed, too, that for his ministerial labors there was hardly a show of compensation. There is scarcely a probability that for thirty-five years' service he received as many hundred dollars.

He made no great pretensions to ability. His endowments were moderate; he was not ambitious; he never aspired to leadership in the Church—not even in his own Presbytery—but he was useful. I know of no one occupying a similar position in the Church who has been more so.

REV. LABAN JONES
(1796-1848)

Sources: "Memoir of Jones and Irving," by Rev. Jesse Anderson.

Laban Jones was born in Frankfort, Hampshire county, Virginia. March 6, 1796. His parents were respectable, and in early life he enjoyed the advantages of religious training and parental restraint. His father and mother were Daniel and Rosanna Jones. His grandfather, John Jones, was for a long time a worthy and devoted member of the Methodist Church, in Virginia. His house was for many years the home of the preachers, as well as a place of religious worship.

Daniel and Rosanna Jones had ten children, eight sons and two daughters. Laban was the fifth son, and in his earlier life was trained to agricultural pursuits. About the year 1816 he lost his father. Of course this was a heavy blow upon a large and dependent family. Previous to the death of his father, however, when he was about eight years old, the family moved, and settled in Henderson county, Kentucky. Here they remained several years. Mr. Jones, on the side of his father, seems to have been connected with families of high character in Virginia. His maternal ancestry were of German origin, and from time immemorial have been distinguished for their quiet and unobtrusive devotion to Christianity.

Mr. Jones's educational advantages were very favorable, for the times. In addition to a fair English education, in 1812 he commenced the study of Latin, in Henderson, with Mr. William Thompson. Mr. Thompson's school, however, was, from some cause, soon discontinued.

In 1813, he resumed his studies under the tuition of Rev. William Grey, a Presbyterian minister, who taught in Morganfield, Union county. With Mr. Grey he seems to have devoted his attention to English pursuits. The author of the memoir says he abandoned the study of Latin, and did not resume it until after he entered the ministry. About this time the family moved to Union county, and settled on a farm about four miles from Morganfield, near the Henderson road. Also, about the same time in 1814, he went to Virginia, for the purpose of acquiring a better education. The author of the Memoir says he went under "unfavorable circumstances." We do not know what those circumstances were. He went, however, to Winchester and Martinsburg, wrote in a Clerk's office, and commenced the study of law. He could not have devoted much attention to the enlargement of his education.

In 1815, he returned to Kentucky, and lived with his parents for several years—or, rather, for the most of those years, with his mother, dividing his time between labor on the farm, history, the English classics, and law. In 1816, upon a certificate from the County Court of Logan county, he was licensed and permitted, as counsel and attorney-at-law, to practice law at all the superior and inferior courts in the Commonwealth of Kentucky. It is supposed, too, that he commenced the practice of law in Morganfield, near to which his family resided. In 1819, he obtained license to practice law in the State of Indiana. It seems doubtful, however, whether he ever carried his practice into that State.

About the year 1820, an event occurred which changed the whole current of Mr. Jones's life. He professed religion under the ministrations of Rev. Henry F. Delaney. Mr. Delaney himself had been a prominent lawyer a number of years in

South-western Kentucky. At some time previous to 1820, he had professed religion, had renounced the practice of law, and entered upon the work of the ministry, and in a few years became one of the most powerful and useful ministers in the Cumberland Presbyterian Church. Such an example would naturally have its influence upon a young convert of ardent, and earnest, and devoted mind. It was characteristic, too, of Mr. Jones, as we shall see, that he did nothing by halves. He at once abandoned his purposed and cherished pursuit—a pursuit which men in this country then considered, as they do now, the stepping-stone to wealth and fame, and determined to forego all its prospects "for the excellency of the knowledge of Christ Jesus our Lord." His whole mind and heart were directed at once to what he had determined to make the pursuit of his life. He traveled as he had opportunity with ministers of the gospel into different parts of the country, and exercised his gifts in exhortation and prayer, and in these exercises succeeded so well that he became encouraged himself to hope for future usefulness, and his friends became satisfied that the work of the ministry was that to which God in his providence and by his Spirit was calling him.

    Whilst the mind of Mr. Jones was thus exercised, and he was making his arrangements for an entrance upon the great work of his life, an incident occurred which was so remarkable, and so trying, that it cannot be overlooked in this sketch. On the 22d day of November, 1822, he was traveling from where he lived up the country, probably to Frankfort, the capital of the State, and about a mile from Hardinsburg, in Breckinridge county, he was met by three desperadoes. These men, it seemed from subsequent development, had been lying in wait for the sheriff of some one of the lower counties, whom they expected to pass that way to Frankfort with the county revenue. Their purpose was to murder the sheriff and take possession of the money. Mr. Jones passed on horseback with saddle-bags about the time they were expecting the sheriff, and not knowing him, or the sheriff for whom they were watching, personally, they supposed him to be the man who was carrying the money. He saw them, but thought of no danger, until one of them seized the rein of his bridle, the others standing one on each side of his horse, and communicated to him the terrible intelligence that they intended to rob and murder him. They took him off into a secluded ravine, in order that undisturbed they might carry out their purpose. On examining his saddle-bags for their contemplated booty, however, they found but a few dollars in money, a pocket-Bible and a hymn-book. The finding of the books, especially, satisfied them that they had made a mistake in the man. The sum of money, too, made it evident that their prisoner was not the sheriff. A difficulty at once arose in relation to what they should do with the man who was in their power. It can be readily understood. If they gave him his liberty he might inform upon them, and have them arrested. Still, they had no motive, aside from their own safety, for taking his life. In the first consultation, two were for his death, whilst the third was for liberating him. The prisoner pleaded for his life; the heart of a second was moved. They then agreed that if Mr. Jones would swear upon his Bible not to disclose the matter for two years they would let him go, adding that in two years they expected to secure money enough, and would then relinquish all such business. He subscribed to the proposition; they gave him back ten dollars of his money, and bade him go.

    It was now his time for doubt and hesitation. He felt that he ought to inform upon the outlaws, and have them arrested in their course of wickedness. Again, he felt restrained by the stipulations into which he had entered, and especially by the oath he had taken upon his Bible. After mature reflection, and conference with those in whose judgment and casuistry he confided, he disclosed the whole matter. The men were arrested and tried, and lodged in the penitentiary of Kentucky. Of course there will be different views of the propriety of Mr. Jones's course in this affair. There can be but one view of its morality. These men were outlaws, professional robbers and murderers. They were enemies to society, and his primary duty to society was to assist in placing them in a situation in which they could not carry out their wicked purposes of robbery and murder. Providentially he was able to do that, and his duty was a plain one. The informal oath was no more binding than a promise extorted by violence. I do not say that it was not binding from its informality, but from the circumstances in which it was taken. It was a trying situation, such a one as rarely happens to a man. He, however, released himself from it in the right way. This is unquestionable.

Says the author of the Memoir: "After the legal adjustment of the sad occurrence we have been just narrating, Brother Jones saw plainly the hand of Providence in his preservation, and felt more forcibly his obligations to God, and that it was his duty to consecrate his energies to the cause of Christianity. Accordingly, in the fall of 1823, he became a candidate for the holy ministry, under the supervision and watch-care of the Anderson Presbytery, in order to identify his efforts more particularly with the Church of his choice. Here he engaged the counsel and instructions of those pious and venerable fathers of the Church who had passed through the revival of 1800, and whose hearts were still glowing with the hallowed fervor of devotion to God and the interests of his kingdom."

In April, 1825, he was licensed by the same Presbytery as a probationer for the ministry. He now commenced his active work, "riding the circuit, and preaching daily to perishing sinners the unsearchable riches of Christ. He studied his theology on the circuit. His labors were arduous and incessant, and the pleasure of the Lord prospered in his hands." In short, it is said that, "as a probationer for the holy ministry, in ability, in zeal, in the true spirit of religion, and in usefulness, he had but few rivals, either in his own or any other Church within the bounds of the Green River country."

In May of 1825 he made his way into the central part of Kentucky, and preached extensively in Mercer and adjoining counties. Cumberland Presbyterians were but little known in that portion of Kentucky. He had, of course, to encounter the customary prejudices. The same spirit which dictated Davidson's "History of the Presbyterian Church in Kentucky," and Dr. Bishop's "Outline," would occasionally develop itself. The people would be suspicious and distrustful, and their suspicions and distrust would rather be encouraged than otherwise. He labored earnestly, not preaching himself, but Christ Jesus the Lord.

In May of 1826 Mr. Jones visited Anderson county, and was instrumental in getting up a considerable revival there. Here he met with similar discouragements to those experienced in other places. Many who were converted under his ministry went and joined other Churches, but, notwithstanding this, he was soon enabled to organize the Hebron Society, which is to this day a flourishing Church." "The first two or three years of his ministry in this country were crowned with abundant success, and hundreds were brought from darkness to light, and from the power of Satan to God."

At the spring meeting of the Anderson Presbytery, on the 14th of April, 1827, he was set apart to the whole work of the ministry, Rev. F. R. Cossitt preaching the ordination-sermon, and Rev. Henry F. Delaney presiding and giving the charge. He immediately returned to Central Kentucky, which he now considered as his proper field of labor. At the fall meeting of his Presbytery, in the same year, he obtained a letter of dismission and recommendation to the Logan Presbytery, within the bounds of which his field of labor properly lay.

The Cumberland Synod met at Russellville, Kentucky, in November of 1827. At that meeting of the Synod, Mr. Jones was appointed to travel at discretion in the United States six months, as an agent of Cumberland College. In October of 1828 he made his settlement with the Treasurer of the College, by paying over one hundred and forty-three dollars and twenty-five cents. These were small proceeds from a year's labor, but they were better than the proceeds of many other agencies engaged about the same time for the same object. It is humiliating even now to think of the manner in which time was thus lost, and labor and influence frittered away, in agencies almost wholly nominal.

About this time some person in his new field of labor, and where he was, in a great measure, a stranger, had the meanness to represent that he had left his widowed mother and his sisters in Union county in a state of destitution and suffering. The matter gave him some trouble, but the calumniator was soon silenced. The facts were produced which spake for themselves.

Mr. Jones would have been thought by strangers, in his earlier ministerial habits, to be imprudent. His temperament was lively, rather impulsive, and sometimes he seemed to speak without reflection. The following summary of rules, however, found among his papers after his death, indicates the care which he observed in trying to correct all errors of this kind, and to conform himself to a most rigid propriety in all his intercourse with society. They ought to be in every minister's book of memoranda:

1. Let your thoughts be serious, chaste, heavenly.
2. Let your conversation be modest, truthful, decent, profitable.
3. Let your works be useful, charitable, holy.
4. Let your manners be unaffected, courteous, cheerful.
5. Let your diet be wholesome, frugally provided, and temperately used.
6. Let your apparel be neat, convenient, suitable to your condition.
7. Let your will be well-disciplined, benevolent, godly.
8. Let your sleep be moderate, quiet, seasonable.
9. Let your prayers be short, devout, fervent, frequent.
10. Let your recreations be innocent, brief, judicious.
11. Let your memory be properly and profitably exercised.
12. You should hear, and learn to be silent.
13. Be silent, and learn to understand.
14. Understand, and learn to remember.
15. Remember, and learn to act accordingly.
16. All that you see, judge not.
17. All that you hear, believe not.
18. All that you know, tell not.
19. All that you can do, do not.

20. Whenever you are about to speak, think first, and attend particularly to what you say, of whom and to whom you speak. You will thereby avoid much evil which results from hasty and injudicious speaking.

These are good rules, and he who followed them in their full import could not have been otherwise than a Christian gentleman.

On the 28th of May, 1829, Mr. Jones was married to Miss Rachel Walker, of Mercer county, Kentucky. His wife is represented to have been an estimable woman, "well calculated to render the domestic circle a scene of perpetual enjoyment." In the fall, after his marriage, he purchased a farm near the foot of the Knobs, in what was then Mercer, but is now Boyle, county. His home seems to have become, in process of time, a sort of theological school on a small scale. Says the writer of the Memoir: "It was during his residence in this place that Brethren Robison, Thomas, Noel, and myself, were rearer up under his immediate tuition. The principles of benevolence were those upon which he acted, and he was frequently heard to remark, publicly and privately, that it was to a man's own interest to be charitable." His motto in this respect was: "There is that giveth and yet increaseth; and there is that withholdeth more than is meet, but it tendeth to poverty."

In the fall of 1829, the Green River Synod constituted the Kentucky Presbytery. The territory embraced the middle and upper portions of the State. The Presbytery held its first meeting at Caldwell's Meeting-house, in Mercer county, commencing the first Thursday in May, 1830. Mr. Jones was the Senior Presbyter, and, although comparatively a young man, was by common consent regarded as the leader and father of the Presbytery. He preached a great deal, and, notwithstanding he now had to make provision for a family, much of his labor, as far as worldly compensation was concerned, went for nothing. He collected wealthy congregations, but they seemed to consider it their first and last duty to take care of themselves. Still he labored, and his labors were blessed.

In 1833, the cholera prevailed in some portions of Kentucky. The alarm and excitement were very great. That year, within the bounds of his operations, and chiefly under his own ministrations, there were seven hundred professions of religion. Time gave proof, too, that in many of those cases the professions were from genuine conversions. Think of it, seven hundred in one year!

In 1833, he sold his farm at the foot of the Knobs, and purchased the Broil farm, near May's mill. Here he lived until 1837, when he moved to Perryville, and engaged in the mercantile business. On his farms, and in his mercantile pursuits, he was, after the manner of the apostle, laboring with his own hands, that he might not be chargeable to the Churches. In this he followed in the footsteps of the old men. It was the order of the times. His mercantile operations, however, proved disastrous. He gave them up, a poorer, but wiser and perhaps better man than when he entered upon them.

In 1844, he settled in Jefferson county. This was his home until he was called to that higher and better home in heaven. In 1847, he became a member of the Board of Publication of the Cumberland Presbyterian Church, and in the course of the summer of that year his preaching is represented as having been unusually spiritual and powerful. Says the author of the Memoir: "I am confident I never heard him preach with such power in all my life. From day to day he appeared to enter more into the work, and every effort from the pulpit bore evident marks of deep thought, and a thorough investigation of his subjects; and, above all, that he maintained intimate communion with God." These gracious developments were precursors of what as to follow. God often works in this way. This is not nature's way, but in such cases it is God's way; the light shines with the greatest brilliancy when approaching its extinction.

Mr. Jones died at his home in Jefferson county, February 20, 1848. His sickness extended from Tuesday to Sabbath, the day of his death. Up to Saturday morning he entertained hope that he would be able to attend his appointment for preaching the following day. His constitution was strong, and resisted the attack with great vigor, but succumbed at last. The good man died with his armor on. It was a call directly from the field on conflict. At his death he was in his fifty-second year, still in the maturity and strength of manhood. His wife and four children survived him. Has the Church taken care of them?

I make two or three extracts from the funeral-sermon, delivered by Rev. Jesse Anderson:

"The death of good men, who have rendered themselves eminently serviceable to the Church and to the world, is to be lamented more than ordinary deaths. Such men are those who, like our beloved Brother Jones, combined at once the elements of true piety and greatness; men who are able ministers of the Word, and the unwearied supporters of the institutions of religion; men who disdain a compromise with error, but who ever stand up for the truth; who count not their lives dear, so that they may win souls to Christ. I say, brethren, that the loss of such men can hardly be estimated, especially when they are taken, as was our beloved brother, in the prime of life, with a constitution naturally strong, and cheeks glowing with indications of health, and a soul fully equal to his physical energies, from a sphere of great usefulness; to whom hundreds within the bounds of Kentucky Presbytery, and elsewhere in the Church, were looking for counsel and guidance—that such a man, under such circumstances, should be marked as a victim of death, and in a few hours sink into the tomb, involves a providential mystery which I dare not undertake to unfold. It is for us meekly to bow in submission to the divine administration, and wait patiently, 'and hope unto the end for the grace that is to be brought unto us at the revelation of Jesus Christ.' Thus much we know, that the death of his saints is precious in the sight of the Lord."

The following is from the closing paragraph of the sermon:

"A few days since I visited the Church at Bethlehem, and saw the place where the remains of our departed and beloved brother had been deposited, to rest in silent slumbers until the morning of the resurrection. My emotions were peculiarly solemn and impressive. A profound awe seized upon my mind, and for a moment so agitated me that I felt as though I dared not approach the sepulchral monument, lest I should intrude upon the hallowed precincts of sainted spirits, and disturb the repose of the departed. At that moment something seemed to whisper, 'Fear not, he loves you still.' I approached the tomb. Naught but the stillness of death reigned there, while I silently gazed upon the mound of earth which hides from my view the form of him I so much loved. I reflected that, when a boy, and a wanderer almost alone in this vale of tears, tossed upon the turbulent ocean of time, regardless of my highest interest, he watched over me, and taught me the way to respectability and honor, to immortality and eternal life. A tear of sorrow started in my eye as I involuntarily cast a look upward, as if in search of the spirit that once animated the lifeless body upon which I had been reflecting. My imagination soon painted his happy release from earth and the toils of the gospel ministry, and saw him ascending to heaven amidst the shouts of angels, while with the prophet I gazed, and cried, 'My father! my father!'"

In 1846, Mr. Jones published, by request of his Presbytery, a biographical sketch of Rev. Samuel Ayres Noel, embodying in the work several of his own sermons. The whole work contains four hundred and thirty-six pages. Mr. Noel was a young man of unusual promise, who was brought into the Church and into the ministry under the influence of Mr. Jones. His career was very short—it was, however, regarded as brilliant. He was ordained by the Kentucky Presbytery in October of 1834, and died in November of 1842.

In 1847, he published a plea for the Cumberland Presbyterian Church. This is a work of five hundred and four pages, and certainly possesses some merit. It is an earnest defense of the Church, to the usefulness and prosperity of which he had devoted the best years of his life. The author of the Memoir denominates it a meritorious work, and one which the Church had long needed. It was especially needed in Kentucky, and no doubt fulfilled a useful mission.

Mr. Jones was evidently a man of great usefulness, zealous, earnest, devoted, and of very respectable ability. He went into a new field; he entered upon a difficult work; and he accomplished a great deal. He did not seek for foundations laid by other men. He laid his own foundation, and saw with pleasure the building rising up. He sowed his own seed, and saw the harvest maturing around him. He introduced a generation of young men into the ministry, who imbibed much of his own spirit. Some of these, with himself, have passed away. Others are following up, with no mean success, the beginnings which were made forty years ago. They have had their troubles, but men who would thwart them, and perhaps think themselves rendering service to God in so doing, may as well make up their minds to the truth that "if this counsel, or this work, be of men, it will come to naught; but if it be of God, they can not overthrow it." Time will decide. God will rule.

Mention has sometimes been made of a peculiarity in his manner as a public speaker. It is difficult to describe it. His biographer says:

> From a disposition, I apprehend, to keep pace with the rapidity of thought, both in his expressions and gestures, he early contracted the habit of protracting his sentences until the inspiration of the lungs was so far exhausted as to cause him to close with a kind of echo, very unnatural, and often very afflictive to those unaccustomed to his ministry. This, however, was soon forgotten by the attentive hearer, and also by those who heard him frequently. He was truly an interesting speaker, although he possessed not that smoothness of articulation, and gracefulness of gesture, calculated to excite the formal and fastidious to rapture and admiration, yet upon many occasions he was truly eloquent, and commanded a train of thought and expression which, for depth and sublimity, I have never heard surpassed by any man.

He gives us an illustration of the effect of his unpolished but strong eloquence:

> I will instance one case out of many which fell under my own observation, as related to me by the gentleman who was chiefly connected with the incident which I am about to relate. The incident occurred at a camp-meeting held at Mount Gilead, Montgomery county, Kentucky. On this occasion the preacher was addressing a large and attentive audience. The gentleman had never heard him before, and at first was so displeased with his unpleasant manner of address that he thought he would leave the congregation. For this purpose he took his hat in hand, and was in the act of departing, when Mr. Jones struck upon a point which drew his attention. He thought he would hear that through, and then retire. But no sooner was that point disposed of than another was introduced equally interesting; after that, another, and still another, came up in exhaustless measure, and at the expiration of nearly two hours and a half, this man was standing with his hat in his hand, lost in astonishment, and intently gazing at this champion of the cross, as he vigorously wielded the weapons of divine truth for the honor and glory of God.

Mr. Jones seems to have been skillful in selecting and improving special occasions. The author of the Memoir attributes this characteristic to "his superior knowledge of human nature." He is doubtless correct in his judgment on this subject. Mr. Jones studied books, but he studied men more. He would use a sort of singularity, or drollery of expression, and his congregation would be excited to an approach to levity. Then again he would give his thoughts and expressions such a turn that, in a few minutes, the same congregation would be bathed in tears. Some men can do this. And in proper hands such ability may be turned to prodigious account. Unskillful hands, however, at such attempts would ruin every thing. This ability belongs to the highest form of the dramatic.

We have an account of a curious case of conviction. At a certain time, Kentucky was visited with a terrible drought. "The earth was parched and cracked with the heat of the sun; the fountains of water were dried up; vegetation was withering and dying; and all nature seemed to be clad in the habiliments of mourning." The people were alarmed, and the Governor of the State very properly, as a man who believed in the exercise of the providence of God, appointed a day of fasting, humiliation, and prayer to be observed throughout the State. It turned out that the day appointed was included in a camp-meeting held at this same Mount Gilead. The people fasted and prayed, and in the forenoon of the day the rain began to fall. The good people felt that prayer was answered. On account of the rain the congregation collected in a large tent for service, and Mr. Jones preached from the text, "The fool hath said in his heart, There is no God." It was a fine occasion for showing off the folly of the fool who would pretend that such a coincidence as they had witnessed was a mere casualty, ignoring the interposition of a wise and good Providence who hears and answers prayer. Says the author of the Memoir: "Many were convicted on that occasion. After service was over, a man, with whom I was intimately acquainted, approached me, evidently enraged at the preacher, who had been, under God, successful in riveting conviction upon his heart." The result of a furious colloquy, however, on his part, was that he was soon bowed at the altar of prayer, a suppliant for mercy. He professed religion before the meeting closed.

My personal acquaintance with Mr. Jones was limited, and my recollections of him are very few. It was such an acquaintance as ministers form at public meetings. I knew nothing, of course, of his domestic or personal habits, and very little of him socially. I heard him preach once, and, I believe, once only. That sermon was delivered at Owensboro, on the occasion of the General Assembly of 1846. My recollection is that he was not a member, but a visitor, and preached one night. It was a better sermon than I expected. It seemed better, no doubt, from the fact that it was almost entirely free from what were called his personal peculiarities. It was an earnest and intelligent exposition of the doctrine of faith.

My first distinct recollection of him goes back to the meeting of the old Cumberland Synod at Russellville, Kentucky, in 1827. At that meeting he was commissioned as an Agent for Cumberland College. Such a commission would make the impression upon the mind of a stranger that he was a very important young man. The night after the adjournment of the meeting was spent by himself and Revs. Henry F. Delaney, John Barnett, David Lowry, and myself, at the same house, the house of a good old man in the neighborhood of Russellville. The introduction left an unfavorable impression upon my mind. It certainly did not lead me to expect what his subsequent life evidently developed. Time and experience no doubt corrected what I thought were social defects. We have proof enough from the preceding sketch, if it has been faithful, that he became an eminently exemplary Christian minister.

He attended the next meeting of the Synod, which was held in Franklin, Tennessee. He delivered an exhortation there, in which he developed the peculiarity of manner in his delivery which afterward became, as we have seen, a matter of extensive remark by those who were in the habit of hearing him.

He was at the meeting of the General Assembly at Princeton, in 1835, and by appointment preached one day in the court-house. I heard the close of the sermon. There were an earnestness and a depth of feeling in his manner which drew me involuntarily to him. Previous impressions were entirely effaced. The congregation, too, were evidently interested and profited. There were no remarks about what came to be called his peculiarity of manner. It would have been a good sermon anywhere.

I saw him at the Assemblies of 1845, 1846, and 1847. This latter meeting occurred about nine months before his death. It was held at Lebanon, Ohio. On Sunday evening it fell to my lot to preach at one of the churches in town. I preached under discouragements. He was appointed to offer prayer at the close. I recollect the manner and spirit of the prayer while I write this. When he prayed especially that the blessing of God might be with and follow the dear brother who had preached to them, an impression was made upon my heart such as I do not easily lose. I never saw him after that evening. He was a good man. Many will be the stars in his crown of rejoicing.

REV. SAMUEL KING
(1775-1842)

Robert King, the father of Rev. Samuel King, was an early settler in North Carolina, and served his country for some time as a captain of volunteers in the war of the revolution. In this position he acquitted himself with honor to himself and the country. He and his family were members of the Presbyterian Church, and highly respected in the community in which they lived.

Samuel King was born in Iredell county, North Carolina, on the 19th of April, 1775. About the year 1791 Mr. King moved to what was then called the "Cumberland Country," and settled in what is now Sumner county, Tennessee. The old gentleman became an elder, and his family members of Shiloh congregation. This congregation was successively for a number of years under the pastoral care of Rev. William McGee and Rev. William Hodge. Mr. McGee was the son-in-law of old Mr. King. An Indian war was then raging in Tennessee. It is said that Samuel King took an active part in repelling the murderous invasions of the Indians. In the year 1795 Mr. King was married to Miss Anna Dixon, of Sumner county. Rev. William Hodge performed the marriage ceremony. Miss Dixon's father had been killed by the Indians. The writer has passed the spot where this murder took place a hundred times. Shortly after his marriage, Mr. King moved to Wilson county, and settled near the Big Spring.

At the time of his marriage, he was a regular member of Shiloh congregation; and feeling it his duty, now that he had become the head of a family, to erect the family altar, and hold family prayers, he did so. He had not, however, kept up the practice of family prayer long, before he became convinced that his religious hope was without foundation. Of course from this time forward the wants of his own soul formed a prominent part of his petitions when bowed at the family altar.

On one of these occasions, while engaged in family worship, he obtained such a discovery, and felt so deeply overwhelmed with a sense of his lost condition, that he ceased praying for others, and for all things else than himself, and continued on his knees to pour out his soul to God for mercy and pardon, until God heard his prayer, and sent peace to his mind. His joy, and his views of the atonement of Christ, and of the Divine goodness were such, that his wife, who at that time had not professed religion, said, "she thought he never would get done saying glory to God."

He soon began to feel great anxiety for his unconverted friends and neighbors, and such was his burden of heart on this subject, that at prayer-meetings, and other social meetings, he was strongly urged by his feelings to get up and talk to the people. When he first commenced these exercises, such were the unction and power attending his words, that many were cut to the heart, fell down, and cried for mercy on the spot.

When Rev. David Rice, the oldest Presbyterian minister in Kentucky, seeing the destitute condition of the congregations in Tennessee, recommended that pious and promising young men should be sought out, and encouraged to exercise their gifts publicly, and prepare themselves for the work of the ministry, Mr. King was one of the first selected. It was not contemplated that these men should go through the ordinary process of education required in the Presbyterian

Church, preparatory to licensure and ordination, The wants of the Church and the circumstances of the country forbade it. Their cases were to be regarded as exceptions to the general rule. He seems, however, to have turned his attention to the work with great hesitation and reluctance. He was uneducated, in the technical sense of the term, had a family, and was poor. The way before him seemed very dark. He felt like the call was from God, but still did not know how he could fulfill its requisitions. He had a brother, a well-educated and most estimable man. There was an old tradition amongst his friends, that in his struggles and misgivings in those days, he sometimes prayed that God would call his brother to the work of the ministry, and excuse him. Still, the great Head of the Church made his own choice, and the suppliant for indulgence was not excused.

The revival ministers, as they were called, encouraged three young men, Alexander Anderson, Finis Ewing, and Samuel King, to prepare written discourses, and to present themselves before the Transylvania Presbytery, at its sessions, in October, 1801. At this Presbytery Mr. Anderson was received as a candidate by a majority of one vote; the others, by a majority of one vote, were rejected as candidates, but continued as catechists. In the fall of 1802 they were all licensed as probationers for the holy ministry.

At the sessions of the Synod of Kentucky, in 1802, Transylvania Presbytery was divided, and Cumberland Presbytery was formed, including the Green River and Cumberland countries. By this Presbytery Mr. King was set apart to the whole work of the ministry in June, 1804.

He was of course one of the minister who were called before the Commission of the Synod of Kentucky, in December of 1805, and proscribed by that body. It is known that the proscribed ministers formed themselves into a Council, which met from time to time, with a view to adopting measures for the promotion of the interests of religion within the bounds of their operations, and keeping the congregations together. These congregations had grown up out of the great revival which had overspread the country. The Council held their last meeting at Shiloh, on the 4th day of October, 1809. Their last hope of a reconciliation with the Church of their fathers had been extinguished, except upon such conditions as seemed to be out of the question, and the subject of organizing an independent Presbytery was agitated. It had been seriously considered before. Two of the members of the Council, however, withdrew; a third hesitated, and Messrs. Ewing and King only were left. Three ministers were considered necessary to the constitution of a Presbytery. They had not the requisite number, and action was postponed. In February of 1810, Messrs. Ewing and King visited Mr. McAdow. They agreed to organize, or rather to reorganize, the old Cumberland Presbytery, which had been dissolved by the Synod of Kentucky. On the 4th day of February, 1810, this important step was taken. It has made the names of Ewing, King, and McAdow, household words in every Cumberland Presbyterian family.

About the year 1812 Mr. King moved from Wilson county, and settled near the Three Forks of Duck River. He remained here until the fall of 1824 or '25, when he moved to Missouri and settled in Clay county. The whole country was new; it had been but recently purchased from the Indians, and the settlements were sparse. In the fall of 1833 he moved again, and settled on the south side of the Missouri River, in Johnson county. Here he resided till his death. This occurred in the fall of 1842. A few weeks before his death, he was attacked with the common fever of the country, while attending a camp-meeting some distance from home. We have the following account of his last sermon, and the attack of fever which followed it. Says the writer:

> I heard him preach his last sermon, and shall never forget it. I remember how he looked as well as if the things had occurred but a week ago. The sermon was preached at Independence Camp-ground, Jackson county, Missouri, about four miles south of the city of Independence
>
> The camp-meeting was in progress. Saturday morning, between ten and eleven o'clock, Father King walked from the camp to the stand, ascended the steps, hymn-book and Bible in hand, and after sitting in a thoughtful, and apparently prayerful mood, a few moments, the congregation being collected and seated, the venerable preacher arose slowly, and placing the Bible upon the hand-board, he opened his hymn-book, and read in that solemn and affecting manner, which thousands may remember, but none can imitate, the beautiful hymn beginning:
>
> 'O Lord, revive thy work
> In Zion's gloomy hour.'
>
> After singing came the prayer, and O, how fervent! What earnestness! What awfully solemn pleading with Jehovah for a visitation of his Spirit, a revival of his work! The prayer being ended, the text was announced: 'O Lord, revive thy work in the midst of the years; in the midst of the years make known; in wrath remember mercy.' The leading points in the sermon were—
>
> 1. The necessity of a revival.
> 2. The means by which a revival could be obtained.
> 3. An exhortation to the Church, urging the members to an immediate use of those means, and encouraging them to expect a gracious revival on that occasion.
>
> The sermon was closed by repeating, most devoutly, the prayer of the text. Such was Father King's last sermon. Its effect upon the congregation was manifested by profound attention on the part of the congregation, and the silent tear, and occasional hearty amen of the more deeply pious members of the Church. I did not know that he was unwell before preaching, but remember that he complained soon after the sermon was closed. He went to the tent, fever arose; the Sabbath came, and many were the inquiries for Father King, but he was unable to leave his bed. The meeting progressed, but the voice of the venerable man of God was heard no more from that sacred stand. At the close of the meeting, he was conveyed to his home in Johnson county, a

distance of fifty-five or sixty miles, and in the course of two or three weeks, he laid aside his mantle on earth for a bright robe in heaven.[25]

It seems that his illness at first was not violent or threatening. On the morning of the day on which he died, he arose as usual, and although feeble, was able to walk about the house. Shortly after he arose, however, he was seized with violent pains, and before noon was a corpse. He was perfectly rational to the last, and his dying words were, "Peace, peace, peace."

The fathers of the Cumberland Presbyterian Church were all laborers, but Mr. King was one of the most laborious among them. As a specimen of his labors, the following may be mentioned. In May, 1834, the General Assembly appointed him, with Messrs. McAdow and Ewing, to visit the churches throughout all the length and breadth of the West and South. From the age and infirmities of these men, the appointment might have been considered rather nominal than otherwise. With Mr. King, however, it was not so. Mr. McAdow was really to infirm, and Mr. Ewing could not leave home. Consequently the whole labor of the appointment, if fulfilled, fell upon Mr. King. It has been said that as far as he was concerned, the appointment was not nominal. His family were then in Missouri. After making suitable arrangements for leaving them as comfortable as possible in that new country, when the appointed time arrived for his departure, he gathered his family around him and commended them to the care of God in solemn prayer, and then set out on his journey in his sixtieth year, on horseback, accompanied by his eldest son, Rev. Robert D. King.

In this tour he traveled through the States of Missouri, Arkansas, Louisiana, Mississippi, Alabama, Tennessee, and Kentucky, and perhaps touched upon some of the more Northern or Eastern States. He was absent from his home and family twenty months. His son, Judge King, says in reference to the occurrence, "God, in his mercy, vouchsafed to keep us all free from harm, and, after the lapse of twenty months, to bring us together again in the flesh." Says my authority: "No accident had befallen his family. No evil had come nigh their dwelling. The guardian angel had spread his broad wings over them, and the everlasting arms were underneath them." In the course of this tour, as I have mentioned, Mr. King met the General Assembly, which held its sessions in 1835, at Princeton, Kentucky. He was elected, I believe, unanimously, the Moderator of the Assembly, after having preached the opening sermon, by the request of Dr. Cossitt, Moderator of the Assembly of 1834.

Mr. King is said to have been the first minister of the gospel who ever preached to the Choctaw and Chickasaw Indians, in their present locality. An incident of great interest is related, which is said to have occurred while he was preaching for the first time to the Choctaws. His son, Judge King, relates it. "While he was addressing a large crowd of the Indians about salvation through Jesus Christ, and communicating to them by means of an interpreter, the interpreter became so convinced of sin, and so overwhelmed by a sense of his guilt in the sight of God, and of his dangerous condition, that he could proceed no farther, but

---

[25]**Ladies' Pearl**, May, 1859.

fell upon his knees, and began to cry aloud for mercy. The preacher paused for a moment. He knew not how to proceed, or what to do. Although he could not speak one word to them in their own tongue, yet he saw that many of them were in tears, and from their sobs and cries, he knew they were praying for mercy. At length the thought occurred to his mind, that although hey could not understand him, nor he them, yet God could hear and understand both; and as the most of his congregation seemed engaged in prayer, he would close the sermon, and kneel down and for a few moments join his Red brethren in prayer. After a short season, and before he arose from his knees, God poured light and comfort into the heart of the interpreter, and he and many others were made happy in the love of Christ."

The labors of Mr. King laid the foundation for the missions which were afterward established among the Choctaws. The mother of Rev. Israel Fulsom, a native minister, was one of the first converts. She is said to have been the first female Choctaw converted to Christianity, and the first to adopt the costume and usages of the whites. At the commencement of the late unhappy war, there were nearly a thousand members of the Cumberland Presbyterian Church among the Choctaws. As one fruit of all this, we have now eleven young Choctaw students in Cumberland University, and seven or eight Choctaw young ladies in Cumberland Female College.

Mr. King spent most of his ministerial life in traveling, and in general labors among the churches. He considered that he could be more useful in that way than in a settled pastorate. There were many circumstances connected with the condition of the Church to encourage such a mode of life, and make it useful. On his part, it was no doubt a wise selection. He was faithful in his attendance upon the judicatures of the Church. Seldom was he absent from the point to which duty called. He belonged to a generation of earnest and faithful men.

I have some personal recollections of Mr. King, which are very interesting to myself. The first time that I recollect to have heard him preach was at Fall Creek, at a camp-meeting, in May, 1819. Fall Creek is in the lower end of Wilson county, Tennessee. The meeting was, on many accounts which need not be mentioned here, an unusually interesting one. He may have preached on Saturday, but if he did, I have no recollection of the sermon. But he preached on Sunday, from John xvii. 3: "And this is life eternal, that they might know thee the only true God, and Jesus Christ, whom thou hast sent." The sermon was a strong argument, and a powerful appeal for the truth of the Christian revelation. I had just become a candidate for the ministry, and the discussion was new to me. The sermon was well adapted to the great crowd who were in attendance, and the impression made was certainly very deep. I heard him preach the same sermon in September following at the Big Spring. It was still a good and great sermon, but was not delivered with so much unction and power as before.

I heard him again, I think, in the fall of 1821. It was at a meeting held at John McLin's, in Sumner county. He preached there on Sunday morning, on his way to Synod. The test was Romans i. 16: "For I am not ashamed of the gospel." including the whole verse. A temporary pulpit and seats had been prepared in the yard. The congregation was large. It was the neighborhood in which Mr. King had been chiefly raised. He was surrounded by a few of his old friends and relatives, and many of their children. The appearance and manner of the preacher were the very expression of solemnity. The sermon was powerful. His voice seemed to shake the assembly. When he was about closing, he turned to those who were sitting in the pulpit behind him, and asked if they had any mourners there. There had been no movement of that kind, however, at the meeting, and the call was omitted.

Mr. King was a member of the first Synod that I ever attended. It was held at the Beech Meeting-house, in Sumner county. I think he did not preach on the occasion. He attended the Synod also of 1825, held at Princeton, Kentucky. This meeting of the Synod is memorable on two accounts. The subject of the division of the Synod, and the organization of a General Assembly, was first discussed there; and the resolution was passed establishing Cumberland College. Upon the establishment of the College, although it was an experiment, there was general unanimity. In regard to the establishment of a General Assembly, as it now exists in the Church, there was a decided difference of opinion. Mr. King was in favor of a General Assembly. Mr. Ewing was present, and was very earnest and very able in his opposition. He favored what was then called a "delegated Synod." The discussion was warm and earnest. Rev. William Barnett was Moderator. Somehow in the heat of that or some other discussion, he and Mr. King came into collision. They were both lion-like men. Neither had ever learned to yield with a good grace. Short words ensued. The occurrence threw a temporary cloud over the meeting. John Barnett wept like a child. The cloud passed off, however, and harmony of feeling was restored. The favorers of a General Assembly were more numerous, and continued to be so until the discussion ended in the organization of this judicature of the Church.

I have mentioned that Mr. King was Moderator of the General Assembly of 1835. He governed the Assembly with energy. Some of the members thought he was arbitrary. He governed, however, in his own way. He had a strong will, and was accustomed to prompt and quiet obedience. The old men were generally vigorous governors. It is no disparagement to them to say that they ruled with a rod of iron. Such an administration was necessary to their times, and God in his providence adapted them to their times. At the close of the Assembly, he visited me at my own home. There he showed himself the kind and gentle father.

Mr. King was a religious man at home. He had a time set apart for private devotion. A portion of each day was spent in this exercise. His son says, "From my earliest recollection, it was his constant custom to read a portion of Scripture, without note or comment, sing a hymn, in which his family joined, and then to lead them in family prayer. Morning and evening he did so, omitting no part of the service, and having every member of the family present. No ordinary circumstance was allowed to interfere with this usage."

He was a poor man, raised a large family, and spent the most of his ministerial life in countries which were new. Of course, from the latter circumstance, it would be supposed that he received but little remuneration for his ministerial labor. Still he faltered not, and whilst he believed and taught that it was the duty of the Church to support the gospel, his own motto was, "To preach, pay or no pay." This was the theory and the practice, too, of other fathers as well as him.

He was the father of ten children—five sons and five daughters. His oldest daughter professed religion at seven years of age, and died in her thirteenth year, in the triumphs of faith. According to the account of her brother, who witnessed the scene, "She rejoiced and praised God aloud, until articulation was hushed in death." Two of his other daughters lived to maturity, and one of them became the wife of Rev. Daniel Patten, of Missouri. Of the history of the two others, the writer has no knowledge. Three of the sons entered the ministry, and are now active and laborious in their profession. They are laboring in Texas. One of them, and the one, too, from whom many of the facts contained in this sketch have been derived, fell a victim to the guerrillas of the cruel war through which we have just passed.

In person, Mr. King was tall and strongly built. His aspect was serious, approaching to severity. His voice was strong, and well adapted to preaching in the open air, to which men of his day were much accustomed. Before I knew him, he had lost two of his front teeth. This of course increased the labor of preaching. It did not, however, injure his articulation. This was sufficiently clear and distinct. His person and manner inspired respect; he would have been observed in any crowd as a man who was concerned with serious things. He belonged to a past age. In the Cumberland Presbyterian Church, at least, it was an age of giants, in their way.

A sermon was delivered at the General Assembly succeeding his death, as a memorial of Mr. King, by Rev. Robert Donnell. The Assembly met that year at Owensboro, Kentucky. The sermon was delivered on Sabbath to a crowded audience. Many who still live will recollect the occurrence.

REV. JACOB LINDLEY
(1774-1857)

Sources: Mrs. C. W. Donnell; Dr. Lutellus Lindley; Manuscript Remains; "The Old Redstone Presbytery," by Joseph Smith, D.D.; Walker's "History of Athens county, Ohio."

Jacob Lindley was born June 13, 1774, in Western Pennsylvania. He was the fifth in descent from Francis Lindley, who was one of the passengers in the May Flower, which landed at Plymouth Rock in 1620.[26] One of his remote ancestors is supposed to have accompanied John Robinson in his emigration from England to Holland, whither they went to escape the violence of the same persecuting hand which at length drove the Puritans of the May Flower and their successors to the American wilderness. The father of Jacob Lindley was Demas Lindley. The father of Demas Lindley emigrated from New England, and settled in Morris county, New Jersey, but at what time it is unknown.

The mother of Jacob Lindley was Joanna Lindley, daughter of Josiah Pruden,[27] and the granddaughter of Rev. John Pruden, an immigrant minister of the gospel from England. Demas Lindley, the father of Jacob Lindley, moved from New Jersey and settled in Western Pennsylvania as early as 1773. I take the following extract from Dr. Smith's "Old Redstone, or Historical Sketches of Western Presbyterianism:"

> The South-western part of Washington county, bordering on Virginia, embraces a fine agricultural region of both sides of Ten-mile Creek. This creek is so named from its entering the Monongahela River ten miles above Redstone Creek. At an early period in the settlement of the country, this section attracted the attention of emigrants from New Jersey. Two respectable elders of the Presbyterian Church from Morris county, in that State, removed to the West about the same time, and settled on Ten-mile. Their names were Jacob Cook and Demas Lindley. The period of their immigration is supposed to have been as early as 1773. Each of these worthy men drew around him in a short time a considerable settlement, known for many years after by the names of Cook's settlement and Lindley's settlement. Mr. Lindley, in the fall and winter of 1774-5, erected a fort and block-house, long known by his name. In fact, it was one of the best forts and

---

[26]Correction submitted by Saundra L. Bennett: Francis Lindley was not on the Mayflower. It is not known exactly where or when Francis Lindley came to America. He was born about 1624 so he was not even alive when the Mayflower came to America.

[27]Correction submitted by Saundra L. Bennett: Joanne Prudden was the daughter of Joseph Prudden not Josiah.

most formidable garrisons between the Monongahela and Wheeling.

These pioneers experienced the perils and hardships which have been common in the early settlements of the great West and South-west. They were compelled to live lives of great self-denial; they were cut off from religious, and a great many, social privileges; they were in constant danger from the tomahawks and scalping-knives of the Indians. At a certain time in the fall of 1777, after a formidable attack by the Indians upon a neighboring fort, and when all the country was in a state of excitement and apprehension from the Indians, there arrived at Fort Lindley a young Presbyterian minister, who came from the same section of country from which the settlers had come.

Amidst such scenes as have been described, and in the year after his father's settlement in Pennsylvania, Jacob Lindley was born.

Mr. Dod, the young minister, whose arrival has been mentioned, entered at once upon the great work in the wilderness to which he had devoted himself. The Sabbath after his arrival he preached and administered the sacrament of baptism. That day Jacob Lindley was baptized. He was in his fourth year. His memory must have been remarkable, and his mind very impressible from divine things. He says of himself: "I never forgot the solemn scene of my baptism, although then only in my fourth year, nor the conversation of my parents, especially of my mother, both before and after my dedication to God in this ordinance. They told me that I belonged to the Lord, and that it was my duty to him to strive to learn his will, and strictly to obey all his commandments. Impressions were made upon my mind which never left me, and which, as a restraining power, ever preserved me from open sin."

At the age of about twelve or thirteen Mr. Lindley connected himself with the congregation of Mr. Dod as a communicant. He was thought, however, by many of his acquaintances and friends to have been a Christian from his seventh year. In 1781 Mr. Dod's neighbors, with one consent, turned out and put up a log-building considerably larger than any dwelling-house in the neighborhood. This was intended for an academy. A school was commenced. There was a department in it for elementary instruction, but the main object was to furnish classical and mathematical instruction to young men and boys somewhat advanced. This is said to have been the first classical and scientific school established in the West. In the course of a year or two, James Hughs, John Brice, Robert Marshall, John Hanna, Daniel Lindley, Jacob Lindley, David Smith, and Francis Dunlavy began their studies in this institution. Some of them were mere beginners; others were sufficiently far advanced for the study of Latin and Mathematics. In process of time they all became ministers of the gospel. Robert Marshall became, after he entered the ministry, entangled in the Unitarian sophistries of Barton W. Stone, and Francis Dunlavy is supposed to be the Dunlavy who afterward joined the Shakers. If so, however, he is known as John Dunlavy in the histories of the times.

At the age of eighteen Mr. Lindley entered what afterward became Jefferson College, at Cannonsburg, Pennsylvania. From thence he went to Princeton, New Jersey, in 1798. He went to Princeton in company with a young friend, James Carnahan. We have the following anecdote in relation to their trip from a short sketch of the life of Dr. Carnahan by his son-in-law. Young Carnahan had no money. "This difficulty," says the narrator, "was partially overcome at the suggestion of Dr. McMillan, of that vicinity, who offered to advance the money as a loan. This offer was at once accepted, and as his friend, Jacob Lindley, was about to start for Princeton, he determined to go in his company.

> A new difficulty arose. Lindley had a horse, bridle, saddle, and saddle-bags, but Carnahan had none of these things, and no money with which to buy them, without impairing his funds, which had been devoted in his mind to the cherished object of completing his education at Princeton. He told this to Lindley, and this generous friend proposed to share his own traveling equipments with him. The plan was: that one should ride the horse five or ten miles, then tie him by the road-side, and proceed on foot; that the other, coming up, would mount the horse, pass his comrade, and at the end of the assigned distance would, in his turn, dismount and proceed on foot. In this way these young men crossed the mountains from a point thirty miles west of the Monongahela River to Princeton, Jew Jersey. By this process, familiarly known in the Western country as ride and tie, the friends traveled thirty-five or forty miles a day, and reached Princeton, November 1, 1798.

These young men graduated in the fall of 1800. From the preceding sketch it needs not surprise the reader to learn that one of them at length became President of his Alma Mater, the College of New Jersey; and the other, first President of the University of Ohio. Young men who could accomplish such a journey in such a manner and for such an object would make their way through the world, and leave their marks behind them.

The following is an extract from a manuscript of Mr. Lindley, giving an account of his feelings upon the occasion of his graduation. He says:

> In the year 1794 I commenced a regular course of collegiate studies, with no other view than to qualify myself for exerting the best and most direct influence upon the souls of sinners for their salvation. As this was my supreme and ultimate object, I made it the touchstone by which I examined every art and science in my long college course-a course, too, which I endeavored to make thorough. I did not expect to find in any of the sciences the most direct avenue to the sinner's heart, conscience, or understanding, for any immediate resources in future efforts, but that I might be able to arm myself with the best weapons for the defense of truth in our warfare against the power of the prince of darkness. After years of close and laborious application I received from the Trustees and Faculty of New Jersey College a diploma, testifying to my fidelity as a student and to the respectability of my scholarship. The night after my final examination was spent in deep sighs, attended with copious tears under a deeply felt consciousness, from all that I had done and learned, of the

vacuity of soul which neither science nor letters could fill, nor in the least degree satisfy.

This is not a common experience of our young men in their college course, and in immediate prospect of their Bachelor's Degree. If it were, our colleges would become fountains of life rather than what they too often are-schools of self-conceit, skepticism, spiritual debauchery, and stepping-stones to death.

In a history of Athens county, Ohio, published in 1869, we have an interesting account of the early labors of Mr. Lindley. After describing his earlier life and the various steps in the progress of his education to his closing his college course at Princeton, the writer says:

> After a course of theological study he was licensed to preach by the 'Washington Presbytery,' and in 1803 he removed to Ohio, settling first at Beverly, on the Muskingum River.
>
> Having been selected by the first Board of Trustees of to organize and conduct that institution, he removed to Athens in 1808, and opened the academy. For several years he had the entire charge of the infant college, which he conducted with distinguished ability and success. He was the prime mover in securing the erection of the college-buildings, and in founding the Presbyterian Church in Athens. He labored here assiduously for about twenty years, during a part of which time he was the only Presbyterian minister in this portion of the State. Dr. Lindley was no common man, but an earnest thinker and conscientious worker. The leading trait in his character was an unswerving devotion to moral principle. His whole life was a continuous effort to promote the welfare of others. He was of an amiable disposition, possessed an eminent degree of sound common sense and an unerring judgment of men. His kindness of heart and known purity of life and conduct gave him great influence with all classes during his long residence at Athens.
>
> One who knew him well says: 'I have seen him go into a crowd of rough backwoodsmen and hunters who used to meet at the village tavern every Saturday, and settle and control them in their quarrels and fights as no other man in that community could do.' His control of the students under his charge was equally extraordinary, and was always marked by gentleness of manner and firmness of purpose. He led a laborious life at Athens, and his works live after him.

In giving a history of the Presbyterian Church in Athens, the writer says:

> The first Presbyterian Society of Athens was organized in the autumn of 1809 by the Rev. Jacob Lindley. The original members of the organization were but nine in number. Public services were held for a time in a little brick school-house; afterward in the court-house until the year 1828, when a brick

church was built. In 1815 the Church numbered forty-seven members, and the revival that year added forty-three. In 1820 there were fifty-three added to the Church, and the whole number of Church-members at that time was one hundred and seventy-seven. The Rev. Jacob Lindley acted as moderator of the session and pastor until about 1828.

In the year 1815 the first degree of Bachelor of Arts awarded in Ohio was conferred by the on Thomas Ewing. He hand entered the institution three years previously, and pursued his studies with great assiduity, spending his later vacations in laying out country roads, surveying, and in similar employments, to enable him by means thus procured to complete his college course.

It will be observed that this occurred under the administration of Mr. Lindley. Thomas Ewing afterward became prominent in the councils of the country. He was for some time a member of Congress, and afterward a member of President Harrison's Cabinet. His descendants are still prominent in the State of Ohio.

During twenty years, from 1808 to 1828, Mr. Lindley was the ruling spirit in the . He was in a great measure both its head and its hands. He shaped its counsels, and performed the most of its labors. The present and succeeding generations owe, and will owe, a debt to these self-denying and laborious pioneers in education, as well as religion, which it will be difficult for them to cancel.

At the expiration of about twenty years he was partially relieved by the appointment of Rev. Dr. Wilson, of Chillicothe, to the presidency, whilst Mr. Lindley agreed to remain a year or two longer as professor of moral philosophy and mathematics.

When he at last left Athens, he spent a year at Walnut Hills, in the neighborhood of Cincinnati, and then a year or two at the Flats of Grace Creek. He was then called to the charge of Upper Ten-mile congregation, within the bounds of which he had been born and raised.

This congregation, or some of its leading men, had commenced a correspondence with Dr. Cossitt, and others of the Cumberland Presbyterian Church, on the subject of their sending missionaries to Western Pennsylvania, before Mr. Lindley took the charge of the congregation. When the missionaries reached there he received them cordially. They held a meeting at his Church. Mr. Chapman, one of the missionaries, describes the meeting as one of great interest. It "was," says he, "awfully solemn. On Sunday we had sixty ro seventy mourners. On Monday there were more than a hundred who distinguished themselves on the anxious seats. It is said that some ten or fifteen obtained comfort." Mr. Lindley found in Donnell, and Chapman, and Burrow, and Morgan, and Bryan, men after his own heart. His proceedings, however, gave offense of course to his former friends, and his Presbytery issued a mandate requiring him to "abstain from any farther ministerial intercourse with the Cumberland Presbyterians." "He received the mandate," says my authority, "with a smile, but declined obedience." At the next meeting of the Presbytery charges were brought against him.. They were all, however, of a frivolous character. The most serious offense alleged was that "he had aided in getting up a camp-meeting in his congregation; had actually had a camp built, and moved his family into it, and share in all the operations of the meeting." Four of his own children professed religion at the camp-meeting in question, and of course he was in no favorable state of mind for making acknowledgments. He attended the Presbytery, and when the charges were read he inquired if they considered him charged with any immorality. The Presbytery decided that the charges did not amount to charges of immorality. He then asked for a letter of dismission, which was granted, and this closed his connection with the Presbyterian Church. He immediately connected himself with the Pennsylvania Presbytery, a new Cumberland Presbyterian Presbytery, which had been organized in Pennsylvania.

Mr. Lindley continued his pastoral connection with the Upper Ten-mile congregation two or three years after he changed his ecclesiastical relations. In process of time, a congregation at Waterford, now Beverly, Ohio, made application to him to come and take charge of them. He informed them promptly and frankly of his change, and also gave the reasons which led to it. The answer was, "Come to us, and we will place ourselves in the same ecclesiastical relations with yourself." It will be recollected that Beverly was the point at which he commenced his ministry, and from which be moved to Athens when called to the charge of the institution there. It seems that he had given the people a promise, that in the event of his leaving Athens, he would return to them, and they now claimed the fulfillment of that promise, though it was something over twenty-five years old. He must have left a deep impression upon the minds of the people in 1808.

In 1837 Rev. Robert Donnell, and his wife, who was the daughter of Mr. Lindley, wrote to him to come to Alabama, and spend his latter days with them. He was becoming old, and himself, and wife, and youngest daughter only remained together of a large family. He complied with the request in part, and removed southward, but still devoted his time to preaching and teaching, as the providence of God opened the way for him. A man of his habits could not have been idle. His daughter married, and on December 4, 1848, he lost his wife. She seems to have been an eminently pious woman. Dr. Lindley gives to Mr. and Mrs. Donnell a minute account of the progress of her illness from day to day, and of her exercises of mind on what proved to be her death-bed. Some extracts are here given from the record of her two last days:

> Dec. 2. Your mother's strength is rapidly failing, but her own words are, 'As the outward man decayeth, the inward man is renewed day by day.'
> Dec. 3. We did not expect, neither did your mother expect, that she would live through the day." (It seems to have been the Sabbath.) "She said, 'This is the day on which Jesus triumphed over death, and took away its sting, and published good news to all the world.' I asked her if she felt any reluctance to pass through the gate of death, through which the Saviour had passed before her. She replied: 'O, no; Jesus is with me, he is my comforter. Yea, though I walk through the

> dark valley of the shadow of death, I will fear no evil, for my Shepherd is with me; his rod and his staff they comfort me.'
>
> Dec. 4. A little before day she requested us to sing *On Jordan's stormy banks I stand, And cast a wishful eye.* Under an excitement which appeared entirely rational, her strength revived to such a degree that she joined us in singing in a loud and distinct voice, and clasping her hands, she strongly and emphatically uttered the words, 'No, never part again.' A little while afterward I asked her if she was now ready and willing to go. She replied: 'I am, with all my heart.' These were her last words.

After the death of his wife, Dr. Lindley spent his time mostly with his children, passing his winters in the South, and his summers in the North. Indeed he seems to have commenced this mode of dividing his time previous to his wife's death. From a letter written in May, 1854, in Pennsylvania, we have the following characteristic account of himself in some of these particulars. He writes thus:

> If I live till June 13th of this year I shall be eighty years of age. I enjoy the best of health; am free from every species of bodily pain; and have strength and action enough to mount a horse from the ground, and to travel any ordinary distance alone in the saddle, or in a buggy. My general practice has been for the last several years to spend the winter in the South, with my children, and the summer season in this country. I come up in the spring by steam-boat, and in the fall I purchase a horse and buggy and return South by land, a distance of eight hundred or a thousand miles. So frequent have been my journeys that I can have a home anywhere on the road, and am therefore everywhere at home. Should any accident befall me in passing, it would not be far from some friend who would take care of me. As to expenses in traveling, I find no difficulty in providing them. After I have used a horse and buggy six months they will sell for about a hundred dollars more in the South then they cost in Pennsylvania. This excess pays my traveling expenses, and leaves something remaining. My children greatly deceive me if they do not desire my company, and take a real pleasure in imparting to all my necessities. They always anticipate my wants, and in such a way as to render a sense of abject dependence impossible. No man can live in this world with fewer fears of want, and less harassed with the cares of life than I do. My sun rises gently in the east, and sinks in smiles behind the western hills.

This experimental picture of old age will very well bear to be place side by side with a chapter of "Cicero de Senectute." The Cato of the moralist was even very far from reaching the sublime and quiet elevation of this Christian subject of our sketch.

In another part of this letter Dr. Lindley refers to an occasion which must have been a matter of great interest to his feelings as well as to the feelings of his children. It occurred the preceding year. Early in the year 1853 his old students, who remained about Athens, determined to express their continued respect for his character as an old instructor and friend by giving him a sort of an ovation. The plan was to have a general convocation of the old students who had been instructed under his administration at the Commencement of the University of Athens in August of 1853. The plan was happily carried out. There was a great concourse of people from the neighboring towns and country. Thomas Ewing, who has been already mentioned as the first graduate of Ohio University, and of the State of Ohio, General Lucius Bird, and other notabilities, made speeches. The old veteran teacher was, however, the central figure, the observed of all observers. He may well be allowed to have said: "I never felt myself and family more highly honored than by that meeting. It was said by those who knew me best thirty years ago, either in what they thought the truth or in flattery, that I had lost nothing in physical or mental energy by the lapse of time. They, however, had not the same opportunity of knowing in that time of high excitement and joyous emotion which I have in my retirement." In spite of all this generous flattery he felt himself to be an old man.

Few men in this rugged world of hard work meet in their declining age with so magnanimous and spontaneous an acknowledgment of the value of their earlier services. It was an evident outpouring of the heart of noble-minded men, who were not quick to forget the faithful instructions and earnest counsels, of the friend of their youth. On this occasion, or some earlier one near this time, Mr. Lindley received the Degree of Doctor of Divinity from the authorities of the University of which he was the acknowledged founder.

The following are extracts from a letter to Mrs. Donnell, dated April 13, 1856. It will be observed that he was then approaching the end of his eighty-second year:

"Last week I went in a buggy to Brownsville, sixteen mils, attended the meeting of Union Presbytery, and returned on Saturday, but was too much fatigued to preach on Sunday, according to appointment. The road was exceedingly rough. As we traveled along the north sides of the hills, where the sun had but little direct influence, the snow was two feet deep.

"Rev. Brother Henderson is appointed to the General Assembly which is to meet in Louisville in May. I am the alternate, but do not expect to go. My health is good, I have a good appetite for food, and sleep well. I am free from pain in every department of the animal, but still am weaker this spring than I ever was before when in health. I have never recovered my strength entirely since my sickness last fall, and would not now attempt to drive two fine horses alone in a buggy to Alabama." He refers to some of his former journeys from the North to the South.

In this letter we find the first decided indications of a failure of strength and a partial failure of health. The machine was becoming old, and notwithstanding its original and long-continued vigor, was beginning to yield to the pressure of so many years. On the 29th of the following January the long and active life of Dr.

Lindley came to an end. I copy the following notice of the occurrence by the Athens County Pioneer Association, organized in December, 1868:

Athens, Ohio,——1857.

Died at the residence of his son, Dr. Lutellus Lindley, of Connellsville, Pennsylvania, on Thursday, the 29th of January, 1857, Rev. Jacob Lindley, D.D., at the advanced age of eighty-three years.

Mr. Lindley resided at this place more than twenty years, during which time he was widely and favorably known as an active and eminently useful member of society. He had the entire charge of the academy here on its first organization in 1808, and conducted it with distinguished ability and success, till it was merged in a college, and others became associated with him as members of the Faculty in the Ohio Univeristy.

During most of the same period he was well known as the only Presbyterian minister in this part of Ohio; and, besides organizing and building up the first Presbyterian Church in Athens, found time to preach at irregular intervals in the surrounding neighborhoods throughout the country, the grateful remembrance of which is still cherished by many of the early settlers in this vicinity. From Athens Mr. Lindley removed to Cincinnati about the year 1828, and perhaps the year following to Western Pennsylvania, soon after which he united with the Cumberland Presbyterian Church, in which he labored ministerially during the rest of his long and useful life.

Notice has been taken in the preceding sketch of Dr. Lindley's change of his ecclesiastical relations. This was an important step in his life, as it is in the life of any manof his age and position in society at the time in which the change occurred. It deserves, therefore, a farther notice. Still this is not the place for a full discussion of the subject, nor is it probable that such a discussion would now be productive of much interest or advantage. Dr. Lindley was, however, always desirous to be understood as not having changed his theological views at the time of his change of relations to the Churches. It is evident, too, from his own account of his early struggles in the formation of his theological opinions, that he would from the beginning have been a Cumberland Presbyterian, had he, in the providence of God, found an established organization holding and preaching such doctrines as he afterward found to be held and preached by Cumberland Presbyterians. Mrs. Donnell says of him:

My father ever seemed desirous that it should be known that his religious sentiments and beliefs underwent no change when he united with the Cumberland Presbyterian Church, as all his writings which relate to these subjects show. He was a Cumberland Presbyterian from the beginning, although he had no knowledge of a people that sympathized with him in his theological views.

This account is no doubt correct. Dr. Lindley was eminently a practical man and an independent thinker. It would have been a difficult matter for him to be at ease within the limits prescribed by the iron logic of Augustinianism. I present a paragraph from his account of his licensure by his Presbytery:

> I must here relate a touching incident connected with my examination. Out of respect, no doubt, to European dignity and literature, a foreigner was invited to conduct the examination. The invitation was accepted, and he entered upon the work with no small pomposity. His gigantic size, gray hairs, sovereign-like manners, and literature of Glasgow renown, rendered him quite formidable to a youthful stranger who had not yet acquired much personal courage. His dictatorial manner and his utter impatience of hearing any explanation of my views were such as almost to crush me to the floor. I was completely overcome, and, with the leave of the Moderator, I withdrew to a log behind the church, and relieved myself a little with a flood of tears. An old American father, Rev. Joseph Patterson, whose heart had often been melted under the tender appeals of Whitefield and the Tennents, came out, took his seat at my side, laid his hand upon my head, bowed down with grief, and addressed me in the following words.

I do not repeat the words. It is not necessary. It is sufficient to say that they were such words as a generous, affectionate ministerial father would know how to address to a sincere, and earnest, and truth-loving young man. The end was, that the Presbytery was willing to give the candidate some latitude of thought, and the sturdy examiner himself, although he had announced his opposition unless a change of views was avowed, came into measures, and the young man was licensed. Dr. Lindley gives us an additional account of his theological struggles at the time of his entrance into the ministry:

> I had been careful to have it known to the Presbytery that although I considered the **Westminster Confession of Faith** as containing more sound theology than had ever before or since its compilation been given in detail by any man or set of men uninspired, yet that there were some views set forth in that worthy volume to which I could not subscribe. And that if they licensed and ordained me, it must be with the understanding that I could not be compelled to teach or preach these objectionable doctrines. There are numbers of living witnesses who can testify that the facts here stated were told to them by members of the Presbytery which brought me forward into the ministry. I have, therefore, the satisfaction of knowing that I cannot be justly charged either with having changed my theological ground or with having deceived my fathers and brethren in the ministry. If I am in error now, I was in error in 1802. And in all places where I have preached for more

than fifty-three years there are witnesses who will testify that my doctrines have been uniformly the same.

The truth is, and it is well enough known now, that the same leaven which was working in the mind of young Lindley was working at the same time in North Carolina in the minds of William McGee and Samuel McAdow, and soon developed itself in the revival in the Green River and Cumberland countries. It was a spirit which leading men in the Church could not tolerate, nor could they condescend to treat with respect, or even to hear with patience, the difficulties or the explanations of their brethren who were as honest and as earnest, and, to say the least, about as capable of reaching and comprehending the truth as themselves. Such men, and, as far as it could be done, their spirit with them, were driven out of the Presbyterian Church under the pressure of those who would rule or ruin. Upon the justice of wisdom of such measures posterity will decide; perhaps the verdict of Providence has already been given.

Dr. Lindley was for many years a professional educator. We will hear a few words from him on the subject of education. He says:

> Had I the control of all the colleges in the world I would admit no young man into the Freshman Class who hd not studied the character of the God of the Bible, and obtained something like a correct knowledge of it. Such a course would immediately bring back the Bible into our common schools, and the Catechism into our families. Then we should all be taught of God. Professors in colleges would no more complain of riots, rebellions, or disorderly conduct among students. The Church would be blessed with a learned and holy ministry, and the world, gently yielding to the spiritual power of the gospel, would be converted by the subordinate agency of the rising generation.

Dr. Lindley believed all this. Such a belief is an evidence of his earnest spirituality. Whether, however, with a fair experiment, expectations so congenial with a good heart, and a sanguine and buoyant spirit, would be realized, may be allowed to be doubtful. Still one thing is certain, there ought to be more religion, and more of the Bible in our best colleges. Any school, or any college, cut off from the influence of these is to dreaded as a fountain whose poisoned waters bring death.

In 1846 Mr. Lindley published a small volume, which he denominated "Infant Philosophy." It is connected with the subject of education. He had raised a large family of children well. He thought that others with skillful and practical measures could do the same thing. This book is intended to be a helper in such a work. It abounds in correct views and wise counsels to parents upon the subject of the early training of children. The work read and thoroughly studied could not be otherwise than a blessing to any family. It ought to be in the hands of every parent, and especially of every mother in the Cumberland Presbyterian Church. There is no parent who might not be greatly profited by its counsels. The author takes the ground that all successful government is commenced in the nursery, and he is right.

Dr. Lindley was married to Hannah Dickey in 1800. She was of Scotch-Irish descent. They had ten children. Six of them still (in 1873) live. The eldest son, Rev. Daniel Lindley, went in 1834 as a missionary under the direction of the American Board of Commissioners for Foreign Missions to Natal, in Eastern Africa, and is still there. He has raised a large family, all born in that country. Mrs. Donnell, the honored relict of Rev. Robert Donnell, still lives at Athens, Alabama. The other children are Dr. Lutellus Lindley, of Pennsylvania; Mrs. Jones, of Hernando, Mississippi; Mrs. Woods, wife of Rev. Leroy Woods, of Illinois; and Mrs. Cowan, of Athens, Alabama. The youngest daughter died, in 1856, in Pontotoc, Mississippi. I have before me a beautiful tribute to her memory, published at the time of her death. She seems to have been a lovely Christian lady. The last week in 1842, in company with two or three brethren, I spent some days at her house in Pontotoc. She was administering its affairs at the time in the absence of her husband. Her generous hospitality made our temporary sojourn very agreeable indeed. I have always preserved a pleasant recollection of those few days.

My personal acquaintance with Dr. Lindley was rather limited. He came into the Church when he was somewhat advanced in life, and our fields of labor were remote from each other. I saw him for the first time at the General Assembly in Princeton, Kentucky, in 1835. He had then been in the Church about three years. He was becoming an old man, and his gray hairs and dignified bearing gave him a venerable appearance. He preached a sermon in the course of the meeting. If family government was not the leading subject of the discourse, he took occasion to give that subject some prominence. He startled the mothers in the congregation by urging that they ought to commence governing their children, at least, by the time they were six months old. The common impression is, that government is early enough if commenced at six years of age, and some never commence at all. The wise old preacher was right. The sooner the twig is bent to the right direction the better. Every sensible parent ought to know this. Dr. Lindley spent a few hours at my house on that occasion. He was kind enough to give me great encouragement in my work. I needed encouragement. I was laboring then, as I have labored a large part of my life, with a clouded future before me.

I think I saw him no more till the Assembly at Lebanon, Ohio, in 1847. Great changes had taken place in the Church in the meantime. There was a stir just then on the subject of a union between us and the New School Presbyterian Church. I do not recollect how he stood upon the question. I was not a member of the Assembly, and my stay was short. We spent only a single morning together. He was at the Assembly at Nashville in 1852. He was there in company with Robert Donnell, but, I believe, was not a member. He was, in a high degree, a genial and companionable old gentleman, a model always in the social and religious circle. His manners were those of the Old School, a school which has far more admirers than imitators. It ought to have imitators. Mrs. Donnell writes of him:

"It will be a great gratification to me to have my father's memory preserved to the world. He was a devoted, humble, self-denying Christian gentleman-a pattern worthy of imitation in all the relations of life."

This is not a mere outpouring of filial affection. The facts presented in this sketch (and many more might be added of the same kind) are a vindication of the truth of every favorable word thus uttered. The memory of such men is a treasure to be cherished by the Church. A long life spent in unfaltering devotion to the great interests of humanity is a spectacle not often presented in this world of selfishness, and sin, and darkness. We thank God, however, that there are some such. They strengthen us in our conflicts with wrong-doing, and encourage the hope that a purer and brighter light will one day shine out from underneath the cloud which hangs over us. Such men are, in the highest sense, benefactors of our race. The earnest teacher and the earnest preacher leave impression behind them which time will not efface. Their influence will never die.

REV. WILLIAM CALHOUN LOVE
(1798-1872)

William Calhoun Love was born in the Grassy Valley, Knox county, East Tennessee, on the 9th day of March, 1798. His father, William Love, was a native of Virginia, having been born and raised in Augusta county, near Staunton. His mother's maiden name was Esther Calhoun. She was born and raised in Abbeville District, South Carolina. She was a relative of John C. Calhoun, the distinguished politician of that State. Mr. Love's father and mother were married in 1785, and settled in Pendleton District, South Carolina. The parents remained in this State until after the birth of their fifth child, some time after which they started for the south-west. Mr. Love left his family for a time in East Tennessee, whilst he himself came to Kentucky, and made a settlement on the waters of Tradewater, in what is now Caldwell county. Whilst the mother and children were in East Tennessee, the subject of this sketch was born. In the settlement of the family in Kentucky it consisted of seventeen members, black and white. Mr. William Love, the father, was a surveyor, and while he was engaged in surveying some lands in what is now Hopkins county, he was killed by some outlaws by the name of Harp. The Harps were a family of brothers who had emigrated from North Carolina, and became a terror to that portion of Kentucky. Their robberies and murders are still recollected by the older inhabitants of Lower Kentucky. The mother was thus left in a land of strangers with a large family of twelve children, white and black. She was a Christian woman, however, and strengthened herself for her burden. Her husband was killed in his thirty-ninth year.

From the manuscript we have the following account of the earliest years of our subject:

> From my earliest years I was taught to pray. How often have I at night covered up my head after retiring, and repeated the little prayer:
>
> *'And now I lay me down to sleep,*
> *I pray the Lord my soul to keep;*
> *And if I die before I wake,*
> *I pray the Lord my soul to take!'*
>
> After I became eight or ten years of age, I frequently retired at night to a certain walnut-tree in the field to pray. I recollect one night while I was engaged in prayer at the root of the tree, a decayed limb, or something which had been lodged in the tree, fell with a considerable noise, and frightened me very much. I verily thought it was the devil. It was some time before I ventured there for prayer again.

In process of time the widow married Joseph Kuykendall, and removed and settled with him near where Hopkinsville now stands. The marriage proved unhappy. The new husband was intemperate, and exceedingly profane. She could not endure the thought of raising her children under such an influence, and left him after an experiment of eighteen months, and returned to her former home. Says the writer of himself in those days:

> I was put in the field to work in crop-time, and in the winter sent to some little three-months' school. I soon learned to read, write, and spell. I was never permitted to swear, or use what were called bad words, or tell stories. On the contrary, I was taught to speak the truth, to go to Church, and when there to keep my seat and behave myself during the service. My mother was a Presbyterian, and had me baptized by old Father Terah Templin, at that time pastor of the congregation of which she was a member. I have a distinct recollection of the appearance of the grave, gray-headed old man. At one time, when he was administering the Lord's-supper, my attention was particularly attracted to him. I made my way up, and stood near him while he was officiating at the head of the table. When some of the old fathers and sisters began to clap their hands and shout, the preacher hastened to the stand, and cried out in the language of Joel, 'Rend your hearts, and not your garments, and turn unto the Lord your God; for he is gracious and merciful, slow to anger, and of great kindness, and repenteth him of the evil.'

His mother, however, became better satisfied with her religious condition after hearing McGready, and Ewing, and others of that class of preachers. Their earnest and experimental style of preaching came more fully home to her heart. She united herself with the revival ministers, as they were called, whilst they were laboring in the capacity of a Council. She died in 1844, in the communion of the Cumberland Presbyterian Church. The most of her children followed in her footsteps.

These details are not so important in themselves, but they are given because they will assist in the explanation of other facts, the account of which will follow. Mr. Love, our subject, grew up to manhood, and by degrees laid aside the habit of retirement for evening prayer, as well as other good habits which he had formed under the guidance of his pious mother. He became a restless and wild young man. He was a fine companion, had a roving disposition, and a great notion of what is called a life of adventure. These developments were, however, temporarily interrupted by the earthquakes of 1811 and 1812. Of the earthquakes we have the following account:

> In December of 1811, the earthquakes commenced on Sunday morning, some time before day. We were all aroused from sleep by a lumbering noise like distant thunder. Immediately the house began to shake, while mother sat up in the bed exclaiming, 'Judgment, the judgments of God upon the world for its wickedness!' We all put on our clothes in great consternation, waiting for daylight. Some time before day the neighbors began to come in, wishing to know mother's opinion of what had occurred, as she was considered among them as a woman of

reading. They got the Bible, and turned it over from passage to passage, and came to the conclusion that it was an earthquake. Their minds were quieted a little. But just after daylight another severe shock occurred. All ran out of the house, which began to reel and crack as though it would fall over every moment. Everything appeared to be in motion. I know not what others thought, but verily I thought the last day had come. I was startled, but still I had but little fear. I had been up to this time like a young ruler: 'All these commandments have I observed from my youth.' The hidden wickedness of my heart had not yet been revealed to me.

Mr. Love's fondness for adventure has been mentioned. The war of 1812 came on, and in the latter part of 1814 a call was made on Kentucky and Tennessee for troops for the defense of New Orleans. He wanted to go upon the expedition which followed the call, but knew that his mother would not give her consent, as he was not yet seventeen. He obtained her consent, however, to make a boating trip, but made his way directly to Smithland, hired himself as a substitute for a man who had been drafted for the service, and was soon on his way to the seat of war. On the 4th of January, 1815, the expedition landed four miles below New Orleans. He shared in the terrible battle of the 8th, lost his bayonet in the conflict, and was very uneasy lest the British would be able to charge over the breastworks of the American lines, and he should be in an awkward predicament without a weapon so much needed in such a case. It turned out that he did not need his bayonet. He was one of the body of troops who were sent across the river to assist in recovering the ground which was supposed to have been lost there. The result of all was, that the unfilial young man reached the home of his mother unhurt. He was received as such wanderers are generally received by forgiving mothers. His own account is, "I met my mother and all the family at the gate, and such joy I had never experienced before as I experienced at that meeting."

This fondness for adventure still continued, and he determined to go to sea. Arrangements were made with Jesse Cobb, of Eddyville, a neighboring town on Cumberland River, to go with him as a hired hand on a trading boat to New Orleans. His purpose was to seek employment at New Orleans on board of a ship as a subordinate officer, or as a private sailor, and thus to commit himself to the perils of a life at sea. A good providence interposed. Before the boat was ready to leave Eddyville he was taken sick with what was then called the winter fever. Before he recovered the boat was gone, and the whole scheme was broken up.

On the 24th of July, 1817, Mr. Love was married to Honor Tison. His wife had been raised in Pitt county, North Carolina, and was six months younger than himself. He bought a farm a few miles from Princeton, and settled on it, but, after one or two unimportant changes, he moved in the winter of 1821 and 1822 to the Western District of Tennessee, and settled in Madison county, or rather what was soon organized into Madison county.

"Here," says her, "I must record with shame and deep contrition of heart that I departed farther than ever before from the way in which my pious mother had taught me to walk. The country was new, the people were strangers to one another, and acquaintances were frequently made and friendships formed around the bottle and over the glass."

He was a popular, companionable, and sprightly man—just such as one as would be expected to be carried away by a current like this. And he was carried too far. In the organization of the militia of the county he was elected an officer of respectable rank. This circumstance increased his temptations. He became, as he says, a prodigal, and started rapidly on the downward road. He had relentings, however, as a man with his early training would almost inevitably have. In the summer or early fall of 1822, James S. Guthrie, Francis Johnston, and the writer, held the first sacramental-meeting that ever was held by Cumberland Presbyterians in what is now Western Tennessee. The meeting was held on the north fork of Forked Deer, near Adley Alexander's. I have mentioned this circumstance elsewhere, but repeat it here for the purpose partly of more particularity. On Sabbath of this meeting, Mr. Guthrie was preaching with great power, on the subject of "pure religion and undefiled before God and the Father." I was in my place in the pulpit, and looking back I saw a man sitting alone on a stump fifteen or twenty steps from the pulpit, weeping like a child. That man was the prodigal, Major William C. Love. What wonders by his providence and by his grace God does work!

In 1824, Mr. Love left Madison county and settled in Gibson, about four miles from where Trenton now stands. After the organization of the county, the first court was held at his house. The following is his account of the accommodations for the occasion:

"I had built a cabin with a passage, and also a stable about twenty feet square, of round logs, mostly beech. As it had never been used, I gave it up for the use of the court. I split some puncheons and arranged them as seats for the court. Then some forks were driven into the ground, and a railing was made for the lawyers. A slab was prepared for their seat, and in front some boards were arranged on forks for their books and for the convenience of writing."

These were primitive preparations for the administration of justice. The ministrations of the gospel were conducted in very much the same primitive manner. The inevitable circuit-rider and camp-meeting of those days followed very soon upon the heels of the settlement. In 1826, a camp-meeting was held in the neighborhood of Mr. Love. It was the first meeting of the kind which was ever held there. He was one of the camp-holders, and, although not yet a professor of religion, and, as we have seen, altogether a man of the world, he entertained more people and kept more horses than any man on the ground. The preachers at that meeting were William Barnett, Robert Baker, Nelson I. Hess, and the writer.

The year 1828 was the great crisis in Mr. Love's life. He says himself, "It was the ever-memorable year in which four things transpired in connection with myself and family. Three of them should never be forgotten in time; and three of them I am sure will be remembered in eternity."

The first was strictly a domestic occurrence. He had, some time previous to this year, joined the Masons.

The second occurrence was his expulsion from the Lodge for card-playing and drinking on the Sabbath-day. He writes opposite to this: "A righteous judgment." If he had not been an honest Christian man he would have left no such record.

"The third," says he, "my last gambling and horse-racing."

The fourth, "My conviction and conversion."

It was a strange succession of events. I suppose the explanation is to be found in the principle that a disease develops itself with such power as partially to spend itself as it approaches a crisis. However we may settle this question, the record no doubt is honestly made, and the whole subsequent life was a cumulative testimony that the conviction and conversion were powerful realities. The following is his account of these latter events:

> Camp-meetings were coming on. The Cumberland Presbyterians held one near my own house. James Stewart, Richard Beard, John C. Smith, John and James McKee, and William Bumpass, were there. I suppose I need not say that there was another there greater than all the rest. It pleased this great, and good, and merciful Being, again to show me that I was a great sinner, and hastening to destruction. I believed and felt that I was the greatest sinner on the ground. Others might have committed more outrageous wickedness, but I had sinned against light and knowledge, had broken so many vows, had so often and so wickedly grieved the Holy Spirit, had so often gone to the altar and then again to the woods for prayer, and had still turned back. These reflections overwhelmed me. I did not know what to do. I was almost ready to say there could be no mercy for me. The good Lord, however, gave me strength and courage once more to seek the salvation of my soul. I there vowed, not in my own strength as heretofore, but in the strength of Israel's God, that I would pray and seek the pardon of my sins as long as I lived, and that I would die pleading for mercy, even if I never obtained it. I was not excited, nor in the altar, but quiet in the camp.

We are not surprised to learn that soon after this experience his mind became calm and peaceful; still he was not satisfied. At another meeting, however, not long after this, he became entirely relieved. It was a quiet, peaceful, and satisfactory conversion. On the following day his wife professed religion. His negro man Cato made profession before the meeting closed. It was, of course, a memorable occasion in the family. In a few weeks the husband and wife presented themselves for examination to the session at a camp-meeting at McLemoresville. The writer was present as Moderator of the session at the time. They were received, and their membership transferred to the congregation in their own vicinity. There was a large number of such cases, as it had been a year of great ingathering.

The following are his reasons, condensed, for uniting with the Cumberland Presbyterians:

1. Their unity and love for one another. This was no small matter with a young convert.
2. Their friendship for other Churches.
3. Their general liberality and open communion.
4. I believed, and loved with all my heart, the doctrines

> which their preachers presented and urged, especially, that Jesus Christ by the grace of God had tasted death for every man.
> 5. Their doctrine of human freedom, which makes men fully responsible for their own conduct.
> 6. The manner in which the righteousness of Christ is presented as the basis of our justification.
> 7. Justification by faith alone; not by baptism, not by works of any kind, but by faith, and if by faith, then by grace.

Of course all these doctrinal principles are to be regarded as crudely received at first, but they afterward became digested into a system, made a part of the spiritual life of our subject. He understood them as well as believed them.

Mr. Love's old companions allowed him three months for a trial of his new life, but supposed that in three months, or at farthest in six, he would break down and be back among them. Instead of this, however, in a few months the subject of the temperance reformation began to be agitated, and he, with a few Presbyterians and Cumberland Presbyterians, organized, it is believed, the first temperance society that was ever organized in Tennessee. It was certainly the first that was organized in West Tennessee. There was opposition. Strange as it may seem, a man who had bidden fair to be a drunkard was found at the head of this temperance movement, in conflict, not merely with men of the world, but with Methodists, Baptists, and, with shame be it said, with some Presbyterians, and Cumberland Presbyterians also. Honor to the memory of the eighteen[28] who then and there commenced the rolling of that ball! The writer knew something of the trial of those days.

In the fall of 1829, Mr. Love was received as a candidate for the ministry by the Hopewell Presbytery. He says of the Presbytery: "It was held at Trenton. I had been sent as a representative by our little Church. Reuben Burrow, Richard Beard, Anthony B. Lambert, Jordan Lambert, William H. Bigham, Robert Baker, William Bumpass, and perhaps others, were in attendance. I had long been in a strait, but my mind was greatly relieved, supposing that if such men as these thought me called to preach it must be so."

He no doubt learned to believe in the experience of his subsequent life that "such men as these," and far wiser and better men, might have been mistaken in this matter. Still, the judgment was unquestionably correct in the particular case.

In March, 1831, he was licensed, the sessions of the Presbytery being held at Bolivar. Two others stood with him and received the Presbyterial commission. One was the present venerable Israel Pickens; the name of a the other is not given. Robert Baker presided. His first regular appointment for preaching was at a school-house about ten miles from his home. In preaching he was very much embarrassed, and his effort was so unsatisfactory to himself, to use his own

---

[28]This was the number that first organized the Temperance Society, at the close of a sermon by Rev. Samuel Hodge.

language, he was so ashamed of himself that as soon as the congregation could be dismissed he left unceremoniously, and rode home without his dinner, thus neglecting to claim even the lowest measure of the laborer's hire.

The following is an account of an experience of the olden time. He had been appointed to a circuit, and at the expiration of the first month says:

> I had been gone from home more than a month, had ridden two hundred and seventh miles, and had preached about twenty-five times. And as this was a six-months' service, the numbers multiplied by six would produce, for miles traveled, sixteen hundred and twenty, and for sermons one hundred and fifty, and yet one dollar and fifty cents was my compensation.

Such a record will startle some of the present generation of preachers. It is not made, however, nor is it repeated here by way of commendation. We may commend the self-denying preacher, but the people receiving the benefits of such labor were guilty before God. Is it not a wonder that God prospered them?

In the month of August, 1836, his wife died. He speaks of this circumstance as the greatest trial of his life. She was no doubt an earnest and devoted Christian woman. She was the mother of several children when her husband entered the ministry. An immense responsibility was upon her, yet she seems always to have borne her burdens with patience and meekness, and as a real helper. The truth is, the man who writes the history of some of the women of those times will write a book to be read. One verse of a favorite song with her was:

> *No, that stream has nothing frightful;*
> *To its banks my steps I bend.*
> *There to plunge will be delightful;*
> *There my pilgrimage will end.*

It was made a part of her obituary notice.

In 1837, Mr. Love moved to Kentucky, and settled in Piney Fork Congregation. His chief object in coming to Kentucky seems to have been that he might secure the aid of his mother in the management of his children. Piney Fork and Bethlehem Congregations were both without pastors. Neither of them had a comfortable house of worship. He calls them, no doubt very appropriately, mere shells of Churches. The Princeton Presbytery itself was small, and very much crippled in its operations. It had but four ministerial members. One of these was a Professor in Cumberland College, another was engaged in the practice of medicine, a third very much embarrassed with the financial affairs of the College, and the fourth was a farmer. About this time Mr. Love took charge of the Bethlehem and Piney Fork Congregations. He was to divide his time equally between them. No specified salary was stipulated.

In July, 1838, he was married a second time, to Miss Catherine Smith. The years 1843 and 1844 he lived near Bethlehem, and taught school in addition to his preaching. Necessity controlled him. In 1844 he resigned the charge of Piney Congregation. The annual compensation for pastoral services was fifty dollars, and sometimes not so much. He felt compelled to look elsewhere for a field of labor.

In October of 1845, he organized the Fredonia Congregation, to which he preached fourteen years in succession. In 1846 he moved to that neighborhood, where he remained to his death. In 1846 he withdrew from his connection with Bethlehem. The salary had been meager enough to produce discouragement. He records it, as upon an average, less than sixty dollars a year. His ministerial labors during the latter years of his life were distributed to the various congregations and destitute neighborhoods within his reach, as circumstances would permit.

In 1861, the cruel civil war came on. His inevitable sympathies and the sympathies of some of his friends ran in different channels. A few of his old friends turned their backs upon him. They were proscriptive; he thought them cruel. Let the charity of silence, however, bury these unholy heart-burnings in oblivion. One of his sons died a prisoner on Johnson's Island. About the same time two of his younger sons, the hope of his old age, were taken from him by death. In addition, in 1864 his home, which was comfortable and well furnished, with nearly every thing which it contained, was consumed by fire. Such a series of disasters produced, says my informant, a depressing effect upon his mind. He nevertheless rallied, and the five last years of his life were years of active labor. In addition to some necessary secular pursuits, he preached frequently on the Sabbath. At the fall session of Princeton Presbytery he was, by a mutual understanding, made the stated supply of Fredonia Congregation. He accordingly preached to them semi-monthly until his death. After the death of Dr. Bird, whose funeral-service he performed, he agreed to preach semi-monthly for the Bethlehem Congregation until a pastor could be procured. This engagement he fulfilled with his accustomed fidelity to his death. Some of the old people said that his pulpit efforts in those last days of his life savored of younger and more vigorous years. One of the elders of Fredonia, who had been in the habit of hearing him for thirty years, reports that "his sermons seemed fresh and new every time."

On the fourth Sabbath in March, 1872, he rode to Bethlehem, about six miles, and returned the same day. He was unwell, and not able to preach. A neighboring minister of the Presbyterian Church supplied the pulpit for him. On Friday following a violent attack of pneumonia developed itself. It soon assumed a typhoid form. Every arrangement, however, had been made. He had set his house in order. His will had been written by himself. He had selected his burial-place, had even given instructions in relation to his coffin and burial-services. Says my informant: "His sufferings were intense and protracted, but his patience and submission were those of a tried Christian. He was scarcely able to speak or hear for days previous to his departure, yet his every and last expression was that of peace and prospective joy. His death was a complete vindication of the truth and power of the Christian religion, as his life had been." He died April 18, 1872.

I have written this sketch on some accounts with a deeper and more tender interest than usual. It will be perceived that the line of the history falls in with the line of my own at various points. I first became slightly acquainted with Mr. Love in my early ministerial life. He then lived in Western Tennessee. I sometimes saw him at my meetings when a circuit-rider in that country. A few years subsequently I knew him as a liberal supporter of camp-meetings near Trenton, while still a man of the old world. Then again, as it has been stated, I believe, I was the Moderator of the session when he and the wife of his youth were received to membership in the Church. I next knew him as a member of the first temperance society of

Trenton, and at his request, with that of others, preached, I suppose, the second temperance-sermon that was ever preached in Western Tennessee. That sermon was delivered in Trenton in the fall of 1828. I was present, according to his record, and according to my own recollection, when he was received as a candidate for the ministry. We were for a short time co-presbyters in 1837 and 1838, and again from 1843 to 1854. I have always regarded him as a remarkable man. He made no pretensions to greatness, in the popular acceptation of that term; but, considering his early life, his habits of life, and his educational advantages, and then the decided change which took place, the unfaltering consistency of that changed life during a trial of forty-five years, and last, though not least, the attainments which he made in scriptural and theological knowledge in the course of his ministry, a ministry at least highly respectable in the sphere in which he moved, I must be allowed to regard him as a remarkable man. There never was a more signal illustration, although a somewhat quiet one, of the sanctifying power of the Christian religion.

It affords me great pleasure in this connection to bear my testimony to one characteristic of Mr. Love which is not always found in the great ministerial brotherhood. I allude to his freedom from that low-minded jealousy and envy which so often poison what should be sources of happiness in society. If he possessed anything of this spirit I never detected it. He loved the Church of his choice; he loved its theology, its measures, and its men.

We see a specimen in his case of what an earnest and willing mind can do under the most unfavorable circumstances. Think of a poor man, with a wife and ten or twelve children at one time dependent on him, performing all the functions of a pastor to one, and sometimes to two, congregations, for the consideration of a hundred, or, at most, a hundred and fifty dollars a year. And yet there are scores of men in the Cumberland Presbyterian Church who are living just such lives to-day. God sees and appreciates their work of faith and labor of love, if the congregations do not. Such men are in their way benefactors of the Church.

That my history may be faithful, however, it is but justice to say here in its place, that the congregations to which our friend and brother whose record we are now considering ministered, under such disadvantages, have made great advances within a few years in their system of operations. They have built good houses of worship, and have, it is believed, become liberal supporters of the ministry and all the institutions of religion. So true it is that while some men sow the seed, others are permitted, in the providence of God, to reap the harvest.

Rev. Samuel McAdow
(1760-1844)

Source: Judge McAdow, Rev. Joel Knight, Foote's **Sketches of North Carolina**.

Samuel Mcadow[29] was born, April 10, 1760, in Guilford county, North Carolina. He was the youngest of eight children, four of whom were boys; the four others were girls. His father, John McAdow, emigrated from Ireland when young, and settled in Guilford. He there married Ellen Nelson, who had also crossed the Atlantic. The father was a farmer, and both the parents were Presbyterians, members of Buffalo congregation, which was at the time under the pastoral care of Dr. David Caldwell. The mother seems to have been a very pious woman, and Mr. McAdow often spoke of her in his subsequent life, bearing testimony to the great excellences of her character and piety of her life. He did not enjoy the benefit of her counsel and watchful care long, as she died when he was about ten years of age. When he was about eleven years of age he professed religion, and was received into the Church by Dr. Caldwell. His early years were divided between the labors of the farm and the school, but when quite young he was placed under the care of Dr. Caldwell, as it would seem, for a regular education. The Revolutionary War, however, came on, and the school was broken up.

After the close of the war he renewed his studies, and completed an academic course. He afterward took a three-years' course in Mecklenburg College, where he completed his education. His father had died in the meantime. On his returning home his step-mother, who occupied the old homestead, prevailed on him to take charge of the farm. He did so, and on the 24th of November, 1788, was married to Henrietta Wheatly. She became the mother of five children, all of whom died young, except one who was living in 1869.

After he professed religion and joined the Church he became seriously impressed with the belief that he ought to prepare himself for the work of the Christian ministry. After having left college, however, and taken charge of the farm, especially after having married and become the head of a family, he, in a great measure, lost those impressions for a time. Still his mind was not long at ease. The impressions returned with increasing force. He left the farm, procured a place near to the residence of Dr. Caldwell, and commenced the study of theology under the guidance of his old teacher. On the 20th of September, 1794, he was licensed to preach by the Presbytery of Orange. This was the oldest Presbytery in North Carolina, having been first constituted in May of 1770. At the time of Mr. McAdow's licensure its ministerial members were, Dr. David Caldwell, James McGready, William Hodge, Henry Patillo, William McGee, and perhaps others.

We have an account of his ordination, but the time is unknown. The information is that he preached after his licensure in different parts of the country until he was ordained, and settled in charge of Hopewell congregation, in Orange county. I find the following in Foote's **Sketches of North Carolina**:

---

[29]the proper spelling of the name is evidently McAdoo, but I follow the usage of the Church Records.

In the year 1796, Mr. McGready, who had been ordained in 1793, removed to Kentucky. In the year 1799 the Presbytery of Orange dismissed Rev. William McGee and Barton W. Stone, a licentiate to Pennsylvania Presbytery, and about the same time the Rev. Messrs. William Hodge, Samuel McAdow, and John Rankin, to remove to the West. The part that these men acted in the succeeding events in the West forms an interesting part in the 'History of the Valley of the Mississippi.'[30]

Mr. McAdow was evidently ordained, therefore, previous to 1799. It has been mentioned also that he was settled after his ordination as pastor of Hopewell congregation in his native State. On the 20th of April, 1799, he lost his wife. This occurred in North Carolina. After the death of his wife, feeling himself to be very much broken up, he turned his attention toward the West, whither several of his old friends in the ministry had gone, and also a number of his relatives. He therefore made his arrangements to remove to Kentucky. He was accordingly dismissed by his Presbytery, as we have seen, for his new destination in 1799. On his way Westward he yielded to the solicitations of friends, and spent the first summer in East Tennessee. During the summer he preached as a supply to the Big Limestone congregation. But when the fall came he resumed his journey to the farther West, feeling that he could not be satisfied until he rejoined his former friends. Of course he did not foresee, but we can now see, that he had a great providential mission to fulfill in the West. A call signed by one hundred and eighteen heads of families for his continuance in East Tennessee as pastor of Big Limestone congregation was presented, but his purpose was fixed. When he reached Kentucky he found his old friends and fellow-laborers engaged in the great revival. The work was just beginning to develop itself in its wonderful power.

In the spring of 1800, he began to preach regularly at Red River, in Logan county, and to the Rockbridge congregation in Christian county. In October of 1800, he was married a second time to Catharine Clark, a very pious lady, of Logan county. The fruit of this marriage was one child, a daughter. His second wife died on the 17th of May, 1804. Being left with two little daughters, one of each family, he committed them to the care of a sister, and engaged in more extensive ministerial operations. He seems to have fully imbibed the spirit of the times; he traveled and preached, extending his tours to the Ohio River, and far into the State of Tennessee. He continued to ride and preach extensively until he was almost entirely disabled from public speaking on account of weakness of lungs. Physicians advised him to desist. His more active ministerial labors, therefore ceased. In July of 1806 he was married a third time. The lady's name was Hannah Cope. There were two sons from this marriage. He now settled in Dixon county, Tennessee, where he owned land. Here he engaged in teaching. His Sabbaths, however, he gave to the work of the ministry. He remained in Dixon county until 1815. This portion of his history brings us to the great work of his life. While he resided in Dixon, on the 4th day of February, 1810, the Cumberland Presbytery was constituted, out of which was grown the Cumberland Presbyterian Church. The

---

[30] Page 376.

transaction took place at his house. The house has become historical. It was an unpretending building on the bank on Jones's Creek, about seven miles from Charlotte. The little fire originated in that obscure spot has kindled a great matter. The good men who prayed and acted there on that occasion had no conception of what the result would be.

In 1815 he sold out his possessions in Dixon, and moved to Jackson county, where he also owned land. Here he remained promoting the interests of religion as he was able until 1828. In the fall of this year he moved to Illinois, and settled in Bond county. Age and infirmities were now settling upon him. His time for any thing like active labor had passed away. Says my informant: "He was, however, still ever ready to do what he could in conducting Sabbath-schools and prayer-meetings, and occasionally preaching. His place was never vacant at the house of God when his health permitted him to attend, and the weather was tolerable. On the 3d day of June, 1839, he lost his third and last wife. From this time he confined himself mostly to his home. His time was spent in reading and meditation. His home was with his eldest son. He seldom left it except in attending public worship. His customary health continued to about the 25th of March, 1844. About that time he became dull, and complained of sleepiness. There was, however, no pain. This condition of things continued until the 30th, when he quietly fell asleep to wake no more. He passed off without a struggle or a groan. His last words were, in answer to a friend, 'All is peace, my work is done, every thing is ready; I have nothing to do, but to die; there is no doubt, no fear.'" He was within a few days of eighty-four years of age. A funeral discourse was delivered by Rev. John Barber, in the course of the sessions of Vandalia Presbytery, a week after his death.

Mr. McAdow lived a quiet, but nevertheless an eventful life. He was not ambitious; he did not seek notoriety, but still one act of his life has made his name a household word in many Christian homes throughout the West and South-west. Even his quiet and unpretending home in Dixon county, Tennessee, as I have said, has become historic. The thoughts of coming generations will cluster around it as the birth-place of great events.

I have some characteristics of Mr. McAdow, and some incidents connected with his life from one of his old friends and later associates. Says my informant:

"Mr. McAdow was a very conscientious man, naturally retiring in his manner, and rather inclined to despondency; often doubting his call to the ministry. After his licensure he yielded to these doubts and other discouragements so far that for a time he declined preaching. And in order to avoid being called out in that way he left the vicinity in which he lived, and made a temporary settlement in one in which he was entirely unknown, and where public religious exercises were very infrequent." Of course, however, Jonah was not long at ease in his retirement. "In his restlessness he found another religious person. They became acquainted, held consultations about the spiritual condition of their neighbors, and concluded to have a prayer-meeting. The prayer-meeting was repeated. It was a new order of things; the people became interested. The interest reacted upon the truant preacher: he commenced preaching to them, and continued it for some time, and at length returned to his former home, and submitted himself to the direction of his Presbytery."

One of his difficulties in relation to preaching seems to have arisen from the same source from which embarrassments in other quarters soon began to develop themselves. There were expressions in the Confession of Faith which were difficult of digestion. The atonement seemed to him, as he understood the Scriptures, to have been a universal provision for the salvation of men. In conformity with this view of the subject the offers and invitations of the gospel seemed to be made unrestrictedly to all, and the Scriptures seemed to make men wholly responsible in the case of their own damnation. But all these views appeared to be in conflict with a literal and consistent interpretation of the Confession of Faith. He was conscientious, and did not know what to do. As it was very proper, he referred the matter to his old friend and theological guide, Dr. Caldwell. Dr. Caldwell was a liberal man. He could not with his temperament and habits of thought have been any thing else. He was not formed by nature, nor had his experience trained him, for Procrustean measures in theology. He advised his pupil to use practical texts, and to confine himself to practical discussions in preaching, and to let these difficult questions take care of themselves. This was certainly wise counsel, but still it did not satisfy the inquirer. As every Scotch-Irishman is, he was wedded to Presbyterianism. Nothing else would do him as a form of religious worship, and mainly as a system of religious doctrines.

After awhile there was a call for his ordination. This created a new trial. Any serious man would have considered it a severe ordeal aside from extraneous difficulties. He was very much dissatisfied with his trial sermon; thought at its close that he would keep quiet until the congregation scattered a little, and then betake himself away, and show himself no more on the occasion. Circumstances did not favor the carrying out of his resolution, and he took a walk to the spring. On his way he passed a group of the leading members of the congregation, and one of them remarked to him that they were consulting on the subject of raising means for the publication of his sermon. Of course this was news to him, but something more was to follow which was to be, if possible, still more astounding.

At the spring he met good Mrs. Dr. Caldwell. She was no doubt a liberal theologian and warm-hearted Christian woman. Addressing herself to him in her kind and encouraging manner, she said: "She thanked the Lord that in his good providence the Church would soon enjoy the services of one so well adapted to the work of the ministry, adding that somehow it was deeply impressed upon her mind that day that God had some important place in the Church for him to fill, some great work for him to do." All this seems to us like an approach to inspiration; still, lest we lay ourselves liable to the charge of fanaticism, we will not call it inspiration. It is nevertheless remarkable that subsequent facts should have so fully coincided with the impression. He was ordained, and, as we have seen, became the pastor of Hopewell congregation.

In the progress of things he seemed to think it due to truth and to himself to set forth his doctrinal views clearly and fully, as they were known not to be in strict conformity with the views prevailing around him. He accordingly made an appointment for that purpose. A large concourse attended. The house of worship could not hold the people, and they repaired to the grove, that all might hear. The sermon was a clear and strong exposition of the truth as he understood it. Persons were living a few years ago who were present on the occasion and heard the discourse. Mr. McAdow seems to have been, from some cause, a favorite in Dr. Caldwell's family. One of the daughters pronounced the sermon unanswerable.

She was a highly educated and intelligent lady. Others were of the same opinion. A gentleman known in early life to the writer, and up at least to the old age of the former, a respected member of the Presbyterian Church, spoke of it as one of the most masterly discussions which he had ever heard. No opposition, however, was excited.

An observation out of the line of the history may be made here. The theological difficulties connected with the early developments of what afterward became the Cumberland Presbyterian Church are generally regarded as the outgrowth of the revival itself. We see, however, from the facts which have just been presented that the seeds were already taking root in North Carolina which subsequently germinated in Kentucky and Tennessee. Messrs. McGready, McGee, Hodge, and McAdow, and also Messrs. Anderson and King, who were brought into the ministry in the West, all emigrated from the same section of North Carolina to this country. A serious man will involuntarily raise the inquiry whether the revival may not have been the outgrowth of the more liberal theology, working inwardly in the hearts of earnest men, than the theology of the revival. This is certainly an aspect of the subject which deserves to be considered. At all events it is certain that the leaven was at work before it developed itself in the licensure of Anderson, Ewing, and King. It is to be observed, too, that the very region of North Carolina in which these men originated shared very extensively the benefits of the great revival. It was the same spirit in the ministry, and the congregations there, which pervaded the Green River and Cumberland countries.

We have another anecdote of Mr. McAdow, as, it will be observed, rather characteristic of the times. At one time after he was settled in Kentucky, he was rather unwell on a particular Saturday. The next day he was to preach according to appointment. From the condition of his health he was inclined to draw back. His wife also thought he was too unwell to preach. He deferred the decision to Sabbath morning. When morning came he was rather shocked at the thought of not preaching. Early in the morning, while the question was still undecided, a colored man, a Christian, and a man of some sprightliness and experience, came in. The colored friend was invited to lead in family prayer. He thanked God in the course of his prayer for what he had done, was doing, and would do, that day. The spirit and matter of the prayer seemed to suggest to the preacher that he must preach, although not well. He did so, and it proved to be a great day of the Son of man among the people. Many were convicted and converted. This occurred at Red River, and was considered on of the precious developments of the revival.

Mr. McAdow seems to have been steadfastly satisfied with the part he acted in the organization of the Cumberland Presbytery. The tradition is, and he himself sanctions it, that when Messrs. Ewing, King, and McLean (Rev. Ephraim McLean was received as a candidate for the ministry by the Transylvania Presbytery at its fall sessions, in October, 1802. On the 4th of October, 1803, he was licensed as a probationer for the ministry, by the Cumberland Presbytery, which had been stricken off from the Transylvania Presbytery a year before. Immediately after the constitution of the new Presbytery, or rather the reorganization of the old Cumberland Presbytery, in 1810, he was ordained. This was the first Presbyterial act of the new organization. He labored with great fidelity and usefulness a few years after the organization of the Presbytery. His race, however, was short. He seems to have been much beloved. Dr. Cossitt says of him, in his **Life and Times of Finis Ewing**, that "After serving the Church efficiently and faithfully for a few years, he died lamented by all who knew him." He left a large and respectable family. Two of his sons have been prominent in the councils of the nation. A grandson is now a beloved young minister in the Church of his fathers.) came to his house in Dixon county to make a final settlement of the question of organizing the Presbytery, Mr. Ewing explained to him the object of their visit, and told him that they had come for his decision, and that they were willing to take that, whatever it might be, as the voice of Providence, and to act accordingly. Mr. McAdow very reasonably replied that the responsibility was too great, and that he could not bear it. The greater portion of the night and of the following day was spent in prayer. After such a struggle he reported himself ready to act. The question was settled. He gives us an account of his feelings upon the occasion. Mr. Ewing does the same thing. It was a fearful responsibility. The men felt it, but as they approached nearer and nearer to the crisis, their confidence evidently increased, that the step to be taken was a necessary one, and one which the providence of God had imposes upon them.

In an interview with a ministerial brother a short time before his death, in reply to an inquiry whether, after a lapse of so many years, he was still satisfied with the proceeding in which he was engaged in the organization of the Presbytery in 1810, he said he had never entertained a doubt on that subject; he believed it was done under the divine sanction, and that God would sustain and bless the Church.

In 1855 his son wrote a letter to a prominent minister in the Church, in relation to his father, from which I make the following extract:

> He was a man of the most fervent piety. Much of his time, especially in the latter part of his life, was spent in meditation and private devotion. He had a strong desire for the welfare and success of the Cumberland Presbyterian Church. This, indeed, seemed to be a matter of chief interest with him. He always believed that he acted in conformity with the immediate counsel of God in the part he took throughout the troubles which led to the constitution of the first Presbytery, and the consequent separation from the Presbyterian Church, and often remarked that it seemed to him that God had lengthened out his life that he might see something of the prosperity of the Church which he had participated in organizing.

Mr. McAdow left a considerable mass of manuscript. The last sermon ever preached by the old man was published in the Theological Medium of 1846. It was delivered when he was near eighty years old. The subject is "Peace with all men, and holiness, without which no man shall see the Lord." A paragraph is extracted and given here as a specimen of his style of preaching. The sentiments as he doubtless understood them himself, and intended them to be understood by his hearers, are correct and exceedingly expressive. He is discussing the subject of holiness:

> But here some will say, The old man has got to preaching up

perfection. Well, my friends, perfection is what is wanted, and without it no one will ever see the face of God in peace; for nothing that is impure can abide in his presence, and where or when is this perfection to be obtained? Do you say, Not till we are ushered into the presence of God by death? Christ says, If we died in our sins, where I am ye cannot come. Therefore we must obtain it in this world, or not at all, and the sooner the better, for we know not how suddenly we may drop off the stage of action into an unchanging eternity. God is perfect, and Christ exhorts us to be perfect, as our Father who is in heaven is perfect. Christ in believers, the hope of glory, is perfect, and John says that 'whosoever hath this hope in him purifieth himself, even as he is pure.' Here is the perfection for which we plead, even purity of heart. Christ says, 'Blessed are the pure in heart, for they shall see God.' The change which Christians undergo from nature to grace is a perfect change; for with such old things have passed away, and, behold, all things are become new. The Spirit of God, which dwells in all true believers, is perfect; and his work, as it relates to the new creation, or inner man, is a perfect work.

The object of the argument is to show that religion must be something real and vital—that it must reach down into the inner heart, and not satisfy itself with a mere external appearance. We see an outcropping of the old spirit of the revival. It is said that, frequently in the progress of the sermon, he shed tears freely, as though feeling that his work was nearly done. How fitting that the sun of a long ministerial life should go down under such circumstances!

I have in my possession several sermons of Mr. McAdow in manuscript. One of them is upon a call to the ministry. It is a long sermon of thirty closely written pages. He enters into the subject very fully. It is discussed negatively, and then positively, and finally objections are answered. He evidently intends to say every thing that can be said upon the question within a reasonable space. The whole discussion takes its coloring from the times. One party required a high grade of learning in the ministry, and would yield nothing to the exigencies of the circumstances. Another party thought that spirituality was the great matter, and that the want of it could not be supplied by any possible human attainments or endowments. Gilbert Tennent had preached and published his famous Nottingham Sermon, on the same subject, fifty years before the time of Mr. McAdow. Mr. Tennent thought, and Mr. McAdow thought with him, that the prospect of money and an easy life called a great many men into the ministry, and that, according to the rule of our Saviour, such men were thieves and robbers. Mr. Tennent said of those who might, perhaps, plead the case of the ministry of Judas in vindication of their course, "I fear that the abuse of this instance has brought many Judases into the ministry, whose chief desire, like that of their great-grandfather, is to finger the pence and carry the bag. But let such hireling, murderous hypocrites take care that they do not feel the force of a halter in this world, and an aggravated damnation in the next."[31]

Indeed Dr. Hodge is candid and honorable enough to represent the New Brunswick Presbytery, of the spirit and measures of which Mr. Tennent was a representative, and the Cumberland Presbytery as occupying analogous ground in their conflicts with the higher authorities of the Presbyterian Church. They were, in fact, cases in which history substantially repeats itself.

Mr. McAdow was not only a preacher, but something of a poet. His poetry seems to have been written for amusement or his own personal improvement. His distrust of himself withheld him from bringing it to the light. I take the liberty of making several extracts. They will give us some insight into the character of the man. I think, too, they will give us a higher appreciation of his ability than what has generally prevailed among us. I take my first extract from an Introduction to what was intended to be a paraphrase, in verse, upon the book of Job. The whole Introduction contains a hundred lines. After acknowledging the dependence of every thing upon God, and the goodness and bounty of the great source of all existence, he commences his invocation thus:

> *Dearest source of light, and life, and love!*
> *Send now thy gracious influence from above.*
> *A poor unworthy worm to thee would look;*
> *Be not thy word to him a sealed book;*
> *But give him ears to hear, and eyes to see,*
> *A tongue to speak, and show its mystery.*
> *Inspire his heart good matter to indite,*
> *In every sentence teach his pen to write.*
> *O let enlivening rays of holy fire*
> *My mind illumine, and my breast inspire!*
> *With skill divine grand myst'ries to explore,*
> *And right extract the metal from the ore.*
> *O guide my thoughts, my grov'ling passions raise,*
> *Nor let me wander in the sacred maze,*
> *Help me the sacred annals to unfold,*
> *And learn a lesson from the days of old*
> *Of humble greatness in prosperity,*
> *Of patient meekness in adversity,*
> *Of sudden changes, sure impending fate,*
> *Which watches our imperfect changeful state;*
> *Of true submission in the midst of ills,*
> *Of acquiescence when our Maker wills.*
> *And if my thoughts essay the holy lay,*
> *Then suffer not my muse to go astray;*
> *But sanctify my hand, my head, my heart,*
> *That all in holy praise my bear a part;*
> *And so direct me when I choose each theme*
> *That truth may come to men, and glory to thy name.*

---

[31]Dr. Hodge's **History of the Presbyterian Church.**

The contemplated paraphrase was commenced, but never finished. It would be an interesting relic if we had it.

We have another poem on the Signs, Forerunners, and Formality of the last Judgment, in two parts. The whole production consists of one hundred and six stanzas of four lines each.

We have still another, addressed to a friend who was thought to be in danger of losing his day of grace. The writer recollects to have heard the old people say when he was a boy that Mr. McAdow was considered very high authority on the subject of the unpardonable sin. There is nothing, however, in the manuscripts which have come to hand on this subject, except the poetical address which has just been mentioned.

It must be mentioned also that there is still another long poem upon the misery of dying in an unconverted state, based upon the first seven verses of the twelfth chapter of Ecclesiastes. This is a long poem, covering several closely written pages. The first twenty-four lines have evidently been lost, and replaced by Mr. McAdow himself at a time subsequent to the first draft, or by another hand. There are two or three other poems, or fragments of poems, less important in their character than those here mentioned.

To the present generation nothing is known of Mr. McAdow except through tradition. A few of the old men and women, survivors of a generation which has nearly passed away, knew him personally. Most of the facts recounted in this sketch have been derived from himself through the agency of a friend and brother in the ministry belonging to this last class. It is probable that no other person now living had them in possession. A surviving son is my authority for the more personal and domestic incidents which have been recorded.

Mr. McAdow was a very different man from either Mr. Ewing or Mr. King, with whom he is always associated in our minds in connection with the organization of the Church. His son writes of him that he was a man on "melancholy temperament." He was evidently quiet and retiring in his habits, not adapted to leadership in any great enterprise, nor ever seeking such a position. His associates were intellectually and physically better adapted to the stormy scenes of life, through which they were called to pass. They were men of war. Many of use who still live had heard their clarion voices calling us to the field of conflict. They were sons of thunder in the pulpit. Mr. Ewing was terrible, too, when he spoke through the press to an offending adversary. They were both heroes in the strife into which the providence of God called them. They fell each with his heavy armor on. We honor, and will honor, their memory. I think, too, we have found that Mr. McAdow, far back in early life, in the midst of the honest Presbyterianism of his fathers, was undergoing a providential training for the important part he was to act amidst the stormy religious scenes of the South-west. The theology, which, after the expiration of twenty years, was embodied in the Cumberland Presbyterian Confession of Faith, was even then taking form in his mind. North Carolina Presbyterians could tolerate it. But when it came into contact with the theology of John Knox, and his more immediate followers, there was a want of affiliation, and a conflict was the result. The history of that conflict is known. The Cumberland Presbyterian Church owes a debt to the memory of Mr. McAdow, which, in the rush and excitement of a stirring age, has been too much overlooked. This imperfect sketch has been intended as a contribution toward the payment of that debt. He deserves a better memorial.

REV. HIRAM MCDANIEL
(1785-1850)

Sources: Manuscript of Miss Jane McDaniel. Minutes of Logan and Anderson Presbyteries.

Hiram Mcdaniel was born August 13, 1785, in Caswell county, North Carolina. His parents were William and Jane McDaniel. His father was a plain, unpretending man, a farmer, and a member of the Methodist Church. His mother, it seems, was not a professor of religion. They raised seven children, of whom Hiram was the fourth in age. His constitution was delicate from childhood; he was regarded with great tenderness by his parents, and was thought to possess promising talents. Under such impressions in relation to his promise, and taking into consideration also his delicate health, they determined to give him a liberal education. He was accordingly sent to one of the best schools in the country, and made rapid progress in the study of the ordinary branches of science, and also in Mathematics. His father and his teacher united in urging him to study the languages. He commenced the study of Latin, but made up his mind that he would never enter one of the learned professions, and that therefore such a course of studies would be useless. Of course he abandoned the course of education which had been urged upon him—a step which he regretted as long as he lived.

Soon after he left school, he engaged as a clerk with a Mr. McCain, a merchant who had some reputation as a book-keeper. It seems that one object of young Mr. McDaniel in this engagement was to acquire a knowledge of book-keeping. He remained in the employment of Mr. McCain until he was about twenty-one. He and his father then made a journey to Kentucky, with a view of buying land, and ultimately settling in that country. He remained in Kentucky, and his father returned to North Carolina, intending to move his family to the West. Something, however, occurred to derange the plan, and the father and family still remained in Carolina. Mr. McDaniel then took charge of a school, in what at that time was Centerville, the county-seat of Livingston county. After teaching a while, he again engaged as a clerk in a store.

On the second of April, 1807, he was married to Miss Catharine Leeper, of Livingston county. Soon after his marriage, the merchant with whom he was engaged dying, he purchased a farm and commenced the business of farming. He soon found himself, however, but poorly adapted to the drudgery of a farm, from his feeble health; and having no assistance, he moved back to Centerville, and engaged in merchandising, at the same time keeping a small tavern, mainly for the accommodation of travelers, as Centerville was situated on the great road leading from Kentucky and Tennessee to the North-west, and the tide of emigration in that direction as just setting in.

In process of time the seat of justice was removed from Centerville to Salem, and Mr. McDaniel fell back to the business of farming, with the assistance of some negroes that he acquired, perhaps through his wife. About this time Mr. McGready began to preach at what was afterward called "Livingston Church." A small congregation of Presbyterians had been organized there, of which old Mr. Leeper was a leading member and an elder. Mr. McDaniel and his wife became deeply concerned on the subject of religion, and in a short time the wife made profession of religion and joined the Presbyterian Church. Mr. McDaniel himself seems to have been a seeker a number of years, and to have professed religion at a Cumberland Presbyterian camp-meeting at Bethlehem, in Caldwell county—a place which God still honors with his presence and grace. Some time previous to his profession of religion, he commenced the practice of family prayer, which he kept up to his death. Very soon after he professed religion his mind began to be exercised on the subject of the ministry. But he had a family, was comparatively poor, and his education did not fill up the measure which he himself had prescribed as a necessary ministerial qualification. He endeavored, of course, to quiet his feelings and excuse himself from the work. He felt, however, that the vows of God were upon him; and after much hesitation, and seeking private counsel from his brethren, he placed himself, as a candidate for the ministry, under the care of the Logan Presbytery. This occurred on the 18th of November, 1819. The sessions of the Presbytery were held at Antioch, in Christian county, Kentucky. By the same Presbytery, at Red River Meeting-house, in Logan county, Kentucky, he was licensed on the 12th day of October, 1820. The discourse which he read was from Phil. ii. 12, 13. At the spring sessions of the Presbytery in 1821, he "was ordered to ride as a missionary in the Christian District. At the fall sessions he was ordered, in conjunction with James Y. Barnett." to ride as a missionary in the same district. In 1822 the Anderson Presbytery was constituted, and Mr. McDaniel, living within its bounds, was transferred to that Presbytery. At Henderson, Kentucky, on the 7th of April, 1824, he was ordained by the Anderson Presbytery. Rev. David Lowry preached the ordination-sermon, and Rev. John Barnett presided and gave the charge.

The winter after he was licensed, Mr. McDaniel visited his father, in North Carolina. He spent most of the winter there, and preached a great deal from house to house. His ministry seems to have been abundantly blessed. A good work commenced at his first appointment, and continued through the winter. My informant says, "He had reason to believe that there were many seals to his ministry," and that "numbers during the winter found peace and joy in believing." He often alluded to this winter as the most happy period of his life. On his return from North Carolina, he preached and attended camp-meetings according to the custom of his fellow-ministers, as he was able.

Two or three years after his licensure, he went as a missionary to Arkansas, and spent a winter there. According to his journal, he visited nearly all the white settlements in the territory, often preaching three times a day. The country was new; his hearers frequently attended preaching with their guns in their hands, and in their buckskin hunting-shirts. The winter was mild for some time, and traveling was agreeable, but suddenly a violent change occurred. He was compelled to cross the Arkansas River. There was no boat sufficient to convey his horse. He crossed, however, by some means, and swam his horse. When he reached the opposite bank the horse was covered with ice. He mounted and set off for his appointment, but soon found that the horse had the blind-staggers. Of course he stopped, and in a few minutes the horse fell in the road and died. He started for his destination with his saddle, saddle-bags, and bridle upon his shoulder. He soon, however, met with a stranger who assisted him forward. He reached his appointment; the people made up twenty-five dollars and bought him a pony, with which he was enabled to consummate his mission.

On his return from Arkansas he found his last negro man declining with the consumption. The man died, and Mr. McDaniel sold his farm in discouragement, intending to move to Mississippi. It seems that a rich relative had urged him to such a removal. He went so far in his preparation that he engaged a steam-boat to convey his family, but a reverse awaited him; the removal was declined; he engaged temporarily in teaching, and had charge for a few months of the Preparatory Department of Cumberland College.

The year in which he was ordained he paid a second visit to his parents, and spent some time with them. His preaching was acceptable, and a number of his relatives professed religion in connection with his ministerial labors, and amongst them his youngest sister.

Some time after this visit, his father purchased a farm for him in North Carolina, and three Presbyterian congregations agreed to employ him as their pastor, assuring him of a competent support; but yielding to other influences, he remained in Kentucky. He made a temporary settlement in Trigg county. Whilst there he engaged in the service of the American Sunday-school Union. In this service he continued three years. One of those years his family spent at Cumberland College, in charge of the boarding-house. This was the collegiate year which closed in September, 1831. In the latter part of his year at the College, he lost a negro boy under very afflicting circumstances. The poor fellow was carelessly playing about the mill while it was in operation, became entangled somehow in the machinery, and was crushed to death. The family felt it very seriously, as one of a series of adverse providences which seemed to be following them. From the College he moved again to Trigg county.

About this time Mr. McDaniel became involved in some difficulties with two or three of his ministerial brethren. A recital of these would be needless and painful. They grew up in some way from the connection of the parties with Cumberland College. The men concerned were all good men, but they misunderstood one another. There was an estrangement of feeling which continued, I suppose, during life, but the worthy men have passed away, and see things now in a different light. It is pleasant to believe, to be assured, that there is an oblivion of all such animosities in heaven.

Some years before his death he sold his farm in Trigg county, and settled in Todd, a few miles below Elkton. He had by this time become so enfeebled by age and infirmities, that he was able to preach but little. He had a pleasant home and lived quietly, preaching when he was able, and otherwise contributing to the interests of the Church in his neighborhood.

In 1848 he had an apoplectic stroke. He had been standing in the sun superintending some domestic matter. Returning to the house and being assisted to bed, he was confined several days. In about two weeks, however, he was restored to his usual health. While confined with his temporary illness, he expressed a wish to live a while longer, that he might preach a sermon which he had prepared on the call of Abraham "to go out to a place which he should afterward receive for an inheritance." He did survive, and it seems was enabled to preach the sermon. One of his last sermons was upon the "Trials of the Christian;" the text, "And he led them forth by the right way, that they might go to a city of habitations." About three weeks before his death, he preached in his own neighborhood, upon the "Beauties and Glories of Heaven." It seemed from the sermon as though he had received a foretaste. Thus says my informant.

Some time previous to his death, notwithstanding his infirmities, he took charge of McAdoo congregation. For this service he was to receive a small salary. In August of his last year he conducted their camp-meeting, and in its progress preached a sermon on the subject of "Faith." It seems to have been a spiritual and effective sermon. On the 26th of November following, 1850, he closed his earthly career. His death was sudden, and of course there were but few circumstances of interest connected with it. We judge of his Christian and ministerial character from his life.

In person, Mr. McDaniel was rather below the medium height. Until late in life his frame was slender; as he approached old age, however, there was a slight tendency to corpulency. His complexion was fair, his hair sandy; his eyes were blue. His carriage and bearing were those of a well-bred gentleman. His wife survived him nearly ten years, and died May 23, 1860. He left six children, all of whom are members of the Church.

My personal acquaintance with Mr. McDaniel extended through a number of years, but it was never intimate. I heard him preach a few times, and occasionally shared the hospitalities of his house. He was a good preacher—not noisy, rather otherwise, but distinct, sensible, and practical. His voice was weak, and his manner deliberate. From these circumstances he was not so well adapted to great popular occasions as some others. The truth is, he was underrated by the Church, as all men of his manner of preaching were in his day. He would have been more popular, and human judgment would have decided more useful, in the Presbyterian Church. Still, God in his providence cast his lot with us: we know that his providence never makes a mistake. He filled up the measure, and accomplished the work, which God appointed. It was creditable to him that, in the midst of many and protracted trials, he was contented with his lot, and devoted to the work which a wise Providence had assigned him.

I have said that he was not so well adapted to popular occasions as some others. Still, some of his sermons attracted a large share of public attention. They were supposed to be favorite sermons with himself, were frequently repeated, and became extensively known through the country in which he lived. One of these sermons was upon Naaman, the Syrian captain, and the Israelitish maid: "Wash and be clean." Another was upon the parable of the Prodigal Son; and still another was upon the parable of the Sower and his Seed. he seemed to have a genius, as he certainly had a taste, for such subjects. The first time I ever heard of him was in connection with a sermon upon the first-mentioned of these subjects, "Wash and be clean." The sermon was delivered soon after his licensure, when he was on his way to North Carolina, upon the occasion of his first visit to that country. He was spoken of as a methodical and correct young preacher. I suppose he preached the sermon occasionally as long as he lived.

He had a great fund of anecdotes for material in conversation, and was consequently a very agreeable companion. For every possible occasion an anecdote seemed to be at hand. They were always innocent, but sometimes very amusing. The wonder was, that with so large and helpless a family as he had through the greater portion of his ministerial life, and the trials which he was called to endure in the loss of property and otherwise, he could keep his spirits up so well, and be so uniformly cheerful and hopeful. He never allowed himself to be worn out and crushed with anxiety in relation to the future of life. It was a happy temperament. A good Providence knows what we need for bearing the burdens of life, and it is not too much to believe that he often endows by nature, and surely trains us by his grace, for the support of those burdens.

REV. WILLIAM MCGEE
(1768-1817)

Rev. William Mcgee was born in Guilford county, North Carolina, in 1768 or 1769. His father was a merchant, and originally a member of the Church of England. His mother was a Presbyterian. After their marriage, however, the father joined the Presbyterian Church, and, with his wife, became a member of a congregation under the care of Rev. David Caldwell. They had five children, of whom William was the youngest. The father died when the son was quite young; but the mother, being an efficient and pious woman, took care of his morals and education. He was kept at school from the time he was ten years old until he was near twenty. He obtained his education, it is supposed, mainly, if not entirely, under the instruction of Dr. Caldwell, pastor of the congregation to which the family belonged.

From the pious instructions which he received, both at home and at school, his mind became early impressed with the necessity of religion. An older brother also in the meantime professed religion, and took pains to direct his mind to that subject. His impressions became very deep. His mind was thoroughly aroused. Says his brother:[32] "His distress was unspeakable, under a conscious sense of the frowns of an angry God which hung over him. This may seem strange to some, when they are informed of the manner of his life prior to this time. I do not believe he ever drank a pint of ardent spirits, or swore a profane oath, in his life. He was the most moral youth I ever saw. It might truly be said of him, as Paul said of himself, 'As touching the law, he was blameless.'"

Notwithstanding his morality, his distress of mind continued for some time. His experience of the bitterness of sin seems to have been very deep.

It is not known at what time he professed religion; nor have we any means of knowing when he was received as a candidate for the ministry, or licensed. In the first public or written notice which we have of him, he appears to be a licentiate, under the care of the Orange Presbytery, in North Carolina. In a record of the proceedings of the Synod of the Carolinas, held at New Providence, in October, 1795, we have the following:

> It appearing to Synod that an ordained missionary was required in the Western Territory, and it being stated that Mr. William McGee, of Orange Presbytery, was willing to take an appointment for that purpose, ordered, that the Presbytery be directed, and they are hereby directed, to ordain Mr. McGee as soon as may be convenient, agreeably to the permission granted to this Synod, in such cases, by the General Assembly at their sessions of last May.

Either before or after his ordination, which is supposed to have taken place in the latter part of 1795, or early in 1796, in conformity with the preceding order of the Synod, Mr. McGee is said to have traveled and preached in Guilford, Orange,

---

[32] The late Rev. John McGee.

and the adjacent counties, with approbation, for some time. He then moved to Holston, and took charge of a congregation, which he served one or two years. He then came to Cumberland, and took charge of a congregation, which was afterward greatly distinguished—the congregation of Shiloh, in what is now Sumner county. The old meeting-house in which he preached stood about a mile from where Gallatin now stands. Here he labored two or three years. Some of the members of the congregation were dissatisfied with the earnest and searching manner in which he held forth, and urged the necessity of a spiritual birth, and wished him to change his mode of preaching. He gave them to understand that he could not do so with a good conscience. The dissatisfaction, however, became so great, that he asked an honorable dismission as a condition of his leaving them and settling elsewhere. The condition was complied with, and he relinquished the charge of the congregation. It is proper, in justice to the memory of all concerned in this unpleasant transaction, to state that the leading persons who opposed Mr. McGee at this time were sympathizers with the Rev. Thomas Craighead, who afterward became distinguished for his opposition to the revival in this country, in 1800, and some of the following years. The congregation was at length divided. A part followed Mr. Craighead, and a part (and much the larger part) remained with Mr. Hodge, the successor of Mr. McGee.

After leaving Shiloh, Mr. McGee settled on Drake's Creek, in the lower end of Sumner county, and took charge of the Beech and Ridge congregations. Whilst he was ministering to these, the Great Western Revival extended into Tennessee. It is understood that he, with his brother, Rev. John McGee, of the Methodist Church, assisted Mr. McGready at the sacramental meeting at Red River Meeting-house, in June, 1800, where the revival first developed itself in full power. At this meeting there seems to have been an extraordinary outpouring of the Spirit of God. "On Monday"—of the meeting—"many had such clear and heart-piercing views of their sinfulness, and the danger to which they were exposed, that they fell prostrate on the floor, and their cries filled the house. In all quarters, those who had been the most outbreaking sinners were to be seen lying on the floor unable to help themselves, and anxiously inquiring what they should do to be saved. In a word, persons of all classes, and of all ages, were to be seen in agonies, and heard crying for redemption in the blood of the Lamb. Twelve precious souls, during the occasion, professed to have passed from death unto life; and many left the place pungently convicted of their sin and danger."

Mr. McGee entered earnestly into the spirit of the revival, and is said to have been "particularly active and useful." In July of 1800 a camp-meeting—the first, it is said, which was ever held in Christendom—was held at Gaspar River Church. "A vast concourse of people flocked to the meeting, from the distance of twenty, thirty, fifty, and even a hundred miles. The ministers who occupied the pulpit on that occasion were James McGready, William McGee, and William Hodge." In September of 1800 Mr. McGready assisted Mr. McGee in holding a camp-meeting at the Ridge Meeting-house, and on the following week Messrs. McGready and McGee assisted Mr. Hodge in a similar meeting at Shiloh. Multitudes attended both meetings, and great effects were produced.

When the difficulties arose in the Transylvania Presbytery, in regard to the licensure and ordination of what were called the "young men," Mr. McGee took a decided stand in favor of the measure. It is not proposed to enter here into a discussion of those old and troublesome questions, but it is plain that the favorers of this were the revivalists, and its opposers the anti-revivalists, of the Presbyterian Church at that time. This is so, or both history and tradition are at fault.

When the Commission of the Synod of Kentucky met in December of 1805, for the purpose of adjudicating upon the proceedings of the Cumberland Presbytery, and demanded a surrender of the "young men" for reexamination, Mr. McGee, with the other older members of the Presbytery, resisted the demand. In consequence of this refusal, and the proclamation of common fame that he with others held doctrines contrary to the Confession of Faith—that they, in effect, denied the doctrine of Election, and held that a certain sufficiency of grace was given to every man, which, if improved, would be increased until he arrived at true conversion, they were cited to appear at the next annual meeting of the Synod to answer for contumacy, and to these doctrinal charges. "Messrs. Hodge, Rankin, and McGee handed in a written refusal to obey the citation, on the ground of its unconstitutionality."

After the meeting of this Commission of Kentucky Synod, we hear no more of Mr. McGee until the 4th day of October, 1809, when what is known in Cumberland Presbyterian History as the Council, met at Shiloh. Messrs. Finis Ewing, Samuel King, and William McGee were present—a number of ordained ministers sufficient for constituting a Presbytery. Mr. McGee, however, informed the Council that he was not satisfied of the propriety of constituting a Presbytery at that time. He was a cautious, and, without doubt, a very conscientious man. Having been identified with the Presbyterian Church from principle, and from infancy, it is no wonder that he hesitated. His difficulties, however, are said to have been theological, rather than constitutional. He had not yet found solid ground between Calvinism and Arminianism.

Mr. Davidson, in his history of the Presbyterian Church in Kentucky, says that in April, 1810, the Presbytery of Transylvania "being made aware of Mr. McGee's distressed state of mind, addressed him an affectionate letter, inviting him to a friendly conference at their next session. Receiving no reply, they repeated the invitation in October; but all their well-meant endeavors were fruitless, for in the fall he joined the independent body." This independent body was the Cumberland Presbytery, which had been constituted in the preceding February. I suppose the "distressed state of mind" to which the historian refers arose from Mr. McGee's theological troubles, from which he seems to have been relieved without the expense and fatigue of a journey to Kentucky.

I recollect very well the accounts given in my early boyhood of his own narrative of his deliverance from these troubles. My recollection is, that the narrative was given at a camp-meeting at Sugg's Creek, in Wilson county, Tennessee. He was silent and thoughtful during the meeting, until the afternoon of Sabbath. After the administration of the sacrament, he called the congregation to the stand, gave them a history of his doubts, fears, and hesitation, which had previously held him back from identifying himself with the new Cumberland Presbytery; his present entire satisfaction that theologically they occupied the true scriptural ground; and that their ecclesiastical course was right, being a necessity imposed upon them. He seemed to be a new man. Many had entertained fears for a while that his usefulness was at an end. The joy was great, and the general impression was overwhelming. He was a great favorite with the common people.

The understanding is, that he had not preached from the time the Cumberland Presbytery was organized, in February, up to the time, a space of several months.

Some time after these occurrences, Mr. McGee moved, and settled near the Three Forks of Duck River. There he remained till his death. Mr. Smith, in his history of the Cumberland Presbyterians, says his death occurred in 1814. Rev. Robert Donnell delivered a sermon upon the occasion of his death, at the Beech Meeting-house, in the fall of 1817. My impression at the time was that his death was a recent occurrence. If so, I suppose it took place rather in 1817. The testimony is that he died in the faith and hope of the gospel. On his death-bed, he is said to have repeated almost constantly the following passage of Scripture: "If the righteous scarcely be saved, where shall the ungodly and the sinner appear?" This was no doubt an expression of the experience of much of his life.

The following sketch of his character is from the pen of the late Rev. Robert Donnell:

> He was a man of deep, penetrating, clear thought, and would not affirm what he did not know; and what he knew, he could say, or make known to others. He has often remarked to me, that he had heard others say that they knew, but could not communicate; but when he knew, he could always communicate. In conversation, he would often recur to the doctrine of Election and Reprobation, which many would say they understood, and would try to explain, but could not. His belief was, that they did not understand it; otherwise they could explain it. Mr. McGee was profound. He thought soberly, deliberated carefully, and executed promptly. He was extremely cautious until he knew what to do; but when questions were settled, the man of energy appeared.
>
> It would be vain and useless for me to attempt a eulogy, and therefore I shall conclude by saying, his head was clear, his heart was warm, his language plain; whilst his figures were bold and striking, his arguments were unanswerable, and his applications were as the application of Nathan to David—'Thou art the man!' His moral character was irreproachable, and his piety undisputed. His seals to his ministry were numerous, and some of them yet live to be his organs in the churches; and by them, 'he being dead, yet speaketh.'

Mr. McGee was, no doubt, an earnest and spiritual preacher. Some anecdotes were told of him which were characteristic. He and another minister, who was not distinguished for spirituality, preached occasionally to the same congregation, which was without a regular pastor. A lady in the congregation became serious on the subject of religion, and applied to the other minister for counsel and guidance. He labored with her for some time, but her mind was not satisfied. She was in the dark, and could find no relief. When he seemed likely to fail entirely, he told her to go to Mr. McGee—that he was a better guide in difficult spiritual cases than himself. She applied to Mr. McGee, was indeed relieved, and became a sincere Christian. She was accustomed to narrate her experience in this respect with great interest.

Again, at a certain large meeting, an old lady had, as she seemed to think, a revelation that Mr. McGee was, under Divine appointment, to perform a particular service. She was, of course, very eager to find him, that she might communicate the revelation, and set him upon the appointed work. When she found him, and made known the object of her mission, his only reply was: "Well, sister, if the Lord did really intend that I should perform this service, why might he not as well have made the revelation to me as to you?" This reply, made in a quiet but dry manner, discouraged the visionary, and she left him.

Mr. Donnell speaks of the boldness of his figures. On of his illustrations is remembered yet. He was preaching at Brown's Ferry, where we now have New Hope Church. The river was, of course, near at hand. He was preaching upon the necessity of combining faith and works. He pointed to the river. "A boatman, says he, "undertakes to cross the river. He uses but one oar. His boat will turn around, but go down the stream. The result is inevitable. But he plies both oars steadily and earnestly. He conquers the current, and makes the desired landing." It will be readily seen that such an illustration, under such circumstances, would be striking.

I recollect something of Mr. McGee's personal appearance and manner of preaching. His complexion was fair, and his hair of a sandy color. He was rather inclined to be corpulent, and I think a stranger would have judged that there was an appearance of indolence in his habits. His eye was dark and piercing, but rather small. He had a good voice, strong and melodious, and well adapted to addressing a crowd. I know the understanding among the old people was, that he preached with great power the experimental and practical truths of the gospel. Thirty years ago, the Christian men and women of this country always mentioned his name with interest. They regarded his memory as a precious legacy to the Church.

Early in life Mr. McGee was married, in North Carolina, to Miss Anna King, sister of the late Rev. Samuel King. His wife survived him, and after his death moved to Missouri, where she died some years ago. They had several children. One son, John McGee, became a candidate for the ministry, and was, perhaps, licensed. He settled in Western Tennessee, in the opening of that country, but soon left for Missouri. From some cause, he did not succeed in the ministry.

REV. JAMES MCGREADY
(1763-1817)

Rev. James Mcgready was of Scotch-Irish descent, and was born in Pennsylvania. When he was quite young, his father moved from Pennsylvania, and settled in Guilford county, North Carolina. Here young McGready passed his early years. He is represented to have been of a thoughtful and serious habit of mind, and otherwise promising, whilst still a youth. An uncle, who was on a visit to his father's family, from Pennsylvania, though that a boy of such habits and promise ought to be educated for the ministry, and prevailed on his parents to allow their son to accompany him to Pennsylvania, with a view to the accomplishment of that object. The more reliable tradition is, that about the time of his commencing his studies preparatory to the work of the ministry, he was convinced by a sermon of a Rev. Mr. Smith, of the unsoundness of his previous religious hopes. Smith, in his history of the Cumberland Presbyterian Church, says that his awakening to a true sense of his spiritual state was attributable to a conversation of two friends, overheard by Mr. McGready, in which they expressed their fears that he was not a truly converted man. Foote, in his Sketches of North Carolina, confirms the latter account. Whatever may have been the means of his awakening, he became an earnest inquirer, and soon, without doubt, a true Christian.

In the fall of 1785, Mr. Smith, who, according to the first tradition, was the means of his awakening, opened a school for the purpose of assisting young men in preparing for the ministry, and young McGready immediately became one of his pupils. He remained here for some time, and then entered a school recently opened by Rev. Dr. McMillan, with whom he had spent some time after his arrival with his uncle from North Carolina. Dr. McMillan's school grew into what is now Jefferson College.

The subject of this sketch having completed his literary and theological course of studies, was licensed to preach by the Presbytery of Redstone, on the 13th of August, 1788, when he was about thirty years of age. In the autumn or winter following, he returned to North Carolina, and on his way spent some time with Dr. John Blair Smith, at Hampden Sidney College in Virginia. Dr. Smith had been extensively connected with a powerful revival of religion, which occurred in his neighborhood about that time, and the mind of Mr. McGready seems to have been deeply affected by what he saw and heard of the manifestations of Divine grace in that revival.

On his arrival in North Carolina, he found the churches in a low state. A great spiritual dearth prevailed, and his preaching was the means of awakening increased interest on the subject of religion. From one of my authorities we have the following: "His labors at an academy under the care of Dr. Caldwell, were instrumental in producing a revival of religion, in which ten or twelve young men were brought into the fold, all of whom became ministers of the gospel, and some of them were subsequently his fellow-laborers in the far West."

About the year 1790 Mr. McGready married, and became the pastor of a congregation in Orange county. "Here he labored with his wonted zeal, and often with great success." His zeal provoked opposition. The cry was raised against him that he was running the people distracted, diverting their attention from their necessary avocations, and creating unnecessary alarm in the minds of those who were decent and orderly in their lives. "A letter was written to him in blood, requiring him to leave the country at the peril of his life; and a number of wicked men and women of the baser sort, on a certain occasion during the week, assembled in his church, tore down the seats, set fire tot he pulpit, and burnt it to ashes." On the following Sabbath, when the congregation met for worship, a scene of confusion and desolation presented itself. He, however, proceeded with the service, using a very appropriate and solemn psalm, and delivering a sermon from the following text: "O Jerusalem, Jerusalem, thou that killest the prophets, and stonest them which are sent unto thee, how often would I have gathered thy children together, even as a hen gathereth her chickens under her wings, and ye would not! Behold your house is left unto you desolate."

In 1796 Mr. McGready left North Carolina for Kentucky. After spending a few months in East Tennessee, he reached his destination, and took the pastoral charge of three congregations in Logan county — Gaspar River, Red River, and Muddy River. These congregations were small, and in a low state of religious interest. There were among them, however, some living and earnest Christians. He made great efforts to arouse his people to a proper sense of their spiritual condition, as well as for the conversion of sinners. In order to effect his object more fully, he presented to the members of his congregation for their approval and signatures, the following preamble and covenant:

> When we consider the word and promises of a compassionate God to the poor lost family of Adam, we find the strongest encouragement for Christians to pray in faith—to ask in the name of Jesus for the conversion of their fellow-men. None ever went to Christ when on earth, with the case of their friends, that were denied, and, although the days of his humiliation are ended, yet, for the encouragement of his people, he has left it on record, that where two or three agree upon earth to ask in prayer, believing, it shall be done. Again, whatsoever you shall ask the Father in my name, that will I do, that the Father may be glorified in the Son. With these promises before us, we feel encouraged to unite our supplications to a prayer-hearing God for the outpouring of his Spirit, that his people may be quickened and comforted, and that our children, and sinners generally, may be converted. Therefore, we bind ourselves to observe the third Saturday of each month, for one year, as a day of fasting and prayer for the conversion of sinners in Logan county, and throughout the world. We also engage to spend one half hour every Saturday evening, beginning at the setting of the sun, and one half hour every Sabbath morning, from the rising of the sun,m pleading with God to revive his work.

To this covenant he and they affixed their names. The writer recollects to have heard the late Dr. Alfred M. Bryan state that his father, and perhaps his mother, were subscribers, among others. In May, 1797, the first signs of promise appeared, in the conversion of a female member of one of his congregations, who had been in the communion of the Church for some time. These favorable indications continued through the summer, but were followed by a temporary reaction through the fall and winter. The following summer the work developed itself more powerfully. On Monday of the sacramental meeting, at Gaspar River Meeting-house, the Spirit of God was poured out abundantly; the congregation became intensely interested on the subject of religion, and during the following week, almost entirely neglected their secular affairs, so great was their solicitude to secure the salvation of their own souls and the souls of others. This was the commencement of the great revival of 1800. For several subsequent years, a history of Mr. McGready would be a history of the revival. He was its leading spirit—I speak of him as a subordinate agent, of course—its most earnest advocate, and powerful promoter.

When the difficulties began to develop themselves, which resulted in the organization of the Cumberland Presbyterian Church, Mr. McGready for a time took a decided stand, as we would have expected, with the revival party. As these difficulties progressed, however, and became more serious than he expected, he faltered. It is, perhaps, not a matter of surprise. He was a Calvinist of the old school. He had received his early theological impressions, and his impressions of ecclesiastical order, from Dr. McMillan and old Red Stone Presbytery, types of the sternest Presbyterianism. He had no idea, it is supposed, when the troubles commenced, that they would become so complicated and embarrassing. Another consideration may be added. Although a man of great power in the pulpit, he was not a man for ecclesiastical conflict. He was not adapted to the leadership of a party. In December of 1805 he was cited, with Revs. Messrs. William Hodge, William McGee, Samuel McAdow, and John Rankin, to appear before the next meeting of Kentucky Synod, to account for their conduct in not submitting the young men for reexamination to the Commission of the Synod. The history of the Commission is known. He succeeded by some means in making his peace with the Synod, and with the Transylvania Presbytery, which he seems to have attended in 1809, for the first time after his citation by the Commission of Synod.

Shortly after Mr. McGready's defection from the Council out of which the Cumberland Presbytery of 1810 grew, he left Logan county, and settled in Henderson county, Kentucky, where he remained until his death, which occurred in February, 1817.

Of his latter years, not much in known. It is known, however, that he continued his ministerial work, with his usual fidelity. But from some cause his labors were not as successful as they had formerly been. This was perhaps partly attributable to such a failure of physical strength and animation as declining age naturally brings. His friends, too, thought that the former unction of his ministry was wanting. It is recorded that in the fall of 1816, a few months before his death, he attended a Cumberland Presbyterian camp-meeting near Evansville, Indiana, where he preached with great power and success. At the close of a very impressive sermon on "The character, history, and end of the fool." he came out of the pulpit, called together the anxious, and prayed for them with great fervency. When he closed, he arose from his knees, and exclaimed with a loud voice, "O blessed be God! I this day feel the same holy fire that filled my soul sixteen years ago, during the glorious revival of 1800."

Mr. McGready was an unusual man. God had evidently endowed him, and raised him up, and given him a spiritual training for a special work. He had great physical strength, and a voice like thunder. In these respects, he was precisely fitted for the field of labor to which Providence assigned him. His early religious experience was well calculated to awaken distrust of the religion of many around him. He had himself built for a time upon a false foundation, and it was very natural that he should fear that others would fall into the same fatal error. He was accordingly terrible upon hypocrites, deceivers, and the self-deceived. Such could hardly stand before his searching and scathing denunciations. And the history of the Church in his time, and the history of his own labors, show very clearly that such a man was greatly needed. Boanerges, sons of thunder, men of a deep and earnest spiritual experience, were the proper ministry for arousing formalists and double-minded Christians, and driving them from their refuges of lies. The Western country, too, in the close of the last, and the commencement of the present century, was filled with open infidelity. Vice was rampant. A bold front was needed to meet them. Mr. McGready's experience, too, was calculated to give him low views of himself. The result was, that notwithstanding his great success as a minister, he was remarkable for his humility. The following is from a sketch of his character, furnished by a ministerial friend:

> From the conduct and conversation of Mr. McGready, there is abundant evidence to believe that he was not only a subject of Divine grace and unfeigned piety, but that he was favored with great nearness to God, and intimate communion with him. Like Enoch, he walked with God; like Jacob, he wrestled with God, by fervent, persevering supplications for a blessing on himself and others, and prevailed; like Elijah, he was very jealous for the Lord of hosts, and regarded his kingdom as the great end of his existence on earth, to which all other designs ought to be subordinate; like Job, he deeply abhorred himself, repenting as it were in dust and ashes, when he was enabled to behold the purity of God, and his own want of conformity to his holy nature; like the apostle Paul, he counted all things but loss for the excellency of the knowledge of Jesus Christ his Lord; and like him, he felt great delight in preaching to his fellow-men the unsearchable riches of Christ. He was remarkably plain in his dress and manners, but very familiar, communicative, and interesting in his conversation. He possessed a sound understanding, and moderate share of human learning. The style of his sermons was not polished, but perspicuous and pointed, and his manner of address was unusually solemn and impressive. As a preacher, he was highly esteemed by the humble followers of the Lamb, who relished the precious truths which he clearly exhibited to their view; but he was hated, and sometimes bitterly reproached and persecuted, not only by the openly vicious and profane, but by many nominal Christians, or formal professors, who could not bear his heart-searching and penetrating addresses, and the indignation of the Almighty against the ungodly, which, as a son of thunder, he clearly presented to the view of their guilty minds from the awful denunciations of the word of truth.

A few of the old people still survive who sometimes heard Mr. McGready in the revival of 1800. They speak even now of his preaching with enthusiasm. They give wonderful accounts of his power in the pulpit, not only in preaching, but in prayer. I have several times heard a very reliable old gentleman, who claimed Mr. McGready as his spiritual father, relate the following circumstance: "On a certain occasion, he was preaching to a large congregation in the woods. A very dark and threatening cloud arose. A storm seemed ready to burst upon them. They had no shelter. The preacher was delivering his message with great earnestness and fervency. Seeing the storm approach, he stopped in the midst of his discourse, and addressed a prayer to God that the storm might be restrained or turned aside. The cloud separated, passing to the right and left, and leaving the congregation undisturbed." All this might have occurred, had no prayer been offered by the preacher. Still the narrator, and no doubt many of the people at the time, believed that God averted the storm in answer to the prayer.

I heard Mr. McGready preach once. I was very young—I suppose in my fourteenth or fifteenth year. The occasion was a funeral-sermon upon the death of his brother, who had lived and died a member of Shiloh congregation in Tennessee. He stood at the foot of a tree in a grove, as the house could not contain the congregation. I have a very distinct recollection of his appearance and manner. He was not boisterous, but rather chaste, solemn, and impressive. Solemnity was most conspicuous in his manner, and he shed tears very freely. It was a solemn day. I suppose it was his last visit to Shiloh, and perhaps to Tennessee.

His sermons were published in two volumes some years after his death, by Rev. James Smith, then of the Cumberland Presbyterian Church. They are good sermons. I have now in my possession one of his manuscript sermons. It is closely and very fully written out, but from age is scarcely legible.

REV. JOHN MORGAN
(1806-1841)

Sources: Manuscripts of Rev. A. Freeman, Rev. Isaac Hague, Mrs. J. R. Brown, Diary.

John Morgan was born May 4, 1806, in Virginia, near Richmond. His parents were John and Sarah Niblet Morgan. He was of Welsh extraction. His mother and the mother of the late President Harrison were cousins, and Mr. Morgan's name was really John Harrison Morgan, but from some cause unknown to the writer, his middle name was dropped in early life, and he was distinguished by his first name only. His educational advantages were very limited, but though seldom attending school, he was a diligent student, studied alone, sometimes taught, and by these means became a respectable scholar. He was, in the most practical sense of the expression, "a self-made man."

Some time in his early life his parents moved to Alabama, and settled in Madison county. But little is known of his boyhood. On the fourth Sabbath in September, 1823, he professed religion, being then in his eighteenth year. This is supposed to have occurred in Alabama. He was licensed to preach on the first of October, 1827, and set apart to the whole work of the ministry first of April, 1828. He was introduced into the ministry by the Tennessee Presbytery.

The first year of Mr. Morgan's ministerial life he spent as an itinerant preacher. His circuit extended through the counties of Limestone and Madison, Alabama, and Franklin and Lincoln counties, Tennessee. According to his own account, it was more than four hundred miles long, and his custom was to preach every day, and sometimes twice, and even thrice a day. Under such exhausting labors, as it would be supposed, his health soon began to fail, and it was found necessary for him to contract his labors. He was therefore directed to divide his time between Athens and Mooresville, Alabama. Here he labored for three years. "During this time," says he, "we experienced many gracious and powerful seasons of refreshing from the presence of the Lord, and witnessed the happy conversion of many precious souls to God." In the course of the first year after his ordination he administered the ordinance of baptism to two hundred and fifty adult persons. This is an indication of the extraordinary success of his early labors.

When he commenced preaching in Athens, there were but three members of the Church in town. At the expiration of his three years the membership numbered near two hundred, and a good house of worship, a brick building, had been erected. His health was still poor, and as he felt that he could be at least temporarily spared from Alabama, he determined to travel to some extent, through the more northern and eastern States, for the twofold purpose of improving his health, and adding to his stock of knowledge.

In the spring of 1831 the call came from Pennsylvania for a visit from some Cumberland Presbyterian preachers to that country. Messrs. Donnell, Chapman, Burrow, Bryan, and Morgan were appointed by the General Assembly of that year to visit Pennsylvania, in conformity with the call. In the latter part of May, Messrs. Morgan and Bryan started for Western Pennsylvania. After attending a meeting in Nashville, of ten days' continuance, which was held in the Market-house, they went to Gallatin, where they remained and preached several days, including the Sabbath. Mr. Morgan's remark is, that there was "some seriousness." From

Gallatin they went to Scottsville, Kentucky, and on through the towns which lay in their way, preaching at night and on the Sabbath, as opportunity presented itself. At Bardstown, Kentucky, they held a four-days' meeting, where "much seriousness was manifested." There they visited the Catholic College, Cathedral, and Nunnery—"finely constructed establishments indeed," says Mr. Morgan in his diary, "and well calculated to deceive and ruin souls." From Bardstown they passed through Lexington, Paris, and on the Washington, where they spent the night and preached. From Washington they went to Maysville, where they preached and spent the night. From Maysville they crossed the river, and for the first time in their lives stood upon "free soil." They shaped their course to Wheeling, preaching in the towns on the road. On the 15th day of July they reached Washington, Pennsylvania. Much curiosity existed to hear a Cumberland Presbyterian preach. Mr. Bryan was sick, and Mr. Morgan preached several times in the Methodist Church to large and attentive congregations.

Mr. Morgan, in connection with the other missionaries, who had all met according to appointment in Western Pennsylvania, attended a number of meetings in the course of the summer and fall, all of which were greatly blessed. Hundreds of persons professed religion, and a number of congregations were organized. The first congregation was organized on the 18th of August. In a few weeks a camp-meeting was held within its bounds, which appears to have been remarkably successful.

In the winter of 1831 and 1832 Mr. Morgan returned to Alabama. He visited Princeton, Kentucky, on his way southward, where he left Mr. John G. Biddle, one of the recent Pennsylvania converts. Mr. Biddle's attention had been turned to the ministry, and he came to Kentucky and entered Cumberland College, with a view to a preparation for that work. Mr. Morgan remained in the South until the spring, and then returned to Pennsylvania.

In the fall of 1832 he took charge of Washington and Bethel congregations. He continued here to the spring of 1834, when he settled in Uniontown, and took charge of the congregation in that place. Here he continued till his death. A considerable portion of the time of his connection with the Uniontown congregation, he was also connected with Madison College, as Professor of Moral and Intellectual Science. Madison College was at that time under the control of the Cumberland Presbyterian Church. In the course of his connection with the Institution he instructed eighteen or twenty young men in theology. He was a member of the General Assembly of 1840, which held its sessions in Elkton, Kentucky, and contributed very greatly by his influence toward the formation of a gigantic scheme for the resuscitation of Cumberland College, the prospects of which had become clouded. The plan, if carried out, would have revived the Institution and placed it on a permanent basis. It was, however, never carried out. He was also a member of the Assembly of 1841, which met at Owensboro, Kentucky. He is said to have delivered his last sermon in March, several months preceding his death, from the text, "For me to live is Christ, but to die is gain." He was fully sensible of his decline, and said through the spring and summer that he would "go with the falling of the leaves." After a tedious illness, he closed his earthly career on Sabbath night, October 17, 1841, in the thirty-sixth year of his age, and the fourteenth of his ministry. From a respected correspondent I have the following in relation to his death:

> I was present with him when he died. He was perfectly calm, and seemed entirely conscious and resigned. I recollect that he took leave of Mrs. Morgan with every mark of affection, but his voice was gone. I could hear nothing but 'Margaret' and 'farewell.' The effort exhausted him, and he soon breathed his last.

From another correspondent I have an account of an interview, which preceded his death a few days. Says the writer:

> Several of us were on the eve of starting to Synod, which was appointed to meet in Greenfield, Washington county. We called to see our esteemed counselor and friend, now rapidly declining. We supposed it might be our last opportunity of seeing him and hearing words from his lips in this life. He now could no more go with us, and lead us to Presbyteries and Synods, and sit as chief among counselors. Some standing at the head of his bed, some at the side, and some leaning on the foot-railing, he said, 'Dear brethren, I can go with you no more to Synod. I should like to go. You have been very kind to me, but we have met, I expect, for the last time. Go, and the Lord be with you! Do the best you can till we meet in the General Assembly and Church of the first-born.' One after another passed out of the room, but still one remained seated near him, held by a ligament which I could not describe. My feelings were tender, and the inquiry of my heart was, 'How can I leave my spiritual guide, father, brother, friend?' While I was thus seated, he fixed his eyes on me and said, 'For some days past the Lord has given me such views of eternity that my mind has been carried away. So delighted and charmed, and even overwhelmed, have I been with these bright visions, that I have felt my strength failing under them, and have been compelled to withdraw my mind from them. O the charming scenes which the Lord has set before me!' These were his last words to me. I arose; we took each other by the hand. It was the last farewell.

I make the following extract from the **Union Evangelist** of November 3, 1841:

> That faithful man of God, Rev. John Morgan, the respected and beloved pastor of the Cumberland Presbyterian congregation in Uniontown, since the spring of 1834, was called from the field of his earthly labors on Sabbath night, October 17, 1841, in the thirty-sixth year of his age, and in the fourteenth of his ministry. * * * In connection with others, he received an appointment from the General Assembly of our Church, convened in Princeton, Kentucky, in May, 1831, to visit some parts of Pennsylvania and New York, and on the 15th of July following he arrived in Washington, Pennsylvania. He was incessant in labors here, and in a section of country south of this; also at other points,

as Pittsburg, Waynesburg, Jefferson, and Wheeling, up to the early part of December, when he returned South, and passing through Marietta and Athens, Ohio, labored successfully at these and other places, which he again visited on his return from Alabama. He reentered the field of labor in Pennsylvania in June, 1832. The ensuing fall he took charge of Washington and Bethel congregations. In the spring of 1834 he resigned his charge here, and settled in Uniontown congregation, where he continued to labor as long as he had strength to preach. He had popular and useful talents, and was a man well suited to the condition and wants of the Church. Wherever he passed he left in his track impressions not soon to be obliterated. With a lucid mind, an unquenchable zeal, a warm heart, and a burning eloquence, he passed through the land like a flame of fire. We may say in truth that he lived fast. His labors soon wore out the frail tabernacle of the mind. All who knew him will bear witness to his urbanity and cheerfulness in the social circle. In the pulpit he was plain in his manner, forcible in his illustrations, and powerful in his appeals; bold, energetic, and faithful; a workman who had not need to be ashamed, rightly dividing the word of truth. He loved revivals of religion, and under God was a happy instrument in promoting them, and leading many to turn from their evil ways. Because of this, he suffered much calumny from the wicked.

The intelligence that such a servant of God, such a soldier of the cross has died on the battle-field, will make the hearts of thousands sad, but we must send forth the unwelcome tidings that Brother Morgan is no more. His congregation has experienced an inexpressible bereavement, our community has lost a valuable citizen, the Church a useful minister, and the cause of education an able advocate. The loss to his family, it were a mockery to attempt to describe. Their grief and mourning, the lamentations of relatives and friends, may be more fitly conceived than expressed. But they sorrow not as those who have no hope. The bereaved family have a better inheritance than silver and gold—the counsels, the example, the prayers of such a husband and father. The widow and her four fatherless children claim, and will doubtless receive, the sympathies and prayers of those who loved the husband and father.

Though his health and been declining for years, Brother Morgan still continued to labor, even beyond his strength. He had, however, seldom attempted to preach for eighteen or twenty months past. His protracted affliction he bore with patience and resignation. He had his right mind—was collected and calm to the last moment. The writer often heard him say that 'Christ had been precious to him, and altogether lovely, when preaching salvation through his name. Now he is precious in my affliction; he is my comfort and my consolation. O there is nothing like communion with God! I know in whom I have believed. My trust is firm. I view the approach of death without fear. I feel myself a poor unworthy creature; Christ is my only dependence. The plan of salvation is just such as man needs. O how well adapted is the Christian's hope to his condition! Nothing else can afford support in affliction, and in the prospect of death.' He sometimes said, when he thought of the Church and of his rising family, he felt a desire to have health again, if it were the Lord's will. The third evening before his death we called to see him, and an aged minister sitting by his side said to him, 'I suppose you remember that our Synod is to meet to-morrow?' 'Yes,' said he, 'I remember it well, but I suppose I shall never meet you again till we meet in the General Assembly and Church of the first-born.' The apostle's language was then quoted, 'For me to live is Christ, but to die is gain.' 'Aye,' said he, 'that is the last text from which I ever preached. Death is a very trying event. It is more than human nature, unsupported, can bear; but human nature, sanctified by Christianity, can bear it. Leaving a rising family is my greatest trial; but the Lord gave them, and if he see fit to call me away, he will take care of them.'

The remains of Mr. Morgan were committed to the tomb on Tuesday, 19th of October. A large crowd assembled at his residence at ten o'clock. The procession from thence to the church was led by sixteen ministers, and embraced the family and relatives of the deceased, his church and congregation, physicians, lawyers, and citizens generally of the town and vicinity. The church was set off with the habiliments of mourning. The crowd being seated, Rev. J. P. Wethee commenced the service by reading the ninetieth Psalm; Rev. David Barclay gave out the hymn, *Why do we mourn departing friends*, etc., and led in prayer. Rev. Milton Bird then delivered the funeral-sermon from Phil. i. 21-24.

One authority says, in relation to the funeral-service: "The audience was the largest I ever saw on such an occasion. The people came from far and near, and all seemed to feel that a great and good man had fallen from the walls of Zion."

I quote again, from the **Union Evangelist**:

Since the existence of our Church, it has never been more sorely bereaved than within the present year. Ewing has fallen in Missouri, Cauby in Illinois, and Morgan in Pennsylvania. This last bereavement falls on a part of the Church which seems least able to bear it. Let us lay these dispensations to heart. Has God a controversy with us? If such afflictions produce no deep impression and salutary reformation, we may expect to be visited still more sorely. Let us take words and return to the Lord with supplication and weeping. In our respective places let us devote ourselves to our duties. Though he feed his people with the bread of affliction, and given them tears to drink in large measure, yet God will not give his heritage to reproach.

Mr. Morgan was on many accounts one of the most interesting young men ever connected with the Cumberland Presbyterian Church. Says a correspondent: "The personal appearance of John Morgan was extremely prepossessing and imposing. He was six feet three inches in height, had black hair, large and brilliant black eyes, and a pale or rather sallow complexion. He was born to command, and without assuming any authority, he was facile princips in Presbytery, Synod, or in any assembly into which he might be thrown."

Although raised, I suppose, in common life, his manners were very fine, rather courtly than otherwise. He was a gentleman evidently without any effort. Such a man could not have been an unkind husband or father. He was just the reverse—loving and loved.

He was for some time connected with the **Union Evangelist** as editor. Some of his editorial productions were worthy of an editor of more experience and higher pretensions as a writer.

It has been already mentioned that he officiated several years as a Professor in Madison College. He possessed great tact in the management of young men. Indeed, he excelled in the management of men generally. I recollect to have heard a prominent lawyer and politician of Kentucky remark, that at the General Assembly of 1840, Mr. Morgan took him into his own garden, and by his controlling influence brought him over to a measure of Church policy in opposition to long-cherished convictions and prejudices—convictions and prejudices which he had considered immovable. Such a man would exert great influence upon the young men of a college.

But the pulpit was Mr. Morgan's forte. There he appeared to greatest advantage. On this subject I quote from a correspondent who was intimate with him, and was capable of forming a correct judgment:

> He was a great preacher—a great pulpit orator. The church in Uniontown was often crowded on ordinary occasions to hear him. He always took an interest in his subject. He felt the force of what he preached. The interest which he felt often kindled up his whole countenance into a flame, and his emotions were communicated to every hearer. At such times the pulpit could hardly contain him, and the whole audience were irresistibly borne along on the tide of thought and feeling. Expressions of deep emotion could be heard on every hand.
>
> My own impression has been that his nervous system was too delicate for his work, and that these overmastering efforts literally wore him out. I have known him to show signs of great prostration after preaching; and when he had delivered some of his best sermons in the morning, he was often unable to get to the church at night. I should have stated that when his emotions were most overpowering, all his action was perfectly natural, and seemed to coincide with his subject and the state of his feelings.

I recollect the first time I ever saw Mr. Morgan. It was at the General Assembly of 1831. I believe he was not a member, but only a visitor. He reached Princeton the evening before the Assembly met, and was appointed to preach that night. We had all heard of him as a young man of fine promise, and of course were anxious to hear him preach. He commenced his sermon with some very felicitous remarks on the subject of being in the neighborhood of a college, and the possibility of his not being able to satisfy so fastidious a taste as might perhaps prevail there. The sermon, however, was good; no one was disappointed. I saw him again at Princeton the following winter, on his way to Alabama. He again attended the Assembly of 1837, at Princeton, as I have already mentioned, and preached an excellent sermon, on Sabbath afternoon, from a passage in the latter part of Revelation. I never met with him after that meeting. At that Assembly he took an active part in the formation of what was for a long time known as "Cumberland College Association." This was an effort made to save the oldest literary institution in the Church.

I give some recollections of Mr. Morgan from another correspondent. The scenes which he described occurred in Pennsylvania:

> I went to a camp-meeting on Father N.'s land. There, for the first time, I saw Mr. Morgan. A tall man, of dark complexion, walked into the preacher's stand. Sitting erect, I carefully surveyed the stranger. His hair was jet-black, his face rather long, his forehead lofty, his shoulders were broad; there was an awe-inspiring power in his countenance—I could not steadily look upon it. I soon learned from the whispers around me that his name was Morgan. He soon arose, and commenced the service of the hour. His manner riveted the attention of all. His text was God's expostulation with his people: 'Come now, and let us reason together, saith the Lord; though your sins be as scarlet, they shall be as white as snow; though they be red like crimson, they shall be as wool.' In the course of the sermon I observed a man who was somewhat noted for skeptical, or rather speculative, principles on the subject of religion. He sometimes rose and stood, then sat down; thus frequently changing his position. All the while, however, his attention was fixed upon the preacher. He seemed to hear every word, and his countenance indicated an intense spiritual struggle. The speaker reasoned, and described the work of God in restoring to the soul its lost purity. His face shone like the face of Moses when he came down from the mount. At last, with his fist clenched and trembling, he darted his long arm toward the stranger. The latter dropped to his seat as though powerless. He yielded to the overwhelming appeal, and wept like a child. The preacher continued. He dwelt upon the character of the soul made white as snow or wool; its exercises here, and its employments in the coming world. Such a description, such words of holy rapture, such bright visions presented of the great white throne and those standing before it, of redeemed and glorified spirits flying in delightful obedience to the great Creator's will throughout his vast dominions, were quite overpowering. 'O, who would not be a Christian!' was the preacher's concluding interrogatory; and then, with a 'God save you, my dear people!' he left the stand.

We have an account of another camp-meeting, held on Upper Ten-Mile. Mr. Morgan preached on an afternoon of one day of the meeting. He seems to have been dissatisfied with his effort, but was appointed to preach again at night. In the sermon of the afternoon, in describing the vices and follies of the times, he found himself carried off into something of a light manner. He closed abruptly, and left the stand in great affliction. At night his text was, "Ye serpents, ye generation of vipers, how can ye escape the damnation of hell?" The introductory hymn was suited to the text. Says our informant, "He discoursed with such clearness and force upon his momentous theme—the place of the damned, the nature and reality of damnation—that he soon found his way to our feelings. The bottomless pit, the ascending columns of smoke and flame, the groans and cries, and unmitigated agonies of doomed spirits, seemed not only a fearful, but a present reality. He closed his sermon, and in the conclusion, raising his eyes to heaven, he cried out, 'O God! who is exposed to this damnation? Sinner, can you escape? Can you resist? God will overtake you—he will hurry you to your doom! You cannot escape! O, God save you from the damnation of hell!' It was the most heart-felt and terrific appeal that I ever heard from the mouth of man. And with this he sank down into his seat, crying, 'O God, O Lord Jesus, save this dear people from the damnation of hell!' Nothing, for some minutes, disturbed the awful stillness but sighs, and sobs, and groans."

We have an account of still another camp-meeting, held in Greene county. The concourse of people was very great, especially on the Sabbath. There seemed to be an organized opposition to the meeting, and great efforts were made to break it up. It seems strange that such should have been the case in the quiet land of Pennsylvania, but we suppose the account faithful. Mr. Morgan was appointed to preach on Sabbath night. Great apprehensions were entertained of the rabble. Every thing indicated a gathering storm. Civil officers were rather with the rowdies than against them. Night came on, however, and the sermon was preached. The text was Moses's invitation to his father-in-law to journey with Israel to the land of promise. It was a memorable night. "More than a hundred persons signified a wish to seek the goodly land." Quiet and order reigned. Victory on the Lord's side seemed complete. The opposition temporarily quailed. But after the service closed at the stand, the rowdies rallied again. At the head of the troop was a large, black negro, called Bob. It was flattering to his vanity to be made a captain, even of such a crowd. They marched around the camp-ground, whooping and yelling, throwing stones at the camps, and in various ways expressing their fiendish spirit. Mr. Morgan passed out and around, so as to meet them, as they moved with their whisky and bludgeons. Coming near, he walked rapidly forward, and meeting the head of their miserable column, he took hold of Bob, and placing a hand on each shoulder, shook him severely, and said, "Bob, you scoundrel, will you persist in this disturbance?" Bob trembled from head to foot, and begging, said, "Mr. Morgan, forgive me, and I will do so no more." Bob kept his word, and his followers quietly slipped off. The troubles of the meeting came to an end.

When Mr. Morgan professed religion, he was an immersionist in sentiment, and had his baptism deferred for some time because there was no stream in the neighborhood suitable for immersion. He chose also to be baptized by a minister who had himself been immersed, and for this purpose went a considerable distance from home for baptism. He seems to have retained his prejudices on this subject until after he entered the ministry. A ludicrous incident in his own ministerial experience directed his attention to a new aspect of the subject. He was called upon to baptize a large negro man in Alabama. The negro, like himself, was an immersionist, and must needs go under the water. The bottom of the creek selected for the administration of the ordinance was very slippery. At the moment of attempting to put the negro under the water, the administrator lost his foothold upon the bottom, and the negro escaped from his hand, and swam out, half drowned, to the opposite side of the stream. Of course the crowd collected to witness the service made themselves merry at the occurrence. A thoughtful man would have considered the inconvenience and incongruity of a rite which rendered him liable to so much embarrassment. Mr. Morgan reviewed his opinions. The result was a total change, and for some years before his death he refused to baptize by immersion under any circumstances.

Mr. Morgan left a wife and four children. The respected widow still lives. The children are all members of the Church except the youngest. His oldest son married the daughter of his old friend and fellow-laborer, Rev. Dr. A. M. Bryan; his second daughter is the wife of Rev. J. R. Brown, of Cherry Grove, Illinois.

REV. HERSCHEL S. PORTER
(1816-1855)

Herschel S. Porter was the son of Rev. Thomas Porter and Nancy Porter. His mother's family name was Lawrence. His paternal grandfather was Captain William Porter. Captain Porter was a Revolutionary soldier, and carried to his grave a large scar upon his face, left by a wound received from a British sword in the war of the Revolution. The Porter family were Scotch-Irish Presbyterians. The family of Dr. Porter's mother were Baptists. His maternal grandfather, Thomas Lawrence, was a deacon in the Baptist Church. He was also a Revolutionary soldier.

Captain Porter moved from Prince Edward county, Virginia, about the year 1794, and settled in what is now Butler county, Kentucky. The maternal grandfather emigrated from the same county in Virginia, but it is not known to the writer at what time. He also settled in Butler county. Rev. Thomas Porter, the father of the subject of this sketch, was raised in Butler county, and spent his life in that portion of Kentucky. Herschel S. Porter was born in Butler county, February 12, 1816.

He commenced going to school when seven years of age. His first instructor was Daniel L. Morrison, a worthy Christian gentleman, and a good instructor. After a while his father moved to Logan county, and taught school himself for two years, and of course the son was one of his pupils. In this school he commenced the study of History and Geography. The custom of boys in those day, at least in that portion of Kentucky, was to labor on the farm in the summer, and attend school in the winter. Young Porter was under the necessity of conforming to this custom. He divided the year between books and the plow. A surviving brother says of him, that "from a child he was a sober, thoughtful, plodding boy, of unbending energy and great fixedness of purpose—so much so, that when he once set his mind upon the accomplishment of an object, he never turned back." He seems to have been chiefly fond of history. An anecdote is told illustrative of this. He and his brother were at work one day in the field. They had both been reading ancient history. The subject of one of Hannibal's great battles came up in conversation. They differed in opinion as to what the facts were according to the history. After discussing the subject for some time, they made a boyish bet, and went to the house to determine the question from the history itself. This incident is of little importance certainly, but it shows that the boy's reading was of a solid kind, and that he was in the habit of thinking of what he read.

Mr. Porter's first Sunday-school instructor was James Stevenson, a pious man, and an elder in the Cumberland Presbyterian Church. Mr. Stevenson had no Sunday-school library. His principal reliance in that way was the Bible. From this he was accustomed to select plain passages, and expound them as well as he could. One of Mr. Stevenson's favorite maxims was, that men should labor for knowledge as the miner digs for his golden treasure. This maxim seems to have made a life-long impression upon the mind of young Porter. After he had reached eminence in the ministry, he was still in the habit of recurring to it as a principle of which he first began to feel the force in a retired country Sunday-school.

After leaving his father's school, young Porter continued his education under several successive instructors. The principal of them was a Mr. Read, who taught an academy near Russellville. There he studied Latin and the ordinary branches of science. With Rev. Mr. McAllen, an Episcopal minister, and graduate of Dublin University, he studied Greek and Mathematics. His education, as far as instruction received from others was concerned, was finished under the care of John D. Tyler, who taught with great success a select high-school, in Montgomery county, Tennessee. He considered Mr. Read, however, as having contributed more toward his education than any other individual.

In the fall of 1832 young Porter professed religion at a camp-meeting at Rock Spring Meeting-house, a few miles from Russellville. He had been serious through the meeting, and on Monday evening was deeply engaged in prayer, with a crowd of others, who had been called together to the mourners' benches. It was a time of deep interest. The Spirit of God was poured out in great abundance. Says a friend, in relation to the occasion: "He rose from his knees with a smile upon his countenance, embraced his friends, and although a modest boy, commenced immediately exhorting sinners to turn to God. This was the brightest day in his history."

In April of 1833 Mr. Porter was received as a candidate for the ministry by the Logan Presbytery. In May of 1835 he was licensed to preach, and in September of 1837 was set apart to the whole work of the ministry, at Glasgow, Kentucky, Rev. Granville Mansfield preaching the ordination-sermon, and Rev. William Harris delivering the charge.

After his ordination he spent three or four years as an itinerant preacher in his own State, traveling through Logan, Warren, Barren, Simpson, Monroe, Cumberland, Butler, and Adair counties. He traveled some time in addition as an agent for Cumberland College. He then spent a year in Fayetteville, Tennessee, preaching to the congregation there. After the close of his term of service in Fayetteville, he made quite an extensive Southern tour, passing through most of the Southern States, and preaching with great acceptance wherever he went. He visited New Orleans, spent some time in Alabama, and returned to Kentucky in 1843. At the General Assembly of that year, which met at Owensboro, Kentucky, the writer of this sketch first became acquainted with him. We were not very remotely related, but had never met before.

From the General Assembly of 1843 he went, in company with Rev. A. M. Bryan, to Western Pennsylvania, and after spending a few months in that country, he was encouraged to undertake the enterprise of collecting a Cumberland Presbyterian congregation in the city of Philadelphia. He accordingly made his first visit to that city in the fall of 1843, and commenced his work. Dr. Bryan is said also to have cooperated with him in his first labors there. He remained in Philadelphia to the spring or summer of 1851. In 1850 he visited the General Assembly, which held its session that year in Clarksville, Tennessee, for the purpose of procuring some assistance in paying for a house of worship which had been erected by his congregation in Philadelphia. Leaving the Assembly, he spent some time in Tennessee and Kentucky, and received very liberal contributions in aid of his object. His labors in his new charge were abundant, and his success greater, perhaps, than could have been expected. He collected a respectable congregation around him, and, as already intimated, through his influence a house of worship was built.

While in Philadelphia he delivered two or three course of scientific lectures, connecting them with his ministerial labors. His object was to set forth the relation of religion to some of the most popular branches of science. His lectures are said to have excited considerable attention, and were highly complimented by the secular press at the time of their delivery.

In 1851 he left Philadelphia, and in the fall of that year settled in Memphis, Tennessee, in compliance with a call of the congregation there. He continued his labors in Memphis to the fall of 1855. On the 5th of October of that year he died, after an illness of but a few days. He had just passed through the labors of an extensive revival in his congregation, in which near a hundred persons had made profession of religion. The most of the labor of the meeting had been performed by himself. The disease which terminated in his death is supposed to have been induced by his excessive exertion, anxiety, and watchfulness, during a series of services kept up two or three weeks. It may be said with truth, and with emphasis, too, that he died at his post, and with his armor on. This last was the most extensive revival which he had ever enjoyed in the prgress of his ministry.

The following is the notice of his death contained in the Memphis Eagle and Enquirer of October 6, 1855:

"With feelings of unfeigned grief we record the death of Rev. Herschel S. Porter, pastor of the Cumberland Presbyterian Church of this city. He died at his residence on Court street, yesterday morning, at four o'clock, of bilious fever, superinduced and aggravated by his exertions in the recent most successful revival at his church. Truly it may be said that Dr. Porter died in the service of his Divine Master, with his harness on. He was about thirty-nine years of age, and a native of Butler county, Kentucky. His early opportunities for acquiring an education were limited, and he was emphatically a self-made man. Since attaining to his majority he has been a close student, and, notwithstanding his few advantages, he had received the honorary degree of D.D. from the Cumberland University, and that of A.M. from Princeton College, Kentucky. He was devoted to science, and was a proficient in the mind-expanding studies of astronomy and geology. His fame as a revivalist is coextensive with the Union. In early life he went to Philadelphia, where he was pastor of a congregation for five years. He has resided in Memphis four years, and has endeared himself to the whole community by his able preaching of the Gospel of Christ, his unaffected piety, and his rare social qualities. His only child, a daughter, died a few weeks ago. He leaves a stricken wife-married in this county-to mourn his early departure to that better land, where we all should strive to follow him, and to which he ever earnestly and eloquently, both by precept and example, pointed the way. When such a man dies, it is like the going out of a great beacon to whose guidance we have been accustomed, and whose place we feel will not easily be supplied."

At the time of Dr. Porter's death, in addition to his pastorate, he held a connection with the Memphis Medical College, as Professor of Natural History. The following is an extract from a record of the proceedings of the Faculty in relation to his death:

> Whereas, in the dispensation of an inscrutable Providence, our much-beloved friend and colleague, Dr. Herschel S. Porter, Professor of Natural History, etc., has been suddenly removed from us by death, we feel that it is due to his many excellent traits of character to give utterance to our sincere and unfeigned sorrow, not only on account of the loss to our

Institution, but tot he community at large; therefore,

Resolved, That by the death of Dr. Porter, the Faculty feel that they have lost a member, not only endeared to them by his gentlemanly bearing and Christian deportment, but also important to the Institution as a learned, able, and popular teacher of the natural sciences.

Resolved, That in their opinion, so many excellent qualities are to be found combined in so high a degree in but few individuals as were exhibited in the character of Dr. Porter, as a learned, liberal, and zealous minister of the gospel; as a promoter of science and all useful knowledge; as an advocate of temperance, order, and morality, and as a member of the community, not only social, kind, and benevolent, but always ready to aid in any and every proper movement or enterprise for the good of his fellow-beings.

Although, as it will be perceived from this sketch, Dr. Porter did not enjoy the advantages of a collegiate education, properly so called, his education was considered equivalent, and accordingly he received the first degree in the arts from Cumberland College in 1841. In 1848 he received the second degree from the same Institution. In 1850 he was honored with the degree of Doctor of Divinity by the Faculty and Trustees of Cumberland University. He was a scholar in the most practical and interesting sense of the word. In 1853 he was Moderator of the General Assembly, and in 1854 was married to Miss Martha A. Persons, of Shelby county, Tennessee.

Dr. Porter published several works-a series of "Astronomical Sermons;" a work on the "Atonement," and a work upon the "Foreknowledge and Decrees" of God. The first is a duodecimo volume of some four hundred pages; the two others are smaller works. At the time of his death he was engaged in preparing a history of the Cumberland Presbyterian Church-a work to the completion of which his friends were looking forward with deep interest.

A few words may be added presenting an outline of the character of Dr. Porter. I mention, then—

1. His energy and perseverance. I combine these as they were combined in him. A poor boy, with little aid from others, he became, by patience, assiduity, and perseverance, a learned man. I say a learned man. He studied the works as well as the word of God, and from his uncommon proficiency in these, he placed himself in an eminent position of usefulness and respectability in society. His eminence was not the award of mere denominational partiality; it was felt and acknowledged by all classes of cultivated minds. His Astronomical Sermons, although every statement in them may not be mathematically correct, and although some of his views may be regarded as rather speculative than otherwise, still indicate a familiarity with the great science upon which they are founded, which is attained by few. And it is true, too, that notwithstanding the Scriptures are not intended to teach us Astronomy and Geology—they have a higher aim—yet, there are both Astronomy and Geology in the Scriptures. The teachings of true science and the teachings of revelation never come in conflict with each other. They originate from the same Divine source. And that is a noble mind which earnestly,

and in any degree successfully, endeavors to understand their connection.

2. His piety. Without doubt he filled up in a high degree the measure ascribed to Barnabas-he "was a good man, and full of the Holy Ghost and of faith." It would seem a matter of course that a Christian minister should be a good man. Observation proves, however, that such men are not always good men. But the subject of this sketch was a pious man. He loved and feared God from his youth. Greatly flattered during his ministry, he still lived the life of an humble follower of Christ. I mention an incident connected with Dr. Porter's childhood. It is related on the best living authority, that when he was baptized in his infancy, the officiating minister (Rev. Alexander Chapman)—one of the holiest of men—made it a subject of special prayer that the child might, at a proper time, be called of God to the ministry of the gospel. The manner of the prayer was so earnest; there was such an expression of faith and power in it, that the narrator, who was present, received an impression from it which remains vivid to this day. It may be remarked, too, that nothing like raving and frantic enthusiasm was connected with the occasion. It was an earnest prayer of an earnest man for an object which lay near his heart. Possibly, I say, possibly, we may see the foreshadowings of Dr. Porter's humble piety, and great eminence and usefulness in that consecrating prayer. Why may we not, if it is indeed true that God hears and answers prayer?

3. His devotion to the Church of his fathers and of his own early choice. Other young men who have acquired some eminence have left us. Their reasons are known to themselves. We have no quarrel with them. For myself, I follow some of them with feelings above those of mere kindness. The world is wide enough for us all. But the subject of this sketch, I suppose, never faltered for a moment in his fidelity to the Communion into which he was baptized, and which when a youth of sixteen he chose for his own immediate Christian brotherhood. I recollect to have heard him remark to the members of the Assembly, in 1850, at Clarksville, that although he had been upon the outposts of the Church for some years, he was willing to go still farther out, if necessity required, to take any station, to engage in any service, which the Church might assign. It is very evident that the single purpose of his life was the promotion, as far as he was able, of the great interests of the Cumberland Presbyterian Church. Still, he was no mere stringent sectarian. He loved his own Church, received its doctrines in good faith, conformed to its order, and labored for its advancement. Still, according to the testimony already given, he was always ready to unite with good and earnest men in any measure for the promotion of the happiness of his race.

4. His modesty and unobtrusiveness were conspicuous. Whilst his pulpit performances were always popular, and his attainments were obviously superior to those of many of his brethren, he never manifested a disposition to present claims to any preference. He had been sixteen years in the ministry before he was a member of the General Assembly; but on the first occasion upon which he was a member, he was elected the Moderator of that body. The dignity and urbanity with which he presided over the Assembly were subjects of remark. He was again a member of the General Assembly in 1855—the last Assembly which met before his death. On that occasion he was appointed to deliver a sermon in reference to the death of two of the fathers of the Church, which had recently occurred (Rev. Thomas Calhoon and Rev. James B. Porter). The sermon was appropriate and impressive. On the same occasion he delivered, by request, a sermon to the young

men of Cumberland University. Still, no claims to preeminence were presented.

5. Dr. Porter was, in the most expressive sense of the phrase, a Christian gentleman. His general bearing, his conversation, his whole intercourse with society, indicated his intellectual, social, and moral culture. There was nothing low, coarse, or vulgar in his conversation or deportment. His character, both public and private, was such as one loves to contemplate. His example was a beautiful model. The memory of such men is to be cherished. They are God's noblest gifts to the Church-she should not be unmindful of their value.

REV. JAMES BROWN PORTER
(1779-1854)

Sources: Rev. C. P. Reed; Smith's **History of the Cumberland Presbyterians**; **Banner of Peace**.

James Brown Porter was born in Guilford county, North Carolina, February 26, 1779. This was one of the darkest periods in our Revolutionary history. The British were making great efforts to subjugate the Carolinas. In the following spring they took Charleston, and the nominal subjugation of South Carolina soon followed. North Carolina was overrun with parties of the enemy who, together with the tories, kept the country in constant agitation and alarm. The British were cruel, but the tories were more cruel still. It was a time which tried men's souls. Reese Porter, the father of James B. Porter, was a brave and patriotic citizen. He, with others, rushed to the rescue of their almost ruined country. After many skirmishes with the enemy, however, they were overpowered, and compelled to surrender themselves as prisoners of war. Reese Porter was a prisoner at the time of the battle at Guilford Court-house. After the battle, however, an exchange of prisoners was made, and he was restored to freedom. Reese Porter was a North Carolina Presbyterian, and that class of men were in the front rank of the patriots of the country. They or their fathers had renounced their homes in Ireland for a free country, and a free religion, and were not willing to give up these here without a struggle. They went into the civil conflict with great earnestness. The Mecklenburg resolutions are matters of history.

In 1785 Mr. Porter, the father, moved to Tennessee, and settled in the vicinity of Haysboro, about six miles north-east of Nashville. At that time, and for some years afterward, the white settlers suffered a great deal from the depredations of the Indians. In the course of this year several persons were killed in the neighborhood of Nashville. Of course times were very dangerous. There were no schools, nor houses of worship. Notwithstanding these discouragements the country filled up, and in process of time, and earlier than could have been expected, schools were established, and houses of worship were built. Reese Porter connected himself with the Presbyterian congregation at Haysboro, of which Rev. Thomas Craighead was pastor. In a few years, however, the revival began to develop itself. Mr. Craighead took a stand against the revival; Mr. Porter sympathized with the revival party, and of course they separated.

In November of 1801, James B. Porter attended a camp-meeting at Shiloh, in Sumner county. Shiloh was celebrated in those days as one of the prominent points at which the revival developed itself. Rev. William Hodge was pastor of the congregation. "It is not uncommon," says my informant, very truly, "for the great Head of the Church to select apparently weak means for the accomplishment of his work." The means selected on this occasion for the accomplishment of a great end was, at least, uncommon. The writer has heard Mr. Porter speak of the occurrence more than once. A Christian young lady was the commissioned angel of mercy. Mr. Porter was a gay young man; had just finished his education, and was expecting to enter in a few days upon his professional studies. Almost, of course, his pride would prompt him to resist as far as possible all serious impressions, with a purpose, perhaps, of attending to these things in future. In this manner he met the first appeal, but still he felt deeply, and wept. He retired from the congregation and prayed in secret. Returning to the congregation with a show of unconcern, the same angel of peace and mercy made a second appeal to his heart. He was no longer able to conceal his feelings, and fell to the floor, and there continued to wrestle and agonize until day-break, when he found peace in believing. He often mentioned the circumstance as an encouragement to young converts to work for the salvation of their friends. This lady was a young convert, and full of zeal. Says my informant, very appropriately: "This interesting case is an illustration of the exclamation of the apostle, 'Behold how great a matter a little fire kindleth!'"

Shortly after Mr. Porter's conversion, he accompanied his mother to South Carolina; his soul being filled with the love of God, and feeling great concern for the salvation of his fellow-men, he sought opportunities to exhort, and, no doubt, in this way awakened many to seriousness, and to feeling the necessity of religion.

On his return he fell in with the celebrated Lorenzo Dow. They attended a meeting together, and Dow was much impressed with Porter's zeal and efficiency. His personal appearance even attracted Dow's attention. He saw also that he was a gifted young man, but he though he saw an object that might hinder his usefulness. He approached young Porter, and said, "Young man, God has a work for you to do, and if you take any step which will hinder you in that work, God will curse you." Then addressing himself to the suspected object, he said, "Young woman, if you cause this young man to neglect that work, God will kill you." This was plain talk, but it was in conformity with Dow's manner.

Mr. Porter was received as a candidate for the ministry by the original Cumberland Presbytery, at Salem Meeting-house, in Sumner county, October 4, 1803. This was the second meeting of the Presbytery. At the same meeting Hugh Kirkpatrick and Ephraim McLean were licensed. At the next regular meeting of the Presbytery, April 3, 1804, he was licensed as a probationer for the gospel ministry. This meeting was held at Shiloh. His licensure was preceded by a critical examination upon the Latin and Greek languages.[33] His education was at least above that of most of the young men who were introduced into the ministry about that time.

From his licensure to 1810 he spent the most of his time as an evangelist. And although a licentiate only, he showed himself in the pulpit a workman who needed not to be ashamed, rightly dividing the word of truth. He was found, too, a safe counselor in those days which intervened between the action of the Commission Kentucky Synod and the constitution of the Presbytery as an independent organization. They were dark days, but the proscribed men labored and waited, and God gave them abundant evidence that their labor was not in vain. His labors were chiefly confined to what is now Middle Tennessee and North Alabama, with an occasional excursion into Kentucky.

Personally, Mr. Porter was a fine specimen of manhood-tall, in his prime,

---

[33]This statement is not made upon the authority of the records, but from the testimony of tradition, which in this case is considered reliable. Mr. Porter was unquestionably a well educated man for the times, and for the country in which he lived.

something more than six feet in height; had a fine face and head, a brilliant and an expressive eye, a large mouth, and a ready tongue. His voice was strong, musical, and melodious; few could sleep under his preaching. In prayer he was devout and impressive. A congregation could not feel otherwise than that they were in the presence of God whilst he was endeavoring to lead them to the throne of grace. In his preaching he confined himself chiefly to experimental and practical subjects, and in presenting subjects of this kind he had few equals and no superiors.

As a presbyter he was wise, prudent, and safe. His counsel was always sought in matters of importance. In questions of difficulty his decisions were generally authoritative. He was especially skillful in training young men for the ministry. Sometimes he was thought to be severe, but really he was not severe; he was no despot. He was no bigot, but he loved the Cumberland Presbyterian Church. He was identified with her interests from the beginning, and was an earnest believer in her doctrine and order. Whilst this was so, however, he embraced in a liberal charity all who loved and honored the name of our Lord Jesus Christ.

The foregoing description of Mr. Porter's person and character is substantially from one who knew him well. Thousands were living twenty years ago who, as far as their knowledge extended, would have confirmed every statement. He was a universal favorite in the Church which he had served, and of which he had been an ornament, so long.

The announcement of his death I find in the **Banner of Peace**, of October 26, 1854. I give it in full:

> Another of the fathers of the Cumberland Presbyterian Church has gone to his reward. Rev. James B. Porter fell asleep in Jesus on the 13th instant, at the residence of his son-in-law, Dr. Sharber, in Spring Hill, Tennessee.
>
> He had been on a decline for some years, and suffered much from loss of memory. He could remember, however, those times of trial through which he had passed in the infancy of our Church as well as if they had transpired but yesterday. He was one of the most eloquent men of his day. When he was in his prime he had probably no superior as a pulpit orator in Tennessee.
>
> We have no time to dwell upon his history. When written, however, it will be found replete with interest. We only add that he died in great peace. He had scarcely a struggle in his departure.

So fades a summer-cloud away,
So sinks the gale when storms are o'er,
So gently shuts the eye of day,
So dies a wave along the shore.
Life's duty done, as sinks the day,
Light from its load the spirit flies;
While heaven and earth combine to say,
How blest the righteous when he dies!

We shall expect a biographical sketch from some one conversant with his history soon. What solemn and earnest calls are the young men of the Church constantly receiving to be up and at work!

In conformity with the preceding request I find the following sketch in the **Banner of Peace**, of November 16, 1854:

Rev. James B. Porter died of paralysis at Spring Hill, Maury county, Tennessee, at six o'clock A.M., on Friday, the 13th of October, A.D. 1854, in the seventy-sixth year of his age.

The history of this great and good man is so intimately interwoven with the history of our branch of the Christian Church as to authorize the conclusion that most, if not all, of your readers are more or less acquainted with him.

Of his early history the writer has been able to learn but little more than that he received quite a liberal education, with an eye to the medical profession, for which he maintained a decided partiality through life. But while pursuing his studies in certain prospect of a most successful and brilliant career, the revival of 1800 was spreading over the land like a mighty, overwhelming flood, and he became one of its early subjects.

Late in the autumn of 1801 he attended a camp-meeting at old Shiloh, in Sumner county, Tennessee, and there, under the convicting power of God's Holy Spirit, he was first led to seek the Lord with all his heart. It was on Tuesday morning, November 24, 1801, about day-break, after spending the entire night in wrestling with God in prayer, the bosom of the surrounding country shrouded in a cold mantle of snow, and while a pious female, now in heaven, together with others, prayed for, and wept over, him, that the Lord spoke peace to his soul. About this time the demand for more laborers was urgent in almost every part of the Cumberland country; and the subject of this sketch soon felt that a dispensation of the gospel was committed to him, and, being encouraged by the revival party of the Cumberland Presbytery, he soon commenced exercising his superior gifts in singing, public prayer, and exhortation. In these public exercises his own soul was signally blessed, sinners were convicted, mourners were converted, and the people of God strengthened and encouraged, so that, prompted by a sense of duty, he presented himself to the Presbytery, and was received as a candidate for the ministry at Salem Meeting-house, in October, 1803. His superior literary and theological attainments at that time may be inferred from the fact that he was licensed to preach the gospel in April of next year.[34]

---

[34]Smith's **History of the Cumberland Presbyterians**.

It was in December of the following year, 1805, that the Commission of Kentucky Synod paid their inquisitorial visit to Cumberland Presbytery. Amongst the ecclesiastical heroes who withstood the high-handed, anti-Presbyterian, and unchristian measures of that body, we find the name of James B. Porter. Amongst other things in the unconstitutional farce enacted by that Commission, it will be remembered that the revival party of the Presbytery were deprived, as far as the action of the Commission could deprive them, of the privileges of their office, and were forbidden to exercise its functions. The result was that, in a spirit of Christian moderation, and of that charity which 'endureth all things,' they refrained from all Presbyterial action for the space of more than four years. Consequently the ordination of our departed father was deferred until after the constitution of the independent Cumberland Presbytery, which proved to be the commencement of the Cumberland Presbyterian Church. In the meantime, however, he filled a sphere of extensive usefulness in the humble character of a circuit-rider; and, as the Commission of Synod had made an unconstitutional effort to silence him, he was furnished by the leading members of the Presbytery with the following, the original of which is now in the hands of the writer:

'We, the majority of Cumberland Presbytery, do conceive from the book of discipline that the power of licensing and ordaining belongs to Presbyteries, and, as the Presbytery did legally license James B. Porter to preach the gospel, and although the Commission of Synod forbade him, we do believe upon the principles of the book of discipline that they had no power to prohibit him, where no charges of immoral conduct were brought against him. And, as we conceive that it is the right of Presbytery to license or forbid to preach, we believe that the said James B. Porter has a lawful and constitutional right to preach the gospel in the bounds of the Cumberland Presbytery, or wherever else God in his providence may call him. Given under our hands, this 11th day of December, 1805.

'JAMES McGREADY,
'WILLIAM HODGE,
'JOHN RANKIN,
'WILLIAM McGEE.'

The writer has also in his possession several copies of Father Porter's reports to the Presbytery and Council, as a circuit-rider, and his diary, besides a number of other documents from which interesting extracts might be made, but he fears it would extend this notice beyond prudent limits. In 1813, the Cumberland, afterward called the Nashville, Presbytery was so divided as to form the Logan and Elk Presbyteries. Of the latter Father Porter was a leading member up to the time it was so divided as to form the Richland Presbytery, in 1834, and of this he remained an honored member and ornament until death called him to his reward in heaven. As a Christian and a minister Father Porter filled up the measure of the inspired description of Barnabas. 'He was a good man and full of the Holy Ghost and of faith.' As a polished and high-toned gentleman he stood unimpeached and unimpeachable through life. As a Presbyter, he was safe in counsel, shrewd in discussion, and without a rival in the art of training young men for the ministry. Was advice called for? he was sure to be selected to give it. Was reproof to be administered? he never failed to do it effectively, and without giving offense. Did a difficulty spring up between brethren? he was emphatically the peacemaker of his Presbytery. In the social circle his easy manner, unfailing good humor, and sparkling, yet sanctified, wit made him unspeakably dear to all his friends. It used to be said, when at camp-meeting, or other religious convocations, any one inquired for a preacher whose whereabouts was not known just then, 'He is with Porter;' and in the main he was found there. But it was as a public speaker, notwithstanding his other excellences, that this man of God was most admired and most useful. His fine, manly form, his calm, pleasant, and expressive countenance, and his smooth and eloquently impressive gesticulation never failed to enchain his audience, whether small or great, while his clarion-like voice, which he kept under the most perfect control, and which never grew hoarse, but was always as smooth as oil, not only fell in music-like tones upon the ear, but entered into, and thrilled, the very soul. He troubled himself and hearers very little with abstruse and difficult theological questions. Religion, experimental and practical, was his theme, and in the exposition of these he had few equals. In his manner of dealing out the terrors of the law he was truly startling; but this was not his forte: he was preeminently 'a son of consolation.' He spent most of his active life as an evangelist, with superior qualifications, however, for the pastoral office.

His domestic virtues were of the highest order. As a son, brother, husband, father, and master, he was affectionate, constant, kind, and indulgent. Father Porter had an excellent constitution, and enjoyed fine health until a few years ago, when he became subject to vertigo, which proved to be the forerunner of a sort of apoplexy or paralysis. Under this disease he lost the use of his tongue and limbs in a great measure, and his mind was greatly impaired.

While able to converse at all, however, he loved to talk about religion; and, when seemingly almost unconscious of surrounding circumstances, if the Saviour's name or cause was mentioned in his presence, it would arouse his mind and fix his attention in a moment. Some days before his departure he became totally helpless and speechless, and so continued till

death released him from the clay, and he was admitted to a seat among the sanctified.
:M******.

In the **Banner of Peace**, of May 26, 1855, I find the following testimonial of Mr. Porter's Presbytery:

Your committee appointed to draft resolutions in reference to the death of Father James B. Porter respectfully submit the following:

Whereas, since the last semi-annual meeting of this Presbytery, it has pleased the King and Head of the Church to remove our venerable father, Rev. James B. Porter, from the toils and trials of the vineyard below to his mansion in the house not made with hands; therefore,

Resolved, That, as one of the fathers of the Cumberland Presbyterian Church, and especially of this Presbytery, we, his sons in the ministry, and his brethren, take occasion hereby to express our admiration of the manner, and would desire to imitate the calm sublimity and conscious rectitude, with which he faced and triumphed over the usurpations and anathemas of ecclesiastical tyranny; the zeal and ability with which he contended for the faith and the interests of the Church of his choice; and especially that sweetness of temper and disposition with which he bore the trials and disappointments incident to ministerial life.

Resolved, farther, That we hereby bear our testimony that by his death this Presbytery has lost one of its safest counselors and most efficient peacemakers, the sweet tones of whose eloquent voice still dwell upon our ears and linger about our hearts, and whose memory is upon perpetual record there.

Resolved, farther, That, while we miss this father of the Church in her councils and from the walls of Zion, we cheerfully submit, and rejoice that, as a ripe shock of corn, he has been gathered into the garner of God, taken from the wilderness below to his home in the city of God above.

Resolved, farther, That, as a token of our respect for the departed, and that the voice with which 'he, being dead, yet speaketh,' may be again heard, some member of the Presbytery be appointed to preach a funeral-sermon to-morrow, at ten o'clock A.M., in the Cumberland Presbyterian Church in this place, and a copy of the foregoing preamble and resolutions be furnished for publication in the **Banner of Peace**. Respectfully submitted,

N. P. MODRALL, Ch'n,
C. P. REED,
S. Y. ANDERSON."

The foregoing report was adopted at the late meeting of the Richland Presbytery, April 21, 1855. Rev. C.P. Reed, by appointment, preached the sermon on Sabbath to a large and attentive audience.

            J. N. EDMISTON, Stated Clerk.

These testimonials are from men who had been associated with Mr. Porter from their early youth in the ministry, or in the councils of the Church, or in both capacities.

It is evident that Mr. Ewing was disposed, in his trials which preceded the organization in 1810, to lean with more than ordinary confidence upon Mr. Porter, and to look with more than ordinary interest to his cooperation. While he was meditating the important step of reorganizing the Cumberland Presbytery, and McGee and McAdow were both hesitating, and not seeming likely to cooperate with him, thus leaving him incompetent according to Presbyterian usage to constitute a Presbytery, he turned his attention to Porter as a counselor and coadjutor. But Porter was only a licentiate. The bold idea was conceived of an organization by two ordained ministers. This, of course, brought up the question, whether ordination conferred by two Presbyters could be considered valid, a sufficient number being thus supplied to constitute a Presbytery.

Whilst this subject was under consideration, Mr. Ewing addressed him the following letter, in which, after setting forth the necessity of decisive action on the part of the friends of the revival, with a view to preserving and perpetuating its fruits, he brings the matter distinctly before his mind:

> For my own part the more I contemplate the thing the more clear I see my way, and the more determined I am 'not to be again entangled with a yoke of bondage.' Therefore I feel determined, for one, to go into a constituted state, if I can get no more than one ordained minister to join me. You may perhaps be startled at this. So was I when I first looked at the subject. But, on a closer and more impartial examination of my aversion to such a measure, I was induced to believe that pride and tradition were the most formidable arguments against it. I therefore was led to giving up the point for the following reasons: First, because the necessities of the Church demand it. Secondly, because there is nothing in God's word forbidding it. Thirdly, because no reformed Church in Christendom except the Presbyterian requires absolutely, and under all circumstances, the number of three ordained preachers to ordain one. Fourthly, because even that Church can depart from their own rule, one of the members of Synod being in that predicament. Therefore, for so doing, we could not feel, nor justly be, reproached from any quarter. I think, notwithstanding, the Presbyterian rule on this subject a good one, and I would not be willing to depart from it under ordinary circumstances. In a case of extreme necessity, however, I would. Whether we will be necessitated to do so I cannot yet tell, for I

have not heard from Mr. McGee, nor Mr. McAdow.

Brother Porter, if you will not think it discourteous I will ask you a question on which I wish you seriously to think, whether it would most wound your pride or your conscience to receive ordination from only two ministers.

I cannot think in my soul of receding and swallowing what I do not believe, nor preach, nor ever expect to preach. Honesty becomes gospel ministers. Yet when I look forward I see numerous difficulties. But when I look again I see the Lord stronger than man-stronger than them all. 'Hitherto the Lord hath helped us.'

This letter was dated December 6, 1809. Two months from its date decisive action was taken. This is a matter of history. We know nothing of the response to the letter, but in April following, at the first regular meeting of the Cumberland Presbytery as an independent organization, James B. Porter was present as a licentiate. The exigency did not occur, which was anticipated as a possibility by Mr. Ewing. Mr. McAdow concurred with himself and Mr. King in the reorganization. Mr. Porter's ordination was one of the first which occurred among the young men after the reorganization. It took place either at this meeting at the Ridge, in April, 1810, or at an early subsequent meeting.

Mr. Porter traveled and preached a great deal in the course of his long ministry of fifty years. No man in the Church was more beloved, and certainly very few were more useful. As it has been intimated already, he was a specimen of the very highest style of manhood physically, intellectually, socially, and spiritually. He would have made a figure in any profession, but he was peculiarly adapted to the profession to which God in his providence, and surely by his Spirit, called him.

The date and some of the circumstances of his death have already been given. At the meeting of the General Assembly following, held at Lebanon, Tennessee, in 1855, by appointment of that body, a sermon was delivered as a memorial of Rev. James B. Porter and Rev. Thomas Calhoon by Rev. Herschel S. Porter, D.D., from the triumphant language of the apostle in view of his departure. The text is familiar to all readers of the New Testament. Both of these good men had died in the interim of that and the preceding. The delivery of the sermon was a solemn hour, and would have been more so if it could have been anticipated that the beloved young preacher who officiated was himself, in the providence of God, to be called away in a few short months.

Mr. Porter was twice married. His first wife was Miss Polly G. Hudson, daughter of Thomas Hudson, Esq., of Haysboro, Tennessee. From her he had four sons. All of them professed religion in early life. She died June 21, 1818, in the triumphs of faith. Thomas Calhoon seems to have been sent for to preach her funeral-sermon. I recollect, in my early religious life, to have heard him speak of the occurrence in the pulpit, and especially of her repeating on her death-bed the closing stanza of one of Watts's sweet but solemn hymns:

Jesus can make a dying-bed
Feel soft as downy pillows are,
While on his breast I lean my head,

And breathe my life out sweetly there.

Her father was an eminent Christian. She seems to have shared largely in his spirit. They both, as well as Mr. Porter himself, were among the first-fruits of the old revival.

His second wife was Mrs. Frances Bond, of Maury county. She was a lady of eminent domestic and Christian worth. An only daughter was the fruit of this marriage. She became the wife of Dr. J. W. Sharber, and still lives. The second Mrs. Porter also preceded her husband to the grave. One son of the first family also lives.

The following personal sketch of Mr. Porter is furnished by Rev. Carson P. Reed. No one was more intimately acquainted with the subject of the sketch. It was, too, one of the last productions of Mr. Reed's life. Says the contributor:

> Mr. Porter's person was an approach to perfection. He was tall, and unusually handsome. His manners were engaging; his conversation always agreeable and instructive. No one could feel otherwise than interested and delighted in his company. His habits were cheerful and pleasant. He addressed himself on all occasions to the circumstances which surrounded him; was never at a loss or embarrassed. As a Christian gentleman he was fully qualified to enter into any company, and, without seeming to know it, commanded respect wherever he went; and notwithstanding he possessed a great flow of spirits, he never compromitted his Christian or ministerial character.
>
> His piety was deep and unquestionable, yet unostentatious. He was fervent in devotion, and his regular seasons for such exercises were carefully observed. Neither family nor secret prayer was neglected, unless under the most forbidding circumstances, and his custom was to go from his knees to the pulpit. It was his habit, too, to seek direction from God in the choice of subjects for the pulpit. He thought that there was such a thing as divine direction in all these matters.
>
> Mr. Porter's appearance in the pulpit was truly commanding and impressive. He carried with him into his public exercises the spirit of a Christian minister. His congregation could hardly refrain from uniting in heart with him in his public prayers. They could hardly feel otherwise than that they were in the presence of God. There were few men who were better adapted to extraordinary occasions. He seemed to be always ready.
>
> In connection with the subject of prayer, a particular incident in the history of his life is worthy of being mentioned. In the course of a camp-meeting at Mount Moriah, held in 1811, two of Mr. Porter's brothers were lying at the point of death, and did both die while the meeting was in progress. One of them was a Christian, and died in the triumphs of faith. The other was an irreligious man. Mr. Porter seemed to lose sight of every thing but the salvation of his brother. All other cares seemed to be

swallowed up in this. His prayers were importunate, and almost incessant for this unconverted dying brother. God evidently heard. The brother obtained a good hope through grace. He died leaving a good testimony behind.

Mr. Porter's care for the sick and dying was always most earnest, and God blessed his labors in their behalf abundantly. In imitation of his divine Master, he 'went about doing good.' All classes of men shared alike in his missions of love and mercy. He exemplified in his daily life what Paul enjoined: 'Rejoice with them that do rejoice, and weep with them that weep.' He was emphatically 'a good man, and,' through his agency, the Spirit of God attending, 'much people were added unto the Lord.' He spent ten or twelve of the first years of his ministerial life as a missionary, or, to use the language of the times, as a 'circuit-rider.' He kindled a fire wherever he went. He planted many churches, and of these many still stand as monuments of his zeal and fidelity. He gloried in the cross of our Lord Jesus Christ, not troubling himself or his hearers much with abstruse speculation, which profit little, but engender a great deal of strife in the Church of God.

During the last twenty years of his life, Mr. Porter was pastor of Mount Moriah congregation, which he had organized in 1810, while yet a young man. It has built its third house of worship, and is still a flourishing congregation. It may be mentioned as an item of interest that this congregation has sent forth sixteen young ministers into the Cumberland Presbyterian Church. Several of these have gone to their reward, and others have grown old in the service. He was similarly connected with Mount Carmel congregation, in Maury county, for a number of years, and also with others for longer or shorter spaces of time. In all these connections he gave eminent satisfaction, proving himself always a workman who needed not to be ashamed, rightly dividing the word of truth. He was my father in the ministry, and long my companion in labor, and my heart clings to his memory with a tender tenacity which is rather strengthened than weakened by time. Yours in Christian labor,

C.P. Reed.

My personal acquaintance with Mr. Porter was not very close, but it extended through about thirty years. I met him mostly in the old Cumberland Synod and in the General Assembly, and occasionally in other circumstances. He was the Moderator of the first Synod of which I was a member. This was held at the Beech Meeting-house, in Sumner county, in 1822. But one circumstance occurred there of which I shall make mention. A camp-meeting followed the Synod, as the custom was in those days. There was a large number of young men, new members in the Synod, at that meeting. There were David Lowry, Robert D. Morrow, F. R. Cossitt, Green P. Rice, and Daniel Buie, not as young as others, but all, I think, new members. Then followed the names of the first representatives of the third generation of preachers in the Church: Carson P. Reed, James S. Guthrie, William S. Burney, Vincent Hubbard, Albert G. Gibson, Aaron Alexander, A. J. Steele, Ezekiel Cloyd, not a young man, but a new member, and the writer. James Y. Barnett was there, but not yet a member. It will be seen that there was a large mass of new material; some of it, too, was rather raw. William Barnett was appointed by the Synod to preach a special sermon to the young members. He was a Boanerges of the times. The sermon was delivered on Saturday afternoon of the meeting. Mr. Porter followed by an impressive exhortation. It was an interesting hour. John Barnett, too, entered very deeply into the spirit of the occasion. He was then in the midst of his better days. He took the young men by the hand, one by one, and wept over them as a father would have wept over his sons in consecrating them to some great and difficult enterprise.

The next occasion which my memory calls up was connected with the meeting of the Synod the following year. The meeting for business was held in Russellville, Kentucky. It was followed by a camp-meeting in the neighborhood. On Sabbath of the camp-meeting, Robert Donnell delivered a funeral-sermon as a memorial of one of the Ewings, who had been a prominent man in the congregation, and in the country around him. I have elsewhere spoken of that sermon. It was one of the most massive productions that I ever heard. Mr. Porter followed with a sermon preparatory to the communion. It was a difficult task to preach to a crowd after such a sermon as had preceded. He sustained himself, however, as few men could have done. He was in the prime of life, and carried with him a large measure of the spirit of the olden time. It was a great day in that country congregation.

In 1828 the old Cumberland Synod met for the last time. The meeting was held in Franklin, Tennessee. At its close it dissolved itself, and called a meeting of the first General Assembly. The act of dissolution was, of course, a solemn act. The older men, who had met annually in a Synodical capacity, could hardly expect to meet often, if ever, again. Mr. Porter offered the concluding prayer. There were not many unfeeling hearts or dry eyes when the prayer closed.

In 1830 Mr. Porter was a member, and also the Moderator, of the General Assembly. This was the second meeting of that judicature. It was held at Princeton, Kentucky. On that occasion I was closely associated with the Moderator, being temporary clerk of the body. Some of the sessions of the Assembly were held in one of the rooms of old Cumberland College. It was an interesting Assembly, and rendered more so than it would have otherwise been, from its being held a few weeks only after the commencement of the publication of the first periodical ever attempted by the Church. This periodical, in about two years, was removed to Nashville, Tennessee, and after assuming a third form broke down in 1840.

In 1838 I moved to Mississippi, taking my little family through the country by land. It was an easy day's travel from the early home of my wife to Spring Hill, the home of Mr. Porter. I was never in the habit of making inconvenient demands of brethren in traveling, but this was a sad day to her, and as Mr. Porter had generally called at the old homestead in passing, and had been a great favorite in the family, it was decided to throw ourselves upon his Christian kindness for the night. I shall never forget the open-hearted manner with which he met us, and the generous hospitality dispensed by himself, his good wife, and his daughter, just developing into womanhood. These constituted the family. He had, no doubt, studied the characteristics of a good bishop, as delineated by the apostle. A cheerful evening, at least, closed up what had been a day of sadness to the travelers.

In 1852, at the Assembly in Nashville, I saw him for the last time. Thirteen years had passed from the time of my seeing him at his own cheerful home at Spring Hill. These years had made terrible inroads upon both body and mind. The palace was a ruin. Still it was a privilege and an unspeakable comfort to know that what of the good and noble man remained seemed to be wholly given up to God. When nothing else could arouse him, a mention of God and his cause always awakened his paralyzed energies to such action as still remained possible. Two years and a half from that time, what had been the mellow voice and manly form were silent and still in death. James B. Porter had become one of the departed fathers.

REV. JOHN P. PROVINE
(1784-1855)

Sources: Autobiography published in **Cumberland Presbyterian Missionary**. Manuscript letter of Rev. J. C. Provine.

Rev. John Provine was born in North Carolina, on the 30th of March, 1784. In 1789 his father moved with his family and settled in Garrard county, Kentucky. The father and mother were both Presbyterians, as the ancestors of the family had been for many generations. His father was an elder in the old Paint Lick congregation of Garrard county. When young John was about eight years of age, his father died from the kick of a horse. Of that afflicting occurrence he gives us the following account in his autobiography, written a short time previous to his death:

> Though it occurred many years ago, and I was quite young, yet I distinctly remember the scene of my father's death—how he talked to the family about religion. When the elders of the Church came to bid him a last farewell, he solemnly gave his family in charge to them, bidding them visit the fatherless and widow, see to it that his children were trained up in the fear of God. The children consisted of three sons and four daughters, and I being the youngest, as was the custom of the Church then, was set apart for the ministry. I remember to have heard my father, in his last counsel given to my mother, say to her, "You must try and educate our son John for the ministry.' The impression then made on my mind has been as lasting as my years.

His mother, in conformity with the dying father's injunction, sent him to a Latin school in the neighborhood, and while he was pursuing his studies, often took occasion to impress on his young mind the necessity of personal religion, especially in her Sabbath evening conversations with her children. He says himself, and no doubt truthfully, "The influences of those fireside talks, the kind admonitions, and gentle warnings that fell from a mother's lips, sunk deep into my heart, and I doubt not contributed in a great degree to preparing the way for the Holy Spirit to do its work."

Notwithstanding these advantages, years passed, and a deep and long struggle was undergone before he experienced that great change which is the first and greatest of all qualifications for the Christian ministry. At a camp-meeting at Cane Ridge—the year is not given—a sister professed religion. The occurrence made a deep impression upon his mind, but he resisted it. At a meeting at Silver Creek, one of the elders of the congregation in which he was raised made a personal appeal to him on the subject of religion. He fell and lay deprived of consciousness for some time. When consciousness returned, he arose with a resolution formed that he would seek the Saviour until he found him. Twelve months, however, were spent in fruitless endeavors to bring himself up to what he considered a proper state of mind and heart for the reception of the mercy of the gospel. Finally, at a prayer-meeting held by one of the elders of the congregation at his mother's house, while the honest man was presenting the promises of the gospel in his artless manner, the subject of this sketch was enabled to claim and appropriate those promises, and, according to his own account, before he was conscious of what he was doing, he was on his feet praising God.

"That night," says he, "I shall never forget; the circumstances are as fresh in my memory as though they had transpired but yesterday. I have forgotten the day of the week, month, and even of the year, but the time when I experienced the full flow of the Christian's hope will be fresh as long as memory retains any thing of the past, for that scene does not grow old with my years."

Mr. Provine now entered upon his preparation for the ministry more earnestly. He attached himself to a Latin school which was taught by Rev. Samuel Finley. A fellow-student and class-mate was Mr. N. H. Hall, who afterward became Rev. Dr. Hall, of Lexington, Kentucky. He and his friend, Mr. Hall, attended the sessions of the Kentucky Synod, at Danville, in the progress of which five ministers, who became leaders of the New Lights, as they were then called, seceded from the Synod. Amongst these was the pastor of his own congregation, Rev. Samuel Houston, who afterward joined the Shakers. Houston persuaded the two young men to leave Mr. Finley's school and enter a school taught by the celebrated Barton W. Stone, in Bourbon county. Here they studied the Greek Grammar and Greek Testament. Mr. Stone was very assiduous in laboring to indoctrinate them into his new theology. Mr. Provine became troubled. The theology of his teacher was in conflict with his Christian experience. When at last he was relieved from these troubles, he left the school, and entered another. Here the doctrine of election and reprobation met him. His theological troubles were renewed. They were of a different kind from the former, but very embarrassing. Mr. Finley advised him to join the Presbytery, and take a regular theological course, that in this way his difficulties might be removed. He declined doing so, however, and resolved to come to Tennessee, and acquaint himself with the views of the people, who afterward became the Cumberland Presbyterians. Mr. Finley advised him, if he could not see his way clear, to embrace the Calvinistic doctrines, to unite with the Methodists, and enter the ministry among them. The result of all was what might have been expected of a conscientious and distrustful man. I give the result in his own words: "Being so much harassed in mind as to what truth was, and finding so much corruption in my heart, I began to feel much discouraged about trying to preach, and finally concluded to abandon all thought on the subject."

Soon after Mr. Provine abandoned his purpose of entering the ministry, he was married to Miss Jane Calhoon, sister of the late Rev. Thomas Calhoon. His marriage occurred on the first day of October, 1807. He joined the Big Spring congregation, in the bounds of which he lived. Still he was not at rest. He was appointed a ruling elder in the congregation, and was frequently sent as a representative to the Presbytery. At the meetings of the Presbyteries in those days, it was customary to have a sermon on a call to the ministry. He was often very unhappy, and at length yielded to persuasion, and made a tour on the circuit with the late Rev. John Barnett. The result, however, was very unsatisfactory to himself. He made up his mind again to abandon all thoughts of entering the ministry, and so reported to Mr. Barnett. The reply was characteristic: "If your conscience can rest easy in view of such a trial as you have made, I would have no such conscience." He went home, however, considering his purpose settled. Soon after he reached home, he was laid upon a bed of sickness, which confined him near three months.

"During my sickness," says he, "I experienced much mental agony in view of the wants of a perishing world, and the great need of some to break to them the bread of life. On my bed of affliction I covenanted with God that I would be his obedient servant in all things, and if he would spare my life, I would do my duty. Being restored to health, I started with Rev. J. L. Dillard on a circuit, and with much fear and trembling gave myself up to the guidance of God, and did what I could to point sinners the way to heaven."

He joined the Nashville Presbytery, as a candidate for the ministry, at its fall meeting in 1814. The meeting was held at Big Spring. The ministers present were David Foster, Hugh Kirkpatrick, Thomas Calhoon, and David McLin. At the next meeting of the Presbytery, which was held at Smith's Fork in the spring of 1815, he read a discourse from John v. 40, which was "sustained as popular preparatory to licensure." Messrs. Kirkpatrick, Calhoon, Foster, and McLin, were appointed a Committee on Examination. The Committee reported that they "had examined Mr. Provine on the Latin and Greek languages, English Grammar, and Divinity." He was accordingly licensed on the 11th day of May, 1815.

On the 14th of October, 1820, he was ordained at the Beech Meeting-house, in Sumner county. Rev. Samuel McSpadden preached the ordination-sermon, and Rev. Thomas Calhoon presided and gave the charge.

Mr. Provine's ministry was confined to Middle Tennessee. His preaching was plain, practical, and forcible. He had a good voice, a dark eye, a very unassuming, but altogether an acceptable manner. His great want was self-confidence. Some men have a great deal too much of this, but he had too little. Still he was an earnest and useful preacher, and a most lovely man.

The first time I recollect to have heard him preach was at the Ridge Meeting-house, in the edge of Robertson county. It was about a year after I professed religion, and I was then teaching my first school in the neighborhood. The text was, "Ye are not your own, for ye are bought with a price; therefore glorify God in your body and in your spirit, which are God's." He was certainly much in the Spirit, and the sermon was very impressive. He spent the night at the house of Rev. Robert Guthrie, a patriarch in his time, with whom I was boarding. He conducted family prayers at night. I recollect distinctly one petition in his prayer: "O Lord, we ask not for riches, nor honor, nor even for long life, but we pray that we may be useful while we live." if I had ever heard such a petition before, it had made no impression upon my mind. But it then made an impression which is vivid now.

I have another anecdote to relate, which is too interesting to be overlooked. In the summer of 1820 Mr. Provine traveled and preached on what was called the Nashville Circuit. A few years later, in the course of my own ministry in Western Tennessee, a pious old lady gave me a history of an occurrence which took place in the summer of 1820, in connection with Mr. Provine's ministry of that year on the circuit. One of his places of preaching was the house of William Orr, on West Harpeth, a few miles from Franklin. There was a very general religious interest in the country at the time. The old lady, with her husband and family, lived then near Franklin, and she and her husband were members of the Presbyterian Church. They had known something of Mr. Provine in his early life in Kentucky. They learned that he was to preach at Mr. Orr's on a particular day, and the mother and several of the children made arrangements to go and hear him. When they were about leaving home, the old lady addressed her children, according to her own account, somewhat thus: "Now, my children, you have heard a great deal of Cumberland Presbyterians, and some of the things which you have heard have been unfavorable. I do not know any thing about them myself, but I knew Johnny Provine when he was a boy, and I believe when you hear him preach, you will hear what he thinks, at least, to be the truth. He was a good boy, and I have no doubt he is a good man."

They went to meeting, and although it was a week-day, the house was crowded. Mr. Provine preached from the following text: "Now then we are ambassadors for Christ, as though God did beseech you by us; we pray you in Christ's stead, be ye reconciled to God." He said afterward that he was very much in the Spirit. The sermon was very impressive. At its close, all the old lady's children that she brought with her were among the mourners. The whole family of children were soon brought into the Church, and some of them now live burning and shining lights. The example of Mrs. Moore might be a valuable lesson to many parents.

In the year 1830 Mr. Provine lost his wife. He calls this, in the style of the antiquated theology, a great crook in his lot. His house was veiled in mourning. On the 24th of January, 1833, he was again married, to Miss Catharine Ralston. He says, no doubt truthfully, that he sought and consummated this marriage with a religious motive.

In 1836 a small speck appeared on his left temple. It soon developed itself into an incurable cancer. Every effort was made for its removal, but in vain. It was the appointed shaft of death. His bodily sufferings were very great. For years the invincible destroyer was engaged at his unceasing work. Nor was the afflicted minister free from the buffetings of Satan. Yet God delivered him, and enabled him, in his own expressive language, "while looking back through this long fight of affliction, to sing of mercy and judgment."

His affliction continued nineteen years. He died July 30, 1855, in his seventy-second year, with unshaken confidence in those precious truths which he had often preached, and which had been his support through so long and painful an affliction. He lies in the same grave-yard with his brother-in-law, Rev. Thomas Calhoon. It is, on many accounts, a sacred spot. Mr. Provine had six children—five sons and a daughter—all of his first family. Two of his sons, says my informant, are in heaven. Two are ruling elders in the Cumberland Presbyterian Church; one is a respected minister, Rev. J. C. Provine, of Nashville, Tennessee.

I saw Mr. Provine for the last time a few weeks before his death. He had been able to attend church at the Big Spring. I went with him to his home, and spent a few hours there. His whole conversation seemed to run in one channel. His mind was evidently engrossed with the prospect of the great event which was just before him. He was an honest, earnest, Christian man, examining always with care the ground on which he stood. The result of his self-examination was the unfaltering faith in which he died.

www.ingramcontent.com/pod-product-compliance
Lightning Source LLC
Chambersburg PA
CBHW071826230426
43672CB00013B/2771